Delphi Cookbook
Second Edition

Over 60 hands-on recipes to help you master the power of Delphi for cross-platform and mobile development on multiple platforms

Daniele Teti

BIRMINGHAM - MUMBAI

Delphi Cookbook
Second Edition

Copyright © 2016 Packt Publishing

All rights reserved. No part of this book may be reproduced, stored in a retrieval system, or transmitted in any form or by any means, without the prior written permission of the publisher, except in the case of brief quotations embedded in critical articles or reviews.

Every effort has been made in the preparation of this book to ensure the accuracy of the information presented. However, the information contained in this book is sold without warranty, either express or implied. Neither the author, nor Packt Publishing, and its dealers and distributors will be held liable for any damages caused or alleged to be caused directly or indirectly by this book.

Packt Publishing has endeavored to provide trademark information about all of the companies and products mentioned in this book by the appropriate use of capitals. However, Packt Publishing cannot guarantee the accuracy of this information.

First published: September 2014

Second edition: June 2016

Production reference: 1280616

Published by Packt Publishing Ltd.
Livery Place
35 Livery Street
Birmingham B3 2PB, UK.

ISBN 978-1-78528-742-8

www.packtpub.com

Credits

Author
Daniele Teti

Reviewer
Roman Yankovsky

Commissioning Editor
Priya Singh

Acquisition Editor
Rahul Nair

Content Development Editor
Deepti Thore

Technical Editor
Mohita Vyas

Copy Editor
Merilyn Periera

Project Coordinator
Shweta H. Birwatkar

Proofreader
Safis Editing

Indexer
Monica Ajmera Mehta

Graphics
Disha Haria

Production Coordinator
Arvindkumar Gupta

Cover Work
Arvindkumar Gupta

About the Author

Daniele Teti is a software architect, trainer, and consultant with over 20 years of professional experience. He writes code in a number of languages but his preferred language for compiled native software, is Object Pascal.

Daniele is an Embarcadero MVP and is a well known Delphi and programming expert in the developers' community. He's the main developer and drives the development of some Delphi open source projects (DelphiMVCFramework, LoggerPro, DORM—"The Delphi ORM", Delphi Redis Client, Delphi STOMP Client, and so on). After writing some articles for the most important programming magazines in Italy and a number of on-line publications, Daniele started to write books. His *Delphi Cookbook*, published in late 2014, has been a bestseller. Daniele wrote his first program when he was 11 year old, and since then happily continues to write software almost every day. Apart from Delphi, he's a huge fan of design patterns, open source, distributed architectures, RESTful architectures, and Android OS. Daniele has been the project manager for a lot of big projects in Italy and in Europe, for private companies and public institutions. When is not busy writing software or writing about programming (for a job or for a hobby), he like to play guitar, write songs, and do voluntary activities. Currently he is CEO of BIT Time Professionals, an Italian company specializing in high level consultancy, training, and development. The company specializes in high performance software, web and mobile solutions, and distributed architecture. Bit Time Professionals is also an Italian leader about indoor proximity solutions using beacon technology, where it provides solutions for museums, supermarkets, art galleries, fairs, and events in general.

Daniele acts as a consultant and teacher for many Italian and European companies, so he travels very often around the world.

Daniele is the technical director for the ITDevCon conference, the biggest European Delphi conference (`www.itdevcon.it`). He's also an international speaker at technical conferences.

Daniele lives in Rome, Italy, with his beloved wife Debora and their little boy Mattia.

> Thank you to my wife Debora and my son Mattia.

About the Reviewer

Roman Yankovsky is a long time Delphi developer who has been working with Delphi since Delphi 2. He has developed and maintained various applications in different industries. Currently he is working with ShareBike, developing a public bike sharing system. Roman is an Embarcadero MVP and a frequent speaker at developer conferences. Most recently, his focus is on the development of productivity tools for developers. He is the author of the FixInsight static analysis tool for Delphi.

www.PacktPub.com

eBooks, discount offers, and more

Did you know that Packt offers eBook versions of every book published, with PDF and ePub files available? You can upgrade to the eBook version at www.PacktPub.com and as a print book customer, you are entitled to a discount on the eBook copy. Get in touch with us at customercare@packtpub.com for more details.

At www.PacktPub.com, you can also read a collection of free technical articles, sign up for a range of free newsletters and receive exclusive discounts and offers on Packt books and eBooks.

https://www2.packtpub.com/books/subscription/packtlib

Do you need instant solutions to your IT questions? PacktLib is Packt's online digital book library. Here, you can search, access, and read Packt's entire library of books.

Why Subscribe?

- Fully searchable across every book published by Packt
- Copy and paste, print, and bookmark content
- On demand and accessible via a web browser

Table of Contents

Preface	**v**
Chapter 1: Delphi Basics	**1**
Introduction	1
Changing your application look and feel with VCL styles and no code	2
Changing the style of your VCL application at runtime	5
Customizing TDBGrid	9
Using owner draw combos and listboxes	16
Making an owner draw control aware of the VCL styles	19
Creating a stack of embedded forms	25
Manipulating JSON	28
Manipulating and transforming XML documents	34
I/O in the 21st century – knowing the streams	44
Creating a Windows service	47
Associating a file extension with your application on Windows	52
Be coherent with the Windows look and feel using TTaskDialog	58
Chapter 2: Becoming a Delphi Language Ninja	**71**
Introduction	71
Fun with anonymous methods – using higher-order functions	72
Writing enumerable types	76
RTTI to the rescue – configuring your class at runtime	80
Duck typing using RTTI	84
Creating helpers for your classes	88
Chapter 3: Knowing Your Friends – the Delphi RTL	**99**
Introduction	99
Check strings with regular expressions	100
Consuming RESTful services using native HTTP(S) client libraries	106
Cope with the encoded Internet world using System.NetEncodings	119

Table of Contents

Save space using System.Zip	126
Decouple your code using a cross-platform publish/subscribe mechanism	129

Chapter 4: Going Cross-Platform with FireMonkey — 137

Introduction	137
Giving a new appearance to the standard FireMonkey controls using styles	138
Creating a styled TListBox	144
Impressing your clients with animations	149
Using master/details with LiveBindings	153
Showing complex vector shapes using paths	165
Using FireMonkey in a VCL application	170
Reinventing your GUI also known as	177
mastering Firemonkey controls, shapes, and effects	177

Chapter 5: The Thousand Faces of Multithreading — 187

Introduction	187
Synchronizing shared resources with TMonitor	188
Talking with the main thread using a thread-safe queue	196
Synchronizing multiple threads using TEvent	199
Displaying a measure on a 2D graph like an oscilloscope	203
Using tasks to make your customer happier	208
Monitoring things using futures	216
Parallelize using the parallel for	222

Chapter 6: Putting Delphi on the Server — 231

Introduction	231
Developing web client JavaScript applications with WebBroker on the server	232
Converting a console application to a Windows service	242
Serializing a dataset to JSON and back	245
Serializing objects to JSON and back using RTTI	250
Sending a POST HTTP request encoding parameters	256
Implementing a RESTful interface using WebBroker	260
Controlling remote application using UDP	277
Using app tethering to create a companion app	283
Creating DataSnap Apache modules	290
Creating WebBroker Apache modules	301
Using native HTTP(S) client libraries	308

Chapter 7: Riding the Mobile Revolution with FireMonkey — 321

Introduction	322
Taking a photo, applying effects, and sharing it	322
Using TListView to show and search local data	331
Using SQLite databases to handle a to-do list	339
Do not block the main thread!	344

Using a styled TListView to handle long lists of data	352
Customizing the TListView	362
Taking a photo and location and sending it to a server continuously	372
Talking with the backend	382
Making a phone call from your app!	390
Tracking the application's lifecycle	395

Chapter 8: Using Specific Platform Features — 401

Introduction	401
Using Android SDK Java classes	402
Using iOS Objective C SDK classes	408
Displaying PDF files in your app	412
Sending Android Intents	418
Letting your phone talk – using the Android TextToSpeech engine	426
Using Java classes in Android apps with Java2OP	430
Doing it in the background, the right way – Android services	433

Index — 447

Preface

If you've been a software developer for a long time, you certainly know how useful a conversation can be with a colleague who has already done something similar to what you are doing and can explain it, as they faced the same problem. It is not possible to put all the possible situations that a developer can face in a book, but many problems are similar at least in principle. This is the reason this book is organized as a cookbook: just like a combination of foods can be adapted and modified to be appropriate for different types of dinner, a "programming recipe" can provide the idea to solve many different problems.

This book is an advanced level guide that will help Delphi developers get a higher expertise in their everyday job. The everyday job, and the quality of your deliverables, is what contributes to the quality of your professional life. If it does not make sense, reinvent the wheel repeatedly, especially when working with a well-established tool, such as Delphi. The focus of the book is to provide readers with comprehensive and detailed examples on how effectively the Delphi software can be designed and written. All the recipes in the book are the result of years of development, training, and consultancy activities in many different fields of the IT industries, from the small systems with thousands of installations to the large systems commissioned by big companies or by the government. It is not a magic book that will solve all your development problems (if you find it, tell me, please!), but can be helpful to get a different point of view on a specific problem, or a hint on how to solve problems.

Armed with the knowledge of advanced concepts, such as high order functions and anonymous methods, generics and enumerable, extended RTTI and duck typing, LiveBindings, multi-threading, FireMonkey, mobile development, server-side development, and so on, you will be pleasantly surprised as to how quickly and easily you can use Delphi to write high quality, clean, readable, fast, maintainable, and extensible code.

I read too many boring programming books, so I tried to maintain a relaxed and light exposition. A small applicability scenario that describes a situation where a particular technology, approach, or design pattern can be used successfully introduces all the recipes. The recipes are not too complex, because otherwise the book may become thousands of pages long, but also not trivial because the IT books' landscape is already full of simple examples with few direct applicability. I tried to do a good tradeoff and I hope to be able to do it.

Preface

Every time I start to read a new book, I ask myself, "Will the author have something interesting to say?", "How much will this book change my point of view about the topics mentioned?", "Is it worth the time spent to read it?" Now, in spite of being from the other side of the river, I worked hard to put as much good quality contents in my books as possible, I hope that will match your expectations.

One last note. Writing hundreds of pages about advanced programming is not an easy task. However, I am very pleased to have done it and I hope you will enjoy reading it at least how I enjoyed writing it.

What this book covers

Chapter 1, Delphi Basics, talks about a set of general approaches that should not be ignored by any Delphi programmer. Some topics are simple and immediate and some are not but all of them should be well understood. By the end of this chapter, the reader is able to use some of the fundamental Delphi techniques related to the RTL, to the VCL, and to the OS integration.

Chapter 2, Becoming a Delphi Language Ninja, focuses on the Object Pascal language. The programming language is the way you talk to the machine, so you must be fluent and know all the possibilities offered. This chapter talks about higher-order functions, practical utilization of the extended RTTI, regular expressions, and other things useful to augment the power of your code and to lower the amount of time spent on debugging.

Chapter 3, Knowing Your Friends – the Delphi RTL, focuses on the Delphi' RTL. There isn't a detailed description of all the Delphi's RTLs (you would need 10 books like this one, which will be particularly boring, I guess) but you can find some recipes that explain some of the most important RTL features and some less know but really useful classes. You'll learn how to use regular expressions, the most popular encoding format used by HTTP base applications, and how to use the built-in data de/compression-related classes.

Chapter 4, Going Cross-Platform with FireMonkey, is dedicated to the FireMonkey framework in general. What you will learn from this chapter can be used in many of the platforms that FireMonkey supports. Moreover, you will learn about non-trivial LiveBindings utilizations.

Chapter 5, The Thousand Faces of Multithreading, talks about thread synchronization and the mechanisms used to obtain this synchronization, such as TMonitor, thread-safe queues, and TEvent. It is also one of the most complex chapters. By the end of this chapter, the reader will be able to create and communicate with background threads, leaving your main thread free to update your GUI (or to communicate with the OS).

Chapter 6, Putting Delphi on the Server, focuses on how well Delphi can behave when running on a server. Some people think that Delphi is a client-only tool, but it is not true. In this chapter, we'll show how to create powerful servers that offer services over a network. Then, in some recipe, we'll also implement a JavaScript client that brings the database data into the user browser. Techniques explained in this chapter open a range of possibilities, especially in the mobile and web area.

Chapter 7, Riding the Mobile Revolution with FireMonkey, is dedicated to the mobile development with Delphi and FireMonkey. If you are interested in mobile development, I think that will be your favorite chapter! Mobile is everywhere, and this chapter will explain how to write software for your Android or iOS device, what are the best practices to use, how to save your data on the mobile, how to retrieve and update remote data, and how to integrate with the mobile operating system.

Chapter 8, Using Specific Platform Features, shows you how to integrate your app with the underlying mobile operating systems beyond what FireMonkey offers. You will learn how to import Java and Objective C libraries in your app and how to use the SDK classes from your Object Pascal code.

What you need for this book

This book talks about Delphi, so you need it. Not all the recipes are available in all the Delphi editions. Typically, the mobile projects can be compiled only if you have Delphi Enterprise or higher (or Delphi Professional plus the mobile add-on, or RAD Studio professional or higher). All the projects are compiled and tested with the latest Delphi version at the time of writing, but many recipes can be compiled also on older versions.

If you want to run the mobile app on a phone or a tablet, you could use the Android emulator or the iOS simulator, but we strongly suggest an actual device to see how the app really behaves. To deploy an iOS app on your device, you also need an Apple computer with MacOSX.

Who this book is for

This book aims to help the professional Delphi developers in their day-to-day job. This book will teach you about the newest Delphi technologies and its hidden gems. It is not a book for a newbie, but the practical approach will help you reach a new level with your Delphi skills. The experienced developer can benefit from this book because nontrivial problems are solved using best practices. Where more than one way is available or the topic is too broad to be explained in the available pages, references are provided to allow you to go deeper in that field. It is a book to have on your desk for the next few years.

Preface

Conventions

In this book, you will find a number of styles of text that distinguish between different kinds of information. Here are some examples of these styles, and an explanation of their meaning.

Code words in text, database table names, folder names, filenames, file extensions, pathnames, dummy URLs, user input, and Twitter handles are shown as follows: "Style manipulation at runtime is done using the class methods of the `TStyleManager` class."

A block of code is set as follows:

```
procedure TMainForm.StylesListRefresh;
var
  stylename: string;
begin
  ListBox1.Clear;
  // retrieve all the styles linked in the executable
  for stylename in TStyleManager.StyleNames do
  begin
    ListBox1.Items.Add(stylename);
  end;
end;
```

When we wish to draw your attention to a particular part of a code block, the relevant lines or items are set in bold:

```
begin
  Application.Initialize;
  Application.MainFormOnTaskbar := True;
  TStyleManager.TrySetStyle('Iceberg Classico');
  Application.CreateForm(TMainForm, MainForm);
  Application.Run;
end
```

Any command-line input or output is written as follows:

```
# cp /usr/src/asterisk-addons/configs/cdr_mysql.conf.sample
   /etc/asterisk/cdr_mysql.conf
```

New terms and important words are shown in bold. Words that you see on the screen, in menus or dialog boxes for example, appear in the text like this: "Add all the columns to TDBGrid by right-clicking and selecting **Columns Editor**".

> Warnings or important notes appear in a box like this.

> Tips and tricks appear like this.

Reader feedback

Feedback from our readers is always welcome. Let us know what you think about this book— what you liked or disliked. Reader feedback is important for us as it helps us develop titles that you will really get the most out of.

To send us general feedback, simply e-mail feedback@packtpub.com, and mention the book's title in the subject of your message.

If there is a topic that you have expertise in and you are interested in either writing or contributing to a book, see our author guide at www.packtpub.com/authors.

Customer support

Now that you are the proud owner of a Packt book, we have a number of things to help you to get the most from your purchase.

Downloading the example code

You can download the example code files for this book from your account at http://www.packtpub.com. If you purchased this book elsewhere, you can visit http://www.packtpub.com/support and register to have the files e-mailed directly to you.

You can download the code files by following these steps:

1. Log in or register to our website using your e-mail address and password.
2. Hover the mouse pointer on the **SUPPORT** tab at the top.
3. Click on **Code Downloads & Errata**.
4. Enter the name of the book in the **Search** box.
5. Select the book for which you're looking to download the code files.
6. Choose from the drop-down menu where you purchased this book from.
7. Click on **Code Download**.

You can also download the code files by clicking on the **Code Files** button on the book's webpage at the Packt Publishing website. This page can be accessed by entering the book's name in the **Search** box. Please note that you need to be logged in to your Packt account.

Once the file is downloaded, please make sure that you unzip or extract the folder using the latest version of:

- WinRAR / 7-Zip for Windows
- Zipeg / iZip / UnRarX for Mac
- 7-Zip / PeaZip for Linux

The code bundle for the book is also hosted on GitHub at `https://github.com/PacktPublishing/Delphi-Cookbook-Second-Edition`. We also have other code bundles from our rich catalog of books and videos available at `https://github.com/PacktPublishing/`. Check them out!

Errata

Although we have taken every care to ensure the accuracy of our content, mistakes do happen. If you find a mistake in one of our books—maybe a mistake in the text or the code—we would be grateful if you could report this to us. By doing so, you can save other readers from frustration and help us improve subsequent versions of this book. If you find any errata, please report them by visiting `http://www.packtpub.com/submit-errata`, selecting your book, clicking on the **Errata Submission Form** link, and entering the details of your errata. Once your errata are verified, your submission will be accepted and the errata will be uploaded to our website or added to any list of existing errata under the Errata section of that title.

To view the previously submitted errata, go to `https://www.packtpub.com/books/content/support` and enter the name of the book in the search field. The required information will appear under the **Errata** section.

Piracy

Piracy of copyrighted material on the Internet is an ongoing problem across all media. At Packt, we take the protection of our copyright and licenses very seriously. If you come across any illegal copies of our works in any form on the Internet, please provide us with the location address or website name immediately so that we can pursue a remedy.

Please contact us at `copyright@packtpub.com` with a link to the suspected pirated material.

We appreciate your help in protecting our authors and our ability to bring you valuable content.

Questions

If you have a problem with any aspect of this book, you can contact us at `questions@packtpub.com`, and we will do our best to address the problem.

1
Delphi Basics

In this chapter, we will cover the following topics:

- Changing your application's look and feel with the VCL style and without any code
- Changing the style of your application at runtime
- Customizing TDBGrid
- Using owner draw combos and listboxes
- Making an owner draw control aware of the VCL styles
- Creating a stack of embedded forms
- Manipulating JSON
- Manipulating and transforming XML documents
- I/O in the 21st century – knowing the streams
- Creating a Windows service
- Associating a file extension with your application on Windows
- Being coherent with the Windows look and feel using TTaskDialog

Introduction

This chapter will explain some of the day-to-day needs of a Delphi programmer. These are ready-to-use recipes that will be useful every day and have been selected ahead of a lot of others because, although they may be obvious for some experienced users, they are still very useful. Even if there isn't specifically database-related code, many of the recipes can also be used (or sometimes, especially used) when you are dealing with data.

Delphi Basics

Changing your application look and feel with VCL styles and no code

Visual Component Library (**VCL**) styles are a major new entry in the latest versions of Delphi. They have been introduced in Delphi XE2 and are still one of the lesser known features for the good old Delphi developers. However, as usual, some businessmen say "looks matter" so the look and feel of your application could be one of the reasons to choose one product over another from a competitor. Consider that with a few mouse clicks, you can apply many different styles to your application to change the look and feel of your applications. So, why not to give it a try?

Getting ready

VCL styles can be used to revamp an old application or to create a new one with a non-standard GUI. VCL styles are a completely different beast to FireMonkey styles. They are both styles, but with completely different approaches and behavior.

To get started with VCL styles, we'll use a new application. So, let's create a new VCL application and drag and drop some components onto the main form (for example, two TButton, one TListBox, one TComboBox, and a couple of TCheckBox).

You can now see the resultant form that is running on my Windows 8.1 machine:

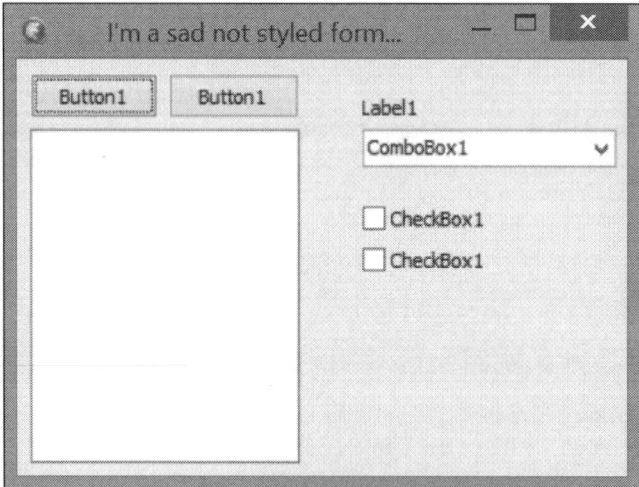

Figure 1.1: A form without style

How to do it...

Now, we've got to apply a set of nice styles by following these steps:

1. Go to **Project | Options** from the menu. Then, in the resultant dialog, go to **Application | Appearance** and select all the styles that we want to include in our application.

2. Using the **Preview** button, the IDE shows a simple demo form with some controls, and we can get an idea about the final result of our styled form. Feel free to experiment and choose the style—or set of styles—that you like. Only one style at a time will be used, but we can link the necessary resources into the executable and select the proper one at runtime.

3. After selecting all the required styles from the list, we've got to select one in the combo box at the bottom. This style will be the default style for our form and will be loaded as soon as the application starts. You can delay this choice and make it at runtime using code if you prefer.

4. Click on **OK**, hit *F9* (or go to **Run | Run**), and your application is styled:

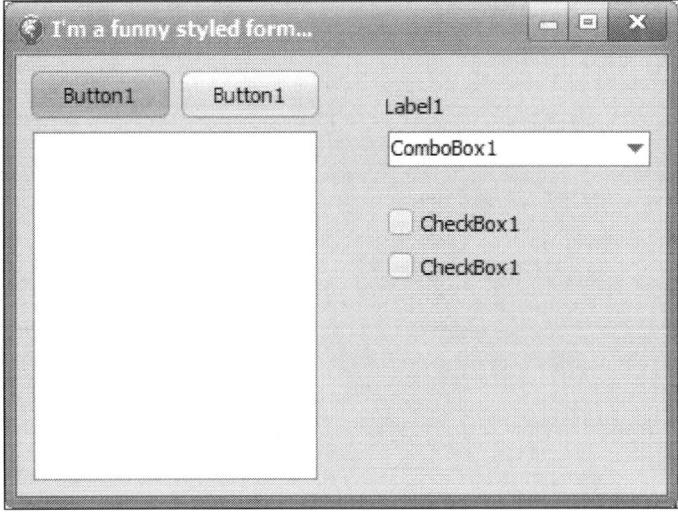

Figure 1.2: The same form as Figure 1.1 but with the Iceberg Classico style applied

Delphi Basics

How it works...

Selecting one or more styles from **Project | Options | Application | Appearance** will cause the Delphi linker to link the style resource into your executable. It is possible to link many styles into your executable, but you can use only one style at a time. So, how does Delphi know which style you want to use when there are more than one? If you check the Project file (the file with the `.dpr` extension) by going to **Project | View Source Menu**, you can see where and how this little magic happens.

The following lines are the interesting section:

```
begin
  Application.Initialize;
  Application.MainFormOnTaskbar := True;
  TStyleManager.TrySetStyle('Iceberg Classico');
  Application.CreateForm(TMainForm, MainForm);
  Application.Run;
end
```

When we've selected the *Iceberg Classico* style as the default style, the Delphi IDE added a line just before the creation of the main form, setting the default style for all the applications using `TStyleManager.TrySetStyle` static methods.

`TStyleManager` is very important class when dealing with VCL styles. We'll see more about it in the upcoming recipe, where you'll learn how to change styles at runtime.

There's more...

Delphi and C++ Builder 10.1 Berlin come with 36 VCL styles available in the folder (with a standard installation):

`C:\Program Files (x86)\Embarcadero\Studio\18.0\Redist\styles\vcl\`

Moreover, it is possible to create your own styles or modify the existing ones using the **Bitmap Style Designer**. You can access it by going to **Tools | Bitmap Style Designer Menu**.

For more details on how to create or customize a VCL style, visit `http://docwiki.embarcadero.com/RADStudio/en/Creating_a_Style_using_the_Bitmap_Style_Designer`.

The Bitmap Style Designer also provides test applications to test VCL styles.

Chapter 1

Changing the style of your VCL application at runtime

VCL styles are a powerful way to change the appearance of your application. One of the main features of VCL styles is the ability to change the style while the application is running.

Getting ready

Because a VCL Style is simply a particular kind of binary file, we can allow our users to load their preferred styles at runtime. We could even provide new styles by publishing them on a website or sending them by e-mail to our customers.

In this recipe, we'll change the style while the application is running using a style already linked at design time, or let the user choose between a set of styles deployed inside a folder.

How to do it...

Style manipulation at runtime is done using the class methods of the `TStyleManager` class. Follow these steps to change the style of your VCL application at runtime:

1. Create a brand new VCL application and add the `Vcl.Themes` and `Vcl.Styles` units to the `implementation main form uses` section. These units are required to use VCL styles at runtime.

2. Drop on the form a TListBox, two TButton, and a TOpenDialog. Leave the default component names.

3. Go to **Project | Appearance** and select eight styles of your choice from the list. Leave the **Default style** to **Windows**.

4. The `TStyleManager.StyleNames` property contains names of all the available styles. In the `FormCreate` event handler, we have to load the already linked styles present in the executable into the listbox to let the user choose one of them. So, create a new procedure called `StylesListRefresh` with the following code and call it from the `FormCreate` event handler:

   ```
   procedure TMainForm.StylesListRefresh;
   var
     stylename: string;
   begin
     ListBox1.Clear;
     // retrieve all the styles linked in the executable
     for stylename in TStyleManager.StyleNames do
     begin
       ListBox1.Items.Add(stylename);
     end;
   end;
   ```

5. In the `Button1Click` event handler, we've to set the current style according to the one selected from the `ListBox1` using the code as follows:

   `TStyleManager.SetStyle(ListBox1.Items[ListBox1.ItemIndex]);`

6. The `Button2Click` event handler should allow the user to select a style from the disk. So, we have to create a folder named `styles` at the level of our executable and copy a `.vsf` file from the default style directory, which, in RAD Studio 10.1 Berlin, is `C:\Program Files (x86)\Embarcadero\Studio\18.0\Redist\styles\vcl\`.

7. After copying, write the following code under the `Button2Click` event handler. This code allows the user to choose a style file directly from the disk. Then, you can select one of the loaded styles from the listbox and click on **Button1** to apply it to application:

```
if OpenDialog1.Execute then
begin
  if TStyleManager.IsValidStyle(OpenDialog1.FileName) then
  begin
    //load the style file
TStyleManager.LoadFromFile(OpenDialog1.FileName);
//refresh the list with the currently available styles
    StylesListRefresh;
    ShowMessage('New VCL Style has been loaded');
  end
  else
    ShowMessage('The file is not a valid VCL Style!');
  end;
end;
```

8. Just to have an idea of how the different controls appear with the selected style, drag and drop some controls on the right-hand side of the form. The following image shows my application with some styles loaded, some at design time and some from the disk.

9. Hit *F9* (or go to **Run | Run**), and play with your application using and loading styles from the disk:

Chapter 1

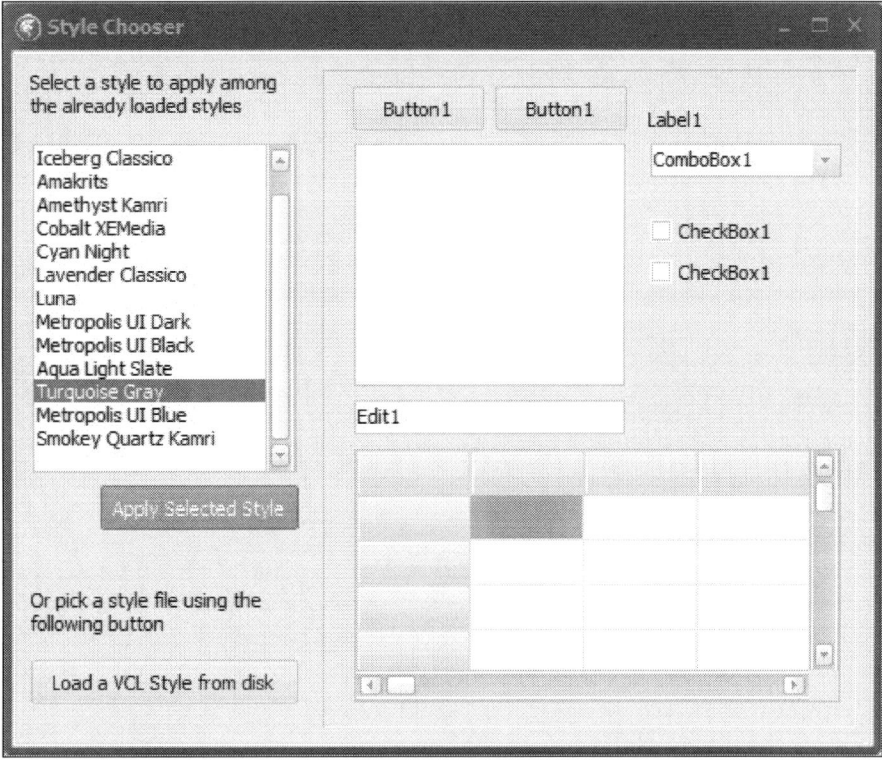

Figure 2.1: The Style Chooser form with a Torquoise Gray style loaded

How it works...

The `TStyleManager` class has all the methods we need to:

- Inspect the loaded styles with `TStyleManager.StyleNames`
- Apply an already loaded style to the running application using the following code:
  `TStyleManager.SetStyle('StyleName')`
- Check whether a file is a valid style using the following code:
  `TStyleManager.IsValidStyle('StylePathFileName')`
- Load a style file from the disk using the following code:
  `TStyleManager.LoadFromFile('StylePathFileName')`

After loading new styles from the disk, the new styles are completely similar to the styles linked in the executable during the compile and link phases and can be used in the same way.

Delphi Basics

There's more...

Other things to consider are third-party controls. If your application uses third-party controls, take care with their style support (some third-party controls are not be style aware). If your external components do not support styles, you will end up with some styled controls (the original included in Delphi) and some not styled (your external third-party controls)!

Go to **Tools** | **Bitmap Style Designer**. Using a custom VCL style we can also:

- Change application colors, such as `ButtonNormal`, `ButtonPressed`, `ButtonFocused`, `ButtonHot`, and others
- Override system colors, such as `clCaptionText`, `clBtnFace`, `clActiveCaption`, and so on
- Font color and font name for particular controls familiar to `ButtonTextNormal`, `ButtonTextPressed`, `ButtonTextFocused`, `ButtonTextHot`, and many others

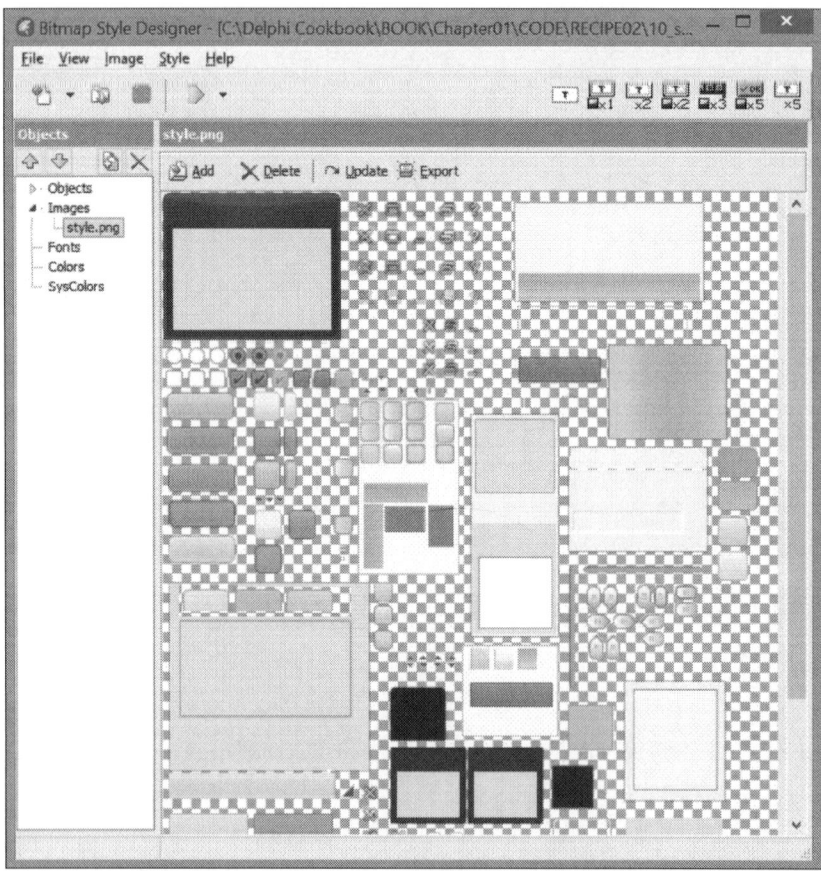

Figure 2.2: The Bitmap Style Designer while it is working on a custom style

Chapter 1

Customizing TDBGrid

The adage "A picture is worth a thousand words" refers to the notion that a complex idea can be conveyed with just a single still image. Sometimes, even a simple concept is easier to understand and nicer to see if it is represented by images. In this recipe, we'll see how to customize TDBGrid to visualize a graphical representation of data.

Getting ready

Many VCL controls are able to delegate their drawing, or part of it, to user code. It means that we can use simple event handlers to draw standard components in different ways. It is not always simple, but TDBGrid is customizable in a really easy way. Let's say that we have a class of musicians that have to pass a set of exams. We want to show the percent of exams already passed with a progress bar and, if the percent is higher than 50, there should also be a check in another column. Moreover, after listening to the pieces played at the exams, each musician received votes from an external examination committee. The last column needs to show the mean of votes from this committee as a rating from 0 to 5.

How to do it...

We'll use a special in memory table from the `FireDAC` library. `FireDAC` is a new data access library from Embarcadero included in RAD Studio since version XE5. If some of the code seems unclear at the moment, consider the in-memory table as a normal TDataSet descendant, which holds its data only in memory. However, at the end of the section, there are some links to the FireDAC documentation, and I strongly suggest that you read them if you still don't know FireDAC:

1. Create a brand new VCL application and drop a TFDMemTable, a TDBGrid, a TDataSource, and a TDBNavigator on the form. Connect all the components in the usual way (TDBGrid connected to TDataSource followed by TFDMemTable). Set TDBGrid's font size to `18`. This will create more space in the cell for our graphical representation.

2. Using the TFDMemTable fields editor, add the following fields and then activate the dataset by setting its `Active` property to `True`:

Field name	Field data type	Field type
`FullName`	`String (size 50)`	Data
`TotalExams`	`Integer`	Data
`PassedExams`	`Integer`	Data
`Rating`	`Float`	Data
`PercPassedExams`	`Float`	Calculated
`MoreThan50Percent`	`Boolean`	Calculated

Delphi Basics

3. Now, add all the columns to TDBGrid by right-clicking and selecting **Columns Editor**. Then, again right-click and select **Add all fields** on the resultant window. Then, rearrange the columns as shown here and give a nice title caption:
    - FullName
    - TotalExams
    - PassedExams
    - PercPassedExams
    - MoreThan50Percent
    - Rating

4. In a real application, we should load real data from some sort of database. However, for now, we'll use some custom data generated in code. We have to load this data into the dataset with the code as follows:

```
procedure TMainForm.FormCreate(Sender: TObject);
begin
  FDMemTable1.AppendRecord(
['Ludwig van Beethoven', 30, 10, 4]);
  FDMemTable1.AppendRecord(
['Johann Sebastian Bach', 24, 10, 2.5]);
  FDMemTable1.AppendRecord(
['Wolfgang Amadeus Mozart', 30, 30, 5]);
  FDMemTable1.AppendRecord(
['Giacomo Puccini', 25, 10, 2.2]);
  FDMemTable1.AppendRecord(
['Antonio Vivaldi', 20, 20, 4.7]);
  FDMemTable1.AppendRecord(
['Giuseppe Verdi', 30, 5, 5]);
  FDMemTable1.AppendRecord(
['John Doe', 24, 5, 1.2]);
end;
```

5. Do you remember? We've two calculated fields that need to be filled in some way. Calculated fields need a form of processing behind them to work. The TFDMemTable, just like any other TDataSet descendant, has an event called `OnCalcFields` that allows the developer to do so. Create the `OnCalcFields` event handler on TFDMemTable and fill it with the following code:

```
procedure TMainForm.FDMemTable1CalcFields(
DataSet: TDataSet);
var
  LPassedExams: Integer;
  LTotExams: Integer;
begin
```

```delphi
    LPassedExams := FDMemTable1.
      FieldByName('PassedExams').AsInteger;
    LTotExams := FDMemTable1.
      FieldByName('TotalExams').AsInteger;
  if LTotExams = 0 then
    FDMemTable1.FieldByName('PercPassedExams').AsFloat := 0
else
      FDMemTable1.FieldByName('PercPassedExams').AsFloat :=
        LPassedExams / LTotExams * 100;

FDMemTable1.FieldByName('MoreThan50Percent').AsBoolean :=
  FDMemTable1.FieldByName('PercPassedExams').AsFloat > 50;
    end;
    end;
```

6. Run the application by hitting *F9* (or by going to **Run | Run**) and you will get the following screenshot:

Figure 3.1: A normal form with some data

7. This is useful, but a bit boring. Let's start our customization. Close the application and return to the Delphi IDE.

8. Go to the **Properties** of TDBGrid and set **Default Drawing** to False.

9. Now, we've to organize the resources used to draw the grid cells. Calculated fields will be drawn directly using code, but the Rating field will be drawn using a 5-star rating image from 0 to 5. It starts with a 0.5 incremental step (0, 0.5, 1, 1.5, and so on). So, drop TImageList on the form, and set Height as 32 and Width as 160.

Delphi Basics

10. Select the TImageList component and open the image list's editor by right-clicking and then selecting **ImageList Editor**. You can find the needed PNG images in the recipe project folder (`ICONS\RATING_IMAGES`). Load the images in the correct order as shown here:

    - Index 0 as `image 0_0_rating.png`
    - Index 1 as `image 0_5_rating.png`
    - Index 2 as `image 1_0_rating.png`
    - Index 3 as `image 1_5_rating.png`
    - Index 4 as `image 2_0_rating.png`

Go to `TDBGrid` events and create the event handler for `OnDrawColumnCell`. All the customization code goes in this event.

Include the `Vcl.GraphUtil` unit, and write the following code in the `DBGrid1DrawColumnCell` event:

```
procedure TMainForm.DBGrid1DrawColumnCell(Sender: TObject;
  const Rect: TRect; DataCol: Integer;
  Column: TColumn; State: TGridDrawState);
var
  LRect: TRect;
  LGrid: TDBGrid;
  LText: string;
  LPerc: Extended;
  LTextWidth: TSize;
  LSavedPenColor, LSavedBrushColor: Integer;
  LSavedPenStyle: TPenStyle;
  LSavedBrushStyle: TBrushStyle;
  LRating: Extended;
  LNeedOwnerDraw: Boolean;
begin
  LGrid := TDBGrid(Sender);
  if [gdSelected, gdFocused] * State <> [] then
    LGrid.Canvas.Brush.Color := clHighlight;

  LNeedOwnerDraw := (Column.Field.FieldKind = fkCalculated)
    or Column.FieldName.Equals('Rating');

  if LNeedOwnerDraw then
  begin
    LRect := Rect;
    LSavedPenColor := LGrid.Canvas.Pen.Color;
    LSavedBrushColor := LGrid.Canvas.Brush.Color;
    LSavedPenStyle := LGrid.Canvas.Pen.Style;
```

```
    LSavedBrushStyle := LGrid.Canvas.Brush.Style;

    if Column.FieldName.Equals('PercPassedExams') then
    begin
      LText := FormatFloat('##0',
        Column.Field.AsFloat) + ' %';
      LGrid.Canvas.Brush.Style := bsSolid;
      LGrid.Canvas.FillRect(LRect);
      LPerc := Column.Field.AsFloat / 100 * LRect.Width;
      LGrid.Canvas.Font.Size := LGrid.Font.Size - 1;
      LGrid.Canvas.Font.Color := clWhite;
      LGrid.Canvas.Brush.Color := clYellow;
      LGrid.Canvas.RoundRect(LRect.Left, LRect.Top,
        Trunc(LRect.Left + LPerc), LRect.Bottom, 2, 2);
      LRect.Inflate(-1, -1);
      LGrid.Canvas.Pen.Style := psClear;
      LGrid.Canvas.Font.Color := clBlack;
      LGrid.Canvas.Brush.Style := bsClear;

      LTextWidth := LGrid.Canvas.TextExtent(LText);
      LGrid.Canvas.TextOut(LRect.Left + (
        (LRect.Width div 2) - (LTextWidth.cx div 2)),
          LRect.Top + ((LRect.Height div 2) -
          (LTextWidth.cy div 2)), LText);
    end
    else if Column.FieldName.
Equals('MoreThan50Percent') then
    begin
      LGrid.Canvas.Brush.Style := bsSolid;
      LGrid.Canvas.Pen.Style := psClear;
      LGrid.Canvas.FillRect(LRect);
      if Column.Field.AsBoolean then
      begin
        LRect.Inflate(-4, -4);
        LGrid.Canvas.Pen.Color := clRed;
        LGrid.Canvas.Pen.Style := psSolid;
        DrawCheck(LGrid.Canvas,
          TPoint.Create(LRect.Left,
          LRect.Top + LRect.Height div 2),
          LRect.Height div 3);
      end;
    end
    else if Column.FieldName.Equals('Rating') then
    begin
```

```
      LRating := Column.Field.AsFloat;
      if LRating.Frac < 5 then
        LRating := Trunc(LRating);
      if LRating.Frac >= 5 then
        LRating := Trunc(LRating) + 0.5;
      LText := LRating.ToString;
      LGrid.Canvas.Brush.Color := clWhite;
      LGrid.Canvas.Brush.Style := bsSolid;
      LGrid.Canvas.Pen.Style := psClear;
      LGrid.Canvas.FillRect(LRect);
      Inc(LRect.Left);
      ImageList1.Draw(LGrid.Canvas,
        LRect.CenterPoint.X - (ImageList1.Width div 2),
        LRect.CenterPoint.Y - (ImageList1.Height div 2),
        Trunc(LRating) * 2);
    end;
  end
  else
    LGrid.DefaultDrawColumnCell(Rect, DataCol,
      Column, State);

  if LNeedOwnerDraw then
  begin
    LGrid.Canvas.Pen.Color := LSavedPenColor;
    LGrid.Canvas.Brush.Color := LSavedBrushColor;
    LGrid.Canvas.Pen.Style := LSavedPenStyle;
    LGrid.Canvas.Brush.Style := LSavedBrushStyle;
  end;
end;
```

11. That's all folks! Hit *F9* (or go to **Run | Run**), and we now have a nicer grid with more direct information about our data:

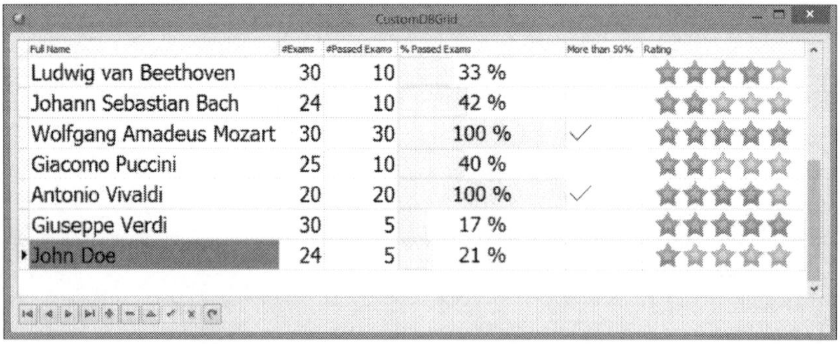

Figure 3.2: The same grid with a bit of customization

How it works...

By setting the DBGrid property `DefaultDrawing` to `False`, we told the grid that we want to manually draw all the data into every cell. `OnDrawColumnCell` allows us to actually draw using standard Delphi code. For each cell we are about to draw, the event handler is called with a list of useful parameters to know which cell we're about to draw and what data we have to read considering the column we are currently drawing. In this case, we want to draw only the calculated columns and the `Rating` field in a custom way. This is not a rule, but this can be done to manipulate all cells. We can draw any cell in the way we like. For the cells where we don't want to do custom drawing, a simple call method, `DefaultDrawColumnCell` that passes the same parameters we got from the event and the VCL code will draw the current cell as usual.

Among the event parameters, there is a `Rect` object (of type `TRect`) that represents the specific area we're about to draw. There is a column object (of type `TColumn`) that is a reference to the current column of the grid and a `State` (of type `TGridDrawState`) that is a set of the grid cell states (for example, `Selected`, `Focused`, `HotTrack`, and many more). If our drawing code ignores the `State` parameter, all the cells will be drawn in the same way, and users cannot see which cell or row is selected.

The event handler uses a **Pascal Sets Intersect** to know whether the current cell should be drawn as a `Selected` or `Focused` cell. Refer the following code for better clarity:

```
if [gdSelected, gdFocused] * State <> [] then
  Grid.Canvas.Brush.Color := clHighlight;
```

> Remember that if your dataset has 100 records and 20 fields, `OnDrawColumnCell` will potentially be called 2000 times! So, the event code must be fast; otherwise, the application will become less responsive.

There's more...

Owner drawing is a really large topic and can be simple or tremendously complex, involving much Canvas-related code. However, often the kind of drawing you need will be relatively similar. So, if you need checks, arrows, color gradients, and so on, check the procedures into the `Vcl.GraphUtil` unit. Otherwise, if you need images, you could use TImageList to hold all the images needed by your grid, as we did in this recipe for the `Rating` field.

The good news is that the drawing code can be reused by different kinds of controls, so try to organize your code in a way that allows code reutilization by avoiding direct dependencies to the form where the control is.

The code in the drawing events should not contain business logic or presentation logic. If you need presentation logic, put it in a separate, testable function or class.

Delphi Basics

Using owner draw combos and listboxes

Many things are organized in a list. Lists are useful when you have to show items or when your user has to choose from a set of possible options. Usually, standard lists are flat, but sometimes, you need to transmit more information in addition to a list of items. Let's think about when you go to choose a font in an advanced text editor such as Microsoft Word or Apache OpenOffice. Having the name of the font drawn in the font style itself helps users make a faster and more reasoned choice. In this recipe, we'll see how to make listboxes more useful. The code is perfectly valid for TComboBox as well.

Getting ready

As we saw in the recipe, *Customizing TDBGrid*, many VCL controls are able to delegate their drawing, or part of it, to user code. It means that we can use simple event handlers to draw standard components in different ways. Let's say that we have a list of products in our store and we have to set discounts on these products. As there are many products, we want to make the processing in a way that our users can make a fast selection between the available discount percentages using a "color code."

How to do it...

1. Create a brand new VCL application and drop a TListBox on the form. Set the following properties:

Property	Value
Style	lbOwnerDrawFixed
Font.Size	14

2. In the listbox Items property, add seven levels of discount. For example, you can use no discount, 10 percent discount, 20 percent discount, 30 percent discount, 40 percent discount, 50 percent discount, 60 percent discount, and 70 percent discount.

3. Then, drop a TImageList component on the form and set the following properties:

Property	Value
ColorDepth	cd32Bit
DrawingStyle	dsTransparent
Width	32
Height	32

4. TImageList is our image repository and will be used to draw an image by index. Load 7 PNG images (size 32 x 32) into TImageList. You can find some nice PNG icons in the respective recipe project folder (ICONS\PNG\32).

5. Create an OnDrawItem event handler for TListBox and write the following code:

```
procedure TCustomListControlsForm.ListBox1DrawItem(
Control: TWinControl; Index: Integer;
Rect: TRect; State: TOwnerDrawState);
var
  LBox: TListBox;
  R: TRect;
  S: string;
  TextTopPos, TextLeftPos, TextHeight: Integer;
const
  IMAGE_TEXT_SPACE = 5;
begin
  LBox := Control as TListBox;
  R := Rect;
  LBox.Canvas.FillRect(R);
  ImageList1.Draw(LBox.Canvas, R.Left, R.Top, Index);
  S := LBox.Items[Index];
  TextHeight := LBox.Canvas.TextHeight(S);
  TextLeftPos := R.Left +
    ImageList1.Width + IMAGE_TEXT_SPACE;
  TextTopPos := R.Top + R.Height div 2 - TextHeight div 2;
  LBox.Canvas.TextOut(TextLeftPos, TextTopPos, S);
end;
```

6. Run the application by hitting *F9* (or by going to **Run | Run**) and you will see the following screenshot:

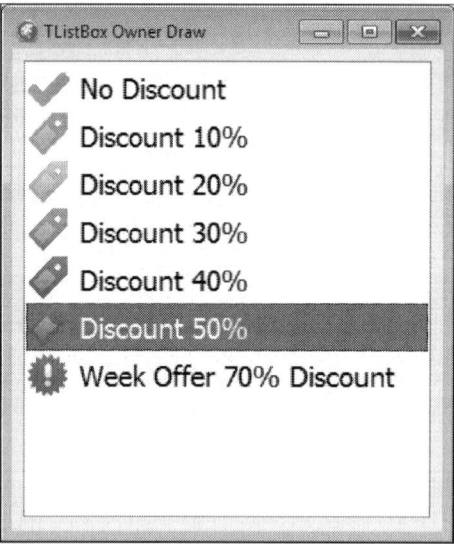

Figure 4.1: Our listbox with some custom icons read from TImageList

How it works...

The `TListBox.OnDrawItem` event handler allows us to customize the drawing of the listbox. In this recipe, we've used TImageList as the image repository for the listbox. Using the `Index` parameter, we've read the correspondent image in TImageList and drawn on the listbox Canvas. After this, all the other code is related to the alignment of image and text inside the listbox row.

Remember that this event handler will be called for each item in the list, so the code must be fast and should not do too much slow Canvas writing. Otherwise, all your GUI will be unresponsive. If you want to create complex graphics "on the fly" in the event, I strongly suggest that you prepare your images the first time you draw the item and then put them in a sort of cache memory (`TObjectList<TBitmap>` is enough).

There's more...

While you are in `OnDrawItem`, you can do whatever you want with the TListBox Canvas. Moreover, the `State` parameter (of type `TOwnerDrawState`) tells you in which states the listbox item is (for example, `Selected`, `Focused`, `HotTrack`, and so on). So, you can use a different kind of drawing, depending on the item state. Check out the *Customizing TDBGrid* recipe to find out about the TDBGrid owner drawing for an example about the State parameter.

If you want to make your code aware of the selected VCL style, changing the color used according to it, you can use `StyleServices.GetStyleColor()`, `StyleServices.GetStyleFontColor()`, and `StyleServices.GetSystemColor()` in the `Vcl.Themes` unit.

The icons used in this recipe are from the Icojam website (http://www.icojam.com). The specific set used is available at http://www.icojam.com/blog/?p=259.

Making an owner draw control aware of the VCL styles

Owner draw controls are powerful. They allow you to completely tune your GUI for the needs of your users and potentially enable your application to display data in a more familiar way. In the end, owner draw controls improve the user experience with your application. However, owner draw controls do not always fit well with the VCL custom styles. Why? Because if you try to draw something by yourself, you could be tempted to use a "fixed" color, such `clRed` or `clYellow`, or you could be tempted to use the operating system color, such as `clBtnFace` or `clWindow`. Doing so, your owner draw controls will be not style aware and will be drawn in the same way regardless of the current VCL style. In this recipe, you'll learn how to make custom graphics remaining being in topic with the selected VCL style.

Getting ready

Let's say you are in charge of developing a controller panel for a hotel's light system. You have a list of lamps to power on, and you, using some hardware, have to power on some lamps by clicking on a button. Customers tell you that buttons should show some additional information about the lamp, for example:

- Served zone (corridor, hall, room number, and so on)
- State (on/off using some fancy graphics)
- The time the lamp was powered on
- The time when electrical problems have been detected, showing a red icon to indicate that the lamp is off even when current supplies the line, so the circuit is interrupted somewhere
- Other custom information not currently known, such as small graphs showing lamp state history during the last 24 hours

Delphi Basics

The question is how to implement this kind of UI. One of the possible ways is to use TDrawGrid and draw all the needed details in each cell, using the cell also as a button. Using TDrawGrid, you have a grid of buttons for free. You have also the greatest flexibility about the information displayed because you are using the `TCanvas` method to custom draw each cell. This is quite a popular solution for this kind of non-standard UI. However, when you deploy this application, the customers ask about the possibility of changing the style of the application to fit the needs of the current user. So, you think about VCL styles, and you are right. However, the graphics drawn into the cells don't follow the currently selected VCL style, and your beautiful application becomes a bad mix of colors. In other words, when users change the selected VCL style, all the controls reflect the new style, but the owner drawn grid, which is unaware to the selected style, doesn't look as nice as the rest of the UI. How to solve this problem? How to draw custom graphics by adhering to the selected VCL style? In this recipe, you'll learn how to do it using the lamp control grid example.

How it works...

At design time, the form looks like the one shown in the following screenshot:

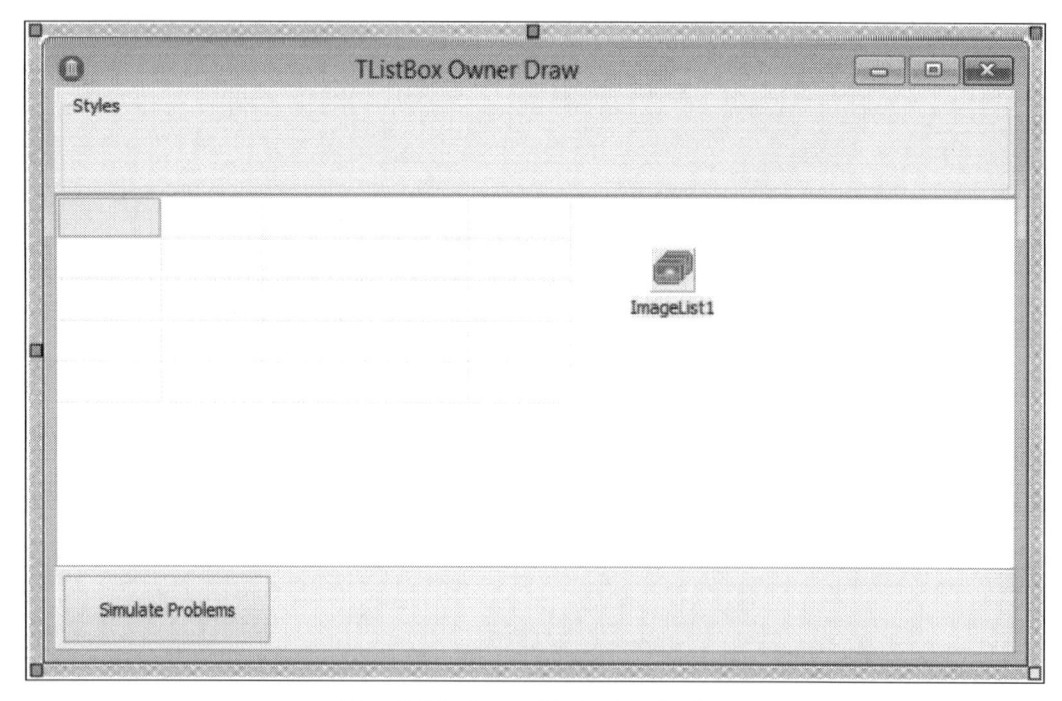

Figure 5.1 The form as it looks at design time

When the form is created, the list of available styles is loaded in the Radio group using code similar to the following one:

```
RadioGroup1.Items.Clear;
RadioGroup1.Columns := Length(TStyleManager.StyleNames);
for LStyleName in TStyleManager.StyleNames do
  RadioGroup1.Items.Add(LStyleName);
RadioGroup1.ItemIndex := 0;
TStyleManager.SetStyle('Windows');
```

Then, a list of the `TLampInfo` object is created and initialized using the information contained in the `Zones` array. After that, the draw grid is initialized according to the `LAMPS_FOR_EACH_ROW` constant. Here's the relevant code:

```
FLamps := TObjectList<TLampInfo>.Create(True);
for I := 1 to LAMPS_FOR_EACH_ROW * 4 do
begin
  FLamps.Add(TLampInfo.Create(Zones[I]));
end;

DrawGrid1.DefaultColWidth := 128;
DrawGrid1.DefaultRowHeight := 64;
DrawGrid1.ColCount := LAMPS_FOR_EACH_ROW;
DrawGrid1.RowCount := FLamps.Count div LAMPS_FOR_EACH_ROW;
```

The `FormCreate` event handler initializes the styles list and the list of the lamps (the model) of the form. Now, we'll see how the other event handlers will use them.

The `TDrawGrid OnSelectCell` event, as the name suggests, is used to address the current "lamp" from the `FLamps` and to toggle its state. That's it. If the lamp is on, then the lamp will be powered down, else the lamp will be powered on. After that, the code forces the grid to redraw using the `Invalidate` method:

```
procedure TMainForm.DrawGrid1SelectCell(Sender: TObject; ACol,
  ARow: Integer; var CanSelect: Boolean);
begin
  FLamps[ACol + ARow * LAMPS_FOR_EACH_ROW].ToggleState;
  DrawGrid1.Invalidate;
end;
```

Delphi Basics

Now, really interesting things happened in the `DrawThemed` method called inside the `TDrawGrid OnDrawCell` event. This method receives information about the coordinates of the cell to draw, and then it draws a button on the canvas using the information contained in the correspond `TLampInfo` instance. The code is quite long, but an interesting concept is that no specific colors are used. When it is necessary to draw something, the code asks `StyleService` to get the correct color according to the current style. This approach is also used for font color and for system colors. Here's a handy table that summarizes these concepts:

Method name	Description
`StyleServices.GetStyleColor(Color: TStyleColor)`	Returns the color defined in the style for the element specified by `Color`
`StyleServices.StyleFontColor(Font: TStyleFont)`	Returns the font color for the element specified by `Font`
`StyleServices.GetSystemColor(Color: TColor)`	Returns the system color defined in the current style

So, when we have to highlight the (pseudo) button, if there are electrical problems on the power line, we will use the following code:

```
if LLamp.ThereAreElectricalProblems then
    LCanvas.Brush.Color := StyleServices.GetStyleColor(scButtonHot)
else
    LCanvas.Brush.Color := StyleServices.GetStyleColor(scWindow);
LCanvas.FillRect(LRect);
```

When we've got to draw normal text, we will use the following code:

```
LCanvas.Font.Color :=
    StyleServices.GetStyleFontColor(sfButtonTextNormal);
LCanvas.TextRect(LRect, LValue, [TTextFormats.tfCenter,
    TTextFormats.tfVerticalCenter]);
```

It is clear that the paradigm is:

▸ Get the current color for the selected element of the UI according to the style
▸ Draw the graphics using that color

Clicking on the **Simulate Problems** button, it is possible to see how the graphics is drawn in the case of problems on the power line. The images are drawn directly from the image list using the following code:

```
procedure TMainForm.DrawImageOnCanvas(ACanvas: TCanvas;
  var ARect: TRect; ImageIndex: Integer);
begin
  ImageList1.Draw(ACanvas, ARect.Left + 4,
    ARect.Top + ((ARect.Bottom - ARect.Top) div 2) - 16,
    ImageIndex);
end;
```

Using this approach, the application created in this recipe, which has a lot of custom graphics, behaves very well even on VCL styles. Here are some screenshots:

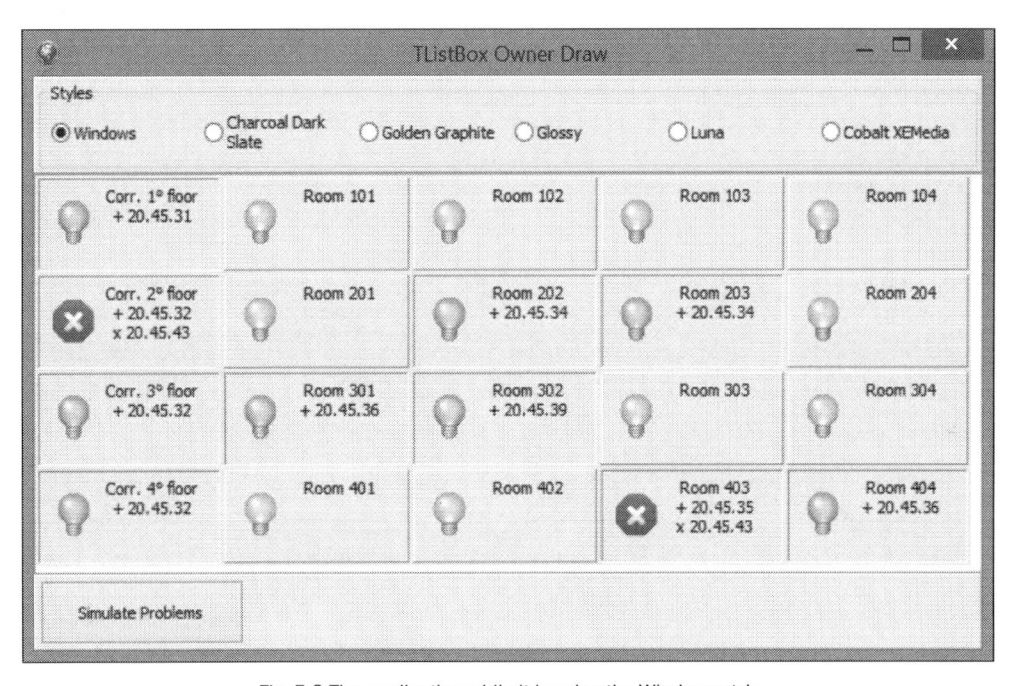

Fig. 5.2 The application while it is using the Windows style

Delphi Basics

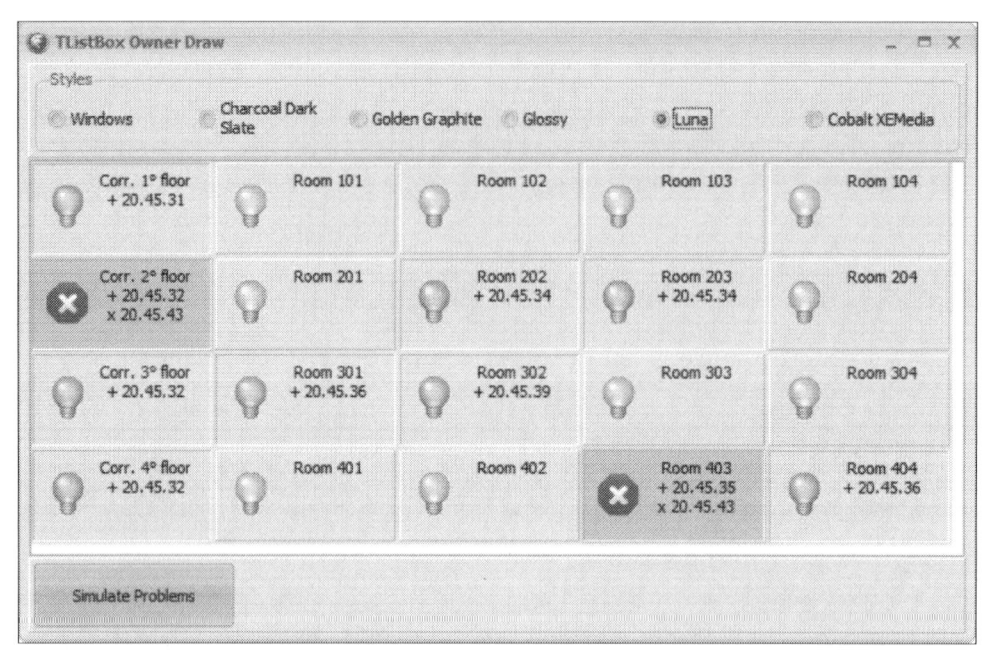

Fig. 5.3 The application while it is using the Luna style

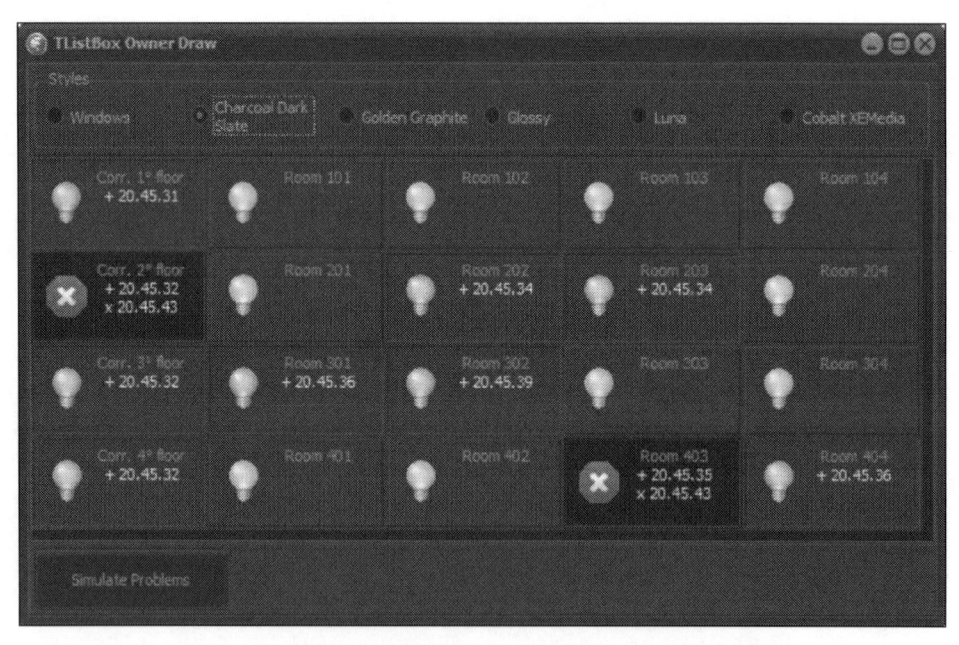

Fig. 5.4 The application while it is using the Charcoal Dark Slate style

As you see, the application correctly draws the owner draw parts of the UI using the right colors from the selected style.

There's more...

The VCL style infrastructure is very powerful. In the case of TWinControl descendants, you can even define specific hooks for you components using `TStyleHook`. `TStyleHook` is a class that handles messages for controls acting as a wrapper for the hooked control. If you have a custom control that you want to be style enabled, inherit from `TStyleHook` and provide custom processing for that control. As examples, see `TEditStyleHook` and `TComboBoxStyleHook`. You need to register the style hook class with the style engine using the `RegisterStyleHook` method as shown in the following code:

```
TCustomStyleEngine.RegisterStyleHook(TCustomEdit, TEditStyleHook);
```

Moreover, the `StyleServices` function returns an instance of `TCustomStyleServices`, which provides a lot of customization methods related to the VCL styles. Check out the related documentation at `http://docwiki.embarcadero.com/Libraries/en/Vcl.Themes.TCustomStyleServices_Methods` to see all the possibilities

Creating a stack of embedded forms

Every modern browser has a tabbed interface. Also, many other kinds of "multiple views" software have this kind of interface. Why? Because it's very useful. While you are reading one page, you can rapidly check another page and still come back to the first one at the same point you left some seconds ago. You don't have to redo a search or use a lot of mouse clicks to just go back to that particular point. You simply have switched from one window to another window and back to the first. I have seen too many business applications that are composed of a bunch of dialog windows. Every form is called with the `TForm.ShowModal` method. So the user has to navigate into your application one form at time. This is simpler to handle for the programmer, but it's less user friendly for your customers. However, giving a "switchable" interface to your customer is not that difficult. In this recipe, we'll see a complete example of how to do it.

Getting ready

This recipe is a bit more complex than the previous recipes. So, I'll not explain all the code but only the fundamental parts. You can find the complete code in the book code repository (`Chapter1\RECIPE06`).

Delphi Basics

Let's say we want to create a tabbed interface for our software that is used to manage product orders, sales, and invoices. All the forms must be usable at the same time, without having to close the previous one. Before we begin, the following screenshot is what we want to create:

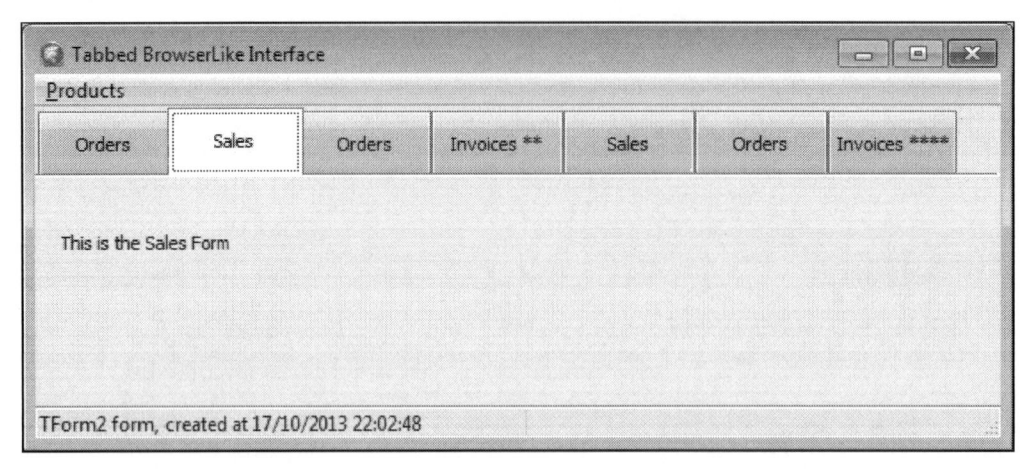

Figure 5.1: The main form containing seven embedded child forms

How it works...

The project is composed of a bunch of forms. The main form has `TTabControl`, which allows us to switch between the active forms. All embedded forms inherit from `EmbeddableForm`. The most important is the method `Show` shown here:

```
procedure TEmbeddableForm.Show(AParent: TPanel);
begin
  Parent := AParent;
  BorderStyle := bsNone;
  BorderIcons := [];
  Align := alClient;
  Show;
end;
```

> Note that all the forms apart from the main form, have been removed from the "Auto-Create Form" list (you can access the list by going to **Project | Options | Forms**).

All the other forms descend from `EmbeddableForm` and are added to `TTabControl` on the main form with a line of code similar to the following one:

```
procedure TMainForm.MenuOrdersClick(Sender: TObject);
begin
  AddForm(TForm1.Create(self));
end;
```

The `AddForm` method is in charge of adding an actual instance of a form into the tabs, keeping a reference to it. The following code shows how it is done:

```
//Add a form to the stack
procedure TMainForm.AddForm(
AEmbeddableForm: TEmbeddableForm);
begin
  AEmbeddableForm.Show(Panel1);
  //each tab show the caption of the containing form and
  //hold the reference to it
  TabControl1.Tabs.AddObject(
    AEmbeddableForm.Caption, AEmbeddableForm);
  ResizeTabsWidth;
  ShowForm(AEmbeddableForm);
end;
```

Other methods are in charge of bringing an already created form to the front when a user clicks on the **Related** tab, and then to close a form when the **Related** tab is removed (check out the `ShowForm` and `WMEmbeddedFormClose` methods).

There is a bit of code, but the concepts are simple:

- When we need to create a new form, add it in the `TabControl1.Tabs` property. The caption of the form is the caption of the tab, and the object is the form itself. This is what the `AddForm` method does with the following line:

    ```
    TabControl1.Tabs.AddObject(AEmbeddableForm.Caption,
      AEmbeddableForm);
    ```

- When a user clicks on a tab, we have to find the associated form by cycling through the `TabControl1.Tabs.Objects` list and bringing it to the front.

- When a form asks to be closed (sending a `WM_EMBEDDED_CLOSE` message), we have to set the `ParentWantClose` property and then call the `Close` method of the correspondent form.

- If the user wants to close a form by closing the corresponding tab (in the recipe code, there is `TPopMenu` connected to `TabControl`, which is used to close a form with a right-click), we have to call the `Close` method on the corresponding form.

- Every form frees itself in the `OnClose` event handler. This is done one time for all the forms in the `TEmbeddableForm.CloseForm` event handler, using the `caFree` action.

Delphi Basics

There's more...

Embedding a form into another `TWinControl` is not difficult and allows us to create flexible GUIs without using `TPageControl` and `Frames`. Probably, for the end user, this multi-tabbed GUI is probably more familiar because all the modern browsers use it, and probably, your user already knows how to use a browser with different pages or screens opened. From the developer's point of view, the multi-tabbed interface allows for much better programming patterns and practices. This technique can also be used for other scenarios where you have to embed one "screen" into another.

More flexible (and complex) solutions can be done involving the use of Observers, but in simple cases, this recipe's solution based on Windows Messaging is enough.

More information about the Observer design pattern can be found at `http://sourcemaking.com/design_patterns/observer/delphi`.

Another interesting solution (that doesn't rely on Windows Messaging and so is also cross-platform) may be based on the `System.Messaging.TMessageManager` class. More information about TMessageManager can be obtained at `http://docwiki.embarcadero.com/Libraries/en/System.Messaging.TMessageManager`.

Code in this recipe can be used with every component that uses `TStringList` to show items (TListBox, TComboBox, and so on) and can be adapted easily for other scenarios.

In the recipe code, you'll also find a nice way to show status messages generated by the embedded forms and a centralized way to show application hints in the status bar.

Manipulating JSON

JSON (JavaScript Object Notation) is a lightweight data-interchange format. As the reference site says, "It is easy for humans to read and write. It is easy for machines to parse and generate." It is based on a subset of the JavaScript programming language, but it is not limited to JavaScript in any way. Indeed, JSON is a text format that is completely language agnostic. These properties make JSON an ideal data-interchange language for many uses. In recent years, JSON has become on a par with XML in many applications, especially when the data size matters, because of its intrinsic conciseness and simplicity.

Getting ready

JSON provides the following five datatypes: `String`, `Number`, `Object`, `Array`, `Boolean`, and `Null`.

This simplicity is an advantage when you have to read a JSON string into some kind of language-specific structure, because every modern language supports the JSON datatypes as simple types or as HashMap (in the case of JSON objects) or List (in the case of JSON arrays). So, it makes sense that a data format that is interchangeable with programming languages is also based on these types and structures.

Since version 2009, Delphi provides built-in support for JSON. The `System.JSON.pas` unit contains all the JSON types with a nice object oriented interface. In this recipe, you'll see how to generate, modify, and parse a JSON string.

How to do it...

1. Create a new VCL application and drop three TButton and a TMemo. Align all the buttons as a toolbar at the top of the form and the memo to all the remaining form client area.
2. From left to right, name the buttons as `btnGenerateJSON`, `btnModifyJSON`, and `btnParseJSON`.
3. We'll use static data as our data source. A simple matrix is enough for this recipe. Just after the start of the implementation section of the unit, write the following code:

```
type
  TCarInfo = (
    Manufacturer = 1,
    Name = 2,
    Currency = 3,
    Price = 4);

var
  Cars: array [1 .. 4] of
    array [Manufacturer .. Price] of string = (
    ('Ferrari','360 Modena','EUR', '250000'),
    ('Ford', 'Mustang', 'USD', '80000'),
    ('Lamborghini', 'Countach', 'EUR','300000'),
    ('Chevrolet', 'Corvette', 'USD', '100000')
    );
```

Delphi Basics

4. TMemo is used to show our JSON files and our data. To keep things clear, create a public property called JSON on the form and map its setter and getter to the Memo1.Lines.Text property. Use the following code:

```
//...other form methods declaration
private
   procedure SetJSON(const Value: String);
   function GetJSON: String;
public
   property JSON: String read GetJSON write SetJSON;
end;

//...then in the implementation section
function TMainForm.GetJSON: String;
begin
   Result := Memo1.Lines.Text;
end;

procedure TMainForm.SetJSON(const Value: String);
begin
   Memo1.Lines.Text := Value;
end;
```

5. Now, create event handlers for each button and write the code that follows. Pay attention to the event names:

```
procedure TMainForm.btnGenerateJSONClick(Sender: TObject);
var
   i: Integer;
   JSONCars: TJSONArray;
   Car, Price: TJSONObject;
begin
   JSONCars := TJSONArray.Create;
   try
      for i := Low(Cars) to High(Cars) do
      begin
         Car := TJSONObject.Create;
         JSONCars.AddElement(Car);
         Car.AddPair('manufacturer',
            Cars[i][TCarInfo.Manufacturer]);
         Car.AddPair('name', Cars[i][TCarInfo.Name]);
         Price := TJSONObject.Create;
         Car.AddPair('price', Price);
         Price.AddPair('value',
            TJSONNumber.Create(
               Cars[i][TCarInfo.Price].ToInteger));
```

```
      Price.AddPair('currency',
        Cars[i][TCarInfo.Currency]);
    end;
    JSON := JSONCars.ToJSON;
  finally
    JSONCars.Free;
  end;
end;

procedure TMainForm.btnModifyJSONClick(Sender: TObject);
var
  JSONCars: TJSONArray;
  Car, Price: TJSONObject;
begin
  JSONCars := TJSONObject.ParseJSONValue(JSON)
                                              as TJSONArray;
  try
    Car := TJSONObject.Create;
    JSONCars.AddElement(Car);
    Car.AddPair('manufacturer', 'Hennessey');
    Car.AddPair('name', 'Venom GT');
    Price := TJSONObject.Create;
    Car.AddPair('price', Price);
    Price.AddPair('value', TJSONNumber.Create(600000));
    Price.AddPair('currency', 'USD');
    JSON := JSONCars.ToJSON;
  finally
    JSONCars.Free;
  end;
end;

procedure TMainForm.btnParseJSONClick(Sender: TObject);
var
  JSONCars: TJSONArray;
  i: Integer;
  Car, JSONPrice: TJSONObject;
  CarPrice: Double;
  s, CarName, CarManufacturer, CarCurrencyType: string;
begin
  s := '';
  JSONCars := TJSONObject.ParseJSONValue(JSON)
                                              as TJSONArray;
  if not Assigned(JSONCars) then
    raise Exception.Create('Not a valid JSON');
```

```
    try
      for i := 0 to JSONCars.Count - 1 do
      begin
        Car := JSONCars.Items[i] as TJSONObject;
        CarName := Car.GetValue('name').Value;
        CarManufacturer :=
          Car.GetValue('manufacturer').Value;
        JSONPrice := Car.GetValue('price') as TJSONObject;
        CarPrice := (JSONPrice.GetValue('value') as
          TJSONNumber).AsDouble;
        CarCurrencyType := JSONPrice.GetValue('currency')
        .Value
        s := s + Format(
          'Name = %s' + sLineBreak +
          'Manufacturer = %s' + sLineBreak +
          'Price = %.0n%s' + sLineBreak +
          '-----' + sLineBreak,
          [CarName, CarManufacturer,
          CarPrice, CarCurrencyType]);
      end;
      JSON := s;
    finally
      JSONCars.Free;
    end;
end;
```

6. Run the application by hitting *F9* (or by going to **Run | Run**).

7. Click on the `btnGenerateJSON` button, and you should see a JSON array and some JSON objects in the memo.

8. Click on the `btnModifyJSON` button, and you should see one more JSON object inside the outer JSON array in the memo.

9. Click on the last button, and you should see the same data as before, but in a normal text representation.

10. After the third click, you should see something similar to the following screenshot:

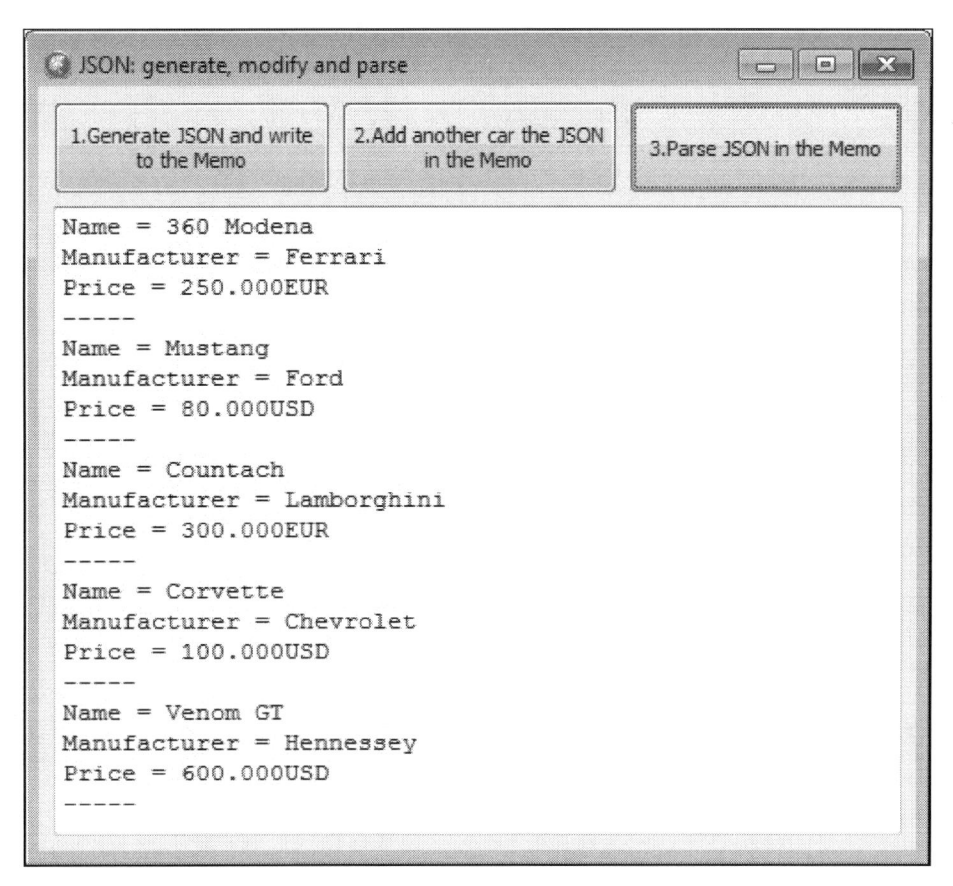

```
JSON: generate, modify and parse

[1.Generate JSON and write to the Memo]  [2.Add another car the JSON in the Memo]  [3.Parse JSON in the Memo]

Name = 360 Modena
Manufacturer = Ferrari
Price = 250.000EUR
-----
Name = Mustang
Manufacturer = Ford
Price = 80.000USD
-----
Name = Countach
Manufacturer = Lamborghini
Price = 300.000EUR
-----
Name = Corvette
Manufacturer = Chevrolet
Price = 100.000USD
-----
Name = Venom GT
Manufacturer = Hennessey
Price = 600.000USD
-----
```

Figure 6.1: Text representation of the JSON data generated and modified

There's more...

Although not the fastest or the most standard compliant on the market, JSON usability is important because other Delphi technologies, such as DataSnap, use it. Luckily, there are a lot of alternative JSON parsers for Delphi, if you find you have trouble with the standard one.

Other notable JSON parsers are:

- SuperObject (https://github.com/hgourvest/superobject)
- The one included in Delphi Web Script library can be found at https://bitbucket.org/egrange/dwscript/
- A fast JSON parser from Andreas Hausladen from https://github.com/ahausladen/JsonDataObjects

Delphi Basics

If your main concern is speed, then check out these alternative JSON parsers.

There are also a lot of serialization libraries that use JSON as a serialization format. In general, every parser has its own way to serialize an object to JSON. Find your favorite. Just as an example, in *Chapter 5, The Thousand Faces of Multithreading,* in the *Using tasks to make your customer happier* recipe you will see an open source library containing a set of serialization helpers using the default Delphi JSON parser.

However, JSON is not the right tool for every interchange or data-representation job. XML has been creating other technologies that can help if you need to search, transform, and validate your data in a declarative way. In JSON land, there is no such level of standardization, apart from the format itself. However, over the years, there is an effort to include at least the XML Schema counterpart in JSON, and you can find more details at `http://json-schema.org/`.

Manipulating and transforming XML documents

XML stands for **eXtensible Markup Language** (`http://en.wikipedia.org/wiki/XML`) and is designed to represent, transport, and store hierarchical data in the trees of nodes. You can use XML to communicate with different systems, and store configuration files, complex entities, and so on. They all use a standard and powerful format. Delphi has had good support for XML for more than a decade now.

Getting ready

All the basic XML-related activities can be summarized with the following points:

- Generate XML data
- Parse XML data
- Parse XML data and modify it

In this recipe, you will see how to carry out all these activities.

How to do it...

1. Create a new VCL application and drop three TButton and a TMemo. Align all the buttons as a toolbar at the top of the form and the memo to the remaining form client area.
2. From left to right, name the buttons `btnGenerateXML`, `btnModifyXML`, `btnParseXML`, and `btnTransformXML`.
3. The real work on the XML will be done by the `TXMLDocument` component. So, drop one instance of the form and set its `DOMVendor` property to `Omni XML`.

4. We will use static data as our data source. A simple matrix is enough for this recipe. Just after the implementation section of the unit, write the code that follows:

   ```
   type
     TCarInfo = (
     Manufacturer = 1,
     Name = 2,
     Currency = 3,
     Price = 4);

   var
     Cars: array [1 .. 4] of
       array [Manufacturer .. Price] of string = (
         (
           'Ferrari','360 Modena','EUR', '250,000'
         ),
         (
           'Ford', 'Mustang', 'USD', '80,000'
         ),
         (
           'Lamborghini', 'Countach', 'EUR','300,000'
         ),
         (
           'Chevrolet', 'Corvette', 'USD', '100,000'
         )
       );
   ```

5. We will use a TMemo to display the XML and the data. To keep things clear, create a public property called Xml on the form and map its setter and getter to the Memo1.Lines.Text property. Use the following code:

   ```
   //...other form methods declaration
   private
     procedure SetXML(const Value: String);
     function GetXML: String;
   public
     property Xml: String read GetXML write SetXML;
   end;

   //...then in the implementation section
   function TMainForm.GetXML: String;
   begin
     Result := Memo1.Lines.Text;
   end;

   procedure TMainForm.SetXML(const Value: String);
   ```

```
begin
  Memo1.Lines.Text := Value;
end;
```

6. Now, create event handlers for each button. For `btnGenerateXML`, write the following code:

```
procedure TMainForm.btnGenerateXMLClick(Sender: TObject);
var
  RootNode, Car, CarPrice: IXMLNode;
  i: Integer;
  s: String;
begin
  XMLDocument1.Active := True;
  try
    XMLDocument1.Version := '1.0';
    RootNode := XMLDocument1.AddChild('cars');
    for i := Low(Cars) to High(Cars) do
    begin
      Car := XMLDocument1.CreateNode('car');
      Car.AddChild('manufacturer').Text :=
        Cars[i][TCarInfo.Manufacturer];
      Car.AddChild('name').Text :=
        Cars[i][TCarInfo.Name];
      CarPrice := Car.AddChild('price');
      CarPrice.Attributes['currency'] :=
        Cars[i][TCarInfo.Currency];
      CarPrice.Text := Cars[i][TCarInfo.Price];
      RootNode.ChildNodes.Add(Car);
    end;
    XMLDocument1.SaveToXML(s);
    Xml := s;
  finally
    XMLDocument1.Active := False;
  end;
end;
```

7. Now, we have to write the code to change the XML. In the `btnModifyXML` click event handler, write the following code:

```
procedure TMainForm.btnModifyXMLClick(Sender: TObject);
var
  Car, CarPrice: IXMLNode;
  s: string;
begin
  XMLDocument1.LoadFromXML(Xml);
  try
```

Chapter 1

```
      Xml := '';
      Car := XMLDocument1.CreateNode('car');
      Car.AddChild('manufacturer').Text := 'Hennessey';
      Car.AddChild('name').Text := 'Venom GT';
      CarPrice := Car.AddChild('price');
      CarPrice.Attributes['currency'] := 'USD';
      CarPrice.Text := '600,000';
      XMLDocument1.DocumentElement.ChildNodes.Add(Car);
      XMLDocument1.SaveToXML(s);
      Xml := s;
    finally
      XMLDocument1.Active := False;
    end;
  end;
```

8. Write the following code under the `btnParseXML` click event handler:

   ```
   procedure TMainForm.btnParseXMLClick(Sender: TObject);
   var
     CarsList: IDOMNodeList;
     CurrNode: IDOMNode;
     childidx, i: Integer;
     CarName, CarManufacturer, CarPrice, CarCurrencyType:
       string;
   begin
     XMLDocument1.LoadFromXML(Xml);
     try
       Xml := '';
       CarsList := XMLDocument1.
         DOMDocument.getElementsByTagName('car');
       for i := 0 to CarsList.length - 1 do
       begin
         CarName := '';  CarManufacturer := '';
         CarPrice := '';  CarCurrencyType := '';
         for childidx := 0 to
           CarsList[i].ChildNodes.length - 1 do
         begin
           CurrNode := CarsList[i].ChildNodes[childidx];
           if CurrNode.nodeName.Equals('name') then
             CarName := CurrNode.firstChild.nodeValue;
           if CurrNode.nodeName.Equals('manufacturer') then
             CarManufacturer := CurrNode.firstChild.nodeValue;
           if CurrNode.nodeName.Equals('price') then
           begin
             CarPrice := CurrNode.firstChild.nodeValue;
   ```

```delphi
              CarCurrencyType :=
                CurrNode.Attributes.
                  getNamedItem('currency').nodeValue;
          end;
        end;
        Xml := Xml +
          'Name = ' + CarName + sLineBreak +
          'Manufacturer = ' + CarManufacturer + sLineBreak +
          'Price = ' +
          CarPrice + CarCurrencyType + sLineBreak +
          '-----' + sLineBreak;
      end;
    finally
      XMLDocument1.Active := False;
    end;
end;
```

9. Finally, write the following code under the `btnTransformXML` click event handler:

```delphi
procedure TMainForm.btnTransformClick(Sender: TObject);
var
  LXML, LXSL: string;
  LOutput: string;
begin
  LXML := TFile.ReadAllText('..\..\..\cars.xml');
  LXSL := TFile.ReadAllText('..\..\..\cars.xslt');
  LOutput := Transform(LXML, LXSL);
  TFile.WriteAllText('..\..\..\cars.html', LOutput);
  ShellExecute(0, PChar('open'),
    PChar('file:///' +
    TPath.GetFullPath('..\..\..\cars.html')), nil,
    nil, SW_SHOW);
end;
```

10. Now, add the following function in your form implementation section:

```delphi
function Transform(XMLData: string; XSLT: string): String;
var
  LXML, LXSL: IXMLDocument;
  LOutput: WideString;
begin
  LXML := LoadXMLData(XMLData);
  LXSL := LoadXMLData(XSLT);
  LXML.DocumentElement.TransformNode(LXSL.DocumentElement,
    LOutput);
  Result := String(LOutput);
end;
```

Chapter 1

11. Run the application by hitting *F9* (or by going to **Run | Run**).
12. Click on the `btnGenerateXML` button, and you should see some XML data in the memo.
13. Click on the `btnModifyXML` button, and you should see some more XML in the memo.
14. Click on `btnParseXML`, and you should see the same data as before, but in normal text representation.
15. After the third click, you should see something similar to the following screenshot:

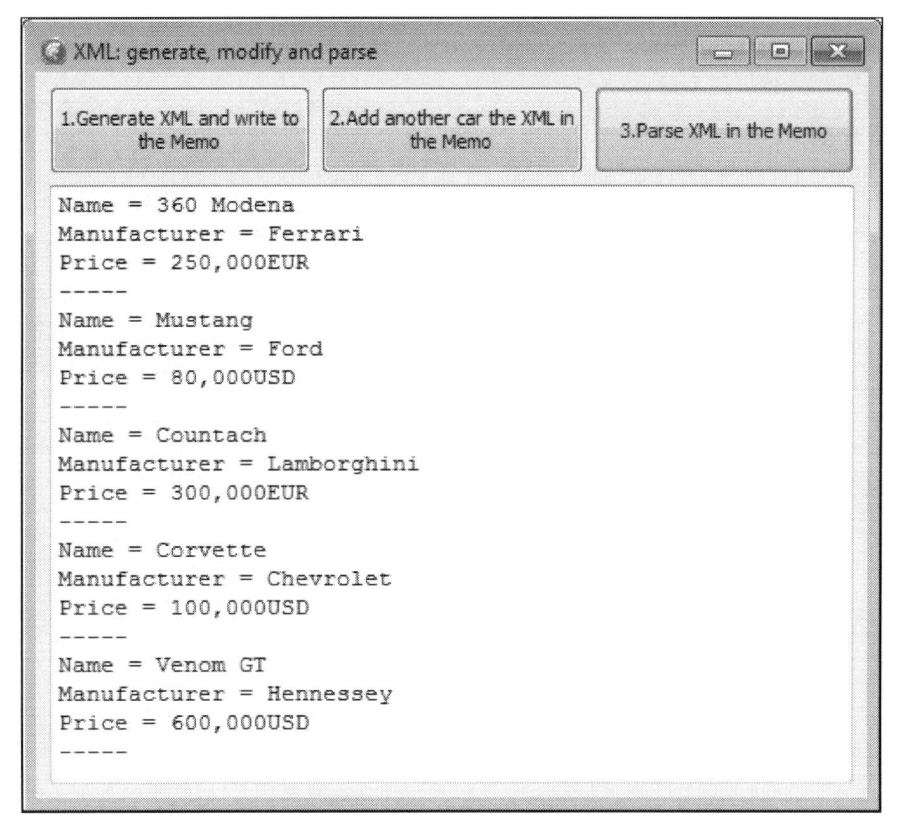

```
XML: generate, modify and parse

1.Generate XML and write to    2.Add another car the XML in    3.Parse XML in the Memo
       the Memo                        the Memo

Name = 360 Modena
Manufacturer = Ferrari
Price = 250,000EUR
-----
Name = Mustang
Manufacturer = Ford
Price = 80,000USD
-----
Name = Countach
Manufacturer = Lamborghini
Price = 300,000EUR
-----
Name = Corvette
Manufacturer = Chevrolet
Price = 100,000USD
-----
Name = Venom GT
Manufacturer = Hennessey
Price = 600,000USD
-----
```

Figure 7.1: Text representation of the XML data generated and modified

16. Now, copy the `cars.xml` and `cars.xslt` files from the respective recipe folder to the parent folder of your project folder and click on the `btnTransformXML` button.

17. The system default browser should appear showing, something like the following screenshot:

Model	Manufacturer	Price
360 Modena	Ferrari	€150,000
Mustang	Ford	€75,000
Countach	Lamborghini	€110,000
Corvette	Chevrolet	€80,000

Sport Cars

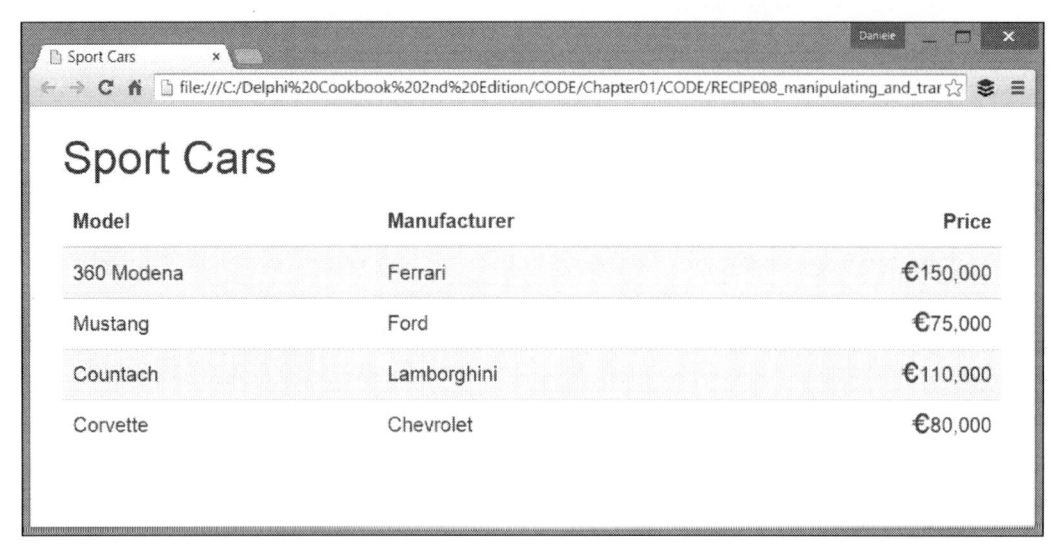

Fig. 7.2 XML data transformed to HTML using a XSLT transformation

How it works...

1. The first button generates the XML representation of the data in our matrix. We've used some car information as sample data.

   > Note that the prices of the cars are not real!!

2. To create an XML attribute, there are three fundamental TXMLDocument methods:
   - `XMLNode := XMLDocument1.CreateNode('node');`
   - `XMLNode.AddChild('childnode');`
   - `XMLNode.Attributes['attrname'] := 'attrvalue';`

   There are other very useful methods, but these are the basics of XML generation.

3. The `btnModifyXML` button loads the XML into the memo and appends some other data (another car) to the list. Then, it updates the memo with the new updated XML. These are the most important lines to note:

   ```
   //Create a node without adding it to the DOM
   Car := XMLDocument1.CreateNode('car');

   //fill Car XMLNode... and finally add it to the DOM
   //as child of the root node
   XMLDocument1.DocumentElement.ChildNodes.Add(Car);
   ```

4. The code under the `btnParseXMLClick` event handler allows us to read the display as normal text the XML data navigating through XML tree.

5. The code under the `btnTransformXMLClick` event handler uses the XSLT transformation in `cars.xslt` and the data in `cars.xml` to generate a brand new HTML page. The XSLT code is as follows:

   ```
   <?xml version="1.0" encoding="UTF-8"?>
   <xsl:stylesheet version="1.0"
     xmlns:xsl="http://www.w3.org/1999/XSL/Transform">
       <xsl:output method="html" version="5.0"
         encoding="UTF-8" indent="yes"/>
     <xsl:template match="cars">
       <html>
         <head>
           <link href="https://maxcdn.bootstrapcdn.com/
             bootstrap/3.3.4/css/bootstrap.min.css"
             rel="stylesheet"/>
           <title>
             Sport Cars
           </title>
         </head>
         <body>
           <div class="container">
           <div class="row">
           <h1>Sport Cars</h1>
             <table class="table table-striped table-hover">
               <thead>
                 <tr>
                   <th>Model</th>
                   <th>Manufacturer</th>
                   <th class="text-right">Price</th>
                 </tr>
               </thead>
               <tbody>
   ```

```
                <xsl:for-each select="car">
                <tr>
                  <td>
                    <xsl:value-of select="name"/>
                  </td>
                  <td>
                    <xsl:value-of select="manufacturer"/>
                  </td>
                  <td class="text-right">
                    <span class="glyphicon glyphicon-euro">
                    </span>
                    <xsl:value-of select="price"/>
                  </td>
                </tr>
              </xsl:for-each>
            </tbody>
          </table>
        </div>
       </div>
      </body>
    </html>
  </xsl:template>
</xsl:stylesheet>
```

There's more...

There are many things to say about XML ecospace. There are XML engines that provide facilities to search data in an XML tree (XPath), to validate an XML using another XML (XML Schema or DTD), to transform an XML into another kind of format using another XML (XSLT), and many others use `http://en.wikipedia.org/wiki/List_of_XML_markup_languages`. The good thing is that just like XML, the DOM object is also standardized. So, every library that is compliant to the standard has the same methods, from Delphi to JavaScript and from Python to C#.

TXMLDocument allows you to select the `DOMVendor` implementation. By default, there are three implementations available:

- MSXML:
    - Is from Microsoft, implemented as COM objects
    - Supports XML transformations
    - Is available only on Windows (so no Android, iOS, or MacOSX)

- Omni XML:
    - Much faster than ADOM and based on the Open Source project.
    - It is cross-platform, so is available on all the supported Delphi platforms. If you plan to write XML handling code on mobile or Mac, this is the way to go.
- ADOM XML:
    - Is a (quite old) open source Delphi implementation
    - Does not support transformations
    - Is available on all the supported Delphi platforms
    - Is still in Delphi for backward compatibility, consider the Omni XML instead

TXMLDocument uses a Windows-only vendor by default. If you are designing a FireMonkey application that is intended to run on other platforms than Windows, select a cross-platform DOM vendor.

XSLT allows you to transform an XML to something else, using another XML as a "stylesheet." As we saw in this recipe, you can use an XML file and an XSLT file to generate an HTML page that shows the data contained in the XML using XSLT to format the data.

The following function loads the XML and an XSLT documents from two string variables. Then, we use the XSLT document to transform the XML document. The code that follows shows this in detail:

```
function Transform(XMLData: string; XSLT: string): String;
var
  LXML, LXSL: IXMLDocument;
  LOutput: WideString;
begin
  LXML := LoadXMLData(XMLData);
  LXSL := LoadXMLData(XSLT);
  LXML.DocumentElement.TransformNode(
    LXSL.DocumentElement, LOutput);
  Result := String(LOutput);
end;
```

This function doesn't know about the output format because it is defined by the XSLT document. The result could be an XML, an HTML, a CSV, or a plain text, or whatever the XSLT defines, but the code does not change.

XSLT can be really useful. I recommend that you go and visit http://www.w3schools.com/xsl/xsl_languages.asp for further details on the language.

I/O in the 21st century – knowing the streams

Many I/O-related activities handle "streams" of data. A stream is a sequence of data elements made available over time. As Wikipedia says, "A stream can be thought of as a conveyor belt that allows items to be processed one at a time rather than in large batches."

At the lowest level, all streams are bytes, but using a high-level interface could obviously help the programmer handle their data. This is the reason why a stream object usually had methods such as `read`, `seek`, `write`, and so on, just to make handling a byte stream a bit simpler.

In this recipe, you'll see some stream utilization examples.

Getting ready

In the good old Pascal days, there were a set of functions to handle the I/O (`AssignFile`, `Reset`, `Rewrite`, `CloseFile`, and many more). Now, we've a bunch of classes. All Delphi streams inherit from `TStream` and can be used as the internal stream of one of the adapter classes (by adapter, I mean an implementation of the `Adapter`, or `Wrapper`, design pattern from the Gang of Four famous book about design patterns).

There are 10 fundamental types of streams.

Class	Use
`System.Classes.TBinaryWriter`	Writer for binary data
`System.Classes.TStreamWriter`	Writer for characters to stream
`System.Classes.TStringWriter`	Writer for a string
`System.Classes.TTextWriter`	Writer of sequence of characters; it is an abstract class
`System.Classes.TWriter`	Writes component data to an associated stream
`System.Classes.TReader`	Reads component data from an associated stream
`System.Classes.TStreamReader`	Reader for stream of characters
`System.Classes.TStringReader`	Reader for strings
`System.Classes.TTextReader`	Reader for sequence of characters; it is an abstract class
`System.Classes.TBinaryReader`	Reader for binary data

You can check out the complete list and their intended use directly on the Embarcadero website at `http://docwiki.embarcadero.com/RADStudio/en/Streams,_Reader_and_Writers`.

As Joel Spolsky says, "You can no longer pretend that "plain" text is ASCII." So, while we write streams, we've to pay attention to which encoding our text has and which encoding our counterpart is waiting for.

One of the most frequent necessities is to efficiently read and write a text file using the correct encoding.

> *"The Single Most Important Fact About Encodings... It does not make sense to have a string without knowing what encoding it uses. You can no longer stick your head in the sand and pretend that "plain" text is ASCII."*
>
> *– Joel Spolsky*
> (`http://www.joelonsoftware.com/articles/Unicode.html`)

The point Joel is making is that the content of a string doesn't know about the type of character encoding it uses.

When you think about file handling, ask yourself, "Could this file become 10 MB? And 100 MB? And 1 GB? How will my program behave in that case?" Handling a file one line at time and not loading all the file contents in memory is usually a good insurance for these cases. A stream of data is a good way to do this. In this recipe, you'll see the practical utilization of streams, stream writers, and stream readers.

How it works...

The project is not complex. All the interesting stuff happens in `btnWriteFile` and `btnReadFile`.

To write the file, `TStreamWriter` is used. `TStreamWriter` (as its counterpart `TStreamReader`) is a wrapper for a `TStream` descendant and adds some useful high-level methods to write to the stream. There are a lot of overloaded methods (`Write/WriteLine`) to allow an easy writing to the underlying stream. However, you can access the underling stream using the `BaseStream` property of the wrapper. Just after having written the file, the memo reloads the file using the same encoding used to write it, and shows it. This is only a fast check for this recipe, you don't need TMemo at all in your real project. The `btnReadFile` simply opens the file using a stream and passes the stream to `TStreamReader` that, using the right encoding, will read the file one line at a time.

Delphi Basics

Now, let's run some checks. Run the program and with the encoding set to ASCII, click on `btnWriteFile`. The memo will show garbage text, as shown in the following screenshot. This is because we are using the wrong encoding for the data we are writing in the file:

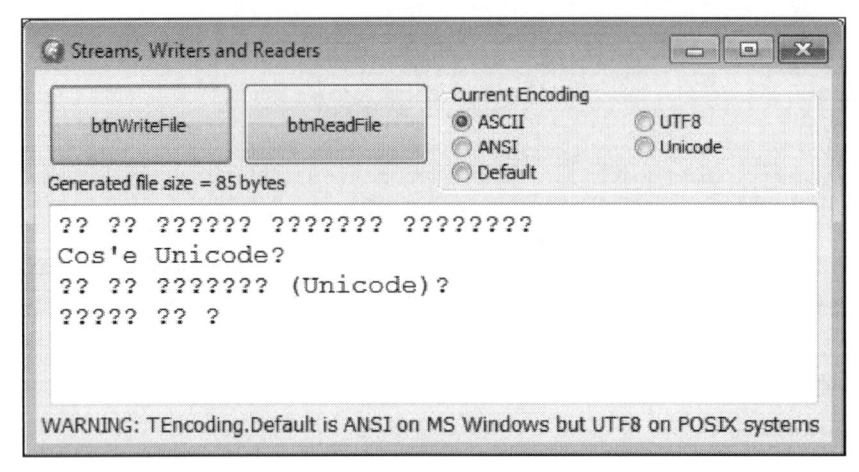

```
Streams, Writers and Readers                                    _ □ ✕

   ┌─────────────────┐  ┌─────────────────┐   ┌ Current Encoding ──────────────┐
   │   btnWriteFile  │  │   btnReadFile   │   │  ◉ ASCII        ○ UTF8         │
   └─────────────────┘  └─────────────────┘   │  ○ ANSI         ○ Unicode      │
                                              │  ○ Default                     │
   Generated file size = 85 bytes             └────────────────────────────────┘

   ┌──────────────────────────────────────────────────────────────────────────┐
   │ ?? ?? ?????? ??????? ????????                                            │
   │ Cos'e Unicode?                                                           │
   │ ?? ?? ?????? (Unicode)?                                                  │
   │ ????? ?? ?                                                               │
   │                                                                          │
   │                                                                          │
   │                                                                          │
   └──────────────────────────────────────────────────────────────────────────┘
   WARNING: TEncoding.Default is ANSI on MS Windows but UTF8 on POSIX systems
```

Figure 8.1: Garbage text written to the file using the wrong encoding. No one line text is equal to the original one. It is necessary to know the encoding for the text before writing and reading it

Now, select **UTF8** from the RadioGroup and retry. By clicking on **btnWriteFile**, you will see the correct text in the memo. Try to change the current encoding using ASCII and click on **btnReadFile**. You will still get garbage text. Why? Because the file has been read with the wrong encoding. You have to know the encoding before to safely read file's contents. To read the text that we wrote, we have to use the same encoding. Play with other encodings to see the different behavior.

There's more...

Streams are very powerful and their uniform interface helps us write portable and generic code. With the help of streams and polymorphism, we can write code that uses `TStream` to do some work without knowing which kind of stream it is!

Also, a less known possibility, if you ever will write a program that needs to access the good old `STD_INPUT`, `STD_OUTPUT`, or `STD_ERROR`, is that you can use `THandleStream` to wrap these system handles to a nice `TStream` interface with the following code:

```
program StdInputOutputError;
//the following directive instructs the compiler to create a
//console application and not a GUI one, which is the default.
{$APPTYPE CONSOLE}
uses
  System.Classes, // required for Stream classes
```

```
  Winapi.Windows; // required to have access to the STD_* handles
var
  StdInput: TStreamReader;
  StdOutput, StrError: TStreamWriter;
begin
  StdInput := TStreamReader.Create(
THandleStream.Create(STD_INPUT_HANDLE));
  StdInput.OwnStream;
  StdOutput := TStreamWriter.Create(
THandleStream.Create(STD_OUTPUT_HANDLE));
  StdOutput.OwnStream;
  StdError := TStreamWriter.Create(
THandleStream.Create(STD_ERROR_HANDLE));
  StdError.OwnStream;
  { HERE WE CAN USE OURS STREAMS }
  // Let's copy a line of text from STD_IN to STD_OUT
  StdOutput.writeln(StdInput.ReadLine);
  { END - HERE WE CAN USE OURS STREAMS }
  StdError.Free;
  StdOutput.Free;
  StdInput.Free;
end;
```

Moreover, when you work with file-related streams, the `TFile` class (contained in `System.IOUtils.pas`) is very useful, and has some helper methods to write shorter and more readable code.

Creating a Windows service

Some kinds of application needs to be running 24/7. Usually, they are network servers or data transfer/monitoring applications. In these cases, you probably start with a normal GUI or console application. However, when the systems start to be used in production, you are faced with a lot of problems related to Windows session termination, reboots, user rights, and other issues related to the server environment.

Getting ready

The way to go, in the previous scenario, is to develop a Windows service. In this recipe, we'll see how to write a good Windows service scaffold, and this can be the skeleton for many other services. So, feel free to use this code as a "template" to create all the services that you will need.

Delphi Basics

How it works...

The project has been created starting from the default project template accessible by going to **File | New | Other | Delphi Projects | Service Application** and then has been integrated with a set of functionalities to make it "real."

All the low-level interfacing with the Windows Service Manager is done by the `TService` class. In `ServiceU.pas`, there is the actual descendant of `TService` that represents the Windows service we are implementing. Its event handlers are used to communicate with the operating system.

Usually, a service needs to respond to the Windows Service Controller commands independently of what it is doing. So, we need a background thread to do the actual work, while the `TService.OnExecute` event should not do any real work (this is not a must, but usually is the way to go). The unit named `WorkerThreadU.pas` contains the thread and the main service needed to hold a reference to the instance of this thread.

The background thread starts when the service is started (the `OnStart` event) and stops when the service is stopped (the `OnStop` event). The `OnExecute` event waits and handles `ServiceController` commands but doesn't do any actual functional work. This is done using `ServiceThread.ProcessRequests(false);` in a while loop.

Usually the `OnExecute` event handler is like this:

```delphi
procedure TSampleService.ServiceExecute(Sender: TService);
begin
  while not Terminated do
  begin
    ServiceThread.ProcessRequests(false);
    TThread.Sleep(1000);
  end;
end;
```

The wait of 1000 milliseconds is not a must, but consider that the wait time should be not too high because the service needs to be responsive to the Windows Service Controller messages. It should not be too low because otherwise the thread context switch may waste resources.

The background thread writes a line in a logfile once a second. While it is in a `Paused` state, the service stops writing. When the service continues, the thread will restart writing the log line. In the service event handlers, there is the logic to implement this change of state:

```delphi
procedure TSampleService.ServiceContinue(Sender: TService;
  var Continued: Boolean);
begin
  FWorkerThread.Continue;
```

```
    Continued := True;
  end;

  procedure TSampleService.ServicePause(Sender: TService;
    var Paused: Boolean);
  begin
    FWorkerThread.Pause;
    Paused := True;
  end;
```

In the thread, there is the actual logic to implement the `Paused` state, and in this case, it is fairly simple: we've to pause the writing of the logfile:

Here's an extract:

```
        Log := TStreamWriter.Create(
          TFileStream.Create(LogFileName,
            fmCreate or fmShareDenyWrite));
        try
          while not Terminated do
          begin
            if not FPaused then
            begin
              Log.WriteLine('Message from thread: ' + TimeToStr(now));
            end;
            TThread.Sleep(1000);
          end;
        finally
          Log.Free;
        end;
```

The Boolean instance variable `FPaused` can be considered thread safe for this use.

Delphi services don't have a default description under the Windows Service Manager. If we want to give a description, we have to write a specific key in the Windows registry. Usually, this is done in the `AfterInstall` event. In our service, this is the code to write in the `AfterInstall` event handler:

```
  procedure TSampleService.ServiceAfterInstall(
  Sender: TService);
  var
  Reg: TRegistry; //declared in System.Win.Registry;
  begin
  Reg := TRegistry.Create(KEY_READ or KEY_WRITE);
  try
     Reg.RootKey := HKEY_LOCAL_MACHINE;
```

```
    if Reg.OpenKey(
      '\SYSTEM\CurrentControlSet\Services\' + name,
      False {do not create if not exists}) then
    begin
      Reg.WriteString('Description',
        'My Fantastic Windows Service');
      Reg.CloseKey;
    end;
  finally
    Reg.Free;
  end;
end;
```

It is not necessary to delete this key in the `AfterUnInstall` event because Windows deletes all the keys related to the service (under `HKEY_LOCAL_MACHINE\SYSTEM\CurrentControlSet\Services\<MyServiceName>`) when it is actually uninstalled.

Let's try an installation. Build the project, open the Windows command prompt, and go to the folder where the project has been built. Then, run this command:

C:\<ExeProjectPath>\WindowsService.exe /install

If everything is ok, you should see this message:

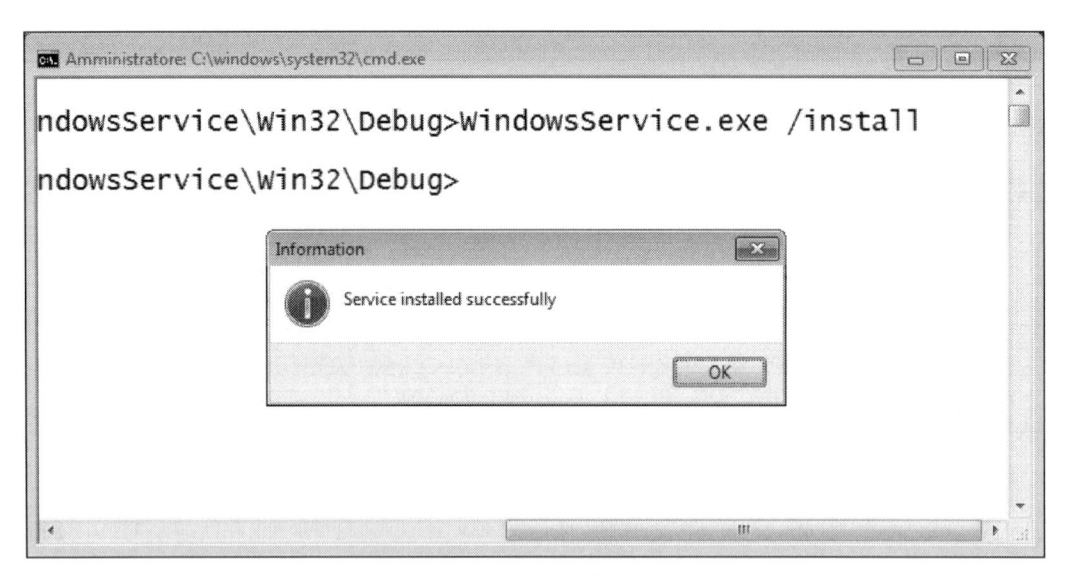

Figure 11.1: The service installation is ok

Now, you can check under the Windows Services Console and you should find the service installed. Click on **Start**, wait for the confirmation, and the service should start to write its logfile.

Chapter 1

Play with **Pause** and **Continue** and check the file activity.

> Some text editors could have a problem with opening the logfile while the service is writing. I suggest that you use a Unix tail clone for Windows.
>
> There are many free choices. Here are some links:
>
> `http://sourceforge.net/projects/tailforwin32/`
> `http://ophilipp.free.fr/op_tail.htm`
> `http://www.baremetalsoft.com/baretail/`

There's more...

Windows Services are very powerful. Using the abstractions that Delphi provides, you can also create an application that, reading a parameter on the command line, can act as a normal GUI application or as a Windows Service.

In the respective recipe folder, there is another recipe called *20_WindowsServiceOrGUI*.

This application can be used as a normal Windows Service using the normal command line switches used so far, but if launched with `/GUI`, it acts as a GUI application and can use the same application code (not `TService`). In our example, the GUI version uses the same worker thread as the service version. This can be very useful also for debugging purposes.

Run the application with the following command:

`C:\<ExeProjectPath>\WindowsServiceOrGUI.exe /GUI`

You will get a GUI version of the service, as shown here:

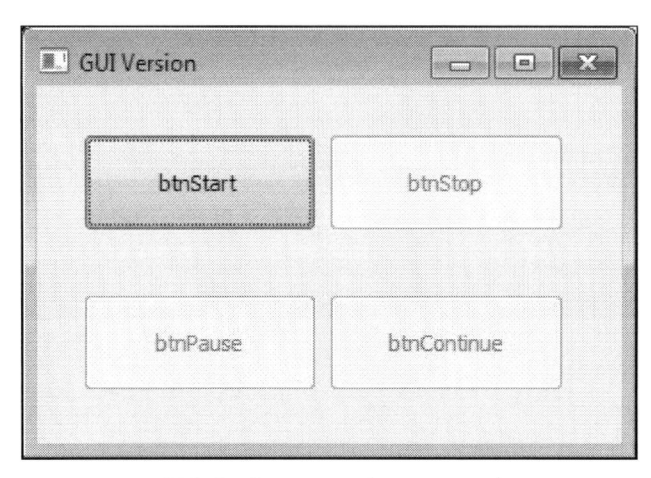

Figure 11.2: The GUI version of the Windows Service

Delphi Basics

Using the TService.LogMessage method

If something happens during the execution of the service that you want to log and you want to log in to the system logger, you can use the `LogMessage` method to save a message. The message can be viewed later using the Windows built-in event viewer.

You can call the `LogMessage` method using an appropriate logging type like this:

```
LogMessage('Your message goes here for SUCCESS',
   EVENTLOG_SUCCESS, 0, 1);
```

If you check the event in the Event Viewer, you will find a lot of garbage text that complains about the lack of "description for the event."

If you really want to use the Event Viewer to view your log message (when I can, I use a logfile and don't care about the Event Viewer, but there are scenarios where the Event Viewer log is needed), you have to use the **Microsoft © Message Compiler**.

The Microsoft © Message Compiler is a tool able to compile a file of messages into a set of RC files. Then, these files must be compiled by a resource compiler and linked into your executable.

More information on Microsoft © Message Compiler and the steps needed to provide the description for the log event can be found at http://www.codeproject.com/Articles/4166/Using-MC-exe-message-resources-and-the-NT-event-lo.

Associating a file extension with your application on Windows

In some cases, your fantastic application needs to be opened with just a double-click on a file with an extension associated with it. This is the case with Microsoft Word, Microsoft Excel, and many other well-known pieces of software. If you have a file generated with a program, double-click on the file and the program that generated the file will bring up pointing to that file. So, if you click on `mywordfile.docx`, Microsoft Word will be opened and `mywordfile.docx` will be shown. This is what we'd like to do in this recipe. The association can be useful also when you have multiple configurations for a program. Double-click on the `ConfigurationXYZ.myext` file, and the program will start using that configuration.

Getting ready

The hard work is done by the operating system itself. We have to instruct Windows to provide the following information:

- The file extension to associate
- The description of file type (it will be shown by Windows Explorer describing the file type)

- The default icon for the file type (in this recipe, we'll use the application icon itself, but it is not mandatory)
- The application that we want to associate
- Let's start!

How to do it...

1. Create a new VCL application and drop two TButton components and a TMemo component. Align all the buttons as a toolbar at the top of the form and the memo to all the remaining form client area.
2. The button on the left-hand side will be used to register a file type, while the button on the right-hand side will be used to unregister the association (cleaning the registry).
3. We have to handle some features specific to Microsoft Windows, so we need some Windows-related units. Under the implementation section of the unit, write this use clause:

   ```
   uses System.Win.registry, Winapi.shlobj, System.IOUtils;
   ```

4. In the implementation section, we need two procedures to do the real work; so just after the uses clause, add this code:

   ```
   procedure UnregisterFileType(
     FileExt: String;
     OnlyForCurrentUser: boolean = true);
   var
     R: TRegistry;
   begin
     R := TRegistry.Create;
     try
       if OnlyForCurrentUser then
         R.RootKey := HKEY_CURRENT_USER
       else
         R.RootKey := HKEY_LOCAL_MACHINE;

       R.DeleteKey('\Software\Classes\.' + FileExt);
       R.DeleteKey('\Software\Classes\' + FileExt + 'File');
     finally
       R.Free;
     end;
     SHChangeNotify(SHCNE_ASSOCCHANGED, SHCNF_IDLIST, 0, 0);
   end;

   procedure RegisterFileType(
     FileExt: String;
   ```

```
      FileTypeDescription: String;
      ICONResourceFileFullPath: String;
      ApplicationFullPath: String;
      OnlyForCurrentUser: boolean = true);
var
   R: TRegistry;
begin
   R := TRegistry.Create;
   try
      if OnlyForCurrentUser then
         R.RootKey := HKEY_CURRENT_USER
      else
         R.RootKey := HKEY_LOCAL_MACHINE;

      if R.OpenKey('\Software\Classes\.' + FileExt,
         true) then begin
         R.WriteString('', FileExt + 'File');
         if R.OpenKey('\Software\Classes\' + FileExt + 'File',
            true) then begin
            R.WriteString('', FileTypeDescription);
            if R.OpenKey('\Software\Classes\' +
               FileExt + 'File\DefaultIcon', true) then
            begin
               R.WriteString('', ICONResourceFileFullPath);
               if R.OpenKey('\Software\Classes\' +
                  FileExt + 'File\shell\open\command',
                   true) then
               R.WriteString('',
                   ApplicationFullPath + ' "%1"');
               end;
            end;
         end;
      finally
         R.Free;
      end;
   SHChangeNotify(SHCNE_ASSOCCHANGED, SHCNF_IDLIST, 0, 0);
end;
```

5. These two procedures allow us to register (and unregister) a file type considering only the current user or all the machine users. Pay attention; if you want to register the association for every user, write your data to:

   HKEY_LOCAL_MACHINE\Software\Classes

6. If you want to register the association for the current user only, write your data to:

   HKEY_CURRENT_USER\Software\Classes

7. On the newest Windows versions, you need administrator rights to register a file type for all the machine users. The last line of the procedures tells Explorer (the Microsoft Windows graphic interface) to refresh its settings to reflect the changes made to the file associations. As a result, for instance, the Explorer file list views will update.

8. We've almost finished. Change the left button name to `btnRegister`, the right button name to `btnUnRegister`, and put the following code on their `onclick` event handlers:

```
procedure TMainForm.btnRegisterClick(Sender: TObject);
begin
  RegisterFileType(
    'secret',
    'This file is a secret',
    Application.ExeName,
    Application.ExeName,
    true);
  ShowMessage('File type registred');
end;

procedure TMainForm.btnUnRegisterClick(Sender: TObject);
begin
  UnregisterFileType('secret', true);
  ShowMessage('File type unregistered');
end;
```

9. Now, when our application is invoked with a double-click, we'll get the file name as a parameter. It is possible to read a parameter passed by Windows Explorer (or the command line) using the `ParamStr(1)` function. Create a `FormCreate` event handler using the following code:

```
procedure TMainForm.FormCreate(Sender: TObject);
begin
  if TFile.Exists(ParamStr(1)) then
    Memo1.Lines.LoadFromFile(ParamStr(1))
  else
  begin
    Memo1.Lines.Text := 'No valid secret file type';
  end;
end;
```

Delphi Basics

10. Now, the application should be complete. However, a nice integration with the operating system requires a nice icon. In the code, the associated file will get the same icon as the main program, so let's change our default icon by going to **Project | Options | Application dialog**, and choose a nice icon. Click on the **Load Icon** button, choose an ICO file, and then select the third item from the resultant dialog:

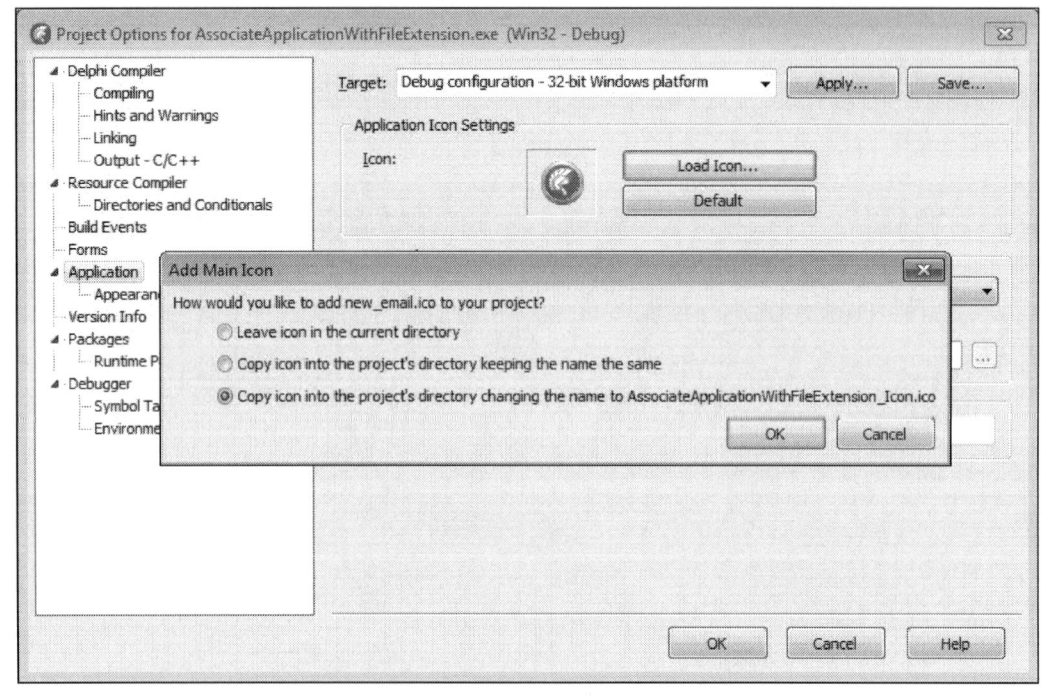

Figure 12.1: Changing the default application icon for our application

11. Now, create some text files with our registered extension `.secret`.

12. These files will appear with the default Windows icons, but in some seconds, they will have a brand new icon.

13. Run the application by hitting *F9* (or by going to **Run | Run**).

14. Click on the **btnRegister** button and close the application. Now, the files get new icons, as shown here:

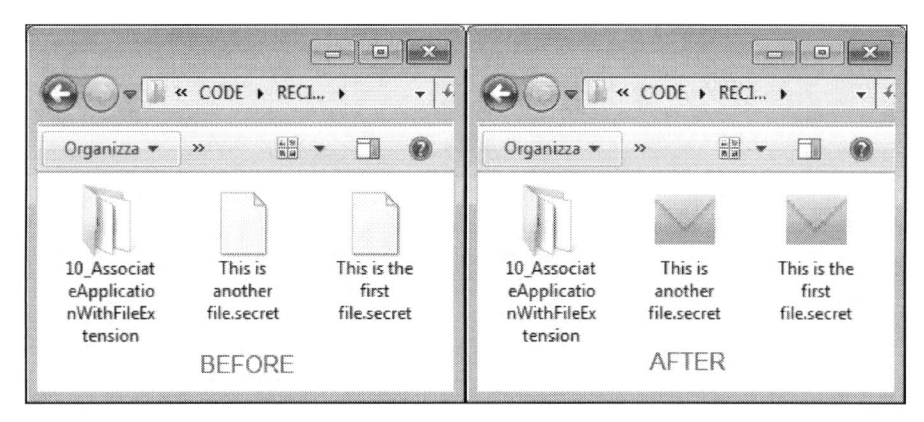

Figure 12.2: The files in Windows Explorer before and after having registered the .secret extension

15. Now, with the application not running, double-click on a `.secret` file. Our program will be started by Windows itself, using the information stored in the registry about the `.secret` file, and we'll get this form (the text shown in the memo is the text contained in the file):

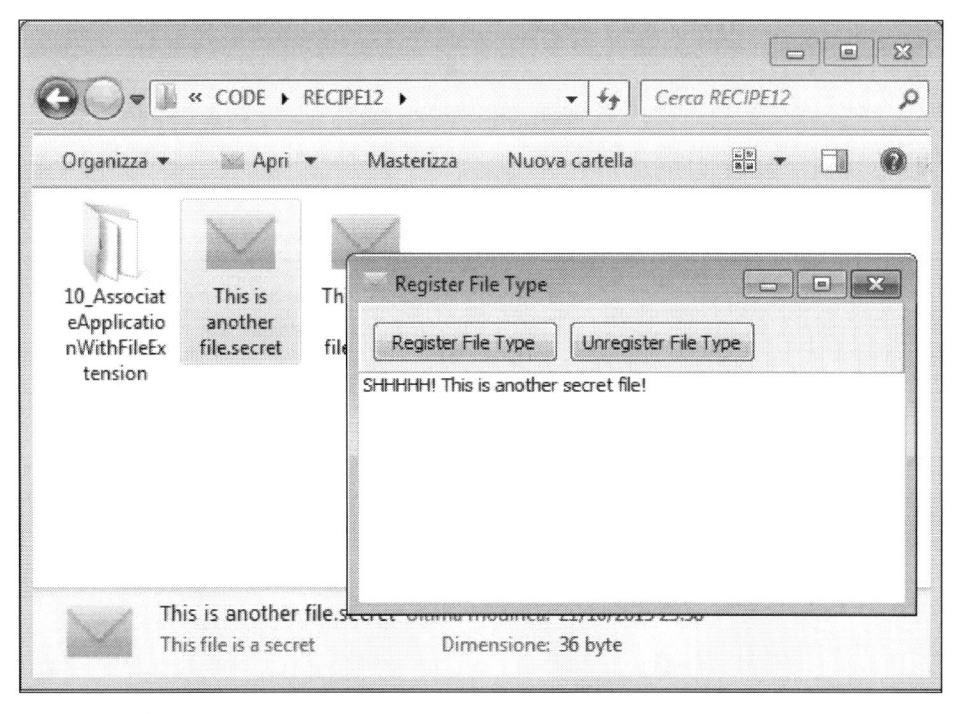

Figure 12.3: Our application, launched by the operating system, while it is showing the contents of the file

Delphi Basics

There's more...

One application can register many file types. In some cases, I've used this technique to register some specific desktop database files to my application (Firebird SQL Embedded database files or SQLite database files). So, a double-click actually was a connection to that database.

Be coherent with the Windows look and feel using TTaskDialog

Version after version, the Windows OS changed its look and feel a lot from the mid 2009 when the first Windows 95 came out. Also the UX guidelines from Microsoft changed a lot. Do you remember the **Multiple Document Interface** (**MDI**) paradigm? It was very popular in the 90s, but now is deprecated and an application seems old also if it has been just released. Indeed, many Windows applications seem stuck in the past in terms of UI and UX. What about dialogs? Our beloved `ShowMessage` and `MessageDlg` are there since Delphi 1, but now, the modern Windows versions use different dialogs to communicate to the users. Many of these standard dialogs contain more than a question and a simple Yes and No. Some dialogs ask something and provide a list of choices using radio buttons; some others have a nice progress bar inside; others have a nice button with an extended explanation of each choice just inside the button. How can our Delphi application can benefit from these new dialogs offered by the OS? In other words, how we can give a coherent look and feel to our dialog windows so that our application does not look old? This recipe shows how to use the `TTaskDialog` component.

Getting started

`TTaskdialog` is a dialog box somewhat like the standard call to `Application.MessageBox` in the VCL but much more powerful. Task Dialog API has been available since Windows Vista and Windows Server 2008, and your application must be theme enabled to use it (go to **Project** | **Options** | **Application** | **Runtime Themes** | **Enable Runtime Themes**).

Besides the usual default set of buttons (**OK**, **Cancel**, **Yes**, **No**, **Retry**, and **Close**), you can define extra buttons and many other customizations. The following Windows API provides task dialogs:

API Name	Description
TaskDialog	This creates, displays, and operates a task dialog. The task dialog contains application-defined message text and title, icons, and any combination of predefined push buttons. This function does not support the registration of a callback function to receive notifications.

API Name	Description
`TaskDialogCallbackProc`	This is an application-defined function used with the `TaskDialogIndirect` function. It receives messages from the task dialog when various events occur. `TaskDialogCallbackProc` is a placeholder for the application-defined function name.
`TaskDialogIndirect`	This creates, displays, and operates a task dialog. The task dialog contains application-defined icons, messages, title, verification checkbox, command links, push buttons, and radio buttons. This function can register a callback function to receive notification messages.

More information about API utilization can be obtained from `https://msdn.microsoft.com/en-us/library/windows/desktop/bb787471(v=vs.85).aspx`.

While the API can be useful in some border cases, the VCL comes with a very nice component that does all the low-level stuff for us. Let's see the sample program that shows how it is simple to create a modern look and feel application.

How it works...

Open the `TaskDialogs.dproj` project and understand how it works.

There are six buttons on the form. The first one shows a simple utilization of the Task Dialog API, while the other five show a different utilization of the `TTaskDialog` component, which wraps that API.

The first button uses the Windows API directly with the following code:

```
procedure TMainForm.btnAPIClick(Sender: TObject);
var
  LTDResult: Integer;
begin
  TaskDialog(0, HInstance,
    PChar('The Title'),
    PChar('These are the main instructions'),
    PChar('This is another content'),
    TDCBF_OK_BUTTON or TDCBF_CANCEL_BUTTON,
    TD_INFORMATION_ICON, @LTDResult);
  case LTDResult of
    IDOK:
      begin
        ShowMessage('Clicked OK');
      end;
    IDCANCEL:
```

```
    begin
        ShowMessage('Clicked Cancel');
    end;
  end;
end;
```

The `TaskDialog` function is declared inside the `Winapi.CommCtrl.pas` unit. So far, you could ask, "Why should I use a component for `TaskDialogs`? Seems quite simple." Yes, it is, if you only want to mimic `MessageDlg`, but things get complicated very fast if you want to use all the features of the Task Dialog API. So, the second button uses the `TTaskDialog` component. Let's see the relevant properties configured at design time for the `tdSimple` component:

```
object tdSimple: TTaskDialog
  Caption = 'The question'
  CommonButtons = [tcbYes, tcbNo]
  DefaultButton = tcbYes
  ExpandButtonCaption = 'More information'
  ExpandedText =
    'Yes, you have to decide something about this question...' +
    ' but I cannot help you a lot'
  Flags = [tfUseHiconMain, tfUseHiconFooter,
    tfVerificationFlagChecked]
  FooterIcon = 4
  FooterText = 'This is an important question...'
  Text = 'To be or not to be, this is the question. To be?'
  Title = 'William ask:'
end
```

> You can check the runtime appearance also at design time by double-clicking on the component over your form, or by selecting **Test Dialog** from the menu over the component. You can access the menu by right-clicking on the component.

As you can see, only the minimum properties have been set, just to show the power of the component. This configuration shows up a dialog with two buttons labelled **Yes** and **No**. The `TTaskDialog` component can be configured at design time using the **Object Inspector**, or can be configured at runtime by code. In this first example, the configuration is defined at design time so that at runtime we only have to call the `Execute` method and read the user response. Here's the code that actually uses the `tdSimple` instance:

```
procedure TMainForm.btnSimpleClick(Sender: TObject);
begin
  tdSimple.Execute; //show the taskdialog
  if tdSimple.ModalResult = mrYes then
```

```
    ShowMessage('yes')
  else
    ShowMessage('no')
  end;
```

Even in this case, it is quite simple, but let's go deeper with the configuration. Let's say that we need a TaskDialog similar to the following screenshot:

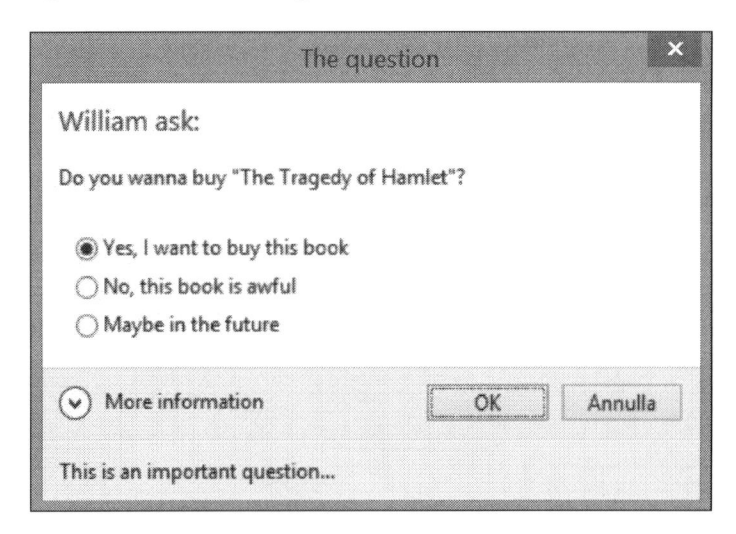

Fig. 12.1 The `TTaskDialog` component is configured to show three radio buttons

Using the plain API is not so simple to do this. So, let's see how to configure the component:

```
object tdRadioButtons: TTaskDialog
  Caption = 'The question'
  DefaultButton = tcbYes
  ExpandButtonCaption = 'More information'
  ExpandedText =
    'Yes, you have to decide something about this question... ' +
    'but I cannot help you a lot'
  Flags = [tfUseHiconMain, tfUseHiconFooter,
    tfVerificationFlagChecked]
  FooterIcon = 4
  FooterText = 'This is an important question...'
  RadioButtons = <
    item
      Caption = 'Yes, I want to buy this book'
    end
    item
      Caption = 'No, this book is awful'
    end
```

```
      item
        Caption = 'Maybe in the future'
      end>
    Text = 'Do you wanna buy "The Tragedy of Hamlet"?'
    Title = 'William ask:'
  end
```

The preceding block of code contains the definition for the three radio buttons. The following code shows the dialog and the retrieval of the result:

```
procedure TMainForm.btnRadioClick(Sender: TObject);
begin
  tdRadioButtons.Execute;
  if tdRadioButtons.ModalResult = mrOk then
    ShowMessage('Selected radio button ' +
      tdRadioButtons.RadioButton.ID.ToString);
end;
```

Even in this case, we have defined the properties at design time so that the runtime code is quite simple. Just note that the user choice is stored in the `RadioButton.ID` property.

The `TTaskDialog.Flags` property can greatly change the behavior of the dialog. Here's the meaning of each element of its set:

Flag set element name	If set...
tfEnableHyperlinks	Content, footer, and expanded text can include hyperlinks
tfUseHiconMain	Uses the custom main icon
tfUseHiconFooter	Uses the custom footer icon
tfAllowDialogCancellation	Permits Task Dialog to be closed in the absence of a **Cancel** button
tfUseCommandLinks	Buttons are displayed as command links using a standard dialog glyph
tfUseCommandLinksNoIcon	Buttons are displayed as command links without a glyph
tfExpandFooterArea	Displays expanded text in the footer
tfExpandedByDefault	Expanded text is displayed when the Task Dialog opens
tfVerificationFlagChecked	The verification checkbox is initially checked
tfShowProgressBar	Displays the progress bar
tfShowMarqueeProgressBar	Displays the marquee progress bar
tfCallbackTimer	Callback Dialogs will be called every 200 milliseconds

Flag set element name	If set...
tfPositionRelativeToWindow	Task Dialog is centered with respect to the parent window
tfRtlLayout	Text reads right to left
tfNoDefaultRadioButton	There is no default radio button
tfCanBeMinimized	The Task Dialog can be minimized

The real power of TaskDialogs comes when you build your dialog at runtime. Let's check what the fourth button does under the hood:

```
procedure TMainForm.btnConfirmClick(Sender: TObject);
var
  LFileName: string;
  LGSearch: String;
const
  GOOGLE_SEARCH = 99;
begin
  LFileName := 'MyCoolProgram.exe';
  tdConfirm.Buttons.Clear;
  tdConfirm.Title := 'Confirm Removal';
  tdConfirm.Caption := 'My fantastic folder';
  tdConfirm.Text :=
    Format('Are you sure that you want to remove ' +
      'the file named "%s"?', [LFileName]);
  tdConfirm.CommonButtons := [];
  with TTaskDialogButtonItem(tdConfirm.Buttons.Add) do
  begin
    Caption := 'Remove';
    CommandLinkHint := Format('Delete file %s from the folder.',
      [LFileName]);
    ModalResult := mrYes;
  end;
  with TTaskDialogButtonItem(tdConfirm.Buttons.Add) do
  begin
    Caption := 'Keep';
    CommandLinkHint := 'Keep the file in the folder.';
    ModalResult := mrNo;
  end;

  if TPath.GetExtension(LFileName).ToLower.Equals('.exe') then
  begin
```

```
      with TTaskDialogButtonItem(tdConfirm.Buttons.Add) do
      begin
        Caption := 'Google search';
        CommandLinkHint := 'Let''s Google tell us what ' +
          'this program is.';
        ModalResult := GOOGLE_SEARCH;
      end;
  end;

  tdConfirm.Flags := [tfUseCommandLinks];
  tdConfirm.MainIcon := tdiInformation;

  if tdConfirm.Execute then
  begin
    case tdConfirm.ModalResult of
      mrYes:
        ShowMessage('Deleted');
      mrNo:
        ShowMessage(LFileName + 'has been preserved');
      GOOGLE_SEARCH:
        begin
          LGSearch := Format('https://www.google.it/#q=%s',
            [LFileName]);
          ShellExecute(0, 'open', PChar(LGSearch), nil, nil,
            SW_SHOWNORMAL);
        end;
    end; //case
  end; //if
end;
```

It seems like a lot of code, but it is simple and can be easily parameterized and reused inside your program. The resultant dialog is as shown:

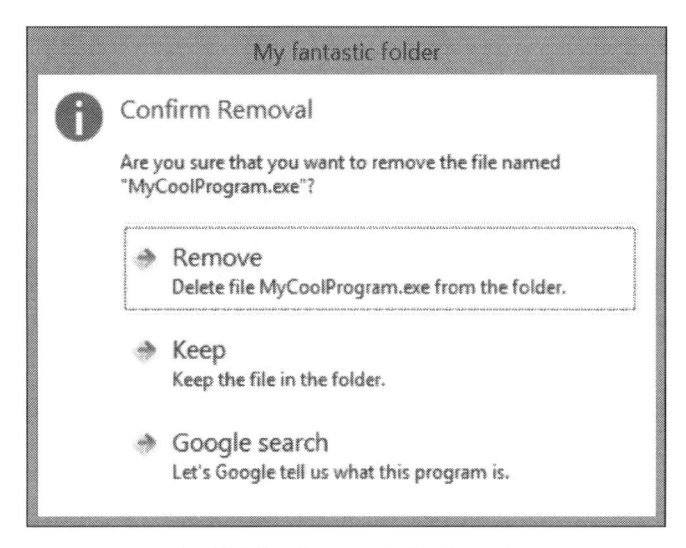

Fig. 12.3 The dialog customized by code

The third choice allows the user to search on Google about the program executable name. This is not a common choice in the `MessageDlg` dialog where buttons are predefined, but using the Task Dialog you can even ask something "strange" to the user (such as "do you want to ask Google about it?")

To achieve a better apparent speed, progress bars are great! The Task Dialog API provides a simple way to use progress bars inside dialogs. The classic Delphi solution relays a custom form with a progress bar and some labels (just like the "Compiling" dialog that you see when you compile a program within the Delphi IDE). However, in some cases, you need some simple stuff done and a Task Dialog is enough. If `TTaskDialog` has the `tfCallbackTimer` flag and `tfShowProgressBar`, the `OnTimer` event will be called every 200 milliseconds (five times a second), and the dialog will show a progress dialog that you can update within the `OnTimer` event handler. However, the `OnTimer` event handler runs in the main thread so that all the related advice applies (if the UI becomes unresponsive, consider a proper background thread and a queue to send information to the main thread).

This is the design time configuration of `TTaskDialog tdProgress`:

```
object tdProgress: TTaskDialog
  Caption = 'Please wait'
  CommonButtons = [tcbCancel]
  ExpandButtonCaption = 'More'
  ExpandedText =
```

```
    'A prime number (or a prime) is a natural number greater'+
      ' than 1 that has no positive divisors other than 1 ' +
      'and itself.'
    Flags = [tfAllowDialogCancellation, tfShowProgressBar,
tfCallbackTimer]
    FooterIcon = 3
    FooterText = 'Please wait while we are calculate prime numbers'
    Text = 'Let'#39's calculate prime numbers up to 1000'
    Title = 'Calculating prime numbers...'
    VerificationText = 'Remember my choice'
    OnButtonClicked = tdProgressButtonClicked
    OnTimer = tdProgressTimer
  end
```

There are two event handlers, one to handle click on the `Cancel` button inside the dialog and one to handle the callback:

```
  const
    MAX_NUMBERS = 1000;
    NUMBERS_IN_A_SINGLE_STEP = 50;

  procedure TMainForm.tdProgressButtonClicked(Sender: TObject;
    ModalResult: TModalResult; var CanClose: Boolean);
  begin
    if not FFinished then
    begin
      tdProgress.OnTimer := nil;
      ShowMessage('Calculation aborted by user');
      CanClose := True;
    end;
  end;

  procedure TMainForm.tdProgressTimer(Sender: TObject;
    TickCount: Cardinal;
    var Reset: Boolean);
  var
    I: Integer;
  begin
    for I := 1 to NUMBERS_IN_A_SINGLE_STEP do
    begin
      if IsPrimeNumber(FCurrNumber) then
        Inc(FPrimeNumbersCount);
      tdProgress.ProgressBar.Position := FCurrNumber * 100
        div MAX_NUMBERS;
      Inc(FCurrNumber);
```

```
    end;

    FFinished := FCurrNumber >= MAX_NUMBERS;
    if FFinished then
    begin
      tdProgress.OnTimer := nil;
      tdProgress.ProgressBar.Position := 100;
      ShowMessage('There are ' + FPrimeNumbersCount.ToString +
          ' prime numbers up to ' + MAX_NUMBERS.ToString);
    end;
  end;
```

To not block the `main` thread, the prime numbers are calculated a few at a time. When the calculation is ended, the callback is disabled by setting the `OnTimer` event handler to `nil`.

In other words, the real calculation is done in the `main` thread, so you should slice your process in to smaller parts so that it can be executed one (small) piece at time.

The following code fires the progress Task Dialog:

```
procedure TMainForm.btnProgressClick(Sender: TObject);
begin
  FCurrNumber := 1;
  FFinished := False;
  FPrimeNumbersCount := 0;
  tdProgress.ProgressBar.Position := 0;
  tdProgress.OnTimer := tdProgressTimer;
  tdProgress.Execute;
end;
```

Here's the resultant dialog:

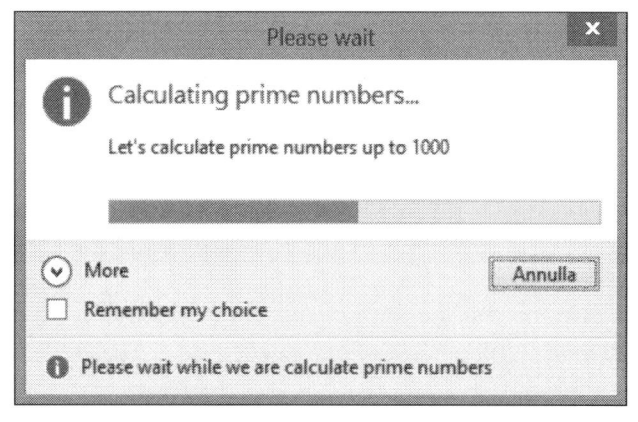

Fig. 12.4 The Task Dialog with an embedded Progress Bar

There's more...

The new Task Dialog API can give your application a fresh breath, but that comes with cost because it works only on Vista or better, with enabled themes. So, how to work around the problem if you need to run the application also in Windows XP or in machine without themes enabled? For button 6, there's a simple code to check whether you can safely use the `TTaskDialog` component or whether you have to come back to normal `ShowMessage` or `MessageDlg`. Here's the event handler for the button 6:

```
procedure TMainForm.btnCheckWinVerClick(Sender: TObject);
var
    LTaskDialog: TTaskDialog;
begin
    if (Win32MajorVersion >= 6) and ThemeServices.ThemesEnabled then
    begin
        LTaskDialog := TTaskDialog.Create(Self);
        try
            LTaskDialog.Caption := 'MY Fantastic Application';
            LTaskDialog.Title := 'The Cook Task Dialog!';
            LTaskDialog.Text :=
                'This is a Task Dialog, so I''m on Vista ' +
                    'or better with themes enabled';
            LTaskDialog.CommonButtons := [tcbOk];
            LTaskDialog.Execute;
        finally
            LTaskDialog.Free;
        end
    end
    else
    begin
        ShowMessage('This is an old and boring ShowMEssage, ' +
            'here only to support old Microsoft Windows OS ' +
            '(XP and below)');
    end;
end;
```

Try to disable the themes for your application and click on button 6.

Obviously, it is strongly suggested that you wrap this code in a function so that you do not have to write the same check code repeatedly.

Downloading the example code

You can download the example code files for this book from your account at http://www.packtpub.com. If you purchased this book elsewhere, you can visit http://www.packtpub.com/support and register to have the files e-mailed directly to you.

You can download the code files by following these steps:

- Log in or register to our website using your e-mail address and password.
- Hover the mouse pointer on the **SUPPORT** tab at the top.
- Click on **Code Downloads & Errata**.
- Enter the name of the book in the **Search** box.
- Select the book for which you're looking to download the code files.
- Choose from the drop-down menu where you purchased this book from.
- Click on **Code Download**.

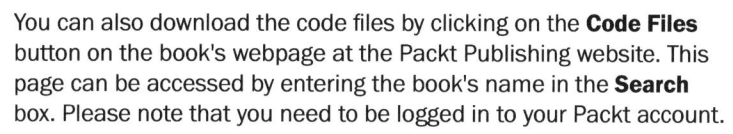

You can also download the code files by clicking on the **Code Files** button on the book's webpage at the Packt Publishing website. This page can be accessed by entering the book's name in the **Search** box. Please note that you need to be logged in to your Packt account.

Once the file is downloaded, please make sure that you unzip or extract the folder using the latest version of:

- WinRAR / 7-Zip for Windows
- Zipeg / iZip / UnRarX for Mac
- 7-Zip / PeaZip for Linux

The code bundle for the book is also hosted on GitHub at https://github.com/PacktPublishing/Delphi-Cookbook-Second-Edition. We also have other code bundles from our rich catalog of books and videos available at https://github.com/PacktPublishing/. Check them out!

2
Becoming a Delphi Language Ninja

In this chapter, we will cover the following recipes:

- Fun with anonymous methods – using higher-order functions
- Writing enumerable types
- RTTI to the rescue – configuring your class at runtime
- Duck typing using RTTI
- Creating helpers for your classes

Introduction

This chapter will explain some of the not-so-obvious features of the language and the RTL that every Delphi programmer should know. Anonymous methods, enumerable types, extended RTTI, and class helpers are powerful tools for every Delphi developer, but usually they are not mastered as they should be. In this chapter, there are ready-to-use recipes that use these concepts to implement something really useful.

Fun with anonymous methods – using higher-order functions

Since Version 2009, the Delphi language (or better, its Object Pascal dialect) supports anonymous methods. What's an anonymous method? Not surprisingly, an anonymous method is a procedure or a function that does not have an associated name. An anonymous method treats a block of code just like a value so that it can be assigned to a variable, used as a parameter to a method or returned by a function as its result value. In addition, an anonymous method can refer to variables and bind values to the variables in the context scope in which the anonymous method is defined. Anonymous methods are similar to closures defined in other languages such as JavaScript or C#. An anonymous method type is declared as a reference to a function:

```
type
  TFuncOfString = reference to function(S: String): String;
```

Anonymous methods (or anonymous functions) are convenient to pass as an argument to a higher-order function. What's a higher-order function?

Wikipedia gives the following explanation (http://en.wikipedia.org/wiki/Higher-order_function).

In mathematics and computer science, a higher-order function (also functional form, functional, or `functor`) is a function that does at least one of the following:

- Takes one or more functions as an input
- Outputs a function

All other functions are first order functions.

Getting ready

In this recipe, you'll see how to use Delphi's anonymous methods with some of the most popular and useful higher-order functions:

- `Map`: This is available in many functional programming languages. This takes as arguments a `func` function and a list of elements `list`, and returns a new list with `func` applied to each element of `list`.
- `Reduce`: This is also known as `Fold`. This requires a combining function, a starting point of a data structure, and possibly some default values to be used under certain conditions. The `Reduce` function proceeds to combine elements of the data structure using the injected function.

   This is used to perform operations on a set of values to get only one result (or a smaller set of values) that represents the *reduction* of that initial data. For example, the values 1, 2, and 3 can be reduced to the single value 6 using the criteria of SUM.

▶ `Filter`: This requires a data structure and a filter condition. This returns all the elements in the structure that match the filter condition.

How to do it...

For the `HigherOrderFunctions.dproj` project, the actual high-order functions are implemented in the `HigherOrderFunctionsU.pas` unit as generic class functions as shown here:

```
type
  HigherOrder = class sealed
    class function Map<T>(InputArray: TArray<T>;
  MapFunction: TFunc<T, T>): TArray<T>;
    class function Reduce<T: record>(InputArray: TArray<T>;
  ReduceFunction: TFunc<T, T, T>; InitValue: T): T;
    class function Filter<T>(InputArray: TArray<T>;
    FilterFunction: TFunc<T, boolean>): TArray<T>;
  end;
```

Let's analyze each of these functions. The `Map` function requires a list of `T` parameters as its input data structure and an anonymous method that accepts and returns the same type of data `T`. For each element of the input data structure, the `MapFunction` is called and another list of data is built to contain all its results.

This is the body of the `Map` function:

```
class function HigherOrder.Map<T>(InputArray: TArray<T>;
    MapFunction: TFunc<T, T>): TArray<T>;
var
  I: Integer;
begin
  SetLength(Result, length(InputArray));
  for I := 0 to length(InputArray) - 1 do
    Result[I] := MapFunction(InputArray[I]);
end;
```

The main form uses the `Map` function in the following way:

```
procedure TMainForm.btnMapCapitalizeClick(Sender: TObject);
var
  InputData, OutputData: TArray<string>;
begin
  //let's generate some sample data
  InputData := GetStringArrayOfData;

  //call the map function on an array of string
```

```delphi
    OutputData := HigherOrder.Map<string>(
      InputData,
      function(Item: String): String
      begin
        //this is the "map" criteria that will be applied to each
        //item to capitalize the first word in the item
        Result := String(Item.Chars[0]).ToUpper + Item.Substring(1);
      end);

    //fill the related listbox with the results
    FillList(OutputData, lbMap.Items);
  end;
```

The `Reduce` function requires a list of `T` as its input data structure and an anonymous method that accepts two parameters of type `T` and returns a value of type `T`. It can also be passed a default for each element of the input data structure, the `ReduceFunction` is called by passing the intermediate result calculated so far and the current element of the list. After the last call, the result is returned to the caller function.

This is the body of the `Reduce` function:

```delphi
class function HigherOrder.Reduce<T>(
InputArray: TArray<T>;
ReduceFunction: TFunc<T, T, T>; InitValue: T): T;
var
  I: T;
begin
  Result := InitValue;
  for I in InputArray do
  begin
    Result := ReduceFunction(Result, I);
  end;
end;
```

The main form uses the `Reduce` function in the following way:

```delphi
procedure TMainForm.btnReduceSumClick(Sender: TObject);
var
  InputData: TArray<Integer>;
  OutputData: Integer;
begin
  InputData := GetIntArrayOfData;
  //sum the input data using as starting value 0
  OutputData := HigherOrder.Reduce<Integer>(InputData,
    function(Item1, Item2: Integer): Integer
    begin
```

```
      Result := Item1 + Item2;
    end, 0);
  lbReduce.Items.Add('SUM: ' + OutputData.ToString);
end;
```

The last implemented function is `Filter`. The `Filter` function requires a list of `T` as its input data structure and an anonymous method accepts a single parameter of type `T` and returns a Boolean value. This anonymous method represents the filter criteria that will be applied to the input data. For each element of the input data structure, the `FilterFunction` is called and if it returns `true`, then the current element will be in the returning list, but not otherwise. After the last call, the filtered list is returned to the caller function.

Here is the body of the `Filter` function:

```
class function HigherOrder.Filter<T>(InputArray: TArray<T>;
    FilterFunction: TFunc<T, boolean>): TArray<T>;
var
  I: Integer;
  List: TList<T>;
begin
  List := TList<T>.Create;
  try
    for I := 0 to length(InputArray) - 1 do
      if FilterFunction(InputArray[I]) then
        List.Add(InputArray[I]);
    Result := List.ToArray;
  finally
    List.Free;
  end;
end;
```

The main form uses the `Filter` function to filter only even numbers. The code is as follows:

```
procedure TMainForm.btnFilterEvenClick(Sender: TObject);
var
  InputData, OutputData: TArray<Integer>;
begin
  InputData := GetIntArrayOfData;
  OutputData := HigherOrder.Filter<Integer>(InputData,
    function(Item: Integer): boolean
    begin
      Result := Item mod 2 = 0; //gets only the even numbers
    end);
  FillList(OutputData, lbFilter.Items);
end;
```

In the recipe's code, there are other utilization samples related to higher-order functions.

There's more...

Higher-order functions are a vast and interesting topic, so in this recipe we only scratched the surface. One of the main concepts is the abstraction of the internal loop over the data structure. Consider this: by abstracting the concept of looping, you can implement looping any way you want, including implementing it in a way that scales nicely with extra hardware. A good sample of what can be done using functional programming is the parallel extension of the good `OmniThreadLibrary` (a nice library to simplify multithreading programming) written by *Primož Gabrijelčič* (http://www.thedelphigeek.com/). This is a simple code sample that executes a parallel function for defining a single iteration with an anonymous method and runs it using multiple threads:

```delphi
Parallel.ForEach(1, 100000).Execute(
    procedure (Const elem: integer)
    begin
      //check if the current element is
      //a prime number (can be slow)
      if IsPrime(elem) then
        MyOutputList.Add(elem);
    end);
```

Writing enumerable types

When the `for...in` loop was introduced in Delphi 2005, the concept of enumerable types was also introduced into the Delphi language.

As you know, there are some built-in enumerable types. However, you can create your own enumerable types using a very simple pattern.

To make your container enumerable, implement a single method called `GetEnumerator`, that must return a reference to an object, interface, or record, that implements the following three methods and one property (in the sample, the element to enumerate is `TFoo`):

```delphi
function GetCurrent: TFoo;
function MoveNext: Boolean;
property Current: TFoo read GetCurrent;
```

There are a lot of samples related to standard enumerable types, so in this recipe you'll look at some not-so-common utilizations.

Getting ready

In this recipe, you'll see a file enumerable function as it exists in other, mostly dynamic, languages. The goal is to enumerate all the rows in a text file without actually opening, reading, and closing the file, as shown in the following code:

```
var
   row: String;
begin
   for row in EachRows('..\..\myfile.txt') do
      WriteLn(row);
end;
```

Nice, isn't it? Let's start.

How to do it...

We have to create an enumerable function result. The function simply returns the actual enumerable type. This type is not freed automatically by the compiler so you've to use a value type or an interfaced type. For the sake of simplicity, let's code to return a record type:

```
function EachRows(const AFileName: String): TFileEnumerable;
begin
   Result := TFileEnumerable.Create(AFileName);
end;
```

The `TFileEnumerable` type is defined as follows:

```
type
   TFileEnumerable = record
   private
      FFileName: string;
   public
      constructor Create(AFileName: String);
      function GetEnumerator: TEnumerator<String>;
   end;
   . . .
constructor TFileEnumerable.Create(AFileName: String);
begin
   FFileName := AFileName;
end;

function TFileEnumerable.GetEnumerator: TEnumerator<String>;
begin
   Result := TFileEnumerator.Create(FFileName);
end;
```

No logic here; this record is required only because you need a type that has a `GetEnumerator` method defined. This method is called automatically by the compiler when the type is used on the right side of the `for...in` loop.

The `TFileEnumerator` type is the actual enumerator and is declared in the implementation section of the unit. Remember, this object is automatically freed by the compiler because it is the return of the `GetEnumerator` call:

```delphi
type
   TFileEnumerator = class (TEnumerator<String>)
   private
      FCurrent: String;
      FFile: TStreamReader;
   protected
      constructor Create(AFileName: String);
      destructor Destroy; override;
      function DoGetCurrent: String; override;
      function DoMoveNext: Boolean; override;
   end;

{ TFileEnumerator }

constructor TFileEnumerator.Create(AFileName: String);
begin
   inherited Create;
   FFile := TFile.OpenText(AFileName);
end;

destructor TFileEnumerator.Destroy;
begin
   FFile.Free;
   inherited;
end;

function TFileEnumerator.DoGetCurrent: String;
begin
   Result := FCurrent;
end;

function TFileEnumerator.DoMoveNext: Boolean;
begin
   Result := not FFile.EndOfStream;
   if Result then
      FCurrent := FFile.ReadLine;

end;
```

The enumerator inherits from `TEnumerator<String>` because each row of the file is represented as a string. This class also gives a mechanism to implement the required methods.

The `DoGetCurrent` (called internally by the `TEnumerator<T>.GetCurrent` method) returns the current line.

The `DoMoveNext` method (called internally by the `TEnumerator<T>.MoveNext` method) returns `true` or `false` depending on whether there are more lines to read in the file or not. Remember that this method is called before the first call to the `GetCurrent` method. After the first call to the `DoMoveNext` method, `FCurrent` is properly set to the first row of the file.

The compiler generates a piece of code similar to the following pseudo code:

```
it = typetoenumerate.GetEnumerator;
while it.MoveNext do
begin
  S := it.Current;
  //do something useful with string S
end
it.free;
```

There's more...

Enumerable types are really powerful and help you to write less, and less error-prone, code. There are some shortcuts to iterate over in-place data without even creating an actual container.

If you have a bounce or integers or if you want to create a non-homogenous `for` loop over some kind of data type, you can use the new `TArray<T>` type as shown here:

```
for i in TArray<Integer>.Create(2, 4, 8, 16) do
  WriteLn(i);
//write 2 4 8 16
```

`TArray<T>` is a generic type, so the same technique works also for strings:

```
for s in TArray<String>.Create('Hello','Delphi','World') do
  WriteLn(s);
```

It can also be used for **Plain Old Delphi Object** (**PODO**) or controls:

```
for btn in TArray<TButton>.Create(btn1, btn31,btn2) do
  btn.Enabled := false;
```

See also

Here is a link to the Embarcadero documentation, which will provide a detailed introduction to enumerable types: http://docwiki.embarcadero.com/RADStudio/en/Declarations_and_Statements#Iteration_Over_Containers_Using_For_statements.

RTTI to the rescue – configuring your class at runtime

Since Delphi 2010, the Delphi RTTI has been greatly expanded. Now, it is comparable to what is called reflection in other languages such as C# or Java. A much-improved RTTI can dramatically change the way you write, or even think about, your code and your architecture. Now, it is possible to write highly flexible code without too much effort.

Getting ready

What we want to do in this recipe is dynamically create a class looking for it by name among the classes that have been linked in the executable (or loaded from dynamic packages). The goal is to change the behavior of the program using only an external file without relying on a lot of parameters and complex configuration code; just create the right class. Wonderful!

Let's say you've developed a program to do orders. Your program allows only one-line orders, so you cannot buy different things in the same orders (this is a sample!). The form is shown in this screenshot:

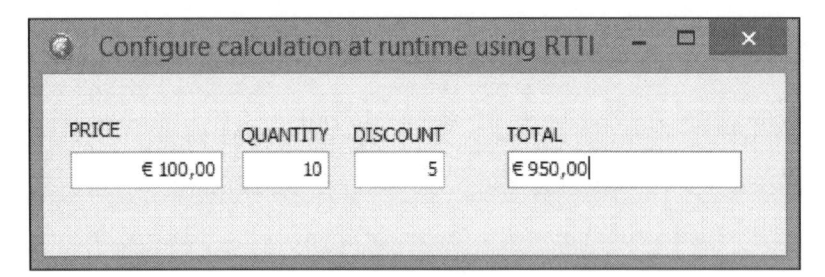

The main form

There is a dataset field connected to each of the `TDBEdit` in the form. The **TOTAL** field is a calculated field and its value is calculated in the `OnCalcFields` dataset.

The calculation is simple:

*total = price * quantity * (1 – discount / 100)*

The customer is happy and you are happy as well.

Now, a new, big customer, the City Mall, wants a customization, "If the total is greater than $1,000, apply another 10 percent discount". Ok, you can create the customized version easily. So far so good, but now you have two different versions to maintain.

Now, another customer, the Country Road Shop says, "If there are more than 10 pieces, the discount must be at least 50 percent". Another customer Spark Industries specifies, "Only at the weekend, all the calculated prices will be cut by 50 percent".

Argh! Four customers and four different version of your software to maintain because of customizations! You get the point; at the beginning things are simple, but when you start to customize something, complexity (and bugs) can arise. Let's fix this problem in this recipe.

How to do it...

The sample customization is simple. However, the difficulty comes in when you have to handle which customization you have to choose among those available. You can define some sort of parameters, sure, but your code will get a lot of if just to understand which calculation to apply. And, even worse, a change in one of your criteria could break something in another. Bad approach!

We can configure our software without `if` statements using RTTI. In this recipe, all the calculus engines are implemented in four different classes in four different units (you can also define all the criteria in only one unit, but it is not mandatory).

In the following table, there is a summary of the customers and the customizations implemented:

Customer	Unit/class name	Calculation criteria
Default (no customization)	CalculationCustomerDefaultU TCalculationCustomerDefault	Result := (Price * Quantity) * (1 - Discount / 100);
City Mall	CalculationCustomer_CityMall TCalculationCustomer_CityMall	Result := (Price * Quantity) * (1 - Discount / 100); if Result > 1000 then Result := Result * 0.90;

Customer	Unit/class name	Calculation criteria

Country Road Shop	`CalculationCustomer_CountryRoad`
	
	`TCalculationCustomer_CountryRoad`
		`if Quantity > 10 then`
		  `if Discount < 50`
		  `then`
		    `Discount := 50;`
		`Result := (Price * Quantity) * (1 - Discount / 100);`

Spark Industries	`CalculationCustomer_Spark`
	
	`TCalculationCustomer_Spark`
		`Result := (Price * Quantity) * (1 - Discount / 100);`
		`if DayOfTheWeek(Date) in [1, 7] then`
		  `Result :=`
		    `Result * 0.50;`

When the program starts, it looks for a configuration file. In the first line of the file, there is a fully qualified class name (`UnitName.ClassName`) that implements the needed calculus criteria. That string is used to create the related class and the instance will be used to calculate the total price when needed. The interesting code is as follows:

```
procedure TMainForm.LoadCalculationEngine;
var
  TheClassName: string;
  CalcEngineType: TRttiType;
const
  CONFIG_FILENAME = '..\..\calculation.config.txt';
begin
  if not TFile.Exists(CONFIG_FILENAME) then
    TheClassName := 'CalculationCustomerDefaultU.' +
'TCalculationCustomerDefault'
  else
    TheClassName := TFile.ReadAllLines(CONFIG_FILENAME)[0];

  CalcEngineType := FCTX.FindType(TheClassName.Trim);
  if not assigned(CalcEngineType) then
    raise Exception.CreateFmt('Class %s not found',
  [TheClassName]);
  if not CalcEngineType.GetMethod('Create').IsConstructor then
    raise Exception.CreateFmt('Cannot find Create in %s',
```

```
  [TheClassName]);

  FCalcEngineObj := CalcEngineType.GetMethod('Create')
.Invoke(CalcEngineType.AsInstance.MetaclassType, [])
.AsObject;
  FCalcEngineMethod := CalcEngineType.GetMethod('GetTotal');
  Label5.Caption := 'Current Calc Engine: ' + TheClassName;
end;
```

`FCalcEngineObj` is a `TObject` reference that holds your actual calculation engine, while `FCalcEngineMethod` is an RTTI object that keeps a reference to the method to call when the calculus is needed.

Now, in the dataset `OnCalcFields` event handler, there is this code:

```
procedure TMainForm.ClientDataSet1CalcFields(DataSet: TDataSet);
begin
ClientDataSet1TOTAL.Value :=
FCalcEngineMethod.Invoke(FCalcEngineObj,
    [ClientDataSet1PRICE.Value,
    ClientDataSet1QUANTITY.Value,
    ClientDataSet1DISCOUNT.Value]).AsCurrency;
end;
```

Run the program and check which calculus engine is loaded. Then stop the program, open the configuration file, and write another `QualifiedClassName` (unit name plus class name), choosing from all those available. Run the program. As you can see, the correct engine is selected and the customization is applied without changing the working code.

On writing the `CalculationCustomer_CityMall.TCalculationCustomer_CityMall` class in the file, you will get the following behavior:

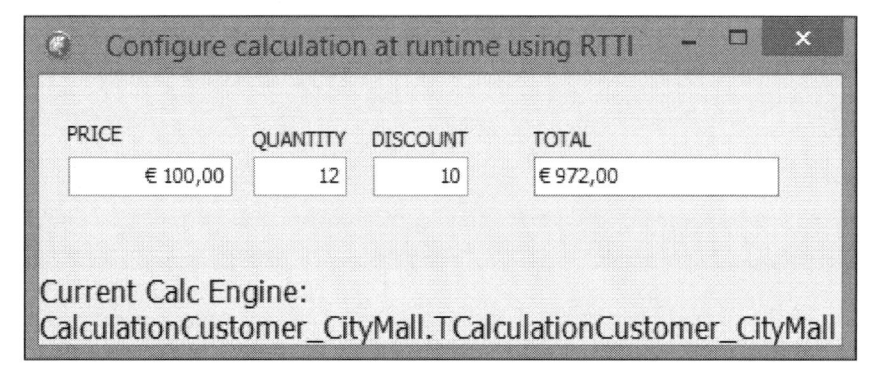

The main form using the customized calculus engine specified in the configuration file

There's more...

RTTI is a really vast topic. There are endless possibilities for using it in smart ways.

Remember, however, that, if the Delphi linker sees that your class is not used in the actual code (because it is used only in the RTTI calls), it could eliminate the class from the executable. So, to be sure that your class will be included in the final executable, write a (even useless) line of code referring to the class. In this recipe, I've included a line of code similar to the following one in every initialization section of the different calculus classes:

```
//. . . other code before
```

initialization

```
//Linker will not remove the class from the final executable
//because now it is used somewhere

TCalculationCustomer_CityMall.ClassName;
```

end.

See also

The documentation from Embarcadero gives more information about extended RTTI: `http://docwiki.embarcadero.com/RADStudio/en/Working_with_RTTI_Index`.

Duck typing using RTTI

> "When I see a bird that walks like a duck and swims like a duck and quacks like a duck, I call that bird a duck."
>
> - James Whitcomb Riley

Clear, isn't it? What may not be so clear is that this approach can be used also in computer programming. Yes, even without an actual duck!

Getting ready

Referring to duck typing, Wikipedia gives the following explanation (`http://en.wikipedia.org/wiki/Duck_typing`).

In computer programming with object-oriented programming languages, duck typing is a style of typing in which an object's methods and properties determine the valid semantics, rather than its inheritance from a particular class or the implementation of an explicit interface.

How can all these concepts be used in everyday programming? This is the question that this recipe aims to answer.

Let's say that you have a form and you want to inform the user that something bad happened by changing all the colorable components to `clRed`. I don't know what the property `Color` means for any control that has that property, I only want to set all the properties named `Color` to `clRed`. How can you achieve this? The naive approach could be to cycle the `Components` property, check whether the current control is a control that I know has a `Color` property, and then cast that control reference to an actual `TEdit` (or `TComboBox`, `TListBox`, or whatever) reference and change the `Color` property to `clRed`. However, what if tomorrow you need to color another kind of control as well? Or you have to change the `Color` property on `TPanels` but the `Font.Color` property on `TEdits`? You get the point, I think. Using the naive approach can raise the complexity of your code. A programmer should hate complexity. More complexity means more time to handle and more time means more money to spend. As usual, the KISS approach is the best one: Keep it simple, stupid!

How to do it...

The code in this recipe allows you to write code like the following snippets. In this snippet, the `Color` property of all controls in the form will be set to `clRed`. I don't know which kind of controls there are on the form, but if they have a property named `Color`, that property will be set to `clRed`:

```
Duck.Apply(Self, 'Color', clRed);
```

In this snippet, the `Caption` property of the controls in the array; if it exists, will be set to `'Hello There'`:

```
Duck.Apply(
  TArray<TObject>.Create(Button1, Button2, Edit1),
  'Caption',
  'Hello There');
```

The following code disables all the `TDataSource` on the form, preventing data editing:

```
Duck.Apply(Self, 'Enabled', False,
  function(Item: TObject): boolean
  begin
    Result := Item is TDataSource;
  end);
```

The following code sets the font name to `Courier New` for some controls:

```
Duck.Apply(TArray<TObject>.Create(Edit1, Edit2, Button2),
    'Font.Name', 'Courier New');
```

Becoming a Delphi Language Ninja

This code works for every kind of control. If you change the `TButton` in `TSpeedButton`, it continues to work. If you change a `TListBox` with a `TComboBox`, the code still works. The concept is simple: if you have a property X then I'll set that property independent of the actual object type.

Let's see the code that actually does the job.

The main `Duck` class is a mere method container (this is the reason its name is `Duck` and not `TDuck`; it is not a real type) declared as shown in the following code:

```
type
   Duck = class sealed
      class procedure Apply(ArrayOf: TArray<TObject>;
PropName: string; PropValue: TValue;
AcceptFunction: TFunc<TObject, boolean> = nil); overload;
      class procedure Apply(AContainer: TComponent;
PropName: string; PropValue: TValue;
         AcceptFunction: TFunc<TObject, boolean> = nil); overload;
   end;
```

Methods are very similar and the second one adds a helper to work with `TComponents`; the real job is done by the first one:

```
class procedure Duck.Apply(ArrayOf: TArray<TObject>;
PropName: string; PropValue: TValue;
    AcceptFunction: TFunc<TObject, boolean>);
var
   CTX: TRttiContext;
   Item, PropObj: TObject;
   RttiType: TRttiType;
   Prop: TRttiProperty;
   PropertyPath: TArray<string>;
   i: Integer;
begin
   CTX := TRttiContext.Create;
   try
      for Item in ArrayOf do
      begin
         if (not Assigned(AcceptFunction)) or
(AcceptFunction(Item)) then
            begin
               RttiType := CTX.GetType(Item.ClassType);
               if Assigned(RttiType) then
               begin
                  PropertyPath := PropName.Split(['.']);
                  Prop := RttiType.GetProperty(PropertyPath[0]);
```

```
          if not Assigned(Prop) then
            Continue;
          PropObj := Item;
          if Prop.GetValue(PropObj).isObject then
          begin
            PropObj := Prop.GetValue(Item).AsObject;
            for i := 1 to Length(PropertyPath) - 1 do
            begin
              RttiType := CTX.GetType(PropObj.ClassType);
              Prop := RttiType.GetProperty(PropertyPath[i]);
              if not Assigned(Prop) then
                break;
              if Prop.GetValue(PropObj).isObject then
                PropObj := Prop.GetValue(PropObj).AsObject
              else
                break;
            end;
          end;
          if Assigned(Prop) and (Prop.IsWritable) then
            Prop.SetValue(PropObj, PropValue);
        end;
      end;
    end;
  finally
    CTX.Free;
  end;
end;
```

This is not very simple, I know, but you can see all the pieces we've already talked about. Obviously, we use RTTI to get the names and set the values of the properties.

The main loop cycles over the array parameter and asks `AcceptFunction` whether the object must be inspected or not. `AcceptFunction` is optional, so the value can be nil. In this case, all the objects are inspected. To allow syntax such as `Font.Name`, there is a small parser that splits the strings and walks through each piece to check whether there is a property with that name. If the last piece (or the only one) is found, then check whether that property is writable; if it is writable, set the property to the passed value. In this way, you can write code that walks through a complex object graph with a simple syntax:

```
Duck.Apply(TArray<TObject>.Create(
DataSource1, DataSource2, Button2), 'DataSet.Active', true);
```

There's more...

Duck typing is a very broad topic and allows you to do wonderful things with a few lines of code. In this recipe's code, there is a bonus recipe project called `DuckTypingUsingRTTIExtended.dproj`, which contains an advanced version of the base recipe. It uses a fluent interface, allows you to select the components that you want to change, and defines what type of change to make on those components; something similar to the following code snippets.

Set all the `Caption` properties of the components on the form to `On All Captions`:

```
Duck(Self).All.SetProperty('Caption').ToValue('On All Captions');
```

Set all the `Text` properties to `'Hello There'` for the components with the name starting with `'Edit'`, using an anonymous method as a filter to select the components:

```
Duck(Self)
.Where(function(C: TComponent): boolean
  begin
        Result := String(C.Name).StartsWith('Edit');
  end)
.SetProperty('Text')
.ToValue('Hello There');
```

Set the `Color` property to `clRed` for all the `TEdit` components on the form. Use an anonymous method to define what to do on the components:

```
Duck(Self).Where(TEdit).Apply(
procedure(C: TComponent)
    begin
       TEdit(C).Color := clRed;
end);
```

In the *bonus* recipe, there are more examples. Feel free to experiment and expand on them.

Creating helpers for your classes

As you know (and if you don't know, you can read the documentation about it), a class helper is a type that can be associated to a class. When a class helper is associated with another class, all the methods and properties defined in the helper are also available in the other class and in its descendants. Helpers are a way to extend a class without using inheritance. However, it is not the same thing as inheritance. In other words, if the `TFooHelper` helper is in the same scope as `TFoo`, the compiler's resolution scope then becomes the original type (`TFoo`), plus the helper (`TFooHelper`). So, if the `TFoo` class defines the `DoSomething` method and the `TFooHelper` (the `TFoo` class helper) defines `DoAnotherThing`, when `TFoo` is used in the same scope as the `TFooHelper`, the `TFoo` instances, and all its descendants, also have the `DoAnotherThing` method.

Getting ready

In this recipe, you'll see how to use class helpers to add iterators (or a sort of iterator) to the `TDataSet` class, so that any other `TDataSet` descendants—even from other vendor— can automatically support this kind of iterator. Moreover, you'll also add a `SaveToCSV` method so that any `TDataSet` can be saved in CSV with only one line of code.

How to do it...

For the `DataSetClassHelpers.dproj` project, let's start to talk about the simpler helper: the `SaveToCSV` method.

The current compiler implementation of class helpers allows only one helper active at a time. So if you need to add two or more helpers at the same time, you have to merge all the methods and properties in a single `helper` class. Your `TDataSet` helper is contained in the `DataSetHelpersU.pas` unit and is defined as follows:

```
TDataSetHelper = class helper for TDataSet
public
   procedure SaveToCSVFile(AFileName: String);
   function GetEnumerator: TDataSetEnumerator;
end;
```

To use this helper with your `TDataSet` instances, you have to add the `DataSetHelpersU` unit in the uses clause of the unit where you want to use the helper. The helper adds the following features to all the `TDataSet` descendants:

Method name	Description
`SaveToCSV`	This allows any dataset to be saved as a CSV file. The first row contains all the fieldnames.
	All the string values are correctly quoted while the numeric values aren't. The resultant CSV file is compatible with MS Excel and can be opened directly into it.
`GetEnumerator`	This enables the dataset to be used as an enumerable type in the `for...in` loops. This removes the necessity to cycle the dataset using the usual `while` loop (so you cannot forget the `DataSet.Next` call at the end of the loop).
	The dataset is correctly cycled from the current position to the end, and for each record the `for` loop is executed.
	The enumerator item type is a wrapper type called `TDSIterator` and is able to access the individual values of the current record using a simplified interface.

Becoming a Delphi Language Ninja

To get an idea about what the helpers can do, check the following code:

```
//all the interface section before

implementation

uses
  DataSetHelpersU; //add the TDataSet helper to the compiler scope

procedure TClassHelpersForm.btnSaveToCSVClick(Sender: TObject);
begin
  //use the SaveToCSVFile helper method
  FDMemTable1.SaveToCSVFile('mydata.csv');
  ListBox1.Items.LoadFromFile('mydata.csv');
end;

procedure TClassHelpersForm.btnIterateClick(Sender: TObject);
var
  it: TDSIterator; //this is the enumerator item type
begin
  //setup the ListBox with some nice headers
  ListBox1.Clear;
  ListBox1.Items.Add(
    Format('%-10s %-10s %8s',
    ['FirstName', 'LastName', 'EmpNo']));
  ListBox1.Items.Add(StringOfChar('-', 30));

  //iterate the dataset in a for..in loop using the helper
  for it in FDMemTable1 do
  begin
    ListBox1.Items.Add(
      Format('%-10s %-10s %8d',
      [
        it.Value['FirstName'].AsString,  //using the default
        it.S['LastName'],    //using the S[fieldname] for strings
        it.I['EmpNo']        //using the I[fieldname] for integers
      ]));
  end;
end;
```

Useful, isn't it? The following screenshot shows the the status of the demo application after the **SaveToCSV** button was clicked. The demo application is seen as running.

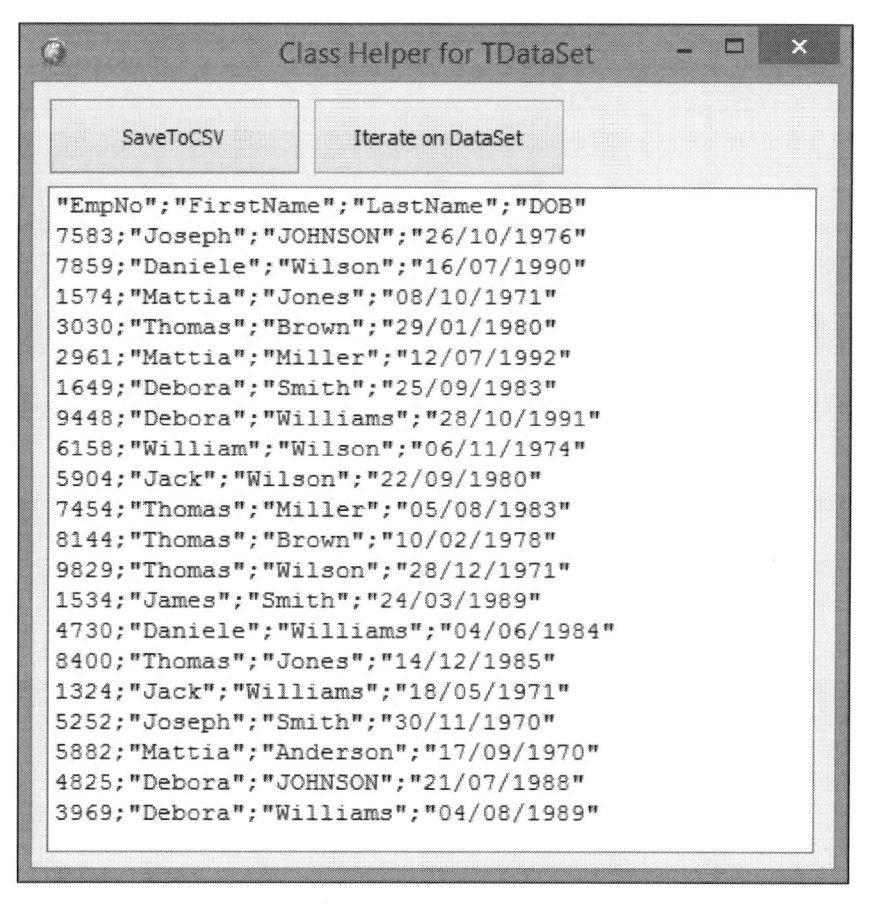

```
"EmpNo";"FirstName";"LastName";"DOB"
7583;"Joseph";"JOHNSON";"26/10/1976"
7859;"Daniele";"Wilson";"16/07/1990"
1574;"Mattia";"Jones";"08/10/1971"
3030;"Thomas";"Brown";"29/01/1980"
2961;"Mattia";"Miller";"12/07/1992"
1649;"Debora";"Smith";"25/09/1983"
9448;"Debora";"Williams";"28/10/1991"
6158;"William";"Wilson";"06/11/1974"
5904;"Jack";"Wilson";"22/09/1980"
7454;"Thomas";"Miller";"05/08/1983"
8144;"Thomas";"Brown";"10/02/1978"
9829;"Thomas";"Wilson";"28/12/1971"
1534;"James";"Smith";"24/03/1989"
4730;"Daniele";"Williams";"04/06/1984"
8400;"Thomas";"Jones";"14/12/1985"
1324;"Jack";"Williams";"18/05/1971"
5252;"Joseph";"Smith";"30/11/1970"
5882;"Mattia";"Anderson";"17/09/1970"
4825;"Debora";"JOHNSON";"21/07/1988"
3969;"Debora";"Williams";"04/08/1989"
```

The form after the SaveToCSV button is clicked

The following screenshot shows the output of the dataset iteration using the helper:

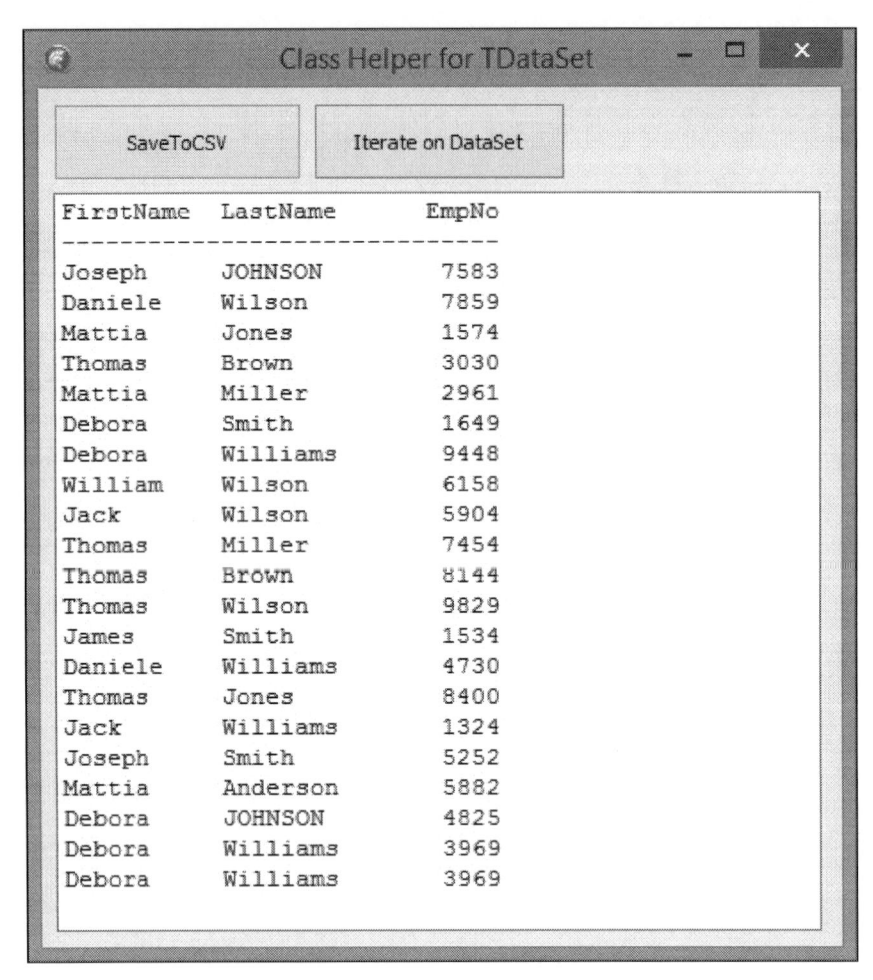

```
Class Helper for TDataSet

    SaveToCSV              Iterate on DataSet

FirstName    LastName        EmpNo
-------------------------------------
Joseph       JOHNSON         7583
Daniele      Wilson          7859
Mattia       Jones           1574
Thomas       Brown           3030
Mattia       Miller          2961
Debora       Smith           1649
Debora       Williams        9448
William      Wilson          6158
Jack         Wilson          5904
Thomas       Miller          7454
Thomas       Brown           8144
Thomas       Wilson          9829
James        Smith           1534
Daniele      Williams        4730
Thomas       Jones           8400
Jack         Williams        1324
Joseph       Smith           5252
Mattia       Anderson        5882
Debora       JOHNSON         4825
Debora       Williams        3969
Debora       Williams        3969
```

The form after the Iterate on DataSet button is clicked; the iteration is used to show dataset data in the listbox.

Let's see the implementation details.

The `SaveToCSV` method has been implemented as shown here:

```
procedure TDataSetHelper.SaveToCSVFile(AFileName: String);
var
  Fields: TArray<string>;
  CSVWriter: TStreamWriter;
  I: Integer;
  CurrPos: TArray<Byte>;
begin
```

```delphi
//save the current dataset position
CurrPos := Self.Bookmark;

Self.DisableControls;
try
Self.First;
//create a TStreamWriter to write the CSV file
CSVWriter := TStreamWriter.Create(AFileName);
try
  SetLength(Fields, Self.Fields.Count);
  for I := 0 to Self.Fields.Count - 1 do
  begin
    Fields[I] := Self.Fields[I].FieldName.QuotedString('"');
  end;

  //Write the headers line joining the fieldnames with a ";"
  CSVWriter.WriteLine(String.Join(';', Fields));


  //Cycle the dataset
  while not Self.Eof do
  begin
    for I := 0 to Self.Fields.Count - 1 do
    begin
      //DoubleQuote the string values
      case Self.Fields[I].DataType of
        ftInteger, ftWord, ftSmallint, ftShortInt,
        ftLargeint, ftBoolean, ftFloat, ftSingle:
          begin
            CSVWriter.Write(Self.Fields[I].AsString);
          end;
      else
        CSVWriter.Write(
          Self.Fields[I].AsString.QuotedString('"'));
      end;

  //if at the last columns, newline, otherwise ";"
  if I < Self.FieldCount - 1 then
    CSVWriter.Write(';')
  else
    CSVWriter.WriteLine;
   end;
   Self.Next; //next record
  end;
```

Becoming a Delphi Language Ninja

```
      finally
        CSVWriter.Free;
      end;

    finally
      Self.EnableControl;
    end;

    //return to the position where the dataset was before
    if Self.BookmarkValid(CurrPos) then
      Self.Bookmark := CurrPos;
  end;
```

The other helper is a bit more complex, but all the concepts have been already introduced in the *Writing enumerable types* recipe, so this should not be too complex to understand.

The method in the class helper simply returns `TDataSetEnumerator` by passing the current dataset to the constructor:

```
function TDataSetHelper.GetEnumerator: TDataSetEnumerator;
begin
  Self.First;
  Result := TDataSetEnumerator.Create(Self);
end;
```

Now, some magic happens in into `TDataSetEnumerator`! Methods to access the current record are encapsulated in a `TDSIterator` instance. This class allows you to access the field values using a limited and simpler interface (compared to the `TDataSet` one).

Here's the declaration of the enumerator and the iterator:

```
TDataSetEnumerator = class(TEnumerator<TDSIterator>)
  private
    FDataSet: TDataSet;     //the current dataset
    FDSIterator: TDSIterator; //the current "position"
    FFirstTime: Boolean;
  public
    constructor Create(ADataSet: TDataSet);
    destructor Destroy; override;
  protected
    //methods to override to support the for..in loop
    function DoGetCurrent: TDSIterator; override;
    function DoMoveNext: Boolean; override;
  end;

//This is the actual iterator
```

```
TDSIterator = class
  private
    FDataSet: TDataSet;
    function GetValue(const FieldName: String): TField;
    procedure SetDataSet(const Value: TDataSet);
    function GetValueAsString(const FieldName: String): String;
    function GetValueAsInteger(const FieldName: String): Integer;
  public
    constructor Create(ADataSet: TDataSet);
    //properties to access the current record
    //values using the fieldname
    property Value[const FieldName: String]: TField read GetValue;
    property S[const FieldName: String]: String
               read GetValueAsString;
    property I[const FieldName: String]: Integer
               read GetValueAsInteger;
  end;
```

The `TDataSetEnumerator` handles the mechanism needed by the enumerable type. However, instead of implementing all the needed methods directly (as you saw in the *Write enumerable types* recipe), you've inherited from the `TEnumerator<T>`, so the code to implement is shorter and simpler. Here's the implementation:

```
{ TDataSetEnumerator }

constructor TDataSetEnumerator.Create(ADataSet: TDataSet);
begin
  inherited Create;
  FFirstTime := True;
  FDataSet := ADataSet;
  FDSIterator := TDSIterator.Create(ADataSet);
end;

destructor TDataSetEnumerator.Destroy;
begin
  FDSIterator.Free;
  inherited;
end;

function TDataSetEnumerator.DoGetCurrent: TDSIterator;
begin
  Result := FDSIterator;
end;

function TDataSetEnumerator.DoMoveNext: Boolean;
```

```
begin
  if not FFirstTime then
    FDataSet.Next;
  FFirstTime := False;
  Result := not FDataSet.Eof;
end;
```

It is clear that the current record is encapsulated by a `TDSIterator` instance that uses the current dataset. This class is in charge of handling real data access to the underlying dataset fields. Here's the implementation:

```
constructor TDSIterator.Create(ADataSet: TDataSet);
begin
  inherited Create;
  FDataSet := ADataSet;
end;

function TDSIterator.GetValue(const FieldName: String): TField;
begin
  Result := FDataSet.FieldByName(FieldName);
end;

function TDSIterator.GetValueAsInteger(
  const FieldName: String): Integer;
begin
  Result := GetValue(FieldName).AsInteger;
end;

function TDSIterator.GetValueAsString(
  const FieldName: String): String;
begin
  Result := GetValue(FieldName).AsString;
end;
```

Let's summarize the relationship between the three classes involved. The class `helper` adds a method `GetEnumerator` to the `TDataSet` instance, which returns the `TDataSetEnumerator`. The `TDataSetEnumerator` uses the underlying dataset to handle the enumerable mechanism. The current element returned by the `DataSetEnumerator` is a `TDSIterator` that encapsulates the dataset's current position, allowing the user code to iterate the dataset using the `for...in` loop.

There's more...

What we discussed for class helpers is valid for record helpers as well. If you find the content of this chapter too difficult, you can refresh your understanding about helpers by (re)reading (and trying it yourself) the `Class` and record helpers section in the Embarcadero DocWiki website (`http://docwiki.embarcadero.com/RADStudio/en/Declarations_and_Statements#Iteration_Over_Containers_Using_For_statements`).

Usually, when I talk about class and record helpers during my live training, just before showing the samples, the attendants ask, "I understand the concepts, but in which cases should I use them?" Now, you saw some nice use cases. However, if you need some others too, read this interesting thread on stack overflows at `http://stackoverflow.com/questions/253399/what-are-good-uses-for-class-helpers`.

3
Knowing Your Friends – the Delphi RTL

In this chapter, we will cover the following recipes:

- Check strings with regular expressions
- Consuming RESTful services using native HTTP(S) client libraries
- Cope with the encoded Internet world using `System.NetEncodings`
- Save space using `System.Zip`
- Decouple your code using a cross-platform publish/subscribe mechanism

Introduction

Don't reinvent the wheel! Many programmers ignore what the big Delphi RTL can offer them. Some old time Delphi lovers continue to write the code like they wrote years ago. The new language features and a better attention to the community, let Embarcadero add many useful classes in the Delphi RTL, and if you don't know them well, risk to reinvent the wheel or simply write inefficient code because you don't have the time to write the correct one. But often the correct one is just in the RTL! To minimize such risks, in this chapter we'll introduce some new or lesser known RTL classes.

Check strings with regular expressions

A **regular expression** (**RegEx**) is a sequence of characters that forms a search pattern where some characters have a special meaning. It's mainly used to match patterns on strings. A simple case is something like this: check whether string A matches the criteria defined in string B. Regular expressions follow a specific language to define the criteria. Regular expressions are not present only in Delphi. Many languages have a regular expression library in their standard built-in library. So, if you don't know what a regular expression is, you can read the general documentation at `http://en.wikipedia.org/wiki/Regular_expression` and then check the Delphi-specific built-in implementation at `http://docwiki.embarcadero.com/RADStudio/Regular_Expressions`.

With regular expressions, perhaps you'll need an external tool to test the most complex ones (just like you want to test a complex query using a database tool instead of changing the SQL in your code over and over again). There are a lot of sites offering this type of tool. One of the most complete websites offering such tools is `http://regex101.com`.

Getting ready

This recipe is a small complete project with specific objectives. It contains a list of checks that could be daunting to code from scratch but are trivial using regular expressions. Just one thing to remember: you always require a RegEx string and an input string to check, and the `RegEx` library gives back the result of the match. In this case, the result is true or false.

Here are some samples of very simple regular expressions with some input strings as a test. In the last column, you can see the result of the match (using the `IsMatch` method). (RegEx can be used to perform smart string replaces as well in order to find another strings and so on, but the concept is the same as the check. You only need to call the right method, as `IsMatch`, `Split`, `Matches`, and so on, to give the right meaning to the RegEx.)

RegEx	RegEx description	Input string	Result
`rocks`	Contains rocks	delphi rocks	True
		rocks	True
		rocks of the mountain	True
`^rocks`	Starts with rocks	delphi rocks	False
		rocks	True
		rocks of the mountain	True
`rocks$`	Ends with rocks	delphi rocks	True
		rocks	True
		rocks of the mountain	False

RegEx	RegEx description	Input string	Result
`^[ABC]3`	Starts with A, B, or C and then there is a 3. Anything after the 3 matches.	A3	True
		B3	True
		C33	True
		F3	False
		A2	False
`^[ABC][01]$`	Starts with A, B, or C and then there is 0 or 1. Then the input ends. No more characters are allowed.	A0	True
		A1	True
		A2	False
		B1	True
		AA0	False
		C3	False
`^\d{2}\.\d{1,3}$`	Starts with 2 digits, then a point, then 1, 2, or 3 digits at the end of the string. N.B. \d matches a digit. It's a shortcut for [0-9].	12.3	True
		123.4	False
		89.123	True
		8.3	False
		34.23	True

How to do it...

The test application is shown in the following screenshot:

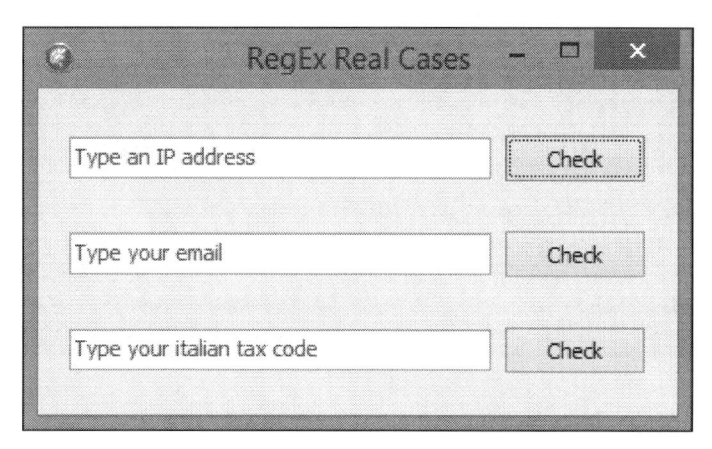

The RegEx recipe main form with some checks on it

Each button checks the value written to the edit at its left. The checks don't test the real validity of the data inserted. They only check the format validity (for example, if the e-mail address is formally valid, the check returns `true` even if the address doesn't really exist).

Open the recipe project called `RegEx.dproj` in the IDE and check the code of the form.

In Delphi, the needed classes and records to work with regular expressions are contained in the `System.RegularExpressions.pas` unit and follow the standard of the regular expression as handled by the Perl language (one of the first languages that started to use RegEx). The unit is included in the implementation section of the form. I suggest putting all your validation code in a separated unit in some testable validator types. However, in this recipe, the validation code is in the form under the event handler (please, do not do this in your production software!).

Let's start from the IP check. Under the `btnCheckIP` button, you can see the following code:

```
procedure TRegExForm.btnCheckIPClick(Sender: TObject);
begin
  if TRegEx.IsMatch(EditIP.Text,
     '^[0-9]{1,3}\.[0-9]{1,3}\.[0-9]{1,3}\.[0-9]{1,3}$') then
    ShowMessage('IPv4 address is valid')
  else
    ShowMessage('IPv4 address is not valid');
end;
```

The code is really simple, only the RegEx needs some more explanation. The regular expression checks a string that starts with 1, 2, or 3 numbers from 0 to 9 ([0-9]{1,3}), then expects a point. Consider that point character in the regex syntax means any character, so if you simply want to check a point, you have to escape the character. This is the reason why in the regular expressions there is a \ before the point (\ is used to escape the successive character).

RegEx continues with the same pattern repeated four times (for the four octets contained in the IPv4 address). The last pattern doesn't expect a point.

> In this case, this regex is enough, but it also considers an IP such as 999.999.999.999 valid, which is not a valid one. For our needs it is okay, but for a complete RegEx to check IPV4 addresses, read http://stackoverflow.com/questions/4890789/regex-for-an-ip-address/30023010#30023010.

Using the static `TRegEx.IsMatch` method, you can easily check whether a string matches a RegEx.

The second check is about the e-mail address. The code used is shown as follows:

```
procedure TRegExForm.btnCheckEmailClick(Sender: TObject);
begin
  // Email RegEx from
  // http://www.regular-expressions.info/email.html

  if TRegEx.IsMatch(
         EditEMail.Text,
         '^[A-Z0-9._%+-]+@[A-Z0-9.-]+\.[A-Z]{2,4}$',
         [roIgnoreCase]) then
    ShowMessage('EMail address is valid')
  else
    ShowMessage('EMail address is not valid');
end;
```

In this case, the RegEx is a little bit more complicated. The string must start with at least a letter from A to Z, with a number from 0 to 9, or with another of the permitted character (., _, %, +, -). The sign + after the square brackets stands for at least one of. Then, there should be a @ sign. After the @ sign, the RegEx checks for letters, numbers, dots, and the minus sign (the domain part of the address) and, as last checks, it looks for two, three, or four letters (.com, .it, .net, and so on). The RegEx syntax is case-sensitive, but an e-mail address validity check must be case-insensitive, so I've put the `roIgnoreCase` modifier on the `IsMatch` to make the RegEx case-insensitive ([A-Z] is considered as [A-Z/a-z]).

As you see, if you can read the RegEx syntax, you can easily understand what the RegEx checks. Obviously, there are really complex RegExes, so before you use them, be sure to be confident with what you are using.

The last button checks the Italian tax code. I also put this example because the criteria are not so complex and it is good to understand the RegEx flexibility.

In Italy, there is a tax code called Codice Fiscale that is assigned to all citizens when they reach a certain age. The criteria are the following:

- 3 letters
- 3 letters
- 2 numbers
- 1 letter
- 2 numbers
- 1 letter
- 3 numbers
- 1 letter

So, for instance, this is a formally valid Italian tax code: RSSMRA79S04H501V. As you see, it is not complex; however, checking it using plain code Delphi can be boring and error prone. Let's build together the RegEx to check it.

Start with 6 letters:

`^[A-Z]{6}`

Then, two numbers:

`^[A-Z]{6}[0-9]{2}`

Then, one letter and two numbers:

`^[A-Z]{6}[0-9]{2}[A-Z][0-9]{2}`

Then, one letter, three numbers, and another one letter. Then, the code must terminate:

`^[A-Z]{6}[0-9]{2}[A-Z][0-9]{2}[A-Z][0-9]{3}[A-Z]$`

Now, the check is really simple:

```
procedure TRegExForm.btnCheckItalianTaxCodeClick(
                                     Sender: TObject);
begin
  if TRegEx.IsMatch(EditTaxCodeIT.Text,
      '^[A-Z]{6}[0-9]{2}[A-Z][0-9]{2}[A-Z][0-9]{3}[A-Z]$',
      [roIgnoreCase]) then
    ShowMessage('This italian tax code is valid')
  else
    ShowMessage('This italian tax code is not valid');
end;
```

After some exercises, you can master the RegEx syntax and you will find it really useful to check and manipulate strings and texts.

The following screenshot shows the sample application while it is checking a wrong e-mail address:

The RegEx sample application while is checking a not valid e-mail address

There's more...

RegEx can be used to perform many string-related tasks. You can match strings, search for strings into another string, split a string using a RegEx as a separator, and so on.

If you work with strings (who doesn't?) do yourself a favor and study regular expressions very well. Just as example. Suppose you have a string with a list of names separated by , or and. Something like: `Daniele, Bruce, Mark and Scott`. Now you want to retrieve only the names. How you can do this?

Here's the regular expression that does the job: `[ ]*,[ ]*|[ ]+and[ ]+`.

To do the actual split, we've to use the following code:

```
procedure MyCoolSplitter;
var
  LNames: TArray<string>;
  LInputString, LName, LRegEx: string;
begin
  //this is the input string, it is also badly formatted...
  LInputString := 'Daniele   , Bruce,  Mark     and   Scott';
  LRegEx := '[ ]*,[ ]*|[ ]+and[ ]+'; //regex to do the splitting
  LNames := TRegEx.Split(LInputString, LRegEx, []);
```

```
    for LName in LNames do
    begin
      ShowMessage(LName); //show each name
    end;
end;
```

Remember to check the Delphi documentation about the built-in RegEx engine syntax at `http://docwiki.embarcadero.com/RADStudio/en/Regular_Expressions`.

Some nice RegEx samples (not Delphi-related) can be found at `http://www.regular-expressions.info/examples.html`.

As a bonus recipe, there is a RegEx tester called `RegExTester.dproj` in the attached code that helps you to exploit all the functionalities. Play with it and become a RegEx Ninja!

Consuming RESTful services using native HTTP(S) client libraries

We live in an interconnected world! A lot of applications now have to exchange data with remote systems. One of the most commonly used and powerful mechanisms to define a communication interface between software over the Internet are RESTful web services (more information about REST and RESTful interfaces will be provided in *Chapter 6, Put Delphi on the Server*, in the recipe *Implementing a RESTful interface using WebBroker*). Usually in Delphi, you can use the INDY suite to access HTTP servers. When dealing with HTTPS, INDY produces some headaches because it doesn't use the same SSL layer of the operating systems, but relies on OpenSSL libraries, so you have to provide a specific version of OpenSSL for each different OS your application supports and you cannot benefit from the security updates from the OSes vendor. This has been a *just-to-keep-in-mind* problem up to April 7, 2014, when the Heartbleed security bug has been disclosed in the OpenSSL cryptography library.

Here's what Wikipedia has to say about it:

> "At the time of disclosure, some 17% (around half a million) of the Internet's secure web servers certified by trusted authorities were believed to be vulnerable to the attack, allowing theft of the servers' private keys and users' session cookies and passwords."

The client applications that use OpenSSL have been affected by this bug. The bug has been fixed on the same day by the OpenSSL team, but the problem was still there for all the deployed applications. Let's think about the problems that this situation produced! Think about your customer that calls you because some "security expert" told him that there is a catastrophic bug in OpenSSL system. Now, he wants an immediate update for all the systems! Then, a call from the second customer, then the third, and so on... arg!

So, to overcome this bad situation Embarcadero developed the native HTTP client library, which is not based on INDY or OpenSSL, but it simply relies on the OS API to implement the HTTP protocol. So, when Microsoft, Apple, or Google releases a new security patch, your application is already updated. Great! You simply rely on the OS security infrastructure and not depend anymore on the OpenSSL dlls!

In this recipe, we'll see how to consume a RESTful interface provided by a sample server using the new native HTTP library introduced in RAD Studio XE8. The server is not HTTPS but the same concepts apply.

Getting ready

This is a showcase recipe. We'll see how to issue HTTP requests to a RESTful server using the new `THTTPClient` class. There is also the `TNetHTTPClient` component, which wraps the `THTTPClient` functionalities in a nonvisual component, but we don't need it now, and the raw `THTTPClient` class is quite high level to be used directly. However, if you want to use the component, the interface is quite similar (almost identical).

Some HTTP considerations

While `GET` and `POST` are by far the most common methods that are used to access information provided by a web server, the **Hypertext Transfer Protocol** (**HTTP**) allows several other (and somewhat lesser-known) methods. Current standard is HTTP 1.1 and is defined by RFC 2616. RFC 2616 defines the following eight methods:

- HEAD
- GET
- POST
- PUT
- DELETE
- TRACE
- OPTIONS
- CONNECT

The `THTTPClient` class supports all these verbs but `CONNECT`, with specific methods that map each verb. To have an idea about the methods provided by the class, see the *There's more...* section.

Knowing Your Friends – the Delphi RTL

How it works...

We use a sample server called `PeopleManagerServer.dproj` located in the `Chapter03\CODE\RECIPE02\Server` folder. Ensure that TCP port 8080 is available on your system and that your local Interbase instance is running. Run the server project. The server is not in the scope of this recipe, so we'll use it just as a black box; however, it handles CRUD and some kind of business logic and searches over a database table called `PEOPLE` contained in a sample database called `DATA.IB`. This server will be developed in *Chapter 6, Put Delphi on the Server* in the recipe *Implementing a RESTful interface using WebBroker*, so if you are curious about its details, read that chapter and then come back here.

Now, open the client project located in `Chapter03\RECIPE02\Client\PeopleManagerClient.dproj`, which is the VCL client for the RESTful service provided by the `PeopleManagerServer`.

In the `FormCreate` event, the `FHTTPClient` is initialized, while in the `FormDestroy` is destroyed:

```
procedure TMainForm.FormCreate(Sender: TObject);
begin
  FHTTPClient := THTTPClient.Create;
  pcMain.ActivePageIndex := 0;
end;

procedure TMainForm.FormDestroy(Sender: TObject);
begin
  FHTTPClient.Free;
end;
```

Note that to use the `THTTPClient` class you have to include `System.Net.HttpClient` (which contains the class definition itself) and the unit `System.Net.URLClient` (which holds common functionality relative to a generic URL Client (HTTP, FTP, and so on).

Run the client, go to the first tab, click on the **Open** button, and you should see something similar to the following screenshot:

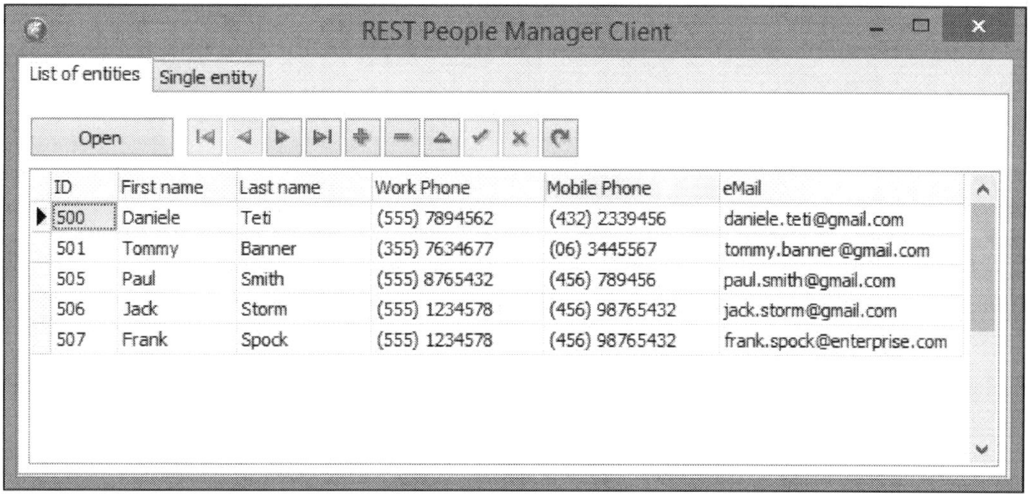

Fig. 3.1: The VCL RESTful HTTP client for the PeopleManagerServer showing the list of people

So, let's see under the hood. Open the main form in the RAD Studio form designer and check the `btnOpen onClick` event handler:

```
procedure TMainForm.btnOpenClick(Sender: TObject);
begin
  dsPeople.Close;
  dsPeople.BeforePost := nil;
  try
    dsPeople.Open;
    dsPeople.First;
  finally
    dsPeople.BeforePost := dsPeopleBeforePost;
  end;
end;
```

`dsPeople` is a `TFDMemTable` (an in-memory table from the FireDAC components suite provided with RAD Studio), so where the data comes from? Let's check the relevant properties of this `TFDMemTable`:

```
object dsPeople: TFDMemTable
  AfterOpen = dsPeopleAfterOpen
  BeforePost = dsPeopleBeforePost
  BeforeDelete = dsPeopleBeforeDelete
  object dsPeopleID: TStringField
    FieldName = 'ID'
```

```
      Size = 255
    end
    object dsPeopleFIRST_NAME: TStringField
      DisplayLabel = 'First name'
      DisplayWidth = 50
      FieldName = 'FIRST_NAME'
      Size = 255
    end
    object dsPeopleLAST_NAME: TStringField
      DisplayLabel = 'Last name'
      DisplayWidth = 50
      FieldName = 'LAST_NAME'
      Size = 255
    end
    object dsPeopleWORK_PHONE_NUMBER: TStringField
      DisplayLabel = 'Work Phone'
      DisplayWidth = 50
      FieldName = 'WORK_PHONE_NUMBER'
      Size = 255
    end
    object dsPeopleMOBILE_PHONE_NUMBER: TStringField
      DisplayLabel = 'Mobile Phone'
      FieldName = 'MOBILE_PHONE_NUMBER'
      Size = 50
    end
    object dsPeopleEMAIL: TStringField
      DisplayLabel = 'eMail'
      DisplayWidth = 50
      FieldName = 'EMAIL'
      Size = 255
    end
  end
```

As you can see, on the `dsPeople` are defined some event handlers and some persistent fields. The persistent fields are used to do the mapping between the JSON objects and the dataset structure (each field has a corresponding property in the JSON objects) and we'll talk about them in a moment. The event handlers allow using the `MemTable` as it was a normal database table, but it consumes the data from a RESTful web service instead of a normal database table. Let's see the code.

Just after the dataset is opened, in the `AfterOpen` event handler we'll issue the request to the server and get the data. The JSON so retrieved is converted and loaded into the dataset using the helpers of `TDataSet` class helpers provided by the unit `ObjectsMappers. pas` contained in the Open Source project `DelphiMVCFramework` (which is at https://github.com/danieleteti/delphimvcframework. More info in *Chapter 6, Put Delphi on the Server*, in the recipe *Implementing a RESTful interface using WebBroker*, so if you are curious about its details, you can read that chapter and then come back here):

```delphi
procedure TMainForm.dsPeopleAfterOpen(DataSet: TDataSet);
var
  LResponse: IHTTPResponse;
begin
  // FHTTPClient is an instance of THTTPClient created in the
  // FormCreate event.
  // Here we are sending a GET request passing the URL, and one
  // ACCEPT header
  LResponse := FHTTPClient.Get(BASEURL + '/people', nil,
    [TNameValuePair.Create('accept', 'application/json')]);

  if LResponse.StatusCode = HTTP_STATUS.OK then
  begin
    // Load JSON data from the body request to the dataset using
    // the TDataSet class helpers provided by the open source
    // library DelphiMVCFramework project
    DataSet.AppendFromJSONArrayString(LResponse.ContentAsString);
  end
  else
  begin
    raise Exception.CreateFmt(ERROR_FORMAT_STRING,
      [LResponse.StatusCode, LResponse.StatusText]);
  end;
end;
```

Now, when we need to delete a record, just before deleting it, we ask the server about the deletion. If some exceptions are raised in the server, the `delete` method also fails on the client and the record remains in the dataset:

```delphi
procedure TMainForm.dsPeopleBeforeDelete(DataSet: TDataSet);
begin
  DeleteRecordOnServer(DataSet);
end;
```

Here's the code for the `DeleteRecordOnServer` method:

```delphi
procedure TMainForm.DeleteRecordOnServer(ADataSet: TDataSet);
var
   LResponse: IHTTPResponse;
begin
   LResponse := FHTTPClient.Delete(BASEURL + '/people/' +
     ADataSet.FieldByName('ID').AsString);
   if LResponse.StatusCode <> HTTP_STATUS.NoContent then
     raise Exception.CreateFmt(ERROR_FORMAT_STRING,
       [LResponse.StatusCode, LResponse.StatusText]);
end;
```

When the user needs to update or insert a new entity in the `BeforePost`, the event handler is executes the following code:

```delphi
procedure TMainForm.dsPeopleBeforePost(DataSet: TDataSet);
var
   LNewlyCreatedResourceURI: string;
begin
   case DataSet.State of
     dsInsert:
       begin
         LNewlyCreatedResourceURI := CreateRecordOnServer(DataSet);
         UpdateDataSetFromURL(LNewlyCreatedResourceURI, DataSet);
       end;

     dsEdit:
       UpdateRecordOnServer(DataSet);

   else
     raise Exception.Create('Invalid state');
   end;
end;
```

This is the code for the methods used in this event:

```delphi
function TMainForm.CreateRecordOnServer(ADataSet:
   TDataSet): string;
var
   LPOSTRequest: IHTTPRequest;
   LResponse: IHTTPResponse;
   LBody: TStringStream;
begin
   LPOSTRequest := FHTTPClient.GetRequest('POST',
     BASEURL + '/people');
```

```delphi
    LPOSTRequest.AddHeader('content-type', 'application/json');
    LBody := TStringStream.Create(ADataSet.asJSONObjectString);
    try
      LPOSTRequest.SourceStream := LBody;
      LResponse := FHTTPClient.Execute(LPOSTRequest);
    finally
      LBody.Free;
    end;
    if LResponse.StatusCode <> HTTP_STATUS.Created then
      raise Exception.CreateFmt(ERROR_FORMAT_STRING,
        [LResponse.StatusCode, LResponse.StatusText]);

    // the server returned the newly created resource
    // in the LOCATION header
    Result := LResponse.HeaderValue['location'];
end;

procedure TMainForm.UpdateDataSetFromURL(AURL: string;
  ADataSet: TDataSet);
var
  LResponse: IHTTPResponse;
begin
  LResponse := FHTTPClient.Get(BASEURL + AURL, nil,
    [TNameValuePair.Create('accept', 'application/json')]);
  if LResponse.StatusCode <> HTTP_STATUS.OK then
    raise Exception.CreateFmt(ERROR_FORMAT_STRING,
      [LResponse.StatusCode, LResponse.StatusText]);

  //load the JSON response body into the current record of the
  //dataset (using the class helpers from the DelphiMVCFramework)
  ADataSet.LoadFromJSONObjectString(LResponse.ContentAsString);
end;

procedure TMainForm.UpdateRecordOnServer(ADataSet: TDataSet);
var
  LPUTRequest: IHTTPRequest;
  LResponse: IHTTPResponse;
  LBody: TStringStream;
begin
  LPUTRequest := FHTTPClient.GetRequest('PUT',
    BASEURL + '/people/' +
    ADataSet.FieldByName('ID').AsString);
  LPUTRequest.AddHeader('content-type', 'application/json');
  LBody := TStringStream.Create(ADataSet.asJSONObjectString);
```

```
    try
      LPUTRequest.SourceStream := LBody;
      LResponse := FHTTPClient.Execute(LPUTRequest);
    finally
      LBody.Free;
    end;
    if LResponse.StatusCode <> HTTP_STATUS.OK then
      raise Exception.CreateFmt(ERROR_FORMAT_STRING,
        [LResponse.StatusCode, LResponse.StatusText]);
  end;
```

As you can see, for simple HTTP requests, you can use the shortcut methods, such as the following:

```
//A simple GET request
LResp := FHTTPClient.Get('http://www.myserver.com/api/customers');

//A simple DELETE request
LResp :=
  FHTTPClient.Delete('http://www.myserver.com/api/customers/1');
```

There are methods that map each HTTP VERBs defined in the HTTP 1.1 protocol (see the *There's more...* section).

If you need to send a more complex request, or if you want to prepare your request and execute it later, you can use the `GetRequest` method as shown in the method `CreateRecordOnServer`. The following code is a smaller example of the `GetRequest` use case:

```
procedure TMyForm.MyComplexRequest;
var
  LPOSTRequest: IHTTPRequest;
  LResponse: IHTTPResponse;
  LBody: TStringStream;
begin
  //get the POST request
  LPOSTRequest := FHTTPClient.GetRequest(
    'POST', 'http://localhost/people');

  //now we can customize the request with headers...
  LPOSTRequest.AddHeader('content-type', 'application/json');
  LPOSTRequest.AddHeader('accept', 'application/json');

  //...and a request body
  LBody := TStringStream
    .Create('{"firstname":"Daniele","lastname":"Teti"');
```

```
    try
      LPOSTRequest.SourceStream := LBody;
      //now, execute the request
      LResponse := FHTTPClient.Execute(LPOSTRequest);
    finally
      LBody.Free;
    end;

    //after the request, we can use the response object (which is an
    //interface instance, so it is reference counted)
    if LResponse.StatusCode <> 201 then
      raise Exception.Create(
        'Invalid response: ' + LResponse.StatusText);
end;
```

Let's come back to the recipe application. The second tab of the `TPageControl` contains all the controls used to do a simple search by ID on the server. Let's write a valid ID in the **EditSearch** edit and click on the **Get by ID** button. The code under the button is quite simple to understand now:

```
procedure TMainForm.btnGetPersonClick(Sender: TObject);
var
  LResponse: IHTTPResponse;
begin
  dsPerson.Close;
  LResponse := FHTTPClient.Get(BASEURL + '/people/' +
    TNetEncoding.URL.Encode(EditSearch.Text));
  if LResponse.StatusCode = HTTP_STATUS.OK then
  begin
    //check if the response is in a supported format (JSON)
    if LResponse
        .HeaderValue['Content-Type']
        .StartsWith('application/json') then
    begin
      dsPerson.Open;
      //unhook the BeforePost event handler because the
      //LoadFromJSONObjectString call could fire it.
      dsPerson.BeforePost := nil;
      dsPerson.Insert;
      //Load the JSON string containing a JSON object into the
      //dataset which has the same structure
      dsPerson.LoadFromJSONObjectString(
        LResponse.ContentAsString);
      dsPerson.Post;
      //hook the event
```

```delphi
      dsPerson.BeforePost := dsPersonBeforePost;
    end
    else
    begin
      //the response content-type is not supported
      ShowMessageFmt('Invalid response format ' +
        '(expected application/json, actual %s',
        [LResponse.HeaderValue['Content-Type']]);
    end;
  end
  else
  begin
    ShowMessageFmt(ERROR_FORMAT_STRING,
      [LResponse.StatusCode, LResponse.StatusText]);
  end;
end;
```

Clicking on the button you should see the data loaded in the `TDBEdits`. Now, you can change the data in the controls and click on the **post** button in the small `TDBNavigator` at the bottom. In the `BeforePost` event of the hooked dataset, called `dsPerson`, there is this code:

```delphi
procedure TMainForm.dsPersonBeforePost(DataSet: TDataSet);
begin
  // only updates allowed here
  if DataSet.State <> dsEdit then
    raise Exception.Create('Invalid dataset state');

  //here we can use the same method used for
  //the dsPeople dataset
  UpdateRecordOnServer(DataSet);
end;
```

There's more...

Lot of stuff in this recipe! Let's give some more detail on the proposed code.

In the source code you saw some reference to a strange `HTTP_STATUS` complex variable. It seems strange, but in Delphi `System.Net.*` there is no list of valid HTTP status codes as a list of constants, so I added it to the `MVCFramework.Commons.pas` unit (there are all the most frequently used codes as defined in http://www.w3.org/Protocols/rfc2616/rfc2616-sec10.html). So you can write `HTTP_STATUS.OK` or `HTTP_STATUS.NOTFOUND` without remembering the status code. Simple but very useful. You can use it also if you want to use other HTTP frameworks.

THTTPClient's methods which directly map the HTTP verbs

This is a small recap of the `THTTPClient` method that maps to the HTTP standard verbs. As you can see, all the methods return an instance of `IHTTPResponse`, which is a reference counted interface reference.

Send the `DELETE` command to url:

```
function Delete(AURL: string; AResponseContent: TStream = nil;
  AHeaders: TNetHeaders): IHTTPResponse;
```

Send the `OPTIONS` command to url:

```
function Options(const AURL: string; const AResponseContent:
  TStream = nil; const AHeaders: TNetHeaders = nil):
  IHTTPResponse;
```

Send the `GET` command to url:

```
function Get(AURL: string; AResponseContent: TStream = nil;
  AHeaders: TNetHeaders = nil): IHTTPResponse;
```

`CheckDownloadResume` checks whether the server has the download resume feature. This is not a one-to-one mapping to the standard HTTP verb but this method relies on the HEAD verb with very small value for `RANGE` header. If the server responds with the data, then it supports the download resume. So, this is a handy method to use in case of large download to check whether the download can be resumed (or split):

```
function CheckDownloadResume(AURL: string): Boolean;
```

Just like the `CheckDownloadResume`, this is not a standard HTTP verb, but it's a handy method that sends the `GET` command to the URL adding the `RANGE` header (used to get a part of the remote resource. It is used to resume interrupted downloads or to split large downloads):

```
function GetRange(AURL: string; AStart: Int64; AnEnd: Int64 = -1;
  AResponseContent: TStream = nil;
  AHeaders: TNetHeaders = nil): IHTTPResponse;
```

Send the `TRACE` command to the URL. The HTTP `TRACE` method returns the contents of client HTTP requests in the entity-body of the `TRACE` response. Please note that attackers could leverage this behavior to access sensitive information, such as cookies or authentication data, contained in the HTTP headers of the request (there is more info about the `TRACE` vulnerability in the next section):

```
function Trace(AURL: string; AResponseContent: TStream = nil;
  AHeaders: TNetHeaders = nil): IHTTPResponse;
```

Send the HEAD command to url:

```
function Head(AURL: string; AHeaders: TNetHeaders = nil):
  IHTTPResponse;
```

Post a raw file without multipart info:

```
function Post(AURL: string; ASourceFile: string;
  AResponseContent: TStream = nil; AHeaders: TNetHeaders = nil):
  IHTTPResponse; overload;
```

Post TStrings values adding multipart info:

```
function Post(AURL: string; ASource: TStrings;
  AResponseContent: TStream = nil; AEncoding: TEncoding = nil;
  AHeaders: TNetHeaders = nil): IHTTPResponse; overload;
```

Post a stream without multipart info:

```
function Post(AURL: string; ASource: TStream;
  AResponseContent: TStream = nil; AHeaders: TNetHeaders = nil):
  IHTTPResponse; overload;
```

Post a multipart form data object. Used to mimic an HTML FORM submit:

```
function Post(AURL: string; ASource: TMultipartFormData;
  AResponseContent: TStream = nil; AHeaders: TNetHeaders = nil):
  IHTTPResponse; overload;
```

Send the PUT command to url:

```
function Put(AURL: string; ASource: TStream = nil;
  AResponseContent: TStream = nil; AHeaders: TNetHeaders = nil):
  IHTTPResponse;
```

The THTTPClient class also supports the standard HTTP verbs PATCH and MERGE.

How to verify that HTTP TRACE is disabled

The TRACE command is a standard HTTP verb defined in the HTTP specification and was considered a "safe" command up until some years ago. However, due to the information disclosed combined with other cross-domain exploits, TRACE is no longer considered safe. See http://www.kb.cert.org/vuls/id/867593 for more information.

So, how can I verify that the TRACE command is disabled? The easiest way to do this is to use telnet. Here's the step-by-step guide to test whether TRACE is enabled on your webserver:

1. Launch telnet with `telnet myserver myport` for example:

    `telnet localhost 80`

2. Now, we can issue the TRACE command for a given URL, for example:

    `TRACE /index.html HTTP/1.0`

3. If you don't see any character on the console while writing, don't worry, it is the `telnet LOCALECHO`, which is disabled. It will work.

If TRACE is enabled, you will get an output that looks something like this:

```
HTTP/1.1 200 OK
Date: Thu, 27 Aug 2015 12:41:14 GMT
Server: Apache/2.4.12 (Win32)
Connection: close
Content-Type: message/http

TRACE /index.html HTTP/1.0

Connection closed by foreign host.
```

If TRACE is disabled, the output will look like this:

```
HTTP/1.1 405 Method Not Allowed
Date: Thu, 27 Aug 2015 12:42:44 GMT
Server: Apache/2.4.12 (Win32)
<some others http header>

Connection closed by foreign host.
```

Cope with the encoded Internet world using System.NetEncodings

Internet is the land of the encodings! URIs are encoded, HTML provide specific encodings, e-mails works because of the mime encoding, and the REST service works because in some way the client and server can talk each other using some sort of encodings! There are many kinds of encoding for different purposes, but in this recipe we will talk about the encodings handled by the classes contained in the `System.NetEncodings.pas` unit.

Getting ready

The unit `System.NetEncodings` contains the following classes:

- `TNetEncoding`: This class is a factory for the actual encoding classes; moreover, it serves as a base class for all the other classes
- `THTMLEncoding`: This class provides methods to encode and decode data in HTML format
- `TURLEncoding`: This class provides methods to encode and decode data in URL encoding
- `TBase64Encoding`: This class provides methods to encode and decode data in the `base64` format

`base64` is a binary-to-text encoding schemes that represent binary data in an ASCII string format by translating it into a radix-64 representation. This kind of encoding is commonly used when there is a need to encode binary data that needs to be stored and transferred over media that is designed to deal with textual data. This kind of encoding mechanism ensures that the data remains intact without modification during transport. `base64` is commonly used in a number of applications, including REST services, e-mail via MIME, in-line data in web pages and to storing complex data in XML or JSON.

Here's an example of base64 encoding:

```
Input text: this is a text
Encoded text: dGhpcyBpcyBhIHRleHQ=
```

HTML is the markup language of the web, and there are different ways to instruct the browser about the character encoding of the document that must be displayed. The web server and the document itself can contain information about native encoding such as ASCII, ISO8859-1, or the most popular UTF-8. These kinds of encodings are called native encoding or charset (handled in Delphi by the `TEncoding` class). In addition to these native character encodings, characters can also be encoded as character references, which can be numeric character references (decimal or hexadecimal) or character entity references.

Escaping also allows for characters that are not easily typed, or that are not available in the document's character encoding, to be represented within element and attribute content. For example, the acute-accented e (é), a character typically found only on Western European and South American keyboards, can be written in any HTML document as the entity reference é or as the numeric references é or é, using characters that are available on all keyboards and are supported in all character encodings.

Here's an example of HTML encoding:

```
Input text: Italian word for "why" is "perché"
Encoded text: Italian word for &quot;why&quot; is
&quot;perch&#233;&quot;
```

Not all the characters can be used in the URLs. This is a big problem when you needs to pass non ASCII text as parameter (for examples `http://www.myserver.com/page.php?q=t/h/i/s` doesn't work). The URL encoding is used to encode the parameters passed over the URL and make them suitable to be sent in such way. Here's an example of URL encoding:

Not encoded parameters in URL: `http://localhost/index?expression=3*4/5`. URL with correctly encoded parameter: `http://localhost/index?expression=3%2A4%2F5`.

In this recipe, we'll download a PNG image encoded as `base64` text, then the binary stream will be reconstructed on the client and the binary contents will be shown on the form in a `TImage` control. The `base64` representation is read by our beloved sample REST server introduced in the previous recipe, so you can open the project called `PeopleManagerServer.dproj` located in the folder `Chapter03\RECIPE02\Server`. Ensure that TCP port 8080 is available on your system and that your local Interbase instance is running. Run the server project. This server provides a resource that returns a `base64` fake photo of the person. So, if the following URL returns the person's information encoded as JSON `GET http://localhost:8080/people/500`.

Then, the following URL returns the person's fake photo (just a PNG file where the person's name has been drawn on some gradient background): `GET http://localhost:8080/people/500/photo`. The photo resource is a `base64` encoded text. Try this yourself with different IDs to see what the response looks like.

Knowing Your Friends – the Delphi RTL

How it works...

Open the project at `Chapter03\RECIPE03\NetEncoding.dproj` and launch it. In the edit section on the left, write `500` (or another valid ID in your database). Now the form should look like the following:

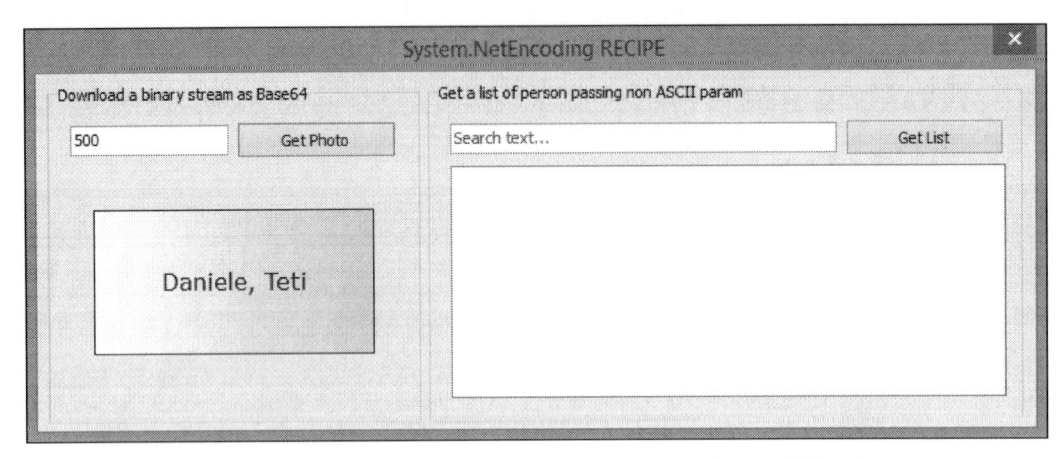

Figure 3.1: The image has been downloaded as base64 text from a REST service and then decoded and loaded in the TImage control

Stop the program and see the code under the **Get Photo** button:

```delphi
procedure TMainForm.btnGetPhotoClick(Sender: TObject);
var
  LHTTP: THTTPClient;
  LResponse: IHTTPResponse;
  LPNGStream: TMemoryStream;
  LPNGImage: TPngImage;
  LURLFormat: string;
begin
  LHTTP := THTTPClient.Create;
  try
    //create the correct URL
    LURLFormat := 'http://localhost:8080/people/%s/photo';
    LResponse := LHTTP.Get(
      Format(LURLFormat,
        [EditPersonID.Text]));

    //check for a valid response
    if LResponse.StatusCode <> 200 then
    begin
      ShowMessage(LResponse.StatusText);
```

```
      Exit;
    end;


    LPNGStream := TMemoryStream.Create;
    try
      //convert response string from base64 to a binary stream
      if TNetEncoding.Base64
           .Decode(LResponse.ContentStream, LPNGStream) = 0 then
        raise Exception.Create('Invalid Base64 stream');

      LPNGImage := TPngImage.Create;
      try
        LPNGStream.Position := 0;
        //load the binary stream into the PNGImage...
        LPNGImage.LoadFromStream(LPNGStream);
        //...and assign it to the TImage control
        Image1.Picture.Assign(LPNGImage);
      finally
        LPNGImage.Free;
      end;
    finally
      LPNGStream.Free;
    end;
  finally
    LHTTP.Free;
  end;
end;
```

Quite simple if you know how to encode and decode the stream to a textual representation, isn't it?

Now, run the application and give attention to the right side of the form. There is another edit button, and a listbox. Here, we can search for people where first name, last name, or e-mail, contains the search parameter. The resource to call is `http://localhost:8080/people/searches?query=<the search string>`.

In our sample database, there are two Germans. So, if we write their last names in the edit, the resultant URL without encoding will be: `http://localhost:8080/people/searches?query=Müller`.

Knowing Your Friends – the Delphi RTL

This is not a valid URL, because it contains non ASCII letters. Let's see the code under the **Get List button**:

```
procedure TMainForm.btnGetPeopleClick(Sender: TObject);
var
  LHTTP: THTTPClient;
  LResponse: IHTTPResponse;
  LURLFormat, LQuery: string;
  LPeople: TObjectList<TPerson>;
  LJArr: TJSONArray;
  LPerson: TPerson;
begin
  LHTTP := THTTPClient.Create;
  try
    LURLFormat :=
      'http://localhost:8080/people/searches?query=%s';
    //encode the parameter
    LQuery := TNetEncoding.URL.Encode(EditSearch.Text);
    //send the HTTP request
    LResponse := LHTTP.Get(Format(LURLFormat, [LQuery]));

    //check for errors
    if LResponse.StatusCode <> 200 then
    begin
      ShowMessage(LResponse.StatusText);
      Exit;
    end;

    //load data into the TListBox
    LPeople := TObjectList<TPerson>.Create(true);
    try
      LJArr :=
        TJSONObject.ParseJSONValue(LResponse.ContentAsString)
          as TJSONArray;

      //convert the json array into list of TPerson using the
      //class Mapper contained in ObjectMappers.pas (from the
      //DelphiMVCFramework project)
      Mapper.JSONArrayToObjectList<TPerson>(LPeople, LJArr);

      //finally load the object list into the TListBox
      lbPeople.Items.BeginUpdate;
      try
        lbPeople.Clear;
```

```
      for LPerson in LPeople do
      begin
        lbPeople.Items.Add(LPerson.ToString +
          ' (' + LPerson.EMAIL + ')');
      end;
    finally
      lbPeople.Items.EndUpdate;
    end;
  finally
    LPeople.Free;
  end;
  finally
    LHTTP.Free;
  end;
end;
```

Use `TNetEncoding.URL.Encode` to encode the parameter (warning: only the parameter value is encoded), the URL is correct, and we can send the HTTP request in a way that the server can understand. So, if we write Müller into the edit, we get the following URL: `http://localhost:8080/people/searches?query=M%C3%BCller`.

This is a valid URL, and it produces the following result:

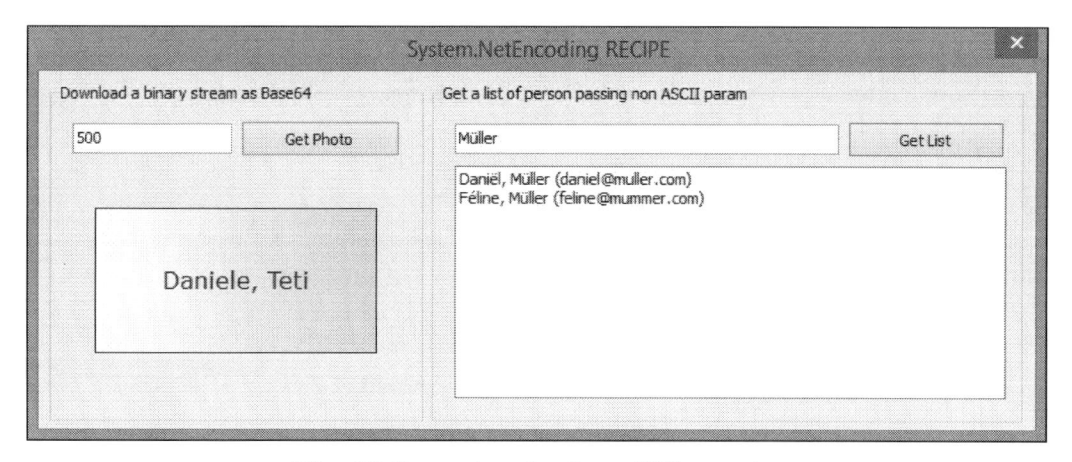

Figure 3.2: The search can handle non ASCII parameters

There's more...

Coping with encodings is not simple, but in a Unicode and distributed world as it is now, we cannot avoid it, so it's worth it to correctly understand how (at least) the most popular encoding works and where it can (or must) be used.

Another interesting application of the `TNetEncoding.Base64` is related to the Data URI (https://en.wikipedia.org/wiki/Data_URI_scheme). Using `base64` and the Data URI scheme you can embed images, scripts, and CSS directly into your HTML. This technique should be used carefully because if the HTML changes but the image doesn't, using embedded images means that the browser cannot properly use the client cache and so the page download time increases.

Also, if you generate HTML content, you should encode the content using `TNetEncoding.HTML` to be sure that all the browsers can correctly display complex characters or symbols and to protect your site from XSS attacks (https://en.wikipedia.org/wiki/Cross-site_scripting#Safely_validating_untrusted_HTML_input).

Save space using System.Zip

Historically, Delphi contains the `TZCompressionStream` and the `TZDecompressionStream` to respectively compress and decompress streams of bytes using the `zlib` format. These classes are quite useful but are quite low level, being simply a stream compressor. In this recipe, we'll use a high-level class to compress and decompress folders and files. It is quite limited in terms of possibilities (you can compress and decompress files and folders, nothing more) but is very simple to use. Just keep in mind that this class is very specialized, so if you need some compression library to work with network protocols or on the fly compression/decompression, don't use this. But if you need a no-brain solution to compress something, this is the way.

The ZIP file format doesn't need presentation. However, some recap can be useful.

> "ZIP is an archive file format that supports lossless data compression. A .ZIP file may contain one or more files or folders that may have been compressed. The .ZIP file format permits a number of compression algorithms, though DEFLATE is the most common. This format was originally created in 1989 by Phil Katz, and was first implemented in PKWARE, Inc.'s PKZIP utility, as a replacement for the previous ARC compression format by Thom Henderson. The .ZIP format is now supported by many software utilities other than PKZIP.
>
> .ZIP files generally use the file extensions ".zip" or ".ZIP" and the MIME media type application/zip. ZIP is used as a base file format by many programs, usually under a different name."

– Wikipedia

In this recipe, we'll see a simple Zipper/UnZipper tool implemented using the `TZipFile` class declared in the `System.Zip.pas` unit.

How it works...

Open the project at `Chapter03\RECIPE04\ZipUnZip\ZipUnZip.dproj` and run it. The GUI is quite simple, click on the button and see the results.

```
System.Zip

   Zip, Get Info and UnZip

Filename         Compressed Size    Uncompressed Size
---------------------------------------------------------
file1.txt                    266                   452
file2.txt                  6.134             2.512.780
file3.txt                     57                    61
file4.txt                     20                   218
```

Figure 4.1 The Zip tool

This little program is a showcase for the `TZipFile` class. In the recipe folder, there is also a test folder called `FolderToZip` with four files inside. These files are zipped, inspected, and unzipped by the code under the button. Let's see it:

```delphi
procedure TMainForm.btnZipUnZipClick(Sender: TObject);
var
  ZF: TZipFile;
  I: Integer;
begin
  MemoSummary.Clear;
  //this single statement zip recursively a folder in a zip file
  TZipFile.ZipDirectoryContents('MyFolder.zip', 'FolderToZip');

  //let's inspect the content of the zip file...
  ZF := TZipFile.Create;
  try
    //open the zip file to read information
    ZF.Open('MyFolder.zip', TZipMode.zmRead);
    MemoSummary.Lines.Add(
      'Filename'.PadRight(15) +
```

```delphi
      'Compressed Size'.PadLeft(20) +
      'Uncompressed Size'.PadLeft(20));
    MemoSummary.Lines.Add(
      ''.PadRight(55, '-'));

    //loop through the compressed file and extract information
    //about name, original size and compressed size
    for I := 0 to ZF.FileCount - 1 do
    begin
      MemoSummary.Lines.Add(
        TEncoding.Default.GetString(ZF.FileInfo[I].FileName)
          .PadRight(15) +
        FormatFloat('###,###,##0', ZF.FileInfo[I].CompressedSize)
          .PadLeft(20) +
        FormatFloat('###,###,##0', F.FileInfo[I].UncompressedSize)
          .PadLeft(20));
    end;
  finally
    ZF.Free;
  end;

  //now actually uncompress the file into a folder
  TZipFile.ExtractZipFile('MyFolder.zip', 'UnzippedFolder');
end;
```

Yes, it is quite simple. Obviously, if you don't need to inspect the ZIP content, all this program becomes as follows:

```delphi
procedure TMainForm.btnZipUnZipClick(Sender: TObject);
begin
  TZipFile.ZipDirectoryContents('MyFolder.zip', 'FolderToZip');
  TZipFile.ExtractZipFile('MyFolder.zip', 'UnzippedFolder');
end;
```

I told you, it is not so flexible, but it is really simple to use. So if you need to decompress an update file for your program and you need only decompression, you can use the `TZipFile` class and don't use external components any more.

There's more...

There are a lot of compressing libraries available for Delphi, but before including a third-party dependency in your project, it's better to check whether the RTL has something usable for our job.

For example, sometimes we need to compress our data, either to reduce network traffic when transmitting or just to save space in storage media.

As explained in the previous chapters, Delphi wraps the `zlib` library into two `TStream` descendant classes: `TZCompressionStream` and `TZDecompressionStream`. To use them, you need to include the `System.Zlib.pas` unit in your use list. In the recipe folder, there is a bonus project that shows you how to compress and decompress generic streams (which can be file stream, a memory stream, or anything that can be wrapped as a stream). Here's the relevant code:

```
procedure TMainForm.Compress(const ASrc, ADest: TStream);
var
  LCompressor: TZCompressionStream;
begin
  LCompressor := TZCompressionStream.Create(ADest);
  try
    LCompressor.CopyFrom(ASrc, 0);
  finally
    LCompressor.Free;
  end;
end;


procedure TMainForm.Decompress(const ASrc, ADest: TStream);
var
  LDecompressor: TZDecompressionStream;
begin
  LDecompressor := TZDecompressionStream.Create(ASrc);
  try
    ADest.CopyFrom(LDecompressor, 0);
  finally
    LDecompressor.Free;
  end;
end;
```

Decouple your code using a cross-platform publish/subscribe mechanism

The publish/subscribe pattern, also known as Observer, is a very popular design pattern. It comes under a lot of different names, but the final scope is always the same: alert someone when something interesting happens to it. In this recipe, we'll see some utilization of the `TMessageManager` class, the publish/subscribe mechanism implemented in the `System.Messaging.pas` unit.

Knowing Your Friends – the Delphi RTL

Getting ready...

What exactly does the cross-platform `TMessageManager` class do? Put simply, it allows you to listen for events and assign actions to run when those events occur. Just like in VCL or FireMonkey, you know about mouse and keyboard events that occur on certain user interactions. These are very similar, except that we can emit events (or send messages) on our own, when we want to, and not necessarily based on user interaction or other mechanisms inside other components. The `TMessageManager` is based on the publish/subscribe model, because we can subscribe to a particular type of message and then publish them.

The other important question is this: why would you use the event model? You already know that in Delphi, the event model allows to decouple the built-in UI code (that's it, the `TButton` code for example) from the business code (your own code), but another benefit to events is that they are a very loose way of coupling parts of your code together. An event can be emitted, but if no code is listening for it, that's okay; it will just be passed unnoticed. This means removing listeners (or event emissions) never results in compile or runtime errors.

`TMessageManager` is the class in charge of the application's message handling, and it manages message dispatching. Its `DefaultManager` property returns an object that acts as an application-wide notification center, and is widely used in mobile development to "listen" for system-generated events (such as `OrientationChanged` and so on). You can call `TMessageManager.DefaultManager` to access the singleton instance of `TMessageManager`. However, in many cases, you will be happy to know that it is possible to create many instances of `TMessageManager`. Once you have an instance of `TMessageManager` (retrieved by the default instance as a singleton or a new instance created with `TMessageManager.Create`), you can call `TMessageManager.SubscribeToMessage` to subscribe message-handling methods to specific types of message. The events hooked to the subscription may be methods of an object or anonymous methods. After you subscribe a method to a type of message, every time there is a call to `TMessageManager.SendMessage` with a message of the target type, the subscribed methods are called. A simple interaction with 1 publisher and 2 subscribers is implemented in the following code:

```
program HelloMessaging;

{$APPTYPE CONSOLE}
{$R *.res}

uses
  System.SysUtils, System.Messaging;

begin
  //subscribe to a String message on the default message manager
  TMessageManager.DefaultManager.SubscribeToMessage(
    TMessage<String>,
```

```delphi
    procedure(const Sender: TObject; const AMessage: TMessage)
    begin
      WriteLn('Called callback1 with value: ',
        TMessage<String>(AMessage).Value);
    end);

  //subscribe to a String message on the default message manager
  TMessageManager.DefaultManager.SubscribeToMessage(
    TMessage<String>,
    procedure(const Sender: TObject; const AMessage: TMessage)
    begin
      WriteLn('Called callback2 with value: ',
        TMessage<String>(AMessage).Value);
    end);

  WriteLn('Let''s send a message to the subscribers...');

  //send a String message to the default message manager
  TMessageManager.DefaultManager.SendMessage(nil,
    TMessage<String>.Create('Hello Messaging'));

  ReadLn; //wait for a return...
end.
```

With this in mind, let's say that our customers ask for an application with some floating tool window showing information about what's happening in the main form. For the sake of simplicity, let's say that the secondary forms must show the text entered in the main form memo. A first naïve approach may imply a deep connection between the first form and all the secondary form instances, so that when the memo change, the main form knows all the secondary forms available and updates the content of the `TLabels`. This approach is really wrong. In such a way, we are coupling the main form with all other forms, and it is also difficult to maintain. Using the `TMessageManager`, instead, all the forms are decoupled from the main form, the code is simple to maintain and new features can be simply added.

Let's see the logic schema:

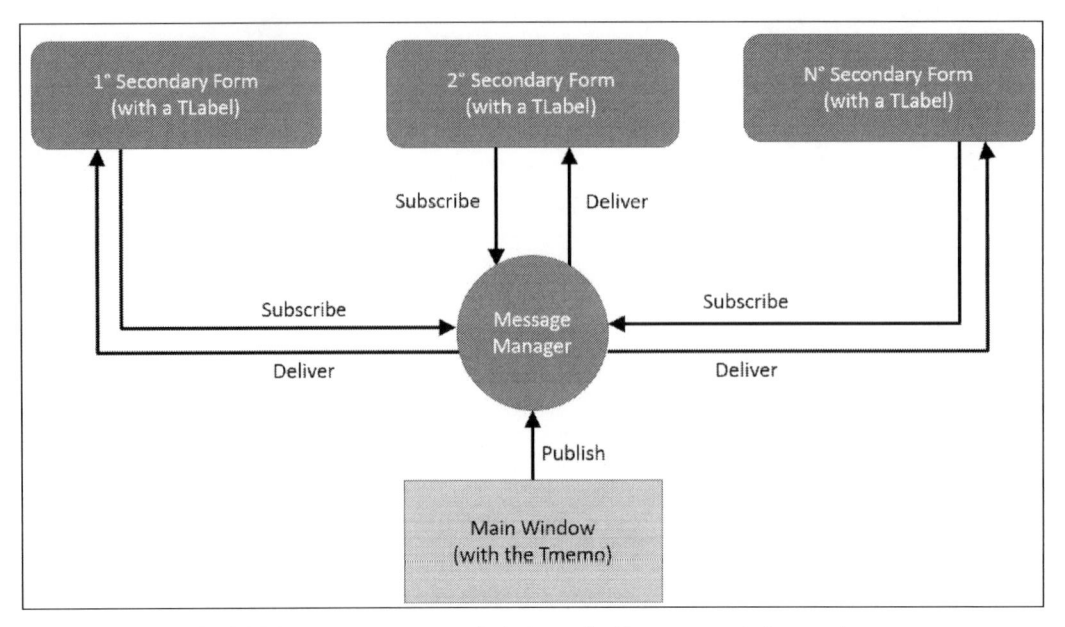

Fig. 3.5 The message manager nicely decouples the component of our system

How it works...

Open the recipe project named `Chapter03\RECIPE05\Messaging.dproj`. The main form is quite simple. There is a memo where we'll write text, and a button that will open a secondary form. The code under these two controls is as follows:

```
uses
   MyMessageManagerU, SecondaryFormU;

procedure TMainForm.btnOpenClick(Sender: TObject);
begin
   TSecondaryForm.Create(Application).Show;
end;

procedure TMainForm.memTextChange(Sender: TObject);
begin
   MessageManager.SendMessage(Self,
      TStringMessage.Create(memText.Lines.Text));
end;
```

The `btnOpenClick` event handler simply creates and shows a new `TSecondaryForm` instance. The `memTextChange` event handler sends a message of the type `TStringMessage` (a type defined in the `MyMessageManager` unit) to the private `TMessageManager` instance. Where is this instance created? Open the `MyMessageManagerU.pas` unit:

```
unit MyMessageManagerU;

interface

uses
  System.Messaging;

type
  //Define a simple message derived from TMessage<String>.
  //Now it is useful only to make the code more readable, but in
  //the future this class can be used to create more complex
  //messages without change the methods interface
  TStringMessage = class(TMessage<String>)
  end;

//the factory to get the message manager
function MessageManager: TMessageManager;

implementation

var
  //private variable to hold the reference to the message manager
  LMessageManager: TMessageManager = nil;

function MessageManager: TMessageManager;
begin
  if not Assigned(LMessageManager) then
  begin
    LMessageManager := TMessageManager.Create;
  end;
  Result := LMessageManager;
end;

initialization

finalization

//free the message manager at the program termination
LMessageManager.Free;

end.
```

Knowing Your Friends – the Delphi RTL

With this simple unit, we can simply write the following:

```
MessageManager.SubscribeToMessage(…
```

To subscribe to this specialized message manager to send messages:

```
MessageManager.SendMessage(…
```

Simple and powerful.

Let's see the consumer of these messages in the following `TSecondaryForm` code:

implementation

uses
   MyMessageManagerU, System.Messaging;

```
procedure TSecondaryForm.btnOpenFormClick(Sender: TObject);
begin
  //just like in the main form, also here we can open other
  //secondary forms
  TSecondaryForm.Create(Application).Show;
end;

procedure TSecondaryForm.FormCreate(Sender: TObject);
begin
  //At the FormCreate we've to register on the MessageManager to
  //be sure that the TStringMessage will be
  //delivered to this instance too.
  FRegID := MessageManager.SubscribeToMessage(TStringMessage,
    procedure(const Sender: TObject; const AMessage: TMessage)
    begin
      lblText.Caption := TStringMessage(AMessage).Value;
    end);
end;

procedure TSecondaryForm.FormClose(Sender: TObject;
  var Action: TCloseAction);
begin
  //at the form close, we have to UnSubscribe
  MessageManager.Unsubscribe(TStringMessage, FRegID, False);
  Action := TCloseAction.caFree;
end;
```

Now, run the project, click four times on the main form's button and rearrange the windows so that you can see all of them. Write some text in the memo and you should see something similar to the following screenshot:

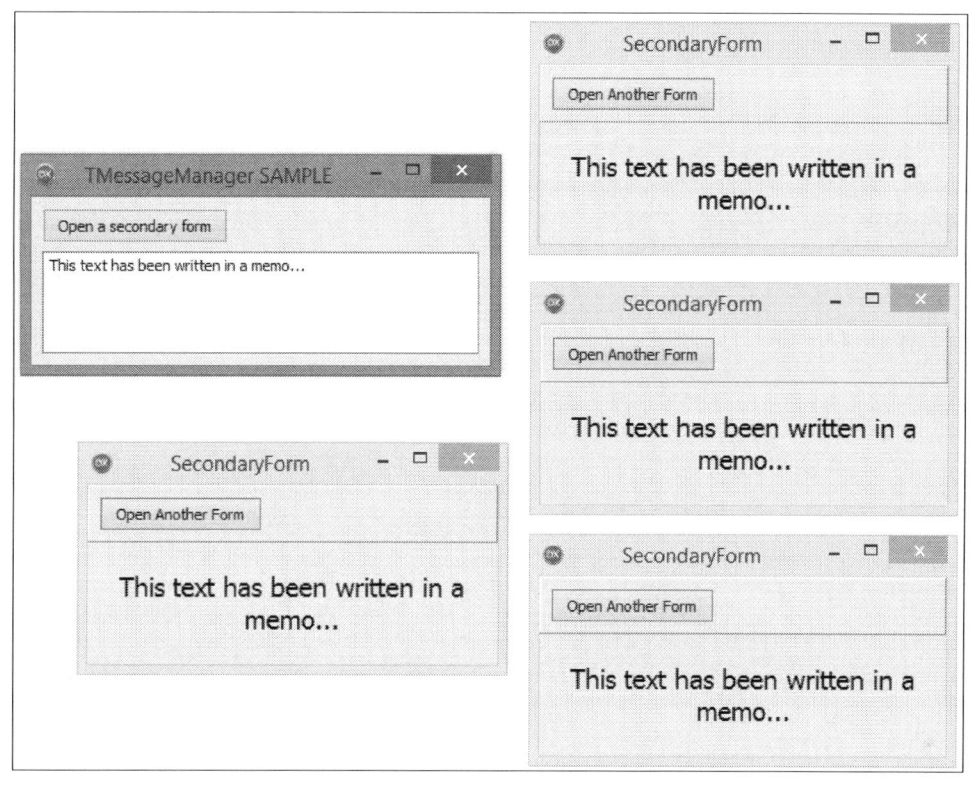

Fig. 3.5 The message is delivered to all the subscribers

There's more...

Messaging is a really large topic. The same concepts we saw in this recipe can be applied also to distributed systems using *Enterprise Message Bus* (see `https://en.wikipedia.org/wiki/Enterprise_service_bus`).

Also within our program, messaging is a great way to decouple our classes and to make software easier to maintain and improve. Another real world use case for object types is within the boundaries of a class. Remember that publishing a message is a synchronous process. Your call to `SendMessage` will not return until each subscriber's `MessageListener` code is run in turn. So your publisher will take longer for the `SendMessage` call to return. About multithreading, consider that `TMessageManager` is not usable in a multithreading environment as is. If you want to create a more complex multi threaded messaging system, you have to manually handle the synchronization between threads.

4
Going Cross-Platform with FireMonkey

In this chapter, we will cover the following recipes:

- Giving a new appearance to the standard FireMonkey controls using styles
- Creating a styled `TListBox`
- Impressing your clients with animations
- Using master/details with LiveBindings
- Showing complex vector shapes using paths
- Using FireMonkey in a VCL application
- Reinventing your GUI also known as mastering Firemonkey controls, shapes, and effects

Introduction

The FireMonkey framework is the app development and runtime platform behind Delphi and C++Builder. FireMonkey has been introduced in these products since Version XE2 (September 2011) and is the first native GPU-powered application platform. The IT world is becoming more multiplatform with each passing year. FireMonkey is a key technology for Embarcadero because it is designed to build multidevice, true native apps for Windows, Mac, Android, and iOS.

Going Cross-Platform with FireMonkey

This chapter explains some of the great features of FireMonkey. These recipes are applicable to the latest RAD Studio versions. FireMonkey is relatively young compared to VCL, so if you have older RAD Studio version, some things may not work as expected, but the fundamental things are still valid. What is exposed in these recipes will be useful on every platform supported by the framework. Some of the OS-related features may not be available everywhere, but the greater part of the concepts are usable on MS Windows, Mac OS X, Android, and iOS. These are ready-to-use recipes that will be useful every day.

Giving a new appearance to the standard FireMonkey controls using styles

Since Version XE2, RAD Studio includes FireMonkey. FireMonkey is an amazing library. It is a really ambitious target for Embarcadero, but it's important for its mid and long-term strategy. VCL is and will remain a Windows-only library, while FireMonkey has been designed to be completely OS and device independent. You can develop one application and compile it anywhere (if anywhere is contained in Windows, OS X, Android, and iOS; let's say that is a good part of anywhere).

One of the main features of FireMonkey is customization through styles. A styled component doesn't know how it will be rendered on the screen, because the style is in charge of it. By changing the style, you can change the aspect of the component without changing its code. The relation between the component code and style is similar to the relation between HTML and CSS: one is the content and another is the display. In terms of FireMonkey, the component code contains the actual functionalities that the component has, but the aspect is completely handled by the associated style. All the `TStyledControl` child classes support styles.

Getting ready

Let's say you have to create an application to find a holiday house for a travel agency. Your customer wants a nice-looking application to search for the dream house for their customers. Your graphic design department (if present) decided to create a semitransparent look-and-feel, as shown in the following screenshot, and you've to create such an interface. How to do that?

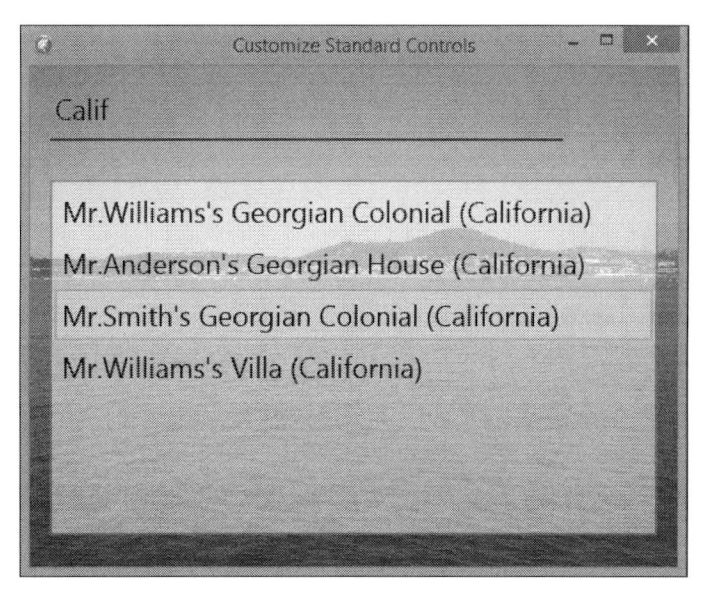

This is the UI we want

How to do it...

In this case, you require some step-by-step instructions, so here they are:

1. Create a new FireMonkey desktop application (navigate to **File | New | Multi-Device Application**).
2. Drop a **TImage** component on the form. Set its **Align** property to **Client**, and use the **MultiResBitmap** property and its property editor to load a nice looking picture.
3. Set the **WrapMode** property to **Fit** and resize the form to let the image cover the entire form.
4. Now, drop a **TEdit** component and a **TListBox** component over the **TImage** component. Name the **TEdit** component `EditSearch` and the **TListBox** component `ListBoxHouses`.
5. Set the `Scale` property of the **TEdit** and **TListBox** components to the following values:
    - **Scale.X**: 2
    - **Scale.Y**: 2

6. Your form should now look like this:

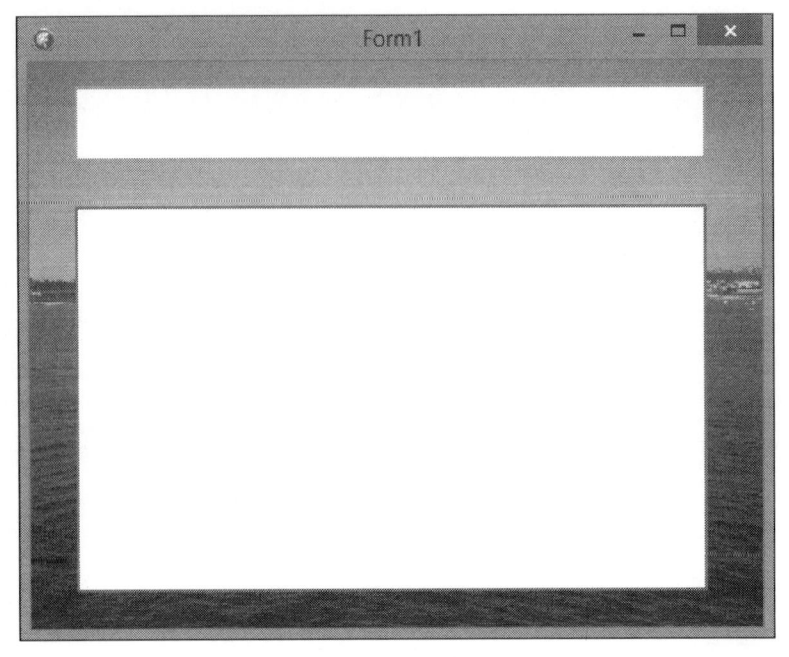

The form with the standard components

> The actions to be performed by the users are very simple. They should write some search criteria in the **Edit** field and click on **Return**. Then, the `listbox` shows all the houses available for that criteria (with a *contains* search). In a real app, you require a database or a web service to query, but this is a sample so you'll use fake search criteria on fake data.

7. Add the `RandomUtilsU.pas` file from the `Commons` folder of the project and add it to the uses clause of the main form.

8. Create an `OnKeyUp` event handler for the **TEdit** component and write the following code inside it:

```
procedure TForm1.EditSearchKeyUp(Sender: TObject;
     var Key: Word; var KeyChar: Char; Shift: TShiftState);
var
  I: Integer;
  House: string;
  SearchText: string;
begin
  if Key <> vkReturn then
```

```
      Exit;

   // this is a fake search...
   ListBoxHouses.Clear;
   SearchText := EditSearch.Text.ToUpper;

   //now, gets 50 random houses and match the criteria
   for I := 1 to 50 do
   begin
      House := GetRndHouse;
      if House.ToUpper.Contains(SearchText) then
         ListBoxHouses.Items.Add(House);
   end;
   if ListBoxHouses.Count > 0 then
      ListBoxHouses.ItemIndex := 0
   else
      ListBoxHouses.Items.Add('<Sorry, no houses found>');
   ListBoxHouses.SetFocus;
end;
```

9. Run the application and try to familiarize yourself with the behavior.

10. Now, you have a working application, but you still need to make it transparent. Let's start with the **FireMonkey Style Designer** (**FSD**).

> Up until XE8, the FSD was probably the less usable part of the RAD Studio IDE. However, after a little improvement in RAD Studio 10 Seattle, in RAD Studio 10.1 Berlin, the designer has been completely redesigned and now is much better.

11. Right-click on the **TEdit** component. From the contextual menu, choose **Edit Custom Style** (general information about styles and the style editor can be found at http://docwiki.embarcadero.com/RADStudio/en/FireMonkey_Style_Designer and http://docwiki.embarcadero.com/RADStudio/en/Editing_a_FireMonkey_Style).

12. Delphi opens a new tab that contains the FSD. However, to work with it, you need the **Structure** pane to be visible as well (navigate to **View | Structure** or *Shift + Alt + F11*).

13. In the **Structure** pane, there are all the styles used by the **TEdit** control. You should see a **Structure** pane similar to the following screenshot:

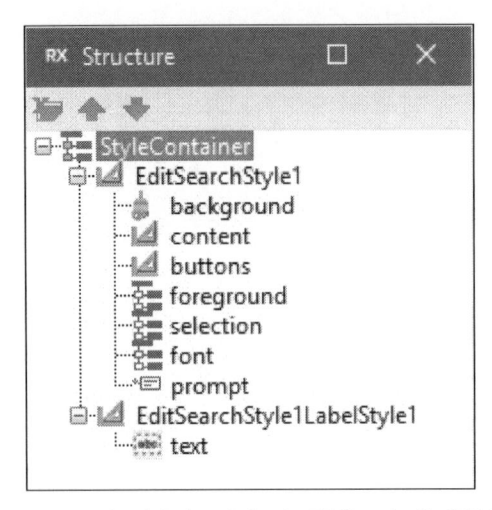

The Structure pane showing the default style for the TEdit control in RAD Studio 10.1 Berlin

14. In the **Structure** pane, open the `EditSearchStyle1` node, select the background sub node, and go to the **Object Inspector**.

15. In the **Object Inspector** window, remove the content of the **SourceLookup** property.

> The background part of the style is **TActiveStyleObject**. A **TActiveStyleObject** style is able to show a part of an image as default and another part of the same image when the component that uses it is active, checked, focused, mouse hovered, pressed, or selected. The image to be used is in the **SourceLookup** property. Our **TEdit** component must be completely transparent in every state, so we removed the value of the **SourceLookup** property.

16. Now the **TEdit** component is completely invisible. Click on **Apply and Close** and run the application. As you can confirm, the edit works but it is completely transparent. Close the application.

17. When you opened the FSD for the first time, a **TStyleBook** component has been automatically dropped on the form and contains all your custom styles. Double-click on it and the style designer opens again.

18. The edit, as you saw, is transparent, but it is not usable at all. You need to see at least where to click and write. Let's add a small bottom line to the edit style, just like a small underline.

19. To perform the next step, you require the **Tool Palette** window and the **Structure** pane visible. Here is my preferred setup for this situation:

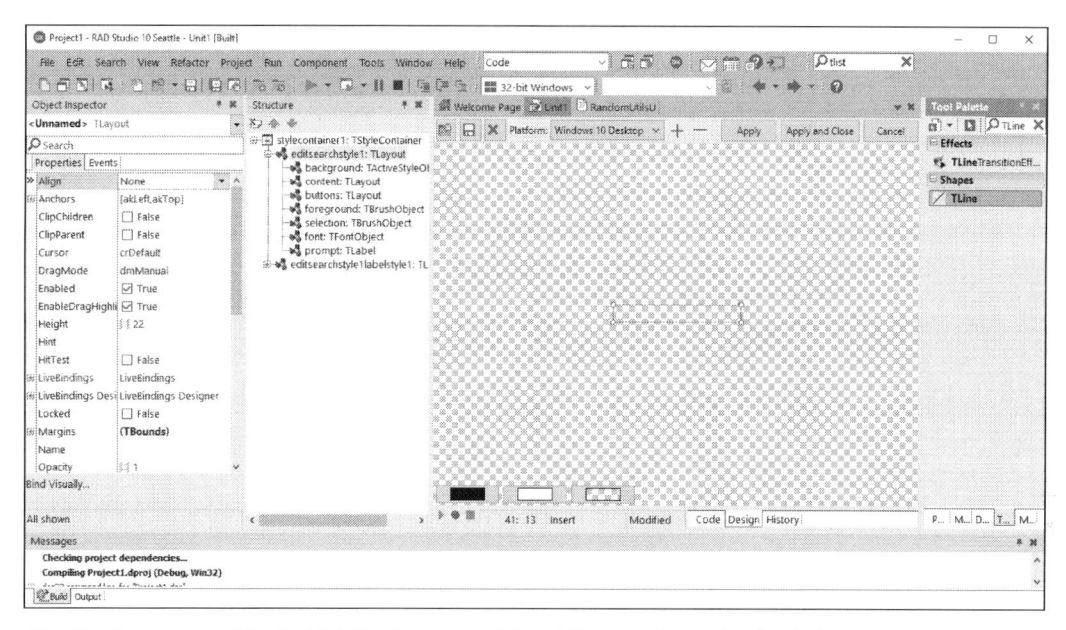

The Structure pane and the Tool Palette window are visible at the same time using the docking mechanism; you can also use the floating windows if you wish

20. Now, search for a **TLine** component in the **Tool Palette** window. Drag-and-drop the **TLine** component onto the `EditSearchStyle1` node in the **Structure** pane. Yes, you have to drop a component from the **Tool Palette** window directly onto the **Structure** pane.

21. Now, select the **TLine** component in the **Structure** pane (do not use the FSD to select the components, you have to use the **Structure** pane nodes). In **Object Inspector**, set the following properties:
    - **Align**: **Contents**
    - **HitTest**: **False**
    - **LineType**: **Bottom**
    - **Opacity**: 0.6

22. Close the FSD tab (or click on **Apply and Close** for versions prior to RAD Studio 10.1 Berlin).

23. Run the application. Now, the text is underlined with a small black line that makes it easy to identify that the application is transparent. Stop the application.

24. Now, you've to work on the listbox; it is still 100% opaque.

Going Cross-Platform with FireMonkey

25. Right-click on the **ListBoxHouses** option and click on **Edit Custom Style**.
26. In the **Structure** pane, there are some new styles related to the **TListBox** class. Select the **listboxhousesstyle1** option, open it, and select its child style, background.
27. In the **Object Inspector**, change the **Opacity** property of the background style to `0.6`. Click on **Apply and Close**.
28. That's it! Run the application, write `Calif` in the **Edit** field and press **Return**. You should see a nice-looking application with a semitransparent user interface showing your dream houses in California (just like it was shown in the screenshot in the *Getting ready* section of this recipe). Are you amazed by the power of FireMonkey styles?

How it works...

The trick used in this recipe is simple. If you require a transparent UI, just identify which part of the style of each component is responsible to draw the background of the component. Then, put the **Opacity** setting to a level less than 1 (0.6 or 0.7 could be enough for most cases). Why not simply change the `Opacity` property of the component? Because if you change the `Opacity` property of the component, the whole component will be drawn with that opacity. However, you need only the background to be transparent; the inner text must be completely opaque. This is the reason why you changed the style and not the component property.

In the case of the **TEdit** component, you completely removed the painting when you removed the **SourceLookup** property from **TActiveStyleObject** that draws the background.

As a thumb rule, if you have to change the appearance of a control, check its properties. If the required customization is not possible using only the properties, then change the style.

See also

If you are new to FireMonkey styles, probably most concepts in this recipe must have been difficult to grasp. If so, check the official documentation on the Embarcadero DocWiki at the URL: `http://docwiki.embarcadero.com/RADStudio/en/Customizing_FireMonkey_Applications_with_Styles`

Creating a styled TListBox

As you saw in the previous recipe, it is possible to style styled controls and completely change their appearance. While in the VCL, the **TListBox** control is a mere wrapper over the correspondent control in the MS Windows API; in FireMonkey, the **TListBox** component is a completely different beast. A **TListBox** component contains a list of `TListBoxItem`, and a **TListBox** item is a `TStyledControl` descendant. This means that every single item in a **TListBox** component can be styled! This feature opens a huge set of new possibilities regarding the use of the control.

Getting ready

In this recipe, you'll see a set of styled `TListBoxItem` components that when added to **TListBox**, changes its appearance completely. Let's say you have a listbox containing a log of events that happened in a monitored remote system. Some events are simply informative, while other events can denote a malfunction. Different kinds of events are shown with different graphics in the listbox. Here are the events:

Type	Appearance
Normal	This is the default option for `TListBoxItem`.
Hint	This has blue colored text on a white background. The text is left aligned but indented by 40 pixels.
Warning	This has black colored text on a white background. There is a small yellow flag on the left-hand side.
Error	This has red colored text over white background. There is a small red flag on the left.

What you require is shown in the following screenshot:

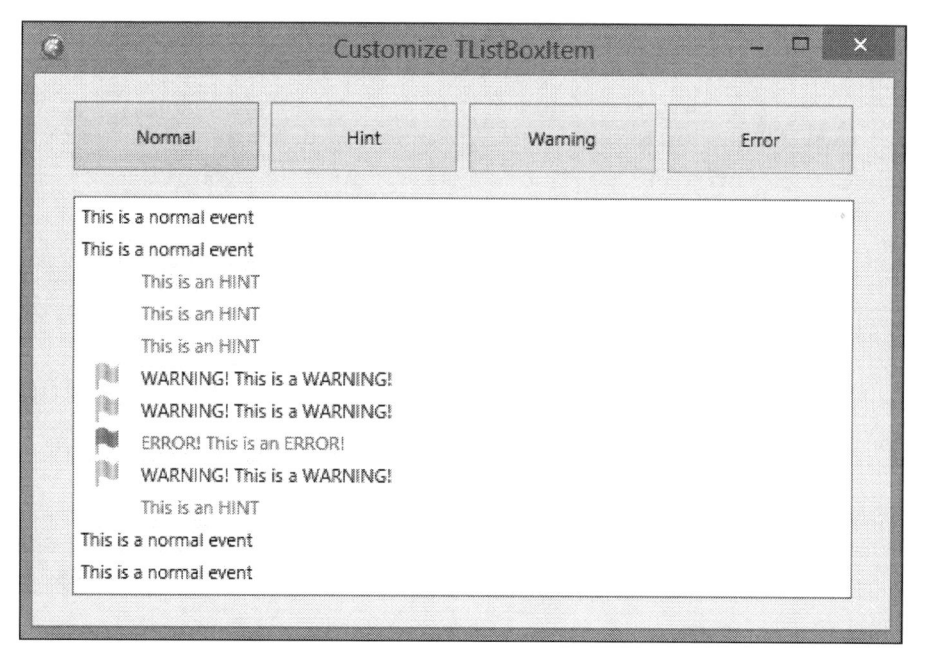

The listbox with some types of event logged

To achieve this result using VCL, you usually rely on owner drawing or some third-party controls. However, with FireMonkey, all these customizations are a matter of style, so they are simpler, faster to implement, reusable, and more flexible.

Going Cross-Platform with FireMonkey

How to do it...

Let's start creating our stunning FireMonkey GUI:

1. Create a new FireMonkey desktop application.
2. Drop four **TButton** components, a **TListBox** component, and a **TStyleBook** component on the form.
3. Double-click on the **TStyleBook** component and open the style editor.
4. Show the **Structure** pane (navigate to **View** | **Structure** or press *Shift + Alt + F11*).
5. Drop three **TLayout** components to create three different styles.
6. Set the **StyleName** property of the three **TLayout** components as follows:
    - errorlistboxitem
    - hintlistboxitem
    - warninglistboxitem

    The **StyleName** property allows you to reference to the style from your form, so we've create three new styles usable from the main form.

7. In every **TLayout** drop a **TText** so that every **TLayout** contains a **TText**. Set the **TText.Align** property to **Client**.
8. Set the **StyleName** property for each **TText** to **eventtext**. Pay attention; every **TText** in each **TLayout**, has the same value in the **StyleName** property. This allows you to use the **StylesData** property independently of the applied style. So you can write `StylesData['eventtext'] := 'Hello World'` and the control that had `StyleName` equal to `eventtext` will be correctly assigned.
9. Now let's work on each style. Select the **hintlistboxitem** style from the **Structure** pane.
10. Now, select the inner **eventtext** component (a **TText** component) and set its **TextSettings.FontColor** property to **Blue** and its **Margins.Left** property to **40**.
11. Select the **warninglistboxitem** style from the **Structure** pane.
12. Now, drop a **TImage** component into the style at the same level of **TText**.
13. Set **TImage.Align** to **MostLeft**.
14. Load a small 32 x 32 icon showing a small yellow flag in its **MultiResBitmap** property (some free icons are provided with the code of the book).
15. Set **TImage.Width** to **40**.
16. Select the **errorlistboxitem** style from the **Structure** pane.
17. Set the **TText.TextSettings.FontColor** property to **Red**.
18. Now, drop a **TImage** component into the style at the same level of **TText**.

19. Set **TImage.Align** to **MostLeft**.
20. Load a small 32 x 32 icon showing a small red flag in its **MultiResBitmap** property.
21. Set **TImage.Width** to **40**.
22. Now, your **Structure** pane should look like this:

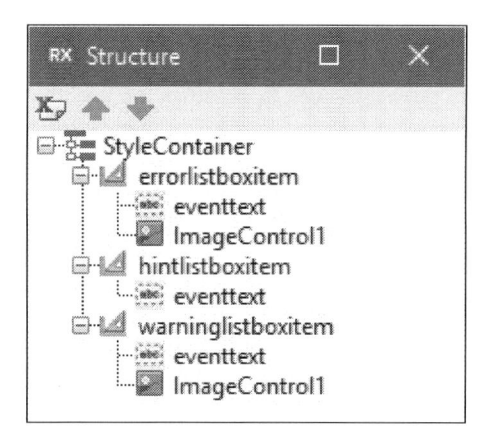

23. Click on **Apply and Close** on the style designer toolbar.
24. Now, the **TStyleBook** component contains all the custom styles. However, currently those styles are not used. Let's use them.
25. Select the form and set **StyleBook** to `StyleBook1`.
26. Go to the form class declaration and add the following private method:

```
procedure TForm1.AddEvent(EventType, EventText: String);
var
  LBItem: TListBoxItem;
begin
  LBItem := TListBoxItem.Create(ListBox1);
  LBItem.Parent := ListBox1;
  if EventType.Equals('normal') then
  begin
    LBItem.Text := EventText;
  end
  else
  begin
    LBItem.StyleLookup := EventType + 'listboxitem';
    LBItem.StylesData['eventtext'] := EventText;
  end;
  ListBox1.AddObject(LBItem);
end;
```

27. Set the button names and captions to the following values:
    - btnNormal (**Caption: Normal**)
    - btnHint (**Caption: Hint**)
    - btnWarning (**Caption: Warning**)
    - btnError (**Caption: Error**)

28. Create four event handlers, one for each **TButton** component, as shown in the following code:

    ```
    procedure TForm1.btnNormalClick(Sender: TObject);
    begin
      AddEvent('normal', 'This is a normal event');
    end;

    procedure TForm1.btnHintClick(Sender: TObject);
    begin
      AddEvent('hint', 'This is an HINT');
    end;

    procedure TForm1.btnWarningClick(Sender: TObject);
    begin
      AddEvent('warning', 'WARNING! This is a WARNING!');
    end;

    procedure TForm1.btnErrorClick(Sender: TObject);
    begin
      AddEvent('error', 'ERROR! This is an ERROR!');
    end;
    ```

29. Hit *F9* and try to click on the buttons, and you should see something like the **Structure** pane shown earlier.

How it works...

By clicking on each button, a new `TListBoxItem` is created (in the **AddEvent** method). Depending on the event type, the correct style is selected from the **TStyleBook** component. There is no need to directly refer to **TStyleBook**, FireMonkey looks automatically to the form's **TStyleBook**. The **StyleLookup** property sets the style used for `TListBoxItem`, while the **StylesData** indexed property contains the values for every style component with **StyleName**. By setting `StylesData['eventtext']`, you are actually setting the **Text** property of the inner **TText** component.

See also

FireMonkey styles are really powerful. The style designer makes working with styles quite simple and once you grasp the foundations of using FireMonkey, styles are addictive! Some links to go deeper with styles are as follows:

- `http://docwiki.embarcadero.com/RADStudio/en/FireMonkey_Style_Designer`
- `http://docwiki.embarcadero.com/RADStudio/en/Customizing_FireMonkey_Applications_with_Styles`
- `http://docwiki.embarcadero.com/RADStudio/en/Working_with_Native_and_Custom_FireMonkey_Styles`

Impressing your clients with animations

Animations are a nice thing. A well done animation, not too intrusive and with good visual information, can explain what is happening on the UI better than a thousand words. In this recipe, you will implement a dual list with the `include<>exclude` paradigm so that what is removed from one list is included in the other list and vice versa. You will use FireMonkey animations.

FireMonkey animations are really simple to use. Some kinds of property type can be animated. Some of these types are color, bitmap, gradient, and floating point number. The most used animation engine is the **TFloatAnimation**. This is used to animate floating point values such as **Opacity**, **Position.X**, **Position.Y**, **Width**, **Height**, and many more.

Going Cross-Platform with FireMonkey

How to do it...

What you want to create is shown in the following screenshot:

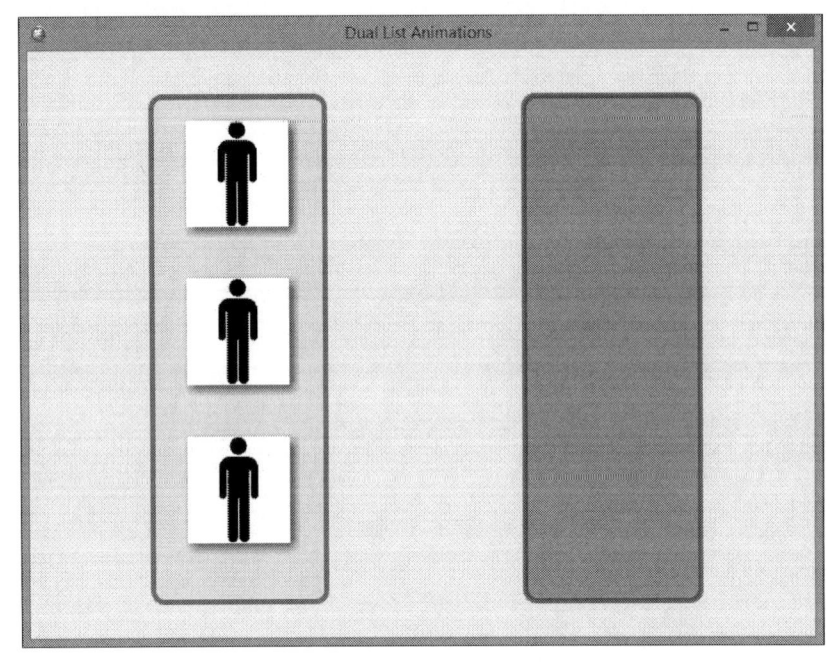

The dual list selection form

There are three images in the left-hand side gray list and zero images in the red list on the right-hand side. Click on an image; the clicked image will slide to the opposite list (gray to red or red to gray) using a nice animation. The steps to reproduce the images are as follows:

1. Create a new FireMonkey desktop application.
2. Drop two **TRectangle** components on the form. Align the first one on the left-hand side and call it **LeftRect**, and the second one to the right-hand side and call it **RightRect**, as shown in the screenshot in the *Getting ready* section of this recipe.
3. Set the properties of the left-hand side rectangle like this:
    - **Fill.Color**: #FFE0E0E0
    - **Fill.Kind**: Solid
    - **Stroke.Thickness**: 5
    - **Opacity**: 0.5
    - **XRadius**: 10
    - **YRadius**: 10

4. Set the properties of the right-hand side rectangle as follows:
    - **Fill.Color**: **Red**
    - **Fill.Kind**: **Solid**
    - **Stroke.Thickness**: 5
    - **Opacity**: 0.5
    - **XRadius**: 10
    - **YRadius**: 10

5. Now, drop three **TImage** components on the form and align them into the left-hand side **TRectangle**.

6. Load some kind of picture or icon into **TImages**. You can use the same images for each **TImage** (as I did) or different images for each **TImage**. It depends on what kind of information you want to transfer to your user.

> In the included source code, you can find an image called `blackman.png` that is the one that I used.

7. Now, for each image, drop **TShadowEffect**. The effect must be owned by the **TImage** component so that in the **Structure** pane, the **TImage** component contains a subnode named **TShadowEffect**. Perform the same action for each **TImage**.

8. Now, set the **Distance** property to 5 for each **TShadowEffect**.

9. Our UI is created. Now you've to write come code. In the FormCreate event, write the following code and declare `FLeftLimit` and `FRightLimit` as private class members of the type `Single`:

```
procedure TDualListForm.FormCreate(Sender: TObject);
begin
   FLeftLimit := LeftRect.ParentedRect.CenterPoint.X
- Image1.Width / 2;
   FRightLimit := RightRect.ParentedRect.CenterPoint.X
- Image1.Width / 2;
end;
```

10. In the `FormCreate` event handler `FLeftLimit` and `FRightLimit` are calculated. The objective is that when the image is clicked, it should start from the left-hand side rectangle and should move to the right-hand side rectangle. If the image is clicked a second time, it should return to the left-hand side (with the same animation).

11. Now, let's use the same event handler for all the three **TImage** components. Create the event handler with a double-click on the **TImage1** component. Fill the event handler with this code:

```
procedure TDualListForm.Image1Click(Sender: TObject);
var
  LImage: TImage;
begin
  LImage := (Sender as TImage);

  if LImage.Tag = 0 then
  begin
    LImage.Tag := 1;
    //Slide the image to the right rectangle
    TAnimator.AnimateFloat(LImage, 'Position.X',
        FRightLimit, 0.8,
          TAnimationType.Out, TInterpolationType.Elastic)
  end
  else
  begin
    LImage.Tag := 0;
    //Slide the image to the left rectangle
    TAnimator.AnimateFloat(LImage, 'Position.X',
        FLeftLimit, 0.8,
      TAnimationType.Out, TInterpolationType.Elastic);
  end;

  //let's make the image a little bigger to mimic
  //a sort of 3D space using Scale property. Check that
  //this animation is delayed and will happen when the move
  //to the right (or to the left) is already started.
  TAnimator.AnimateFloatDelay(LImage, 'Scale.X',
        1.2, 0.2, 0.2);
  TAnimator.AnimateFloatDelay(LImage, 'Scale.Y',
        1.2, 0.2, 0.2);

  //Back to the original dimension using delay
  TAnimator.AnimateFloatDelay(LImage, 'Scale.X',
         1, 0.2, 1);
  TAnimator.AnimateFloatDelay(LImage, 'Scale.Y',
         1, 0.2, 1);
end;
```

12. As you can see, I've used the `TImage.Tag` property to keep a track of the current position. It would be better to have an external data model to hold this kind of visual state instead of putting this information in the graphical components, but for this demo, it's okay.
13. Now, connect the same `TImage1.OnClick` event handler to `TImage2.OnClick` and `TImage3.OnClick` as well. In this way, you can centralize the behavior in a single event handler.
14. Run (navigate to **Run | Run** or press *F9*) and start clicking on the images.

How it works...

This recipe is very simple and is a good example of how animations can be used to gain not only visual wow effect (that probably may even disturb your user in some cases), but also some informative content.

The approach is simple: when the user clicks, communicate using animations that something happened and make it mime the real physical world. This is about the eBook reader applications on your smartphones. Is it strictly required to show a *page turning animation* when you change pages? No! However, it makes it clear to the user what is happening. Your animation should be used for the same goal.

See also

Some useful basic information about animations can be read on the Embarcadero DocWiki:

- `http://docwiki.embarcadero.com/RADStudio/en/FireMonkey_Animation_Effects`
- `http://docwiki.embarcadero.com/RADStudio/en/Using_FireMonkey_Animation_Effects`

Using master/details with LiveBindings

When you have a customer with his/her orders or an invoice with his/her items, you have a **master/details** (**M/D**) relationship. In this recipe, you will learn how to use the new LiveBindings technology to show an M/D relationship.

As explained in the Embarcadero wiki:

> *"LiveBindings is a data-binding feature supported by both the VCL and FireMonkey frameworks in RAD Studio. LiveBindings is an expression-based framework, which means it uses bindings expressions to bind objects to other objects or to dataset fields."*

LiveBindings is a very nice technology and can be used in VCL applications also, but its main targets are FireMonkey applications. Indeed, it is the only way to do automatic data binding in the FireMonkey framework. If you don't know what LiveBindings is or what its strengths are, I suggest you stop here and read the article in the Embarcadero wiki at http://docwiki.embarcadero.com/RADStudio/en/LiveBindings_in_RAD_Studio.

What we want to do in this recipe is create a simple but complete FireMonkey application that handles a sort-of M/D relationship. Usually, this kind of thing involves the use of some databases. In this case, however, we are abandoning the SQL-based approach (that uses two or more datasets) in favor of a purely object-oriented approach. In other words, you will use a list of objects instead of a simple SQL query, and the relationships are child objects contained in the main object, not another query. Keep in mind that if for this simple example, the OOP approach may seem not necessary, when you deal with a lot of logic the classic DataSet approach rapidly becomes unmanageable, while the OOP approach tends to be really stable and easily maintained and understood by a third programmer.

Getting ready

The simple UML class diagram generated by Delphi is shown here:

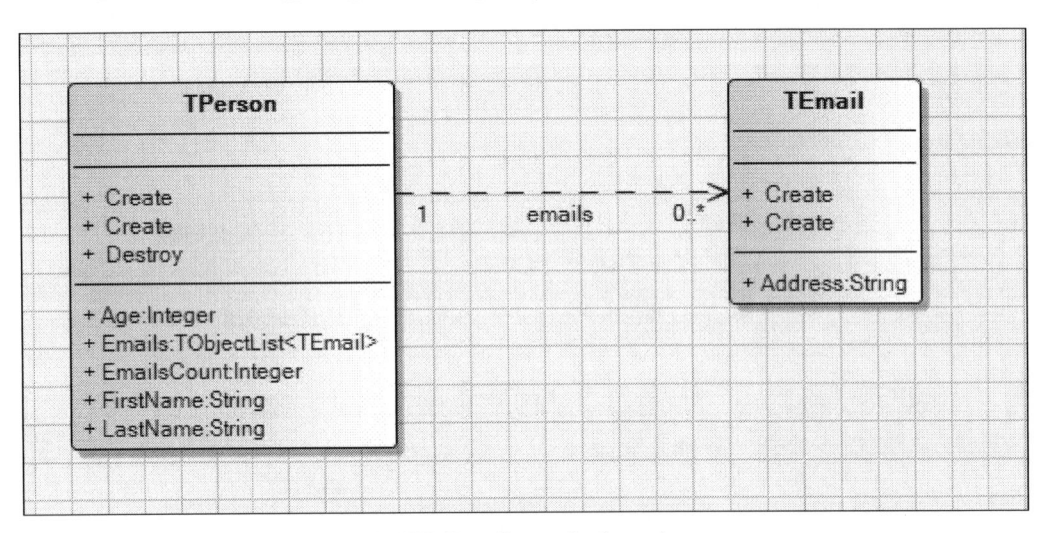

The UML class diagram for the recipe

The main list of objects contains the **TPerson** instances. Each **TPerson** instance, as shown in the preceding diagram, contains a variable number of e-mails. So, the **TPerson** class has a property called **Emails** that is a list of **TEmail** instances. Instead of filtering all the e-mails and showing only the e-mails related to the selected person (as usually happens in the classic SQL programming), you'll show only the e-mails of that person; no filters are involved. The e-mails are already tied to the person. In this recipe, the difference between the TDataset approach and the vobject-oriented approach will be clear. The final application is shown in the following screenshot:

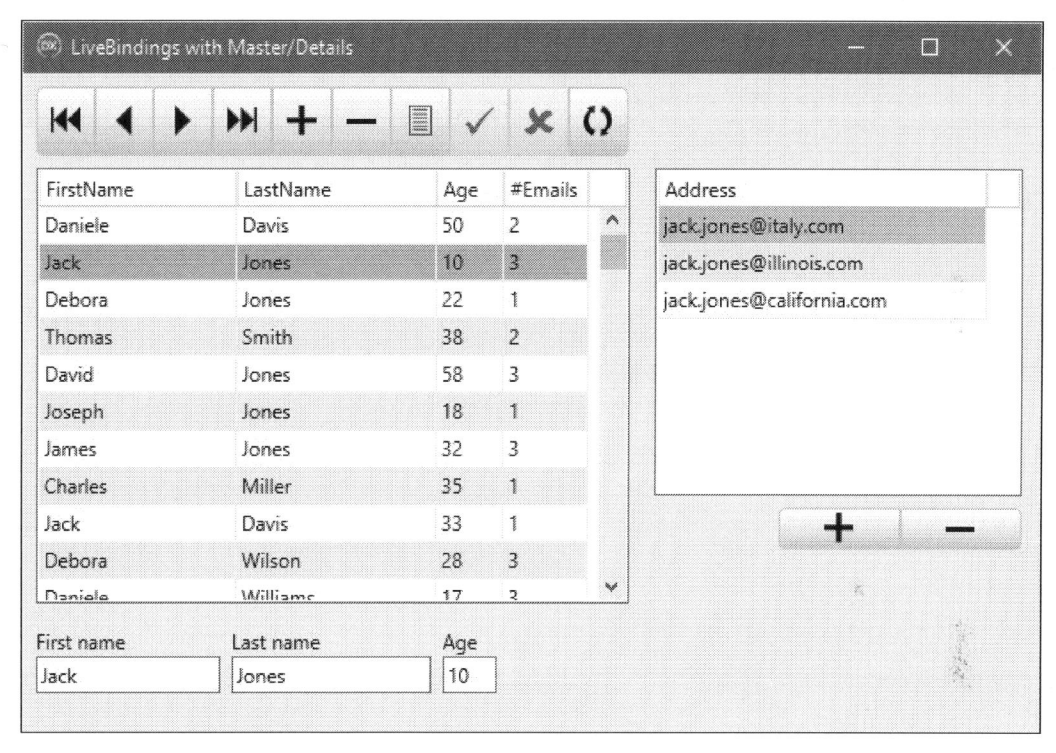

Fig. 4.2 The final aspect of the M/D application that is able to manage people and the related e-mails

How to do it...

Let's start:

1. Create a new FireMonkey HD desktop application and name the main form `MainForm`.
2. Drop two **TGrid** components on the form and name them `grdPeople` and `grdEmails`. Set the **Options.AlternatigRowBackground** property to **True** for both the components. Set the **Options.RowSelection** to **True** for the `grdPeople`.

3. Drop two **TProtypeBindSource** components in the form and name them `bsPeople` and `bsEmails`.

4. Double-clicking on **bsPeople** shows its field definitions. Using the **Add** (the first button from the left-hand side) button, add four fields as shown in the following screenshot:

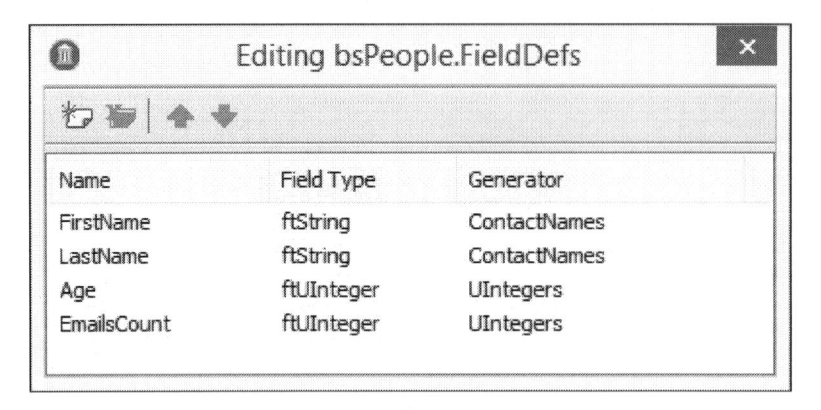

Name	Field Type	Generator
FirstName	ftString	ContactNames
LastName	ftString	ContactNames
Age	ftUInteger	UIntegers
EmailsCount	ftUInteger	UIntegers

Editing bsPeople.FieldDefs

5. Close the field definition of **bsPeople**.

6. Double-clicking on **bsEmails** shows its field definitions. Using the **Add** (the first button from the left-hand side) button, add the **Address** field as shown here:

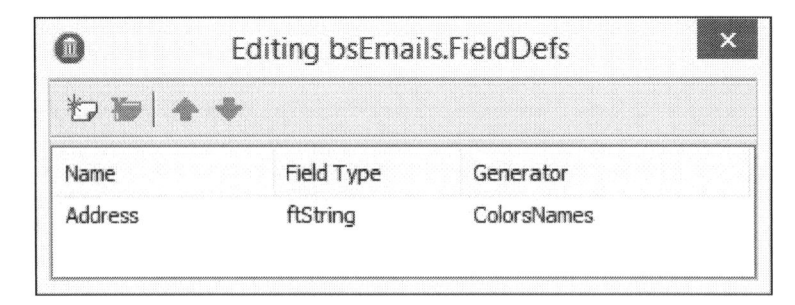

Name	Field Type	Generator
Address	ftString	ColorsNames

Editing bsEmails.FieldDefs

7. Close the field definition of **bsEmails**.

8. Drop a **TBindNavigator** component on the form and connect its **DataSource** property to **bsPeople**.

9. Drop another **TBindNavigator** component on the form and connect its **DataSource** property to **bsEmails**. Then, set all the elements inside its **VisibleButtons** property to `False` and set only **nbInsert** and **nbDelete** to **true** (this will allow you to insert or remove any e-mail from a person).

10. Now, drop three **TEdit** components on the form and name them **EditFirstName**, **EditLastName**, and **EditAge**.

11. Our UI is almost ready. Add some labels and arrange the controls as show in the figure 4.2.

12. Now the interesting part begins.
13. Navigate to **View | LiveBindings Designer**.
14. The window shows the famous **LiveBindings Designer**. All the **LiveBindings Enabled** controls with their properties will be shown.
15. On the left-hand side toolbar, there are a set of buttons useful to change the disposition and zoom of the diagram. Use the buttons; they will save your sanity!
16. Identify the **bsPeople** element and drag and drop all its elements on `grdPeople`. You can also drag only the * column, but columns are not created at design time. So, if you want (as usually you will) to change the aspect of the grid columns, drag every field one by one.
17. Perform the same action (as done for **bsPeople**) with the **bsEmails** and `grdEmails`.
18. Now, you've to connect the editable field of the **bsPeople** component to the **TEdits** component.
19. Connect `bsPeople.FirstName` to `EditFirstName.Text`.
20. Connect `bsPeople.LastName` to `EditLastName.Text`.
21. Connect `bsPeople.Age` to `EditAge.Text`.
22. Do not connect the `EmailsCount` field. This field is a read-only field, mapped to a read-only property, and used to show the number of e-mail addresses related to the current person. This technique can be quite useful when you have to show how many rows are contained in an invoice, how many orders are related to a customer, and so on.
23. If you run the application now, you will see some fake data is generated. You will also notice that there is no M/D relationship between people and e-mails. We are about to fix this in a moment. Close the application and go back to Delphi.
24. Add a new unit, name it `BusinessObjectsU.pas`, and add the following code to it:

```
unit BusinessObjectsU;

interface

uses System.Generics.Collections;

type
  TEmail = class
  private
    FAddress: String;
    procedure SetAddress(const Value: String);
  public
    constructor Create; overload;
```

```
    constructor Create(AEmail: String); overload;
    property Address: String
             read FAddress write SetAddress;
  end;

  TPerson = class
  private
    FLastName: String;
    FAge: Integer;
    FFirstName: String;
    FEmails: TObjectList<TEmail>;
    procedure SetLastName(const Value: String);
    procedure SetAge(const Value: Integer);
    procedure SetFirstName(const Value: String);
    function GetEmailsCount: Integer;
  public
    constructor Create; overload;
    constructor Create(const FirstName, LastName: string;
          Age: Integer); overload; virtual;
    destructor Destroy; override;
    property FirstName: String
             read FFirstName write SetFirstName;
    property LastName: String
             read FLastName write SetLastName;
    property Age: Integer read FAge write SetAge;
    property EmailsCount: Integer read GetEmailsCount;
    property Emails: TObjectList<TEmail> read FEmails;   end;

implementation

uses System.SysUtils;

constructor TPerson.Create(const FirstName, LastName:
                                      string; Age: Integer);
begin
  Create;
  FFirstName := FirstName;
  FLastName := LastName;
  FAge := Age;
end;

// Called by LiveBindings to insert a new Person
constructor TPerson.Create;
begin
```

```delphi
  inherited Create;
  FFirstName := '<name>';
  //initialize the emails list
  FEmails := TObjectList<TEmail>.Create(true);
end;

destructor TPerson.Destroy;
begin
  FEmails.Free;
  inherited;
end;

function TPerson.GetEmailsCount: Integer;
begin
  Result := FEmails.Count;
end;

procedure TPerson.SetLastName(const Value: String);
begin
  FLastName := Value;
end;

procedure TPerson.SetAge(const Value: Integer);
begin
  FAge := Value;
end;

procedure TPerson.SetFirstName(const Value: String);
begin
  FFirstName := Value;
end;

constructor TEmail.Create(AEmail: String);
begin
  inherited Create;
  FAddress := AEmail;
end;

// Called by LiveBindings to insert a new Email
constructor TEmail.Create;
begin
  Create('<email>');
```

```
   end;

   procedure TEmail.SetAddress(const Value: String);
   begin
      FAddress := Value;
   end;

end.
```

25. Now, go to the `TMainForm` declaration and add the following code in the `private` section:

```
private
   FPeople: TObjectList<TPerson>;
   bsPeopleAdapter: TListBindSourceAdapter<TPerson>;
   bsEmailsAdapter: TListBindSourceAdapter<TEmail>;
   procedure PeopleAfterScroll(Adapter: TBindSourceAdapter);
   procedure LoadData;
```

26. Create the `PeopleAfterScroll` and `LoadData` methods in the implementation section (you can use *Ctrl + Shift + C* to generate the empty method body; check all the others keyboard shortcuts at http://docwiki.embarcadero.com/RADStudio/en/Default_Keyboard_Shortcuts):

```
procedure TMainForm.LoadData;
var
   I: Integer;
   P: TPerson;
   X: Integer;
begin
   for I := 1 to 100 do
   begin
      // create a random generated person
      P := TPerson.Create(
        GetRndFirstName,
        GetRndLastName,
        10 + Random(50));

      // add some email addresses (1..3) to the person
      for X := 1 to 1 + Random(3) do
      begin
         P.Emails.Add(
           TEmail.Create(P.FirstName.ToLower + '.' +
                         P.LastName.ToLower +
              '@' + GetRndCountry.Replace(' ', '').ToLower +
              '.com'));
```

```
    end;
    FPeople.Add(P);
  end;
end;

procedure TMainForm.PeopleAfterScroll(
                  Adapter: TBindSourceAdapter);
begin
  bsEmailsAdapter.SetList(
    bsPeopleAdapter.
      List[bsPeopleAdapter.CurrentIndex].Emails, False);
  bsEmails.Active := True;
  bsEmails.First;
end;
```

27. On the main form, create the `FormCreate` and `FormDestroy` event handlers with this code:

    ```
    procedure TMainForm.FormCreate(Sender: TObject);
    begin
      Randomize;
      FPeople := TObjectList<TPerson>.Create(True);
      LoadData;
      bsPeopleAdapter.SetList(FPeople, False);
      bsPeople.Active := True;
    end;

    procedure TMainForm.FormDestroy(Sender: TObject);
    begin
      FPeople.Free;
    end;
    ```

28. Now, show the main form, select **bsPeople**, and create the event handler for the `OnCreateAdapter` event. This event is called when the `TPrototypeBindSource` method has to decide whether to use fake randomly-generated data or your real data. You have to handle this event and plug the code to provide your data. Write the following code in the event handler:

    ```
    procedure TMainForm.bsPeopleCreateAdapter(Sender: TObject;
              var ABindSourceAdapter: TBindSourceAdapter);
    begin
      bsPeopleAdapter := TListBindSourceAdapter<TPerson>.
            Create(self, nil, False);
      ABindSourceAdapter := bsPeopleAdapter;
      bsPeopleAdapter.AfterScroll := PeopleAfterScroll;
    end;
    ```

29. On the main form, select **bsEmails** and create the event handler for the `OnCreateAdapter` event:

    ```
    procedure TMainForm.bsEmailsCreateAdapter(Sender: TObject;
               var ABindSourceAdapter: TBindSourceAdapter);
    begin
      bsEmailsAdapter := TListBindSourceAdapter<TEmail>
                             .Create(self, nil, False);
      ABindSourceAdapter := bsEmailsAdapter;
    end;
    ```

30. If you run the application, you should see a working form showing an M/D relationship, or better a *has a* relationship, because a person has a list of e-mails. Stop it and add a small trick.

31. If you try to add a new e-mail, the new line is added in the **TGrid** component. I hate data entry directly into grids! In some cases, it is a great feature, but in many cases, it only shows a badly designed UI (this is not the case if you are developing a spreadsheet!). So, let's create `TBindSourceNavigator` to show a dialog to add a new e-mail.

32. Select the `TBindSourceNavigator` component named **bnEmails**, create an event handler for the `BeforeAction` event, and then write the following code:

    ```
    procedure TMainForm.bnEmailsBeforeAction(Sender: TObject;
               Button: TNavigateButton);
    var
      email: string;
    begin
      if Button = TNavigateButton.nbInsert then
        if InputQuery('Email', 'New email address', email) then
        begin
          bsEmailsAdapter.List.Add(TEmail.Create(email));
          bsEmails.Refresh; // refresh the emails list
          bsPeople.Refresh; // refresh the email count
          Abort; //inhibit the normal behavior
        end;
    end;
    ```

33. Now, run the application and try to add a new e-mail; you'll see a nice dialog comes up.

34. That's all folks!

How it works...

There are a few concepts involved in LiveBindings, but these concepts must be well understood to create a working application. Let's analyze this application.

Chapter 4

At the beginning, the `TPrototypeBindSource` components are initialized with the `TListBindSource<T>` instances so that they show actual data instead of fake data. Then in the `FormCreate` event handler, you created the actual list of objects that will contain your people and load some data in it using the `LoadData` method. This method loads some random data but in a real application, it should read data from some query or from some web service. This is one of the LiveBindings strengths; you can visualize your data wherever its origin is. You are no more tied to `TDataSet`!

After loading the data, you set the **bsPeople** list of objects to your people and then activated it. This is okay for one single list of data, but how do you handle the M/D relationship?

In the `bsPeople.OnCreateAdapter` event, you set an `AfterScroll` event handler for `bsPeopleAdapter` (the internal adapter used by `TPrototypeBindSource`). This event is called when the selected person changes. So, you can handle the data visualization on the e-mail grid from this event. The code in this event handler is self-explanatory:

```
procedure TMainForm.PeopleAfterScroll(
                  Adapter: TBindSourceAdapter);
begin
  //sets the email object list to the emails of the
  //selected person in the bsPeopleAdapter. The adapter
  //is automatically deactivated when the underling list is
  //changed, so you don't need to set its Active property to False
  bsEmailsAdapter.SetList(
    bsPeopleAdapter.
      List[bsPeopleAdapter.CurrentIndex].Emails, False);
  //here the bsEmails is no more active, let's activate it
  bsEmails.Active := True;
  bsEmails.First;
end;
```

Usually, working with the internal adapter of `TPrototypeBindSource` is a bit messy because you have to write something like this:

```
//sets a new list of objects as data source
(bsPeople.InternalAdapter as TListBindSourceAdapter<TPerson>).
  SetList(MyList);
```

Saving a reference when you are creating the actual adapter in the `OnCreateAdapter` method saves a lot of casting and makes code more readable. There are other solutions, but I really like this one.

There's more...

LiveBindings is a relatively new technology. It has changed a lot since its introduction in Delphi XE2, at least in the high-level components. The good old Delphi programmer seems to not completely understand its power (probably because `TDataSet` along with VCL really does a good job for classic client/server applications), but there is still time to explore the capabilities. However, when you use FireMonkey, LiveBindings is mandatory, so I strongly suggest you try it because, sooner or later, you will have to use it for some mobile stuff or some general FireMonkey applications.

There are many things to say about LiveBindings—we've only scratched the surface. For example, if you are building a big project and you have to handle or show some kind of recurrent entities, such as customers, orders, invoices, or users, you can create a `TListBindSourceAdapter<T>` descendant, compile it in a package, and install it in the tool palette so that every time you require it, you can simply drag and drop it on your data module or form.

See also

Here are some links where you can find more information about LiveBindings:

- *XE3 Visual LiveBindings: User defined objects* at `http://blogs.embarcadero.com/jimtierney/2012/12/11/31961`
- *LiveBindings GridColumns* at `http://www.youtube.com/watch?v=K6Xu90Rtbys`
- *TBindSourceDB* at `http://www.malcolmgroves.com/blog/?p=1072`
- *TAdapterBindSource and binding to Objects* at `http://www.malcolmgroves.com/blog/?p=1084`
- *Updating Objects via an Adapter* at `http://www.malcolmgroves.com/blog/?p=1186`
- *Formatting your Fields* at `http://www.malcolmgroves.com/blog/?p=1226`
- *XE3 Visual LiveBindings: Samples* at `http://blogs.embarcadero.com/jimtierney/2012/10/21/31944`
- If you are interested in the core of LiveBindings, you can read an old article of mine that is still valid at `http://www.danieleteti.it/2011/08/30/in-the-core-of-livebindings-expressions-of-rad-studio-xe2/`

Showing complex vector shapes using paths

One of the biggest advantages of FireMonkey compared to VCL is its vector-based nature. Various visual parts can be created in FireMonkey using vector based graphic (even if in some cases, using a bitmapped approach can be faster). In terms of vectorial graphics, there is a nice language called **Scalable Vector Graphics** (**SVG**) that allows you to define primitive shapes using a set of coordinates and not a raster image. So, you can stretch the image without losing its resolution, because the image is not actually stretched, but completely redrawn using the new coordinates. That's it; the SVG file is made up of coordinates and mathematical formulae to join them.

Inside the SVG language, there is an element called SVG path. The path element is used to define a path. So, what's a path?

A path is a sequence of instructions to draw something using primitives. Think of an SVG path as a language into another language (let's say a sort of internal DSL).

The following commands are available for path data:

- M: This represents the `moveto` command (without drawing)
- L: This represents the `lineto` command (like M but drawing)
- H: This represents the `horizontal lineto` command
- V: This represents the `vertical lineto` command
- C: This represents the `curveto` command
- S: This represents the `smooth curveto` command
- Q: This represents the `quadratic Bézier curve` command
- T: This represents the `smooth quadratic Bézier curveto` command
- A: This represents the `elliptical Arc` command
- Z: This represents the `closepath` command

All of these commands can also be expressed with lowercase letters. Uppercase letters mean absolutely positioned and lowercase means relatively positioned.

So, the path `M50 0 L100 100 L0 100 Z` means:

- Move the pen to X50 Y0
- Draw a line from the current point to X100 Y100
- Draw a line from the current point to X0 Y100
- Close the path drawing a line to the origin point (X150 Y0)

It draws a triangle like the following:

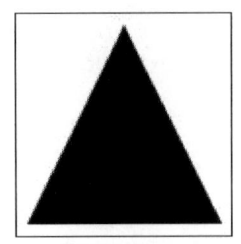

The triangle drawn by the sample path data

Getting ready

In the FireMonkey framework, there is a component called **TPath** (it is defined in the FMX.Objects.pas unit; do not confuse it with the **TPath** component defined in the System.IOUtils.pas unit). The **TPath** component is able to interpret and show an SVG path. In this recipe, you'll see how to use it to draw complex vector shapes and fonts.

Let's say you want to monitor a continuous stream of data, maybe a value read from some kind of hardware or some value related to finance stock quotes. You want fresh data pushed from the right-hand side and oldest data removed from the left-hand side. At any time, you can see the last 20 values scrolling from right to left. This is shown in the following screenshot:

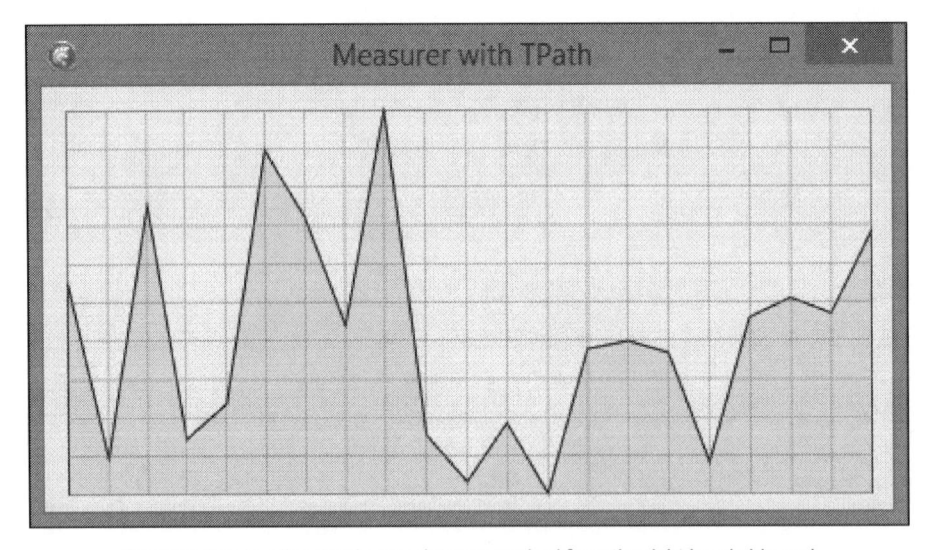

Scrolling data in a line graph; new data are pushed from the right-hand side and old data are removed from the left-hand side

Usually, in order to write something like this, you require some third-party components or you have to write a lot of code to write all the values and axes and deal with proportional issues. Using the **TPath** component, you don't have to do all this! The **TPath** component with a proper SVG PATH is completely in charge to stretch and redraw your graphic in order to fit the drawing area.

How to do it...

Let's create this application step-by-step:

1. Create a new FireMonkey desktop application.
2. Drop a **TPanel** component on to the form. In the **TPanel** component, put a **TPath** component and set its **Align** property to **alClient**. Now, the **TPath** component should fit into the **TPanel** component.
3. Drop another **TPath** component onto the first one and again, set its **Align** property to **alClient**.
4. Now you should have **TPanel** with two nested **TPath** components inside it.
5. Show the structure of the form (*Shift + Alt + F11*).
6. Name the first **TPath** component as `PathValues` and the second **TPath** component as `PathAxis`.
7. Drop a **TTimer** component on the form and double-click on it. Into the `OnTimer` event handler, write the following code:

    ```
    procedure TMainForm.Timer1Timer(Sender: TObject);
    begin
      FValuesQueue.Add(Trunc(Random * 100));
      RefreshGraph;
    end;
    ```

8. Set the **Timer Interval** property to **50**.
9. Now, go to the code editor and declare a private form instance variable:

    ```
    FValuesQueue: TList<Integer>;
    ```

10. Create the `FormCreate` and `FormDestroy` event handlers and fill them with the following code:

    ```
    procedure TMainForm.FormCreate(Sender: TObject);
    var
      I: Integer;
      svggrid: string;
    begin
      FValuesQueue := TList<Integer>.Create;
      for I := 0 to 19 do
    ```

```
      FValuesQueue.Add(0);

   svggrid := '';
   for I := 0 to FValuesQueue.Count - 1 do
      svggrid := svggrid + ' M' + I.ToString + ',0 V100';
   for I := 1 to 10 do
      svggrid := svggrid + ' M0,' +
                   IntToStr(I * 10) + ' H20';
   PathAxis.Data.Data := svggrid;
end;

procedure TMainForm.FormDestroy(Sender: TObject);
begin
   FValuesQueue.Free;
end;
```

11. So far, you've declared and initialized your data container (the `TList<Integer>` item named `FValuesQueue`); now let's do something with its data. Create a private procedure named `RefreshGraph` and fill it with the following code:

```
procedure TMainForm.RefreshGraph;
var
   I: Integer;
   svg: string;
begin
   svg := 'M0,100 ';
   if FValuesQueue.Count > 19 then
   begin
      svg := svg + 'L0,' +
             (100 - FValuesQueue.First).ToString;
      FValuesQueue.Delete(0); //remove the first
   end;

   for I := 0 to FValuesQueue.Count - 1 do
   begin
      svg := svg + ' L' + I.ToString + ',' +
             (100 - FValuesQueue[I]).ToString;
   end;

   svg := svg + ' L' +
      IntToStr(FValuesQueue.Count - 1) + ' 100 ';
   PathValues.Data.Data := svg;
end;
```

12. Run the application.

Chapter 4

13. Are you disappointed with the performance? In this case, the debugger load on the execution speed is heavy. So, to check the real drawing speed, run it without the debugger (*Shift + Ctrl + F9*).
14. You should now see the graph scrolling at a good speed.

How it works...

The architecture is simple—the timer is the (fake) data producer that fills the list. Then, the list is used to draw the graph. After drawing the graph, the first list element is removed, waiting for the next one.

In a real-world application, some tuning may be necessary and in this case, a classic producer/consumer pattern is more suited to do this compared to a simple **TTimer**. However, in this sample, a normal **TTimer** component is enough.

A good thing to note is that you have a fixed coordinate system when drawing the values in the graph. You don't have to worry about form size, relative or absolute coordinates, and so on. All the details are handled by the **TPath** component.

So, if you'd like to add another scrolling graph of a different size, you could use the same `SVG PATH` data to show the same graph on another area.

Let's add another `TPanel->TPath->TPath` triad on the form and make the **TPanel** component bigger than the previous one. With a little change in the code (the full code is available), you can have something like this:

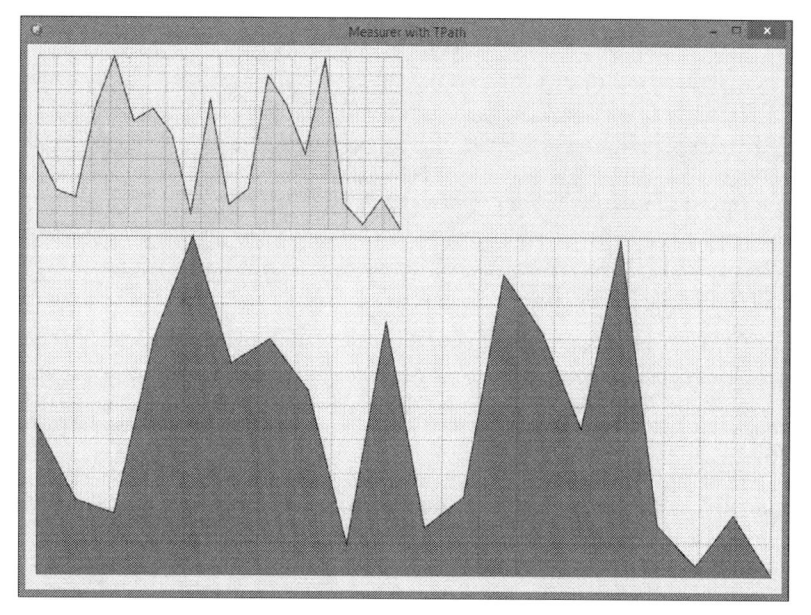

Another scrolling graph showing the same values added without changing the drawing code

There's more...

The `SVG PATH` data can be very useful. If you require complex `SVG PATH` data, I suggest that you use a proper editor to generate the path. There is a nice online editor that can generate this kind of information called Method Draw and it's available at `http://editor.method.ac/`. The `SVG PATH` data can be also used to drive animations using the `TPathAnimation` component.

The producer/consumer cited in this recipe is a classic concurrency pattern. You can find more information on this at `http://javarevisited.blogspot.it/2012/02/producer-consumer-design-pattern-with.html`.

Using FireMonkey in a VCL application

As you probably know, VCL is incompatible with FireMonkey. What does this mean? Embarcadero explains in the DocWiki:

> "FireMonkey (FMX) and the Visual Component Library (VCL) are not compatible and should not be used together in the same module. That is, a module should be exclusively one or the other, either FireMonkey or VCL. The incompatibility is caused by framework differences between FireMonkey (FMX) and VCL."

However, there is still something that can be done to use FireMonkey functionalities in a VCL application.

It's very probable that a VCL application could gain benefits by using some components or functionalities present only in the FireMonkey framework. So what could be the solution? One solution is to create a Windows DLL that contains all the FireMonkey code and exposes a set of raw functions to access them. Then, the VCL application can load the DLL and call the exposed functions. Let's see this in action.

This recipe requires familiarity with some advanced Delphi concepts, so there will not be a step-by-step section; I'll only talk about the project code.

How to do it...

Let's begin!

1. Open the recipe project group called `UsingFMXfromVCL.groupproj`. The group contains two projects:
    - A VCL application (`vclmainproject.exe`) that is your legacy application
    - A DLL project (`fmxproject.dll`) that contains all the FireMonkey stuff

Chapter 4

2. To get an idea about the projects, navigate to **Project | Build all Projects**, select the `vclmainproject.exe` file, and hit *F9* to run it. The `fmxproject.dll` file has been compiled in the same folder of `vclmainproject.exe`. You should see the form shown here:

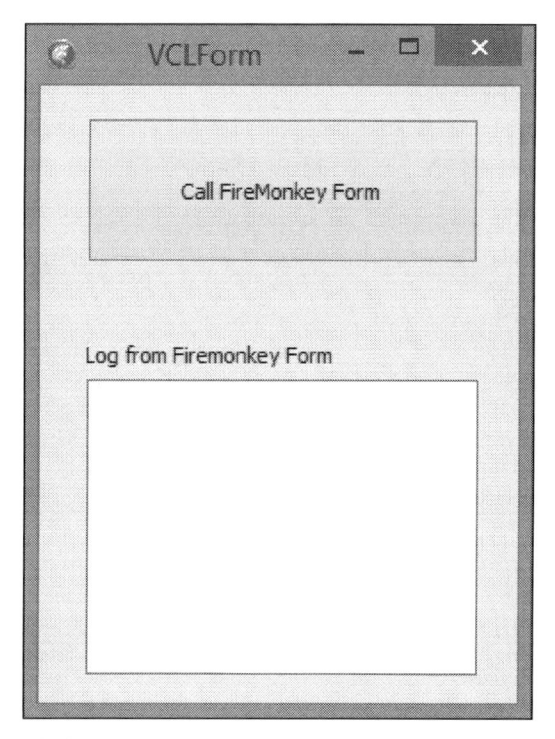

The VCL form that will use the DLL containing the FireMonkey code

3. By clicking on the **Call FireMonkey Form** button, you can call the FireMonkey DLL that will show a FireMonkey form that is able to send to the main form some information using a callback (we'll talk about this in a moment). The callback makes your project a little bit difficult, but being able to send something to the caller is a fundamental part of any integration.

4. If you click on the button and play with the FMX controls, you should get something like this:

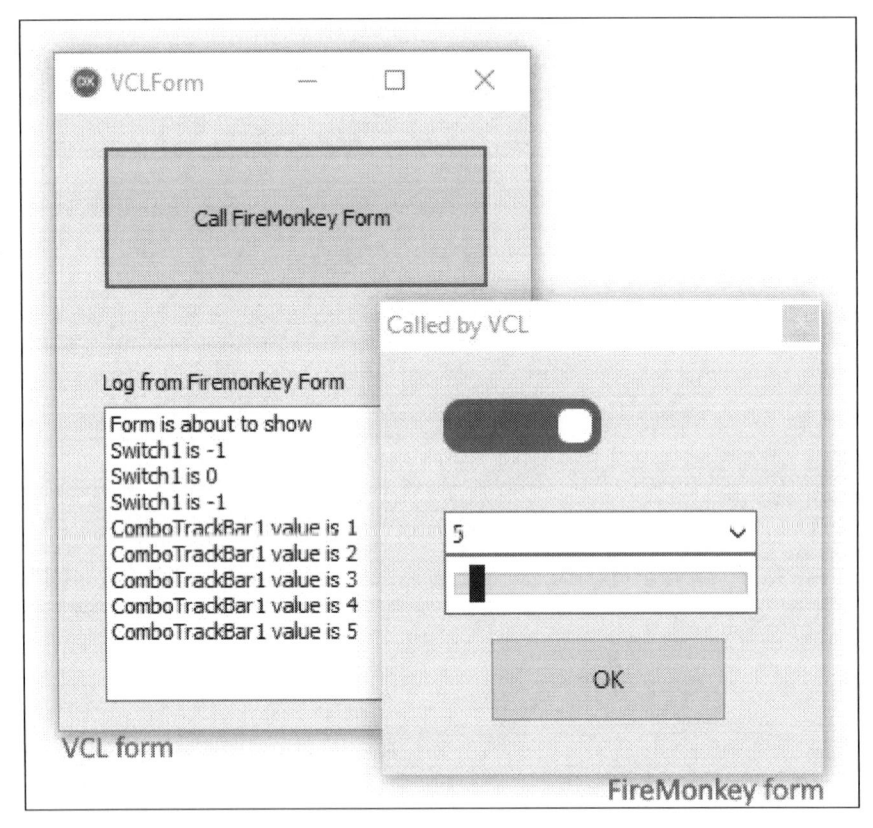

The FireMonkey form used by the VCL application

How it works...

The `CommonsU.pas` unit is shared between the VCL and FMX projects and contains the declaration for the callback function, as shown here:

type
    TDLLCallback = **procedure**(**const** Value: String);

The `DLLImportU.pas` unit is used only by the VCL project (because it needs to import the `DLL` functions). It is really simple and refers to the `TDLLCallBack` declaration:

unit DLLImportU;

interface

uses

```
  CommonsU;

procedure Execute(const Caption: String;
         Callback: TDLLCallback); stdcall; external 'fmxproject';
```

implementation

end.

These two files are the *bridge* between the VCL project and the FMX project. Now, let's see how the VCL project calls the FireMonkey DLL.

Using the **Project Manager**, select the VCL project main form. The `Button Click` event handler calls the `Execute` external function with the following code:

```
procedure MyCallBack(const Value: String);
begin
   VCLForm.ListBox1.Items.Add(Value);
   VCLForm.ListBox1.Update;
end;

procedure TVCLForm.btnCallFMXClick(Sender: TObject);
begin
   Execute('Called by VCL', MyCallBack);
end;
```

Notice that the `MyCallBack` procedure is not a form method, but a simple procedure. This is the reason because inside it I used instance name of the form, `VCLForm`, and cannot use the implicit `Self` reference. Also, a normal string and a function pointer are passed to the `Execute` function. Notice that the function pointer is `MyCallBack` and not `MyCallBack()` (with parenthesis, it means call the procedure and without parenthesis it means the address of).

The VCL project doesn't require further explanation. Let's switch to the FMX DLL. Using the Project Manager, select the `fmxproject.dll` file and navigate to **Project | View Source**.

The `library` project file contains the exported functions and the startup code to show the FMX form. Its code is shown here:

```
library fmxproject;

uses
   System.ShareMem, Winapi.Windows,
   System.SysUtils, System.Classes,
   FMXMainForm in 'FMXMainForm.pas' {Form1},
```

```
    CommonsU in 'CommonsU.pas';

{$R *.res}

procedure Execute(const Caption: String;
                  Callback: TDLLCallback); stdcall;
var
  frm: TForm1;
begin
  frm := TForm1.Create(nil);
  try
    frm.Caption := Caption; //use the passed string as Caption
    frm.FCallback := Callback; //link callback as form property
    frm.ShowModal;
  finally
    frm.Free;
  end;
end;

{ This is exported function that will be used by the VCL form }
exports Execute;

begin

end.
```

As you can see, the `callback` pointer has been assigned to a `form` property to be accessible from it. How will the FMX form use the `callback` pointer? In this recipe, it uses the `callback` pointer to send some information about the components on it to the main VCL form.

This is the relevant code of the main VCL form:

```
type
  TForm1 = class(TForm)
    btnClose: TButton;
    Switch1: TSwitch;
    ComboTrackBar1: TComboTrackBar;
    procedure btnCloseClick(Sender: TObject);
    procedure Switch1Switch(Sender: TObject);
    procedure ComboTrackBar1Change(Sender: TObject);
    procedure FormShow(Sender: TObject);
    procedure FormClose(Sender: TObject;
                        var Action: TCloseAction);
```

```
    private

    public
       {This is the function pointer to the main VCL form callback}
       FCallback: TDLLCallback;
    end;

implementation

{$R *.fmx}

procedure TForm1.ComboTrackBar1Change(Sender: TObject);
begin
  //send the value of TComboTrackBar
  FCallback('ComboTrackBar1 value is ' +
            ComboTrackBar1.Value.ToString);
end;

procedure TForm1.FormClose(Sender: TObject;
                           var Action: TCloseAction);
begin
  //inform the main form about FMX form closing
  FCallback('Form is about to close');
end;

procedure TForm1.FormShow(Sender: TObject);
begin
  //inform the main form about FMX form showing
  FCallback('Form is about to show');
end;

procedure TForm1.Switch1Switch(Sender: TObject);
begin
  //inform the main form about the state of the Switch
  FCallback('Switch1 is ' + Switch1.IsChecked.ToString);
end;
```

The FMX-side code is not complex, and you can use whatever complex data structure you want to send information from the FMX form to the VCL form. A good and simple solution for this is to define a simple textual protocol to allow a single callback to bring multiple types of information. For this kind of thing, I used to use a JSON-serialized string. If the data that you have to transfer is a lot, or the data transfer rate is critical, you can use a specific record and use a pointer to it to share information between the `dll` and the main program (in this way you save the JSON generate/parse time). If the values sent by the callback are many, you can queue the values and process them as soon as possible; this is something like the producer/consumer design pattern.

There's more...

This recipe follows the *official* approach and uses two different projects (one VCL and one FireMonkey) to use the FireMonkey framework from a VCL application.

What if you have a legacy project where you'd like to use a FireMonkey DLL, but the legacy project is not in Delphi VCL (let's say it is in C#, Visual C++, Python, or any other language that can load a DLL)? You can still use the same approach, but you cannot use Delphi-specific data types. So your strings should be `PChar` and so on. You can find more information on this at `http://delphi.about.com/od/objectpascalide/a/dlldelphi.htm`.

Just to be clear, keep in mind that mixing FireMonkey and VCL forms in the same application isn't officially supported. However, there are a number of libraries that aim to integrate VCL and FireMonkey forms in the same project.

Here's a short list in no particular order:

- *TFireMonkeyContainer* at `https://parnassus.co/open-source/tfiremonkeycontainer/`
- *MonkeyMixer* by *LaKraven Studios Ltd* at `https://github.com/LaKraven/MonkeyMixer`
- *Delphisorcery* at `https://bitbucket.org/sglienke/dsharp` (using `DSharp.Windows.FMXAdapter.pas`)

In the recipe, you used a function pointer as a callback. If you want to know more about this type and other types of callback, check the link: `http://www.delphi-central.com/callback.aspx`.

Chapter 4

Reinventing your GUI also known as mastering Firemonkey controls, shapes, and effects

As you have surely understood at this point, FireMonkey is a completely new graphic library, which allows a completely new way to think about your GUI. During my FireMonkey training, one of the first exercises that I give to the class is: "Please, look for the strangest FireMonkey control in the Tool Palette." It is quite a strange exercise but the reason is really important: you must realize as soon as possible that FireMonkey is not a cross platform VCL, it is a new beast with new possibilities and new things to know. So you have to rethink your GUI architecture because many *patterns* used in the last 5, 10, 15, or more years of VCL development, now maybe simply obsolete or are no more the best things to do. For instance, you have to display a pie chart with some user interaction and some nice visual effects. When the user moves the mouse over a pie slice, the slice gets highlighted and some information is shown to the user. How can you achieve that? In VCL, there are two ways: write your own code (a lot of) or use a third-party control. In FireMonkey, there is also a third way: use the primitive shapes to create it using no third-party controls and a very little amount of code. This is a recurring pattern in FireMonkey. This is the reason because probably your FireMonkey application needs a lot fewer third-party controls that the VCL one. To show you how this is possible, in this recipe we'll create a simple pie chart with such aspect and user behavior. Here's a screenshot of the application we'll build:

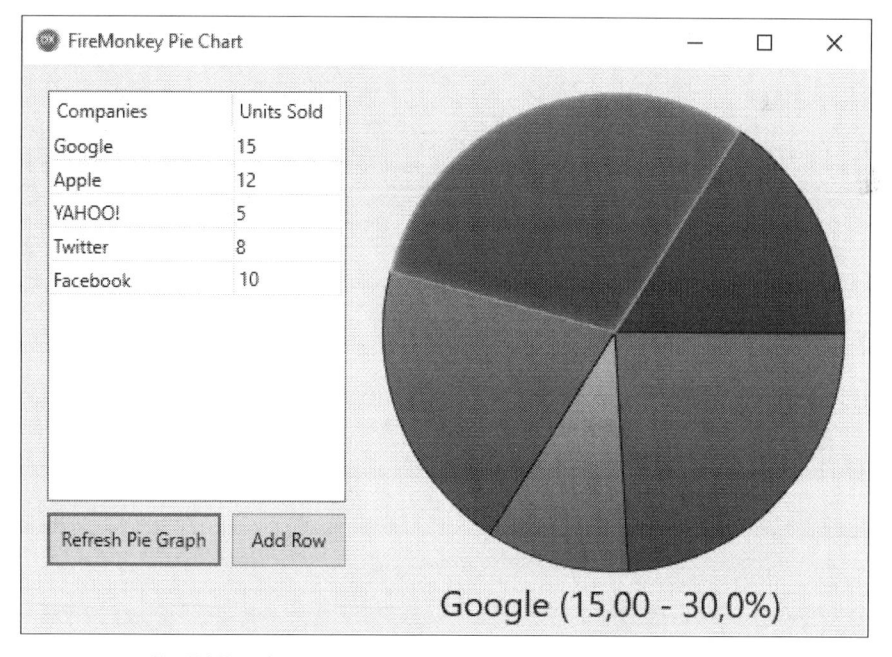

Fig. 7.1 The pie chart generated using only FireMonkey components

Getting ready

The first steps to design your GUI is to slow down and think about it. We need a pie chart isn't it? So, is there a primitive shape packaged as component in the FireMonkey library able to draw a slice of a pie? Yes, there is the `TPie` control. But we need a variable number of slices, and all the slices must be stacked one over the other to make a full pie. Where we could put these dynamically created slices? Obviously, in a `TLayout`! This is the basic idea behind the recipe. Let's talk about the recipe code in detail.

How it works...

Open the *Reinventing your GUI also known as mastering Firemonkey controls, shapes, and effects* of *Chapter 4*, named `PieChart.dproj`. The main form is quite simple; there is a `TStringGrid` to allow the user to write the data, a `TButton`, which actually starts the (re)generation of the chart, another button to add a new row in the grid, a `TLabel` to show some additional information when the user moves the mouse over the single slice, and the `TLayout` we already talked about. Here's the main form at design time:

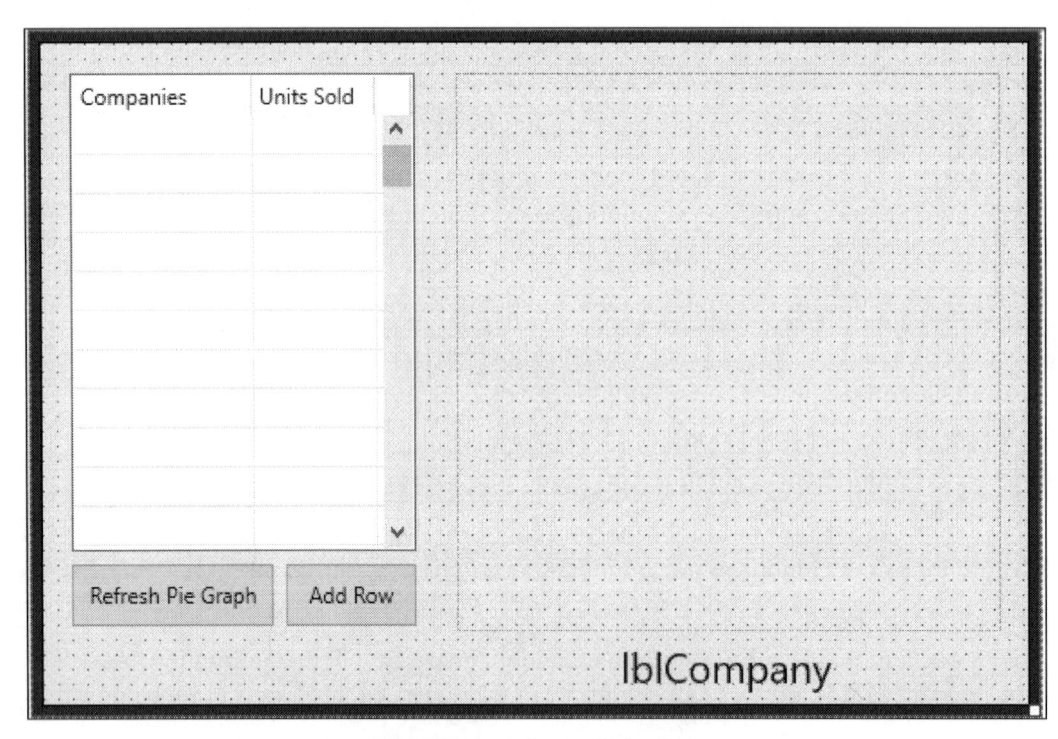

Fig. 7.2 The main form at design time

In the `FormCreate` event handler, the initialization code creates the `TDictionary<String, Extended>`, which will contain the data represented in the chart. Moreover, considering this is a sample, the data is generated randomly and used to fill the grid. Here's the `FormCreate` code:

```
procedure TMainForm.FormCreate(Sender: TObject);
begin
  Randomize;
  FDataDict := TDictionary<String, Extended>.Create;
  sgData.RowCount := 5;
  sgData.BeginUpdate;
  try
    sgData.Cells[0, 0] := 'Google';
    sgData.Cells[1, 0] := RandomRange(2, 20).ToString;
    sgData.Cells[0, 1] := 'Apple';
    sgData.Cells[1, 1] := RandomRange(2, 20).ToString;
    sgData.Cells[0, 2] := 'YAHOO!';
    sgData.Cells[1, 2] := RandomRange(2, 20).ToString;
    sgData.Cells[0, 3] := 'Twitter';
    sgData.Cells[1, 3] := RandomRange(2, 20).ToString;
    sgData.Cells[0, 4] := 'Facebook';
    sgData.Cells[1, 4] := RandomRange(2, 20).ToString;
  finally
    sgData.EndUpdate;
  end;
  lblCompany.Text := '';
end;
```

As you can see, the generated data is about some companies so that each row in the grid will contain the **Company name** and **Units Sold** of something. Now, interesting things happen under the **Refresh Pie Chart** button. Here's the code:

```
procedure TMainForm.btnRefreshPieClick(Sender: TObject);
var
    LPie: TPie;
    LCurrAngle, LGrad: Single;
    LIdx: Integer;
    LRefColor: TAlphaColor;
    LPair: TPair<String, Extended>;
begin
  // Loads the data from the string grid and put them in the
  // dictionary using the company name for the key and the
  // units sold as the value.
```

```
  LoadData(FDataDict);

  // Get the total for all the companies using an
//higher order function
  FTotalValue := HigherOrder
    .Reduce<Extended>(FDataDict.Values.ToArray,
      function(A, B: Extended): Extended
      begin
          Result := A + B;
      end, 0);

  // remove all the TPie already present into the TLayout
   // The first time there aren't child, but from the second time
   // yes, so let's remove all the TPie from the TLayout
  lytPie.DeleteChildren;

  LCurrAngle := 0;
  LIdx := 0;
  lytPie.BeginUpdate;
  try
    //looping through the dictionary and create each TPie
    for LPair in FDataDict do
    begin
      //some math to know how many degree each pie slide must be
      LGrad := 360 * LPair.Value / FTotalValue;

      //Build the pie slice, che the BuildPieSlice for details
      LPie := BuildPieSlice(LPair.Key);
      LPie.StartAngle := LCurrAngle;
      LPie.EndAngle := LCurrAngle + LGrad;
      LCurrAngle := LCurrAngle + LGrad;
      LRefColor := GetColor(LIdx);

      //Setup some nice gradients color to give
      //a sort of fake 3D effect to each slice
      SetupGradient(LPie.Fill, LRefColor);

      //Let's give some dynamicity to the chart
      //with some effects
      InjectEffects(LPie, GetColor(LIdx));
      Inc(LIdx);
    end;
  finally
    lytPie.EndUpdate;
  end;
end;
```

There's quite a lot of stuff in this method! Let's analyze the interesting parts of it.

After having loaded the data into the dictionary, we're using a higher order function to summarize the total for the units sold by all the companies. This function is a part of the *Fun with anonymous methods – using higher-order functions* of *Chapter 2*. It is a Reduce function, which is used here to do a sum. So that the result of the function is the total of all the units sold.

Having the total we can start with the loop to create each `TPie` and add it into the `TLayout`. Each `TPie` starts its slice where the previous one ends. So that the nth slice has its `StartAngle` equal to the `EndAngle` of the previous slice.

Here's the code for the `BuildPieSlice` method and the other methods used by it:

```
function TMainForm.BuildPieSlice(AIdentifier: String): TPie;
begin
  //create the pie as child of TLayout
  Result := TPie.Create(lytPie);
  Result.Parent := lytPie;
  //setup some events to give interactivity
  Result.OnMouseEnter := OnPieEnter;
  Result.OnMouseLeave := OnPieLeave;
  //We need the company name to which each pie is referred to
  Result.TagString := AIdentifier;
  //Align to the parent so that all the TPie are aligned
  //and stacked one over the other
  Result.Align := TAlignLayout.Contents;
end;

procedure TMainForm.OnPieEnter(Sender: TObject);
var
  LKey: String;
  LPie: TPie;
  LValue, LPercValue: Extended;
begin
  LPie := Sender as TPie;
  //move the current TPie to the front so that the effects
  //applied effect are not covered by the other TPie
  LPie.BringToFront;
  LKey := LPie.TagString;
  //gets the value for the company to which the pie
  //refers to and calculate the percentage over the total
  LValue := FDataDict.Items[LKey];
  LPercValue := LValue / FTotalValue * 100;
  //display the data in the TLabel
```

```pascal
    lblCompany.Text := Format('%s (%.2f - %2.1f%%)',
      [LKey, LValue, LPercValue]);
end;

procedure TMainForm.OnPieLeave(Sender: TObject);
begin
    //clear the TLabel when the mouse leave the TPie
    lblCompany.Text := '';
end;
```

The color of each `TPie` is provided by a function contained in the `ColorsUtils.pas` unit. This unit contains a static array of colors and some functions to manipulate them. Here's the code:

```pascal
const
    Colors: TArray<TAlphaColor> = [$FF4285F4,$FFFBBC05,
          $FF34A853,$FFEA4335,$FFA90FF4,$FF9F3C00];

function GetColor(AIndex: Integer): TAlphaColor;
begin
    //Gets a color from the list
    Result := Colors[AIndex mod Length(Colors)];
end;

function GetDarkerColorByPercent(AColor: TAlphaColor;
          ADarkerPercent: Integer): TAlphaColor;
begin
    //returns a color which is a
    //percentage darker than the input
    Result := InterpolateColor(AColor, TAlphaColorRec.Black,
      ADarkerPercent / 100);
end;

function GetLighterColorByPercent(AColor: TAlphaColor;
          ADarkerPercent: Integer): TAlphaColor;
begin
    //returns a color which is a
    //percentage lighter than the input
    Result := InterpolateColor(AColor, TAlphaColorRec.White,
      ADarkerPercent / 100);
end;
```

Nothing complex here, but the RTL `InterpolateColor` function is quite interesting. This function is used by the `TColorAnimation` effect (and other classes) and has this prototype:

```
function InterpolateColor(const Start, Stop: TAlphaColor;
T: Single): TAlphaColor;
```

The function interpolates color value between colors `Start` and `Stop` at time moment `T`. So when `T` = 0, the result is equal to `Start` and when `T` = 1, the result is equal to `Stop`. Interesting, but we need a function that is able to create a lighter or a darker color, starting from one given color. How can we use the `InterpolateColor` to do that? Quite simple.

What is the darkest color in the world? Black (which, as you know, strictly speaking is not even a color). So if I need to create a color which is 20 percent darker than standard red, I can use `InterpolateColor` to create a new color that *tends* to be dark but it is only at 20 percent of the transition. The code looks like the following:

```
TwentyPercDarker := InterpolateColor(
TAlphaColorRec.Red,
TAlphaColorRec.Black,
   0.2);
```

We use the same approach to create a lighter color. What's the lightest color in the world? White! So the code here is:

```
TwentyPercLighter := InterpolateColor(
TAlphaColorRec.Red,
TAlphaColorRec.White,
   0.2);
```

Simple and effective!

There are two more interesting methods to explain in the main form. The first one is `SetupGradient`. Given a `TBrush` and a reference color, this method sets up the brush to use the color gradient, which starts from the reference color and ends at a color 50 percent darker:

```
procedure TMainForm.SetupGradient(ABrush: TBrush;
                                  ARefColor: TAlphaColor);
begin
   ABrush.Kind := TBrushKind.Gradient;
   ABrush.Gradient.Color := ARefColor;
   ABrush.Gradient.Color1 :=
      GetDarkerColorByPercent(ARefColor, 50);
end;
```

The last method is `InjectEffects`, which adds effects and animations to the `TFmxObject` passed in. These effects are triggered when the mouse moves over the control and are:

- An inner glow
- A color animation of the Stroke, from black to a reference color
- A size animation of the Stroke thickness to make the border more evident

Here's the code which inject the effect to the `TFmxObject` passed in

```
procedure TMainForm.InjectEffects(AComponent: TFmxObject;
                                  ARefColor: TAlphaColor);
var
   LEffect: TInnerGlowEffect;
   LColorAnimation: TColorAnimation;
   LBoldAnimation: TFloatAnimation;
begin
   // Glow effect when MouseOver
   LEffect := TInnerGlowEffect.Create(AComponent);
   LEffect.Enabled := False;
   LEffect.Trigger := 'IsMouseOver=True';
   LEffect.Parent := AComponent;
   LEffect.GlowColor := TAlphaColorRec.White;
   LEffect.Opacity := 0.5;
   LEffect.Softness := 0.5;

   // Stroke.Color animation when MouseOver
   LColorAnimation := TColorAnimation.Create(AComponent);
   LColorAnimation.PropertyName := 'Stroke.Color';
   LColorAnimation.Enabled := False;
   LColorAnimation.Trigger := 'IsMouseOver=True';
   LColorAnimation.TriggerInverse := 'IsMouseOver=False';
   LColorAnimation.Parent := AComponent;
   LColorAnimation.StartValue := TAlphaColorRec.Black;
   LColorAnimation.StopValue :=
      GetLighterColorByPercent(ARefColor, 20);

   // Stroke.Thickness animation when MouseOver
   LBoldAnimation := TFloatAnimation.Create(AComponent);
   LBoldAnimation.PropertyName := 'Stroke.Thickness';
   LBoldAnimation.Enabled := False;
   LBoldAnimation.Trigger := 'IsMouseOver=True';
   LBoldAnimation.TriggerInverse := 'IsMouseOver=False';
   LBoldAnimation.Parent := AComponent;
   LBoldAnimation.StartValue := 1;
   LBoldAnimation.StopValue := 2;
end;
```

Chapter 4

With some code and a bit of cleverness, we've created a not-so-bad pie chart using only the basic FireMonkey shapes, effects, and animation. The same concepts can be used in other situations. For instance, now that we know how to create this pie chart, how difficult could it be to create a histogram? Very simple! You have to use `TRectangle` instead of `TPie` and linear distance instead of degrees! Yes, FireMonkey is very flexible and really pays back the time spent to get confident with it.

Now, launch the program, click on the **Refresh Pie Chart** button and see the chart. Move the mouse over the slices and see how the behaviors implemented make the GUI nice to see. You can also add a new row in the grid, put other data, and hit the **Refresh Pie Chart** button once more to see how it changes.

There's more...

It's quite important to know all the layouts available in FireMonkey. As the Embarcadero documentation says:

> "FireMonkey layouts are containers for other graphical objects that can be used to build complex interfaces with visual appeal. The FireMonkey layouts extend the functionality of TControl to control the arrangement, sizing, and scaling of their child controls, and offer the possibility to manipulate a group of controls as a whole."

In this recipe, we spoke about the basic `TLayout`; however, there are a lot of layouts. Here's a link to understand the basics about them: `http://docwiki.embarcadero.com/RADStudio/en/FireMonkey_Layouts_Strategies`.

The way you arrange controls inside the layouts is also important. This link can help you get in touch with the basics of FireMonkey: `http://docwiki.embarcadero.com/RADStudio/en/Arranging_FireMonkey_Controls`.

5
The Thousand Faces of Multithreading

In this chapter, we will cover the following topics:

- Synchronizing shared resources with `TMonitor`
- Talking with the main thread using a thread-safe queue
- Synchronizing multiple threads using `TEvent`
- Displaying a measure on a 2D graph like an oscilloscope
- Using tasks to make your customer happier
- Monitoring things using futures
- Parallelize using the parallel for

Introduction

Multithreading can be your biggest problem if you cannot handle it with care. One of the fathers of the Delphi compiler used to say:

> *"New programmers are drawn to multithreading like moths to flame, with similar results."*
>
> – Danny Thorpe

The Thousand Faces of Multithreading

In this chapter, we will discuss some of the main techniques to handle single or multiple background threads. We'll talk about shared resource synchronization and thread-safe queues and events. The last three recipes will talk about the **Parallel Programming Library** introduced in Delphi XE7, and I hope that you will love it as much as I love it. Multithreaded programming is a huge topic. So, after reading this chapter, although you will not become a master of it, you will surely be able to approach the concept of multithreaded programming with confidence and will have the basics to jump on to more specific stuff when (and if) you require them.

Synchronizing shared resources with TMonitor

`TMonitor` is a record used to synchronize threads. Just to be clear, we are talking about `System.TMonitor`, not `Vcl.Forms.TMonitor`.

Since Delphi 2009, the `TObject` instance size has been doubled to make room for an additional 4 bytes. What are these 4 bytes for? They provide `TMonitor` support!

Now, every `TObject` descendant can be used as a lock. The type that allows this is the `System.TMonitor` record, which implements a generic monitor synchronization structure.

Getting ready

In this recipe, you'll face one of the classic multithreading problems—concurrent access to a shared file. Specifically, you'll have a lot of threads writing some information on a file—the same file—and all the threads have to be synchronized for this. Otherwise, the file will not be accessible due to locking, which will cause exceptions in your program code. This problem can be solved in a lot of ways, but `TMonitor` offers the simplest solution. Let's start.

How to do it...

Follow these step-by-step instructions to synchronize shared resources with `TMonitor`:

1. Create a new **VCL Forms Application** (navigate to **File | New | VCL Forms Application**).
2. Drop a **TButton**, **TListBox**, and **TTimer** component on the form.
3. Name the **TButton** component as `btnStart` and change the value of **Caption** to `Multiple writes on a shared file`.

4. Add a new unit to the project, call it **FileWriterThreadU.pas**, and add the following code to it:

```
unit FileWriterThreadU;

interface

uses
   System.Classes, System.SyncObjs,
   System.SysUtils, System.IOUtils;

type
   TThreadHelper = class helper for TThread
   public
      function WaitFor(
ATimeout: Cardinal): LongWord; platform;
   end;

   TFileWriterThread = class(TThread)
   private
      FStreamWriter: TStreamWriter;
   protected
      procedure Execute; override;
   public
      constructor Create(
AStreamWriter: TStreamWriter);
   end;

implementation

{$IF Defined(MSWINDOWS)}
uses
   Winapi.Windows;
{$IFEND}

constructor TFileWriterThread.Create(
AStreamWriter: TStreamWriter);
begin
   FStreamWriter := AStreamWriter;
   inherited Create(False);
end;

procedure TFileWriterThread.Execute;
var
   I: Integer;
```

```
      NumLines: Integer;
begin
  inherited;
  NumLines := 11 + Random(50);
  for I := 1 to NumLines do
  begin
    TThread.Sleep(200);
    //here we are locking the shared resource
    TMonitor.Enter(FStreamWriter);
    try
      FStreamWriter.WriteLine(
Format('THREAD %5d - ROW %2d',
[TThread.CurrentThread.ThreadID, I]));
    finally
      //unlock the shared resource
      TMonitor.Exit(FStreamWriter);
    end;
    if Terminated then
      Break;
  end;
end;

function TThreadHelper.WaitFor(
ATimeout: Cardinal): LongWord;
begin
{$IF Defined(MSWINDOWS)}
  Result := WaitForSingleObject(Handle, ATimeout);
{$ELSE}
  raise Exception.Create('Available only on MS Windows');
{$IFEND}
end;

initialization

Randomize; // we'll use Random function in the thread

end.
```

5. Go back to the form and add the following units in the `interface` `uses` section:
   - System.Generics.Collections
   - FileWriterThreadU

6. In the `private` section of the form, declare the following variables:

   ```
   private
     FOutputFile: TStreamWriter;
     FRunningThreads: TObjectList<TFileWriterThread>;
   ```

7. In the `FormCreate` and `FormClose` event handlers, add the following code:

   ```
   procedure TMainForm.FormCreate(Sender: TObject);
   begin
     FRunningThreads := TObjectList<TFileWriterThread>.Create;
     FOutputFile := TStreamWriter.Create(
       TFileStream.Create('OutputFile.txt',
         fmCreate or fmShareDenyWrite));
   end;

   procedure TMainForm.FormClose(Sender: TObject;
     var Action: TCloseAction);
   var
     Th: TFileWriterThread;
   begin
     for Th in FRunningThreads do
       Th.Terminate;
     FRunningThreads.Free; // Implicit WaitFor...
     FOutputFile.Free;
   end;
   ```

   With the preceding code, you created a data structure to hold the thread list and file access. The `FOutputFile` variable is your shared resource for all the threads.

8. Create the `OnClick` event handler for `btnStart` and add the following code to it:

   ```
   procedure TMainForm.btnStartClick(Sender: TObject);
   var
     I: Integer;
     Th: TFileWriterThread;
   begin
     for I := 1 to 10 do
     begin
       Th := TFileWriterThread.Create(FOutputFile);
       FRunningThreads.Add(Th);
     end;
   end;
   ```

   The preceding code creates 10 threads that will contend for the shared resource `FOutputFile`.

9. Now, threads can run without problems but the UI doesn't have any information about their jobs. We want to check whether a thread is still running or is already terminated. So, let's create the event handler for the `Timer1.OnTimer` event using the following code:

```
procedure TMainForm.Timer1Timer(Sender: TObject);
var
  Th: TFileWriterThread;
begin
  ListBox1.Items.BeginUpdate;
  try
    ListBox1.Items.Clear;
    for Th in FRunningThreads do
    begin
      if Th.WaitFor(0) = WAIT_TIMEOUT then
        ListBox1.Items.Add(
          Format('%5d RUNNING', [Th.ThreadID]))
      else
        ListBox1.Items.Add(
          Format('%5d TERMINATED', [Th.ThroadID]))
    end;
  finally
    ListBox1.Items.EndUpdate;
  end;
end;
```

The preceding code will iterate over the thread list and check the state of each of them. The resultant check will fill the `ListBox1` component.

10. Run the application and click on the button (the only button present on the form). You should see something like the following:

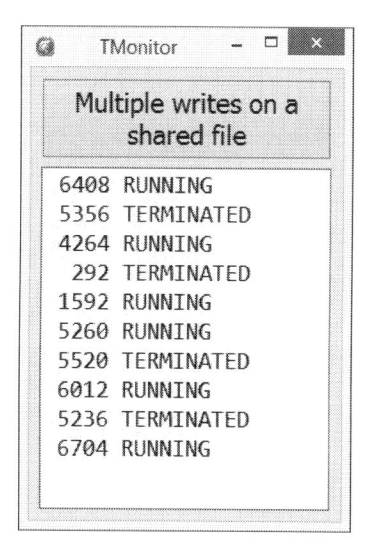

The main form showing thread statuses

11. `ListBox1` contains thread statuses. When all threads terminate, you can open the file and see that each of them wrote information without interference from the others; no crashes, no data loss. Your multithreading application is working alright.

12. If you want to see the file while the threads are writing it, you can use one of the Unix tail clone options for Windows suggested in the *Creating a Windows service* recipe of *Chapter 1, Delphi Basics*.

How it works...

The `btnStart` event creates 10 threads and puts each of them in a simple generic list declared as `TObjectList<TFileWriterThread>`. This list will be used to iterate over the threads when terminating or checking the status of threads. Threads are not configured with `FreeOnTerminate` because we require a live reference to check their status.

The real work is done in the `Execute` method of `TFileWriterThread`. Let's check it out:

```
procedure TFileWriterThread.Execute;
var
  I: Integer;
  NumLines: Integer;
begin
  inherited;
  //decide how many numbers to write
  NumLines := 11 + Random(50);
  for I := 1 to NumLines do
  begin
```

```
      //wait a bit of time to simulate a higher workload
      TThread.Sleep(200);
      //acquire the lock on FStreamWriter.
      TMonitor.Enter(FStreamWriter);
      try
        //only one thread at time can execute this code
        FStreamWriter.WriteLine(
          Format('THREAD %5d - ROW %2d',
            [TThread.CurrentThread.ThreadID, I]));
      finally
        //Be sure to release the lock. Otherwise all threads
        //will hang waiting for acquire the lock
        TMonitor.Exit(FStreamWriter);
      end;
      //if thread is terminated exit from the loop
      if Terminated then
        Break;
    end;
end;
```

Another important piece of code is under the `TTimer` event handler:

```
procedure TMainForm.Timer1Timer(Sender: TObject);
var
  Th: TFileWriterThread;
begin
  ListBox1.Items.BeginUpdate;
  try
    ListBox1.Items.Clear;
    for Th in FRunningThreads do
    begin
      //check if the thread if still running. Method WaitFor has
      //been introduced by a class helper in the
      //FileWriterThreadU.pas file, it is not part of TThread
      if Th.WaitFor(0) = WAIT_TIMEOUT then
        ListBox1.Items.Add(Format('%5d RUNNING',
          [Th.ThreadID]))
      else
        ListBox1.Items.Add(Format('%5d TERMINATED',
          [Th.ThreadID]))
    end;
  finally
    ListBox1.Items.EndUpdate;
  end;
end;
```

The `WaitFor` method used in the `TTimer` event handler is not part of the standard `TThread` class but has been introduced using a class helper. This is because the standard `WaitFor` method present on the `TThread` class doesn't provide a timeout for the waiting, so it waits forever. If you want to check whether a thread is terminated or simply if you want to have the GUI responsive while waiting for the thread termination, you cannot do it using the `WaitFor` method. So, we added a new `WaitFor` method that provides a timeout. When you are calling `WaitFor(0)`, you are only asking whether a thread is still running. This is another good utilization of class helpers.

There's more...

Monitors are not a Delphi-specific concept; Wikipedia mentions it as follows:

> "Monitors were invented by C. A. R. Hoare and Per Brinch Hansen, and were first implemented in Brinch Hansen's Concurrent Pascal language."

To have a clear understanding of what a Monitor is and what's its main utilization, please read the Wikipedia article at http://en.wikipedia.org/wiki/Monitor_%28synchronization%29.

As a plus, a `TMonitor` class used in a smart way allows you to create a sort of "new language construct". Consider the following code:

```delphi
procedure ExecWithLock(const ALockObj: TObject;
const AProc: TProc);
begin
System.TMonitor.Enter(ALockObj);
try
AProc();
finally
    System.TMonitor.Exit(ALockObj);
end;
end;
```

Using the preceding code, it is possible to write something like the following:

```delphi
ExecWithLock(Obj,
    procedure
    begin
        //Here you have thread safe access to Obj
    end);
```

Cool, isn't it?

Talking with the main thread using a thread-safe queue

Using a background thread and working with its private data is not difficult, but safely bringing information retrieved or elaborated by the thread back to the main thread to show them to the user (as you know, only the main thread can handle the GUI in VCL as well as in FireMonkey) can be a daunting task. An even more complex task would be establishing a generic communication between two or more background threads. In this recipe, you'll see how a background thread can talk to the main thread in a safe manner using the `TThreadedQueue<T>` class. The same concepts are valid for a communication between two or more background threads.

Getting ready

Let's talk about a scenario. You have to show data generated from some sort of device or subsystem, let's say a serial, a USB device, a query polling on the database data, or a TCP socket. You cannot simply wait for data using `TTimer` because this would freeze your GUI during the wait, and the wait can be long. You have tried it, but your interface became sluggish... you need another solution!

In the Delphi RTL, there is a very useful class called `TThreadedQueue<T>` that is, as the name suggests, a particular parametric queue (a FIFO data structure) that can be safely used from different threads. How to use it? In the programming field, there is mostly no single solution valid for all situations, but the following one is very popular. Feel free to change your approach if necessary. However, this is the approach used in the recipe code:

1. Create the queue within the main form.
2. Create a thread and inject the form queue to it.
3. In the thread `Execute` method, append all generated data to the queue.
4. In the main form, use a timer or some other mechanism to periodically read from the queue and display data on the form.

How to do it...

Open the recipe project called `ThreadingQueueSample.dproj`. This project contains the main form with all the GUI-related code and another unit with the thread code.

The `FormCreate` event creates the shared queue with the following parameters that will influence the behavior of the queue:

- `QueueDepth = 100`: This is the maximum queue size. If the queue reaches this limit, all the push operations will be blocked for a maximum of `PushTimeout`, then the `Push` call will fail with a timeout.

- `PushTimeout = 1000`: This is the timeout in milliseconds that will affect the thread, that in this recipe is the producer of a producer/consumer pattern.
- `PopTimeout = 1`: This is the timeout in milliseconds that will affect the timer when the queue is empty. This timeout must be very short because the pop call is blocking in nature, and you are in the main thread that should never be blocked for a long time.

The button labeled **Start Thread** creates a `TReaderThread` instance passing the already created queue to its constructor (this is a particular type of dependency injection called constructor injection).

The thread declaration is really simple and is as follows:

```
type
  TReaderThread = class(TThread)
  private
    FQueue: TThreadedQueue<Byte>;
  protected
    procedure Execute; override;
  public
    constructor Create(AQueue: TThreadedQueue<Byte>);
  end;
```

While the `Execute` method simply appends randomly generated data to the queue, note that the `Terminated` property must be checked often so the application can terminate the thread and wait a reasonable time for its actual termination. In the following example, if the queue is not empty, check the termination at least every 700 milliseconds ca:

```
procedure TReaderThread.Execute;
begin
  while not Terminated do
  begin
    TThread.Sleep(200 + Trunc(Random(500)));
    // e.g. reading from an actual device
    FQueue.PushItem(Random(256));
  end;
end;
```

So far, you've filled the queue. Now, you have to read from the queue and do something useful with the read data. This is the job of a timer. The following is the code of the timer event on the main form:

```
procedure TMainForm.Timer1Timer(Sender: TObject);
var
  Value: Byte;
begin
```

The Thousand Faces of Multithreading

```
      while FQueue.PopItem(Value) = TWaitResult.wrSignaled do
      begin
        ListBox1.Items.Add(Format('[%3.3d]', [Value]));
      end;
      ListBox1.ItemIndex := ListBox1.Count - 1;
    end;
```

That's it! Run the application and see how we are reading the data coming from the threads and showing the main form. The following is a screenshot:

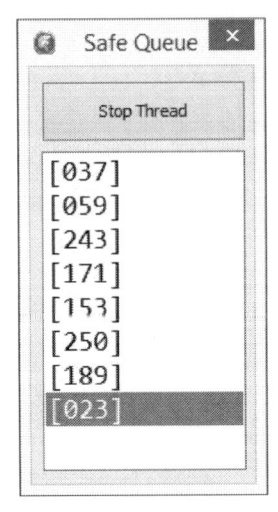

The main form showing data generated by the background thread

There's more...

The `TThreadedQueue<T>` is very powerful and can be used to communicate between two or more background threads in a consumer/producer schema as well. You can use multiple producers, multiple consumers, or both. The following screenshot shows a popular schema used when the speed at which the data generated is faster than the speed at which the same data is handled. In this case, usually you can gain speed on the processing side using multiple consumers.

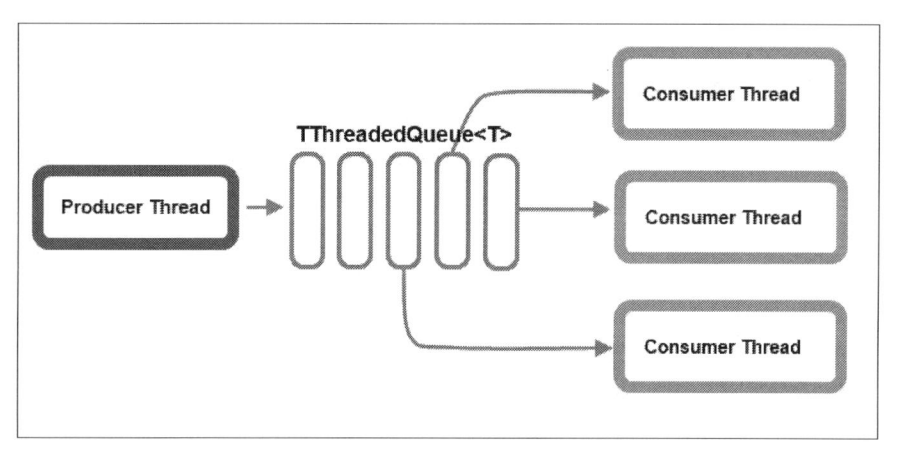

Single producer, multiple consumers

Synchronizing multiple threads using TEvent

The synchronization details we discussed so far were related to a data flow that is generated in the background thread context and has to be used in another thread. The other thread can be the main thread or another background thread. In this recipe, you'll use a simple synchronization mechanism called event that can be useful when you have to notify a new state, not necessarily new data. Obviously, the new state could also mean *there is new data to handle*. In such cases, the state change alerts you about new data being available.

Getting ready

The recipe scenario is simple: you have a lot of running threads that are doing something for you. You want to know when all of them are terminated. In this case, you can use a `TEvent` object (this is a tiny wrapper around an OS `Event` object).

How to do it...

This recipe is a bit articulated, so we'll not discuss steps to recreate it. Please open the recipe project code named `ThreadsTermination.dproj`; let's comment on it together.

The GUI is minimal; there is a button to run the threads and a list box to show the current state of threads. The `FormCreate` event initializes a list to hold the threads that will be used later. When you click on the button, the program launches five threads. Each thread waits for a random amount of time then generates a random number that should represent your output data. The main thread has to be notified about the thread termination. The thread code is as follows:

```
unit MyThreadU;

interface

uses
  System.Classes, System.SyncObjs;

type
  TMyThread = class(TThread)
  private
    FEvent: TEvent;
    FData: Integer;
  protected
    procedure Execute; override;
  public
    constructor Create(AEvent: TEvent);
    destructor Destroy; override;
    property Event: TEvent read FEvent;
    function GetData: Integer;
  end;

implementation

uses System.SysUtils;

constructor TMyThread.Create(AEvent: TEvent);
begin
  FEvent := AEvent;
  inherited Create(False);
end;

destructor TMyThread.Destroy;
begin
  FreeAndNil(FEvent);
  inherited;
end;

procedure TMyThread.Execute;
```

```
begin
  TThread.Sleep(2000 + Random(4000));
  FData := Random(1000);
  // This call sets the internal event state to signaled
  FEvent.SetEvent;
end;

function TMyThread.GetData: Integer;
begin
  Result := FData;
end;

end.
```

In the thread, the constructor is injected a `TEvent` instance. When the thread does its job, it calls the `SetEvent` method on the event instance. This call sets the internal event state to signaled. What's that for? It is required because the main thread is waiting for this change. To be more precise, it is waiting to know when all the threads have called their `SetEvent` methods. The following function is used to check whether there are any running threads:

```
function TMainForm.AreThereThreadsStillRunning: Boolean;
var
  H: THandleObject;
begin
  Result := TEvent.WaitForMultiple(
    Handles, 1, True, H) = wrTimeout;
end;
```

In the preceding code, the variable `Handles` is an array containing all the `Events` that have to be checked for termination.

The button event handler requires a bit of explanation. The code is as follows:

```
procedure TMainForm.btnStartClick(Sender: TObject);
var
  i: Integer;
  Evt: TEvent;
begin
  if (FThreads.Count > 0) and AreThereThreadsStillRunning then
  begin
    ShowMessage('Please wait, there are threads still running');
    Exit;
  end;
  FThreads.Clear;
  for i := 0 to High(Handles) do
  begin
```

```
        Evt := TEvent.Create;
        Handles[i] := Evt;
        FThreads.Add(TMyThread.Create(Evt));
    end;
    ListBox1.Items.Add('Threads running');
    Timer1.Enabled := True;
end;
```

When the user clicks on the button, the application checks whether there are any running threads from previous clicks. If so, inform the user with a `ShowMessage` and exit. If there are no running threads, the code fills the thread list with five threads. Each thread has its own `TEvent` instance to talk to. The reference to the `TEvent` variable is passed to the threads, but the threads have a property of accessing it during its runtime.

What is the best way to read the thread status? In a `TTimer` class, the code under the `OnTimer` event is the following; consider that this timer is normally disabled:

```
procedure TMainForm.Timer1Timer(Sender: TObject);
var
    th: TMyThread;
begin
    if not AreThereThreadsStillRunning then
    begin
        Timer1.Enabled := False;
        ListBox1.Items.Add('All threads terminated');
        for th in FThreads do
        begin
            ListBox1.Items.Add(
                Format('Th %4.4d = %4d',
                    [th.ThreadID, th.GetData]));
        end;
    end;
end;
```

With this last procedure, you retrieved the thread status; when all threads finished running, you also retrieved the *calculated* value.

There's more...

The event object is used to send a signal to a thread indicating that a particular event has occurred inside another thread. The event does not carry information; it simply informs that *something has happened*. It is simple, but can be useful in creating very complex synchronization mechanisms between two or more threads.

Events can be in a signaled state or not. If you want to have a deeper knowledge about the event objects and its utilization, visit the following links:

- `http://msdn.microsoft.com/en-us/library/windows/desktop/ms682655(v=vs.85).aspx`
- `http://docwiki.embarcadero.com/RADStudio/en/Waiting_for_a_Task_to_Be_Completed`

Displaying a measure on a 2D graph like an oscilloscope

An **oscilloscope** is a type of electronic test instrument that allows the observation of constantly varying signal voltages. Usually, information is shown as a two-dimensional plot graph of one or more signals as a function of time. In this recipe, you'll implement a type of oscilloscope to display data generated by a background thread. Obviously, in this recipe, you'll not create an accurate oscilloscope, rather a nice real-world utilization of retrieving data and using it continuously in the GUI.

Getting ready

You'll use the `TThreadedQueue<Extended>` class to bring out data from the background thread to the main thread. The approach is similar to that shown in the recipe *Talking with the main thread using a thread-safe queue*, but in this case, we've to show data in a complex way—on a 2D graph showing only the last n data retrieved.

The Thousand Faces of Multithreading

How to do it...

This recipe has a background thread acting like an *analogic signal generator* that is able to generate a sine style stream of data and a graph that plots these data. The resulting application is as follows:

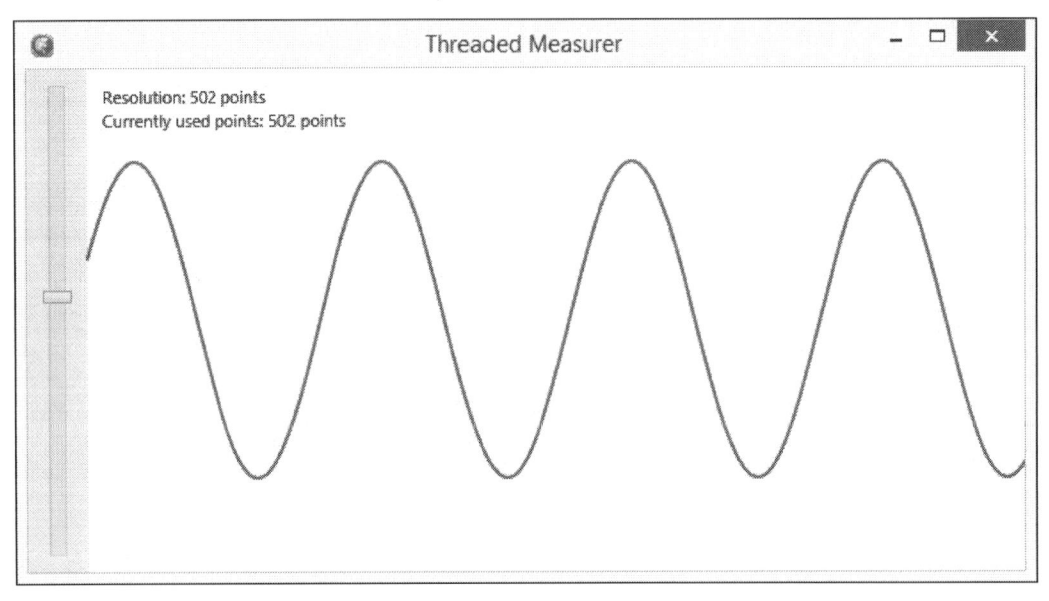

The main form showing a sine function generated by a background thread

You can adjust the resolution of the plot (number of points used to draw the sine) using the track bar on the left-hand side. Let's see the most important parts.

The thread used as a signal generator is very simple. As shown in the following code, it uses the `System.Math.Sin` function to generate a sine wave form. Every 10 milliseconds ca, a new value is appended to the queue; this value is the sample you get from the measured system. The code is as follows:

```
procedure TSignalGeneratorThread.Execute;
var
   Value: Extended;
begin
  inherited;
  Value := 0;
  while not Terminated do
  begin
    TThread.Sleep(10);
    FQueue.PushItem(Sin(Value) * 100);
```

```
      Value := Value + 0.05;
      if Value >= 360 then
        Value := 0;
    end;
  end;
```

Being a classic producer/consumer, this architecture has to deal with the classic problem of a queue being full and not accepting any data until someone starts to dequeue from it. At regular intervals, a `TTimer` dequeues all the values from the queue and appends them to a different queue living in the main thread.

This queue must have a fixed size, so if there are more values than what is defined by the resolution, the oldest values are dequeued until the queue size is equal to the maximum length permitted. This adjustment is done in the timer event handler with the following code:

```
procedure TMainForm.Timer1Timer(Sender: TObject);
var
  Value: Extended;
  QueueSize: Integer;
begin
  // put readed values in the display list...
  // max FMaxValuesCount values
  while FValuesQueue.PopItem(QueueSize, Value) =
                                       TWaitResult.wrSignaled do
  begin
    FDisplayList.Add(Value);
  end;
  // remove values from the head of the list...
  while FDisplayList.Count > FMaxValuesCount do
  begin
    FDisplayList.Delete(0);
  end;
  // RefreshGraph;
  pb.Repaint;
end;
```

The actual values are plotted on a simple 2D graph using `TPaintBox` as canvas. Remember that only the main thread should repaint and call paint procedures. The following is the code in the `OnPaint` event used to draw the plot:

```
procedure TMainForm.pbPaint(Sender: TObject; Canvas: TCanvas);
var
  Values: TPolygon;
  I: Integer;
  XStep: Extended;
  YCenter: Integer;
```

```delphi
begin
  // prepare scene
  Canvas.BeginScene;
  Canvas.Stroke.Kind := TBrushKind.Solid;
  Canvas.Stroke.Thickness := 1;

  // setup the canvas with a white background
  Canvas.Fill.Color := TAlphaColorRec.White;
  Canvas.FillRect(RectF(0, 0, Canvas.Width, Canvas.Height),
 0, 0, [], 1);

  // write the blue top-left labels
  Canvas.Fill.Color := TAlphaColorRec.Blue;
  Canvas.FillText(RectF(10, 10, Canvas.Width, 40),
    'Resolution: ' + MaxValuesCount.ToString + ' points',
 False, 1, [],
    TTextAlign.Leading, TTextAlign.Leading);
  Canvas.FillText(RectF(10, 25, Canvas.Width, 40),
    'Currently used points: ' +
    FDisplayList.Count.ToString + ' points', False, 1, [],
    TTextAlign.Leading, TTextAlign.Leading);

  // preparing points to draw
  SetLength(Values, FDisplayList.Count);
  XStep := Canvas.Width / FDisplayList.Count;
  YCenter := Canvas.Height div 2;
  for I := 0 to FDisplayList.Count - 1 do
  begin
    Values[I].X := XStep * I;
    Values[I].Y := YCenter - FDisplayList[I];
  end;

  // setup the points aspect
  Canvas.Stroke.Thickness := 2;
  Canvas.Stroke.Color := TAlphaColorRec.Red;
  // draw the points
  DrawOpenPolygon(Canvas, Values, 1);

  // actually update the canvas
  Canvas.EndScene;
    end;
```

FireMonkey Canvas does not allow you to draw an *open* polygon. An open polygon is a shape composed of 2 or more line segments, where the first and the last points are not connected directly. Here, we need an open polygon, so how to do it? Here's the code of the `DrawOpenPolygon` method:

```
procedure TMainForm.DrawOpenPolygon(const Canvas: TCanvas;
  const Points: TPolygon; const AOpacity: Single);
var
  I: Integer;
  LPath: TPathData;
begin
  if Length(Points) = 0 then
    Exit;
  LPath := TPathData.Create;
  try
    LPath.MoveTo(Points[0]);
    for I := 1 to High(Points) do
      LPath.LineTo(Points[I]);
    Canvas.DrawPath(LPath, AOpacity);
  finally
    LPath.Free;
  end;
end;
```

There's more...

Showing dynamically changing data is always a challenge and is a typical synchronization problem if you have to read from a blocking and very fast data source. However, using queues in an efficient way can help to reach the correct architecture. If you have very high concurrency (many consumers or many producers) or a very high producer speed compared to the consumer's speed, you may have some performance improvements using lock-free data structures.

Unluckily in Delphi, there are no ready-to-use lock-free data structures; however, there are very good libraries, even open source, that implement it in the context of multithreaded programming. One of the most popular libraries, although at the time of writing it is only for the Windows platform, is the open source `OmniThreadLibrary` from my friend Primož Gabrijelčič (http://www.omnithreadlibrary.com/).

Using tasks to make your customer happier

Since RAD Studio XE7 Delphi and C++ Builder developers can use **Parallel Programming Library** (**PPL**). What is PPL? PPL is a part of the Delphi RTL that provides facilities multithreading (or parallel) programming.

PPL is available for all the platforms supported by Delphi and provides a number of advanced features for running tasks, joining tasks, waiting on groups of tasks to process, and so forth. PPL is not only a different way to create threads, but is a different way to manage threads as well. Why? Because to manage all of these features (tasks, futures, parallel for, joining, and so on), there is a thread pool that self-tunes automatically (based on the load on the CPUs), so you do not have to care about creating or managing threads for this purpose.

The good news is that PPL is quite simple to use and doesn't require big changes to your application. You can use this library by including `System.Threading` in your application or app. This unit is made up of several features that can be included into new and existing projects.

So the question is: "How and when I can use the PPL?" Well, in all the cases where you usually need to use a thread, you should consider a task. This doesn't mean that you will not create threads anymore, but in many cases you will end up using some sort of task instead of a normal thread.

In this recipe, we'll develop a reusable asynchronous library to accomplish a very recurrent need: start a background operation and be informed, in the main thread, when the background process ends successfully or not.

Using plain PPL, a very recurrent code is similar to the following:

```
procedure TMainForm.btnITaskClick(Sender: TObject);
var
   LTask: ITask;
begin
   LTask := TTask.Run(
     procedure
     var
       LResult: Integer;
     begin
       Sleep(1000); //do something useful here...
       LResult := Random(100); //some kind of "result"

       //Queue the execution in the main thread
       TThread.Queue(nil,
         procedure
         begin
```

```
      TaskEnd(LResult); //TaskEnd is called in the UI thread
        end);
    end);
end;
```

Quite simple now, but things get a bit more complicated when you have many tasks running and you have to handle exceptions. So a bit layer to increase the usability can be useful. Here's the `Async.Run<T>!`.

A complete call to the `Async.Run<T>` method is made up of three anonymous methods:

- **A background task**: This is a function returning some kind of data. It runs in a background thread using a PPL task.
- **A success callback**: This is a procedure that gets the result of the background task. It runs in the main UI thread.
- **An error callback**: This is a procedure that gets the exception raised by the background task, if any. It runs in the main UI thread.

This small library can be used in the following way:

```
Async.Run<String>(
    function: String
    begin
        //This is the "background" anonymous method. Runs in the
        //background thread, and its result is passed
        //to the "success" callback.
        //In this case the result is a String.
    end,
    procedure(const Value: String)
    begin
        //This is the "success" callback. Runs in the UI thread and
        //gets the result of the "background" anonymous method.
    end,
    procedure(const Ex: Exception)
    begin
        //This is the "error" callback.
        //Runs in the UI thread and is called only if the
        //"background" anonymous method raises an exception.
    end);
```

In this case, the data returned by the background function is a string but, being `Async.Run<T>` a generic method, you can change the type to whatever you want.

The Thousand Faces of Multithreading

Getting ready

In this recipe, we'll create the `Async` library and a testbed program for it. Our objective is to exercise the library with some use cases to see how it works.

How it works...

Open the project `AsyncTaskSample.dproj` and let's talk about the `AsyncTask.pas` unit.

Here's the unit with some comments:

```delphi
unit AsyncTask;

interface

uses
  System.SysUtils,
  System.Threading; //The PPL unit

type
  //the "background" task
  TAsyncBackgroundTask<T> = reference to function: T;

  //the "success" callback
  TAsyncSuccessCallback<T> = reference to
                  procedure (const TaskResult: T);

  //the "error" callback
  TAsyncErrorCallback = reference to
                  procedure (const E: Exception);

  //the default "error" callback if the user does not provide it
  TAsyncDefaultErrorCallback = reference to
                  procedure (const E: Exception;
                             const ExptAddress: Pointer);

  //the main class
  Async = class sealed
  public
    class function Run<T>(Task: TAsyncBackgroundTask<T>;
      Success: TAsyncSuccessCallback<T>;
```

```delphi
    Error: TAsyncErrorCallback = nil): ITask;
  end;

var
  //default "error" callback. It is a public var so that the
  //programmer can override the default behavior
  DefaultTaskErrorHandler: TAsyncDefaultErrorCallback = nil;

implementation

uses
  System.Classes;

class function Async.Run<T>(Task: TAsyncBackgroundTask<T>;
  Success: TAsyncSuccessCallback<T>;
  Error: TAsyncErrorCallback): ITask;
var
  LRes: T;
begin
  //the background task starts here
  Result := TTask.Run(
    procedure
    var
      Ex: Pointer;
      ExceptionAddress: Pointer;
    begin
      Ex := nil;
      try
        LRes := Task(); //run the actual task
        if Assigned(Success) then
        begin
            //call the success callback passing the result
          TThread.Queue(nil,
            procedure
            begin
              Success(LRes);
            end);
        end;
      except
        //let's extend the life of the exception object
        Ex := AcquireExceptionObject;
        ExceptionAddress := ExceptAddr;

        //queue on the main thread to call the error callback
```

```
            TThread.Queue(nil,
      procedure
      var
         LCurrException: Exception;
      begin
         LCurrException := Exception(Ex);
         try
           if Assigned(Error) then
            Error(LCurrException) //call the "error" callback
            else
            DefaultTaskErrorHandler(
                  LCurrException, ExceptionAddress);
         finally
           //free the exception object. It is necessary
                //because we "extended" the natural life
                //of the exception object beyond the except block
                FreeAndNil(LCurrException);
         end;
      end);
         end; //except
      end); //task.run
end;

initialization

//this is the default error callback
DefaultTaskErrorHandler :=
   procedure(const E: Exception;
              const ExceptionAddress: Pointer)
   begin
     ShowException(E, ExceptionAddress);
   end;

end.
```

Now that we know how the `Async.Run<T>` is implemented, let's see how to use it. Open the main form and check the code under each button. Let's start with the button `btnSimple`:

```
   procedure TMainForm.btnSimpleClick(Sender: TObject);
   begin
      Async.Run<Integer>(
         function: Integer //long operation in the background
         begin
            Sleep(2000);
```

```
      Result := Random(100);
    end,
    procedure (const Value: Integer) //show the result in the UI
    begin
      //write the result in a memo in the form
        Log('RESULT: ' + Value.ToString);
    end);
end;
```

The long (and in this case fake) operation is executed in the anonymous method as a function that returns an integer. When the function ends, its return value is passed to the other anonymous method, which is a procedure, and runs in the UI thread so that it can interact with the user. If you run the program and click on this button, you can verify that the UI is not frozen while the long operation (actually a `Sleep(2000)` call) is running.

The second button is named `btnWithException` and shows how to handle exceptions that may be raised inside the background thread:

```
procedure TMainForm.btnWithExceptionClick(Sender: TObject);
begin
  Async.Run<String>(
    function: String
    begin
      raise Exception.Create('This is an error message');
    end,
    procedure (const Value: String)
    begin
      // never called
    end,
    procedure (const Ex: Exception)
    begin
      Log('Exception: ' + sLineBreak + Ex.Message);
    end);
end;
```

Quite simple, isn't it? If something goes wrong in the background, the related exception object is passed to the error callback. Pay attention that the error block is not a standard Delphi except block, it is just an anonymous method that gets an `Exception` object, so, for instance, a raise; call to `reraise` the current exception is not allowed.

The Thousand Faces of Multithreading

The next button called `btnExceptionDef` shows the library's abilities to handle the exception raised in the background even if the programmer doesn't handle it directly or forgot to do it:

```
procedure TMainForm.btnExceptionDefClick(Sender: TObject);
begin
  Async.Run<String>(
    function: String
    begin
      raise Exception.Create(
         'Handled by the default Exception handler');
    end,
    procedure(const Value: String)
    begin
      // never called
    end);
end;
```

Clicking on this button, you will see the Delphi standard exception message. In some cases, this can be enough, but if you need some custom handling, you can simply pass the specific callback or override the default behavior assigning another default handler to the global variable `DefaultTaskErrorHandler`.

The last button does something actually useful: it gets the current time from a rest service. The button is called `btnRESTRequest` and this is the code behind it:

```
procedure TMainForm.btnRESTRequestClick(Sender: TObject);
begin
  Async.Run<String>(
    function: String
    var
      LHTTP: THTTPClient;
      LResp: IHTTPResponse;
    begin
      LHTTP := THTTPClient.Create;
      try
          LResp := LHTTP.Get('http://www.timeapi.org/utc/now');
        if LResp.StatusCode = 200 then
          begin
        Result := LResp.ContentAsString(TEncoding.UTF8)
          end
          else
          begin
        raise Exception.CreateFmt(
                    'Cannot get time. HTTP %d - %s',
```

```
            [LResp.StatusCode, LResp.StatusText]);
       end;
     finally
        LHTTP.Free;
     end;
   end,
   procedure(const DateAndTime: String)
    begin
     Log('Current Date Time: ' + DateAndTime);
   end,
   procedure(const Ex: Exception)
   begin
      Log('Exception: ' + sLineBreak + Ex.Message);
   end);
end;
```

At this point, the code should be clear. In the background task the actual rest call is executed, if the server replies with a 200 OK HTTP status, then the response body is passed to the success callback, otherwise an exception is raised explaining that the error happened.

There's more...

The PPL greatly simplifies multithreading programming. However, the biggest advantage is the `ThreadPool`, which does the dirty job of creating, destroying, and reusing the background threads. So, please, don't see the PPL as a different way to create threads, it is a powerful mechanism to correctly handle multiple threads without saturating the CPUs. Remember then when you ask the PPL to start a task, the task may not start immediately. This is because the `ThreadPool` may decide to put your task in the waiting queue and actually start it ASAP, but not now. The great thing is that this is actually not a problem but a feature, because, otherwise, you will easily saturate CPU's resources. In my own experience, in complex situations, you cannot simply start a thread when you need it, but you have to inform the *thread manager* that you need a thread and then it can start it ASAP. This *threads manager* was absent in Delphi RTL before the PPL, so this is the reason I greatly appreciate the PPL `ThreadPool`.

Here's some useful links to get started with the PPL concepts and classes:

- http://docwiki.embarcadero.com/RADStudio/en/Using_the_Parallel_Programming_Library
- http://docwiki.embarcadero.com/RADStudio/en/Using_TTask_from_the_Parallel_Programming_Library
- http://www.danieleteti.it/using-dynamic-arrays-and-parallel-programming-library-part-1/

Monitoring things using futures

Futures are a great tool in the tool chest of every programmer. But, wait! What's a future?

Well, while a task can be seen as a sort of asynchronous procedure, a future can be seen as an asynchronous function. However, while using task, the process is quite clear (it runs in the background and uses some sort of messaging to talk to the other thread) the future is a bit more complex. When should I get the return value of the future? Let's talk about futures with an example. You can use futures to run tasks on a separate thread and then forget about them, but often, you'll want to use the result of the task. The future function returns an `IFuture<T>` reference that you can use to request the result of type `T`. The reference is like the ticket that a dry cleaner gives you: at any time you can use it to request your clean dress, but if your dress isn't clean yet, you'll have to wait. Similarly, you can use the reference value to request a future's result, but if the future isn't done computing the result, you'll have to wait.

In this recipe, we'll develop a simple application able to convert money between any currency and euros. So, you will set the source currency type, set the amount of money and then with the press of a button you can convert the value in euros. Quite simple. However, this application gets the currency rates from a web service, so there is some delay in every conversion. But, let's talk about the process.

You	Program
Select the source currency type	Do nothing
Write the amount of money to be converted	Do nothing
Press the button	▸ Call the web service using the selected currency symbol ▸ Wait for the response (let's say some seconds) ▸ Parse the response ▸ Calculate the result ▸ Show the result in a TEdit

As you can see, the program waits for the input for a long time while you are writing the data. Should we do it better? Sure!

Chapter 5

Getting ready

How could we improve the program flow to optimize the user wait periods making the program faster?

When the user selects the currency type, we could already have the conversion rates for that currency, but we cannot block the main thread while the user is using the UI because it is a bad practice and upsets the user. So, what we want to do is to start the request for the conversion rates in the background, and in this case, a future is really the perfect solution.

We'll implement this process in our recipe.

You	Program
Select the source currency type	Run a future in parallel, which gets the conversion rates for the selected currency. The UI remains responsive.
Write the amount of money to be converted	Do nothing but the future is running and likely will terminate before you push the button to get the conversion.
Press the button	Calculate the result using the future result (if the future is still running, the user has to wait, but usually this is not the case)
	Show the result in a `TEdit`

How it works...

Let's open the project **CurrencyRatesCalculator.dproj**. The GUI is quite simple and is shown here:

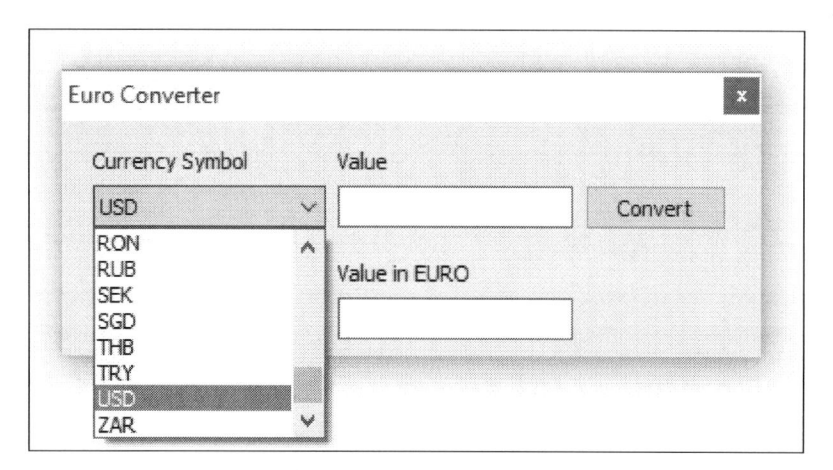

Fig 6.1 CurrencyRatesCalculator GUI

The first problem we've to cope with is: how many and which currency types will be available in the combo? Well, we'll use a nice free RESTful service to get the conversion rates available at `http://fixer.io`, and this service has a set of API to interact with. For instance, to get the latest foreign exchange reference rates in the JSON format, we can call the following request:

```
GET http://api.fixer.io/latest
```

This obtains the following response:

```
{
base: "EUR",
rates: {
AUD: 1.4825,
BGN: 1.9558,
BRL: 3.966,
CAD: 1.4229,
CHF: 1.0844,
CNY: 6.8239,
CZK: 27.031,
DKK: 7.4602,
GBP: 0.701,
HKD: 8.2833,
HRK: 7.6278,
HUF: 309.96,
IDR: 14529.52,
ILS: 4.1473,
INR: 70.7492,
JPY: 131.28,
KRW: 1234.46,
MXN: 17.7282,
MYR: 4.5803,
NOK: 9.2035,
NZD: 1.6296,
PHP: 50.231,
PLN: 4.2411,
RON: 4.4438,
RUB: 69.3309,
SEK: 9.2796,
SGD: 1.5093,
THB: 38.199,
TRY: 3.0165,
USD: 1.0688,
ZAR: 14.8862
}
}
```

Therefore, in the rates object, we have all the currencies the service can handle. We've to issue a request in the `FormCreate`, elaborate the response, and then set the `Combo.Items` property to the list of currencies available. Obviously, we do not want to block the user in the `FormCreate` event (it is really bad practice) so the program uses our nice `AsyncTask.pas` developed in the recipe to get the list without blocking the GUI. Here's the code in the `FormCreate` event handler:

```
procedure TMainForm.FormCreate(Sender: TObject);
begin
  Async.Run<TStringList>(
    function: TStringList
    var
          LHTTP: THTTPClient;
          LResp: IHTTPResponse;
          LJObj: TJSONObject;
          LJRates: TJSONObject;
          I: Integer;
    begin
          LHTTP := THTTPClient.Create;
      try
        //send the request and parse the json response
        LResp := LHTTP.Get('http://api.fixer.io/latest');
        LJObj := TJSONObject.ParseJSONValue
                    (LResp.ContentAsString(TEncoding.UTF8))
                      as TJSONObject;
      try
        //gets the json object 'rates' and
        //loop through the property names
        LJRates := LJObj.GetValue<TJSONObject>('rates');
        Result := TStringList.Create;
        for I := 0 to LJRates.Count - 1 do
        begin
            //add each names in the resulting TStringList
    Result.Add(LJRates.Pairs[I].JsonString.Value);
end;
        //sort the list
      Result.Sort;
        finally
    LJObj.Free;
        end;
        finally
      LHTTP.Free;
        end;
    end,
```

```
    procedure(const Strings: TStringList)
    begin
            //set the list as the items property of the combobox
            cbSymbol.Items.Assign(Strings);
    end);
end;
```

Now, when the program starts, there are no delays and as soon as the request terminates, the cbSymbol combo box fills up with all the available currency symbols. Now, we have to start a future when the user selects a currency from the list. Here's the relevant code:

```
procedure TMainForm.cbSymbolClick(Sender: TObject);
begin
  StartFuture;
end;

procedure TMainForm.StartFuture;
var
  LBaseSymbol: String;
begin
  EditResultInEuro.Clear;
  if cbSymbol.ItemIndex < 0 then
    Exit;

  LBaseSymbol := cbSymbol.Text;
  FConversionRate := TTask.Future<Currency>(
    function: Currency
    var
            LHTTP: THTTPClient;
            LResp: IHTTPResponse;
            LJObj: TJSONObject;
    begin
            LHTTP := THTTPClient.Create;
            try
                //send the request using the
                //selected currency symbol
                LResp := LHTTP.Get(
                        Format('http://api.fixer.io/latest?base=%s&symbols=EUR',
                            [LBaseSymbol]));
                //parse the response and get the rate
                LJObj := TJSONObject.ParseJSONValue
```

```
                              (LResp.ContentAsString(TEncoding.UTF8))
                              as TJSONObject;
               try
      Result := LJObj.GetValue<TJSONNumber>('rates.EUR')
                           .AsDouble;
               finally
                    LJObj.Free;
               end;
            finally
                 LHTTP.Free;
            end;
       end);
  end;
```

When the user selects a currency in the combo, the future starts. Then, the user writes a value in the `EditValue` and the future is running in parallel. Then, the user clicks on the button to get the conversion. At this point, the future may be terminated or not, but our code is not affected by this. We are just reading the future return value, that's it. If the future is terminated, we simply read the value; if the future is not terminated, the read is blocked until it terminates. Here's the code under the `btnConvert`:

```
  procedure TMainForm.btnConvertClick(Sender: TObject);
  begin
    if not Assigned(FConversionRate) then
    begin
      ShowMessage('Please, select a currency symbol');
      Exit;
    end;
    EditResultInEuro.Text :=
      //simply "read" from the future
         //No synchronization or checks are needed
      FormatCurr('€ #,###,##0.00', FConversionRate.Value *
      StrToFloat(EditValue.Text));
  end;
```

Run the program, check how the combo gets filled with the available currency kinds without slowing down the program startup. Now, select a currency symbol, write a value in the edit, and check the button. As you can see, there are no slowdowns. If your network is fast enough when you click on the button to get the conversion, the future is already finished, so that you don't advise the delay. Here's a screenshot of the program running:

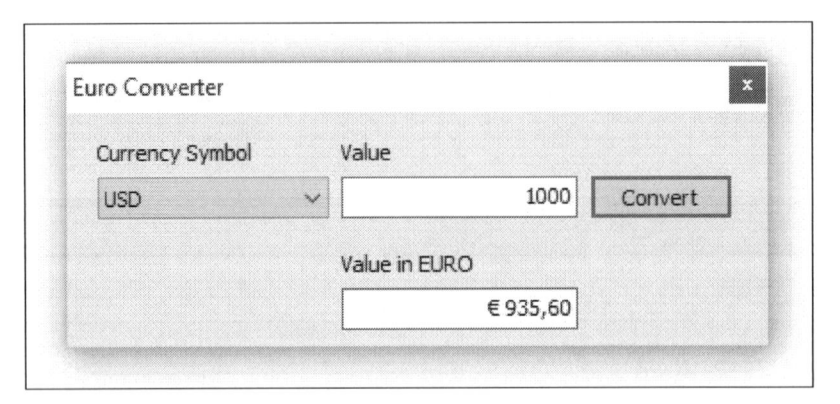

Fig 6.2 The program running

There's more...

Futures are not as ubiquitous as tasks are, but in some kinds of situations, you really can simplify your code using them. Remember that an IFuture is a descendant of ITask so you can use all the methods already used in the previous recipe to check whether the future is finished. However, in some cases, such as that exposed in this recipe, this is simply not needed. Here's some documentation about futures:

Using TTask.IFuture from the Parallel Programming Library (http://docwiki.embarcadero.com/RADStudio/en/Using_TTask.IFuture_from_the_Parallel_Programming_Library).

Tutorial on *Using Futures from the Parallel Programming Library* (http://docwiki.embarcadero.com/RADStudio/en/Tutorial:_Using_Futures_from_the_Parallel_Programming_Library).

Parallelize using the parallel for

One of the first loops that any programmer starts to know is the for loop. In this recipe, we'll see a particular type of for loop: the parallel one. To be clear, this parallel for loop is not a new language feature but is a sort of it implemented as a static class method.

The parallel for loop is part of the Parallel Programming Library and is implemented by the `TParallel` class. Here's one of its (overloaded) versions and a utilization example:

```
//declaration
class method TParallel.&For(ALowInclusive, AHighInclusive:
Integer; const AIteratorEvent: TProc<Integer>): TLoopResult;

//used as follows
TParallel.&For(1,10,
  procedure(Index: Integer)
  begin
    //executed 10 times with index 1..10
  end);
```

What is different about the classic `for`? The difference is that the anonymous method passed to the `for` method is executed on different threads concurrently; this is the reason it's a parallel for, as the for block is executed in parallel. This means that you cannot be sure that execution with index 5 runs before execution with index 6, they are just parallel. Another important consideration is that all the code inside the for block must be synchronized with the shared resources eventually used, because, actually each of them runs in a different thread context.

A good question is: "What happens if I start a parallel for from 1 to 10,000? Will 10,000 threads will be created?". No, absolutely not. This will cause a huge performance degradation, at first, and then will eventually crash your program (depending on your OS and the stack size defined for each thread). Here, the `TThreadPool` does its job queuing the execution and maintaining the thread's number at a right level. Therefore, the 100,000 executions will be serialized and executed in a finite number of threads depending on available CPUs cores and the current load on them.

Similar to the parallel for there is the parallel join which is really a variation of the parallel for, we'll use `TParallel.Join` in this recipe. What does `TParallel.Join` do? It gets an array of `TProc` to execute and return an `ITask` interface to check when execution ends. Then, in the background, executes them in parallel using the `TThreadPool`.

Here's a utilization sample:

```
procedure TMainForm.Button1Click(Sender: TObject);
var
  LProcs: ITask;
begin
  LProcs := TParallel.Join([
    procedure
    begin
      // do something
    end,
```

```
      procedure
      begin
        // do something
      end,
        procedure
        begin
          // do something
        end]);
    LProcs.Wait(INFINITE);
  end;
```

In this example three anonymous methods are executed in parallel. Then, the last call to wait waits indefinitely for their termination.

Now, let's say that we have to generate some sort of summary data and generate a file for each customer in the database. Doing it serially is quite simple, but we will not use all the CPU cores to elaborate. Just one after the other. Considering the power and the cores provided by the current devices (computer, smartphone, or tablets) is a not optimized+ approach. Let's use the `TParallel.Join` to optimize it.

Getting ready

We've to generate one text file for each customer in the database containing a list of its sales. The filename should contain the customer code, which is something like `customer_00123.txt`. Consider that in many cases, the connection and login phases are the slower operations when dealing with a short connection to the database. So we've to handle this problem too. Luckily, FireDAC provides pooled connections, and they are a must when using concurrent database accesses in multithread scenarios. Let's start by checking the recipe's code.

How it works...

As already mentioned, we have to access the database using a connection pool. FireDAC has the concept of connection definition. A connection definition describes how to store and use FireDAC connection parameters and what a connection definition means. To specify connection parameters, an application must use a connection definition. The connection definition is a set of parameters. Depending on the kind of connection definition, a connection may also be pooled.

FireDAC supports three connection definition kinds:

Connection	Definition
Temporary	This has no name, is not stored in a connection definition file, and is not managed by the FDManager. It is defined directly on TFDConnection component and cannot be used as Pooled.
Private	This has a unique name, is managed by the FDManager, but is *not* stored in a connection definition file. It can be used as a pooled connection inside the sample application.
Persistent	This has a unique name, is managed by the FDManager, and is stored in a connection definition file. It can be used as pooled also in different applications. In this case, each application has its own pool.

In this case, we can use a persistent or private connection definition. We'll go for a private connection definition. Here's the code (reusable at 100 percent) used to define a connection definition that can be used in pool:

```
procedure TMainForm.DefinePrivateConnDef;
var
   LParams: TStringList;
begin
   LParams := TStringList.Create;
   try
     LParams.Add('Database=employee');
     LParams.Add('Protocol=TCPIP');
     LParams.Add('Server=localhost');
     LParams.Add('User_Name=sysdba');
     LParams.Add('Password=masterkey');
     LParams.Add('Pooled=true'); //can be pooled!
     FDManager.AddConnectionDef(CONNECTION_DEF_NAME, 'IB',
   LParams);
   finally
     LParams.Free;
   end;
end;
```

Now, we can use this connection definition in each `TFDConnection` simply assigning its `ConnectionDefName` property to the name of the connection definition:

```
var
   LConn: TFDConnection;
begin
   LConn := TFDConnection.Create(nil);
   LConn.ConnectionDefName := CONNECTION_DEF_NAME;
   LConn.Open;
   //use the connection
```

In our case, we will call the `DefinePrivateConnDef` procedure in the `FormCreate` event.

Our GUI is quite minimal. We've only a button that starts the parallel processing. Let's see the code under this button:

```
procedure TMainForm.btnStartClick(Sender: TObject);
var
   LConn: TFDConnection;
   LQry: TFDQuery;
   LTasks: TArray<TProc>;
   LProcs: ITask;
   i: Integer;
begin
   LConn := TFDConnection.Create(nil);
   try
     LConn.ConnectionDefName := CONNECTION_DEF_NAME;
     LConn.Open;
     LQry := TFDQuery.Create(LConn);
     LQry.Connection := LConn;
     LQry.Open('SELECT * FROM CUSTOMER ORDER BY CUST_NO');
     LQry.FetchAll;
      //prepare the array to contain all the TProc
     SetLength(LTasks, LQry.RecordCount);
     i := 0;
     while not LQry.Eof do
     begin
        //define each TProc passing the CustNo to work on
       LTasks[i] := MakeProc(LQry.FieldByName('CUST_NO')
   .AsInteger);
        LQry.Next;
        Inc(i);
     end;
   finally
     LConn.Free;
```

```
    end;

    //create the output folder
    TDirectory.CreateDirectory(OUTPUT_FOLDER);

    //TParallel.Join is blocking but we don't want block the GUI, so
    //we call it inside a task
    TTask.Run(
      procedure
      begin
        //start the parallel processing
        LProcs := TParallel.Join(LTasks);
        //wait for finish
        LProcs.Wait(INFINITE);
        //inform the user that we've finished
        TThread.Queue(nil,
          procedure
          begin
            ShowMessage('Summary files generated successfully');
            btnStart.Enabled := True;
          end);
      end);
    btnStart.Enabled := False;
end;
```

Following the comments, the code should be quite simple to understand. Particularly interesting is the `MakeProc` function and what it really does.

`TProc` doesn't have parameters, but we've to pass a different value (the `CUST_NO` field) to each of them, so here we're using a second order function to configure an anonymous method using the scope capture feature. Moreover, this method contains the actual code that creates the file reading from the `SALES` table.

Here's the `MakeProc`:

```
function TMainForm.MakeProc(const CustNo: Integer): TProc;
begin
  Result :=
    procedure
    var
      LConn: TFDConnection;
      LQry: TFDQuery;
      LOutputFile: TStreamWriter;
      LFName: string;
    begin
```

```
            LConn := TFDConnection.Create(nil);
            try
               LConn.ConnectionDefName := CONNECTION_DEF_NAME;
               LFName := TPath.Combine(OUTPUT_FOLDER,
         Format('customer_%.8d.txt', [CustNo]));
               LOutputFile := TFile.CreateText(LFName);
               try
      //Some fake delay to mimic a heavy computation...
                  Sleep(1000);
                  LQry := TFDQuery.Create(LConn);
                  LQry.Connection := LConn;
                  //gets the data
                  LQry.Open('SELECT * FROM SALES WHERE CUST_NO = ? ' +
                     'ORDER BY ORDER_DATE, PO_NUMBER', [CustNo]);
                  //write the output file one record by line
                  while not LQry.Eof do
                  begin
                     //GetRow().DumpRow() is an handy FireDAC method
                     //to dump a row from a table.
                     //In a real word application you probably need
                     //a more complex formatting code
                     LOutputFile.WriteLine(LQry.GetRow().DumpRow(True));
                     LQry.Next;
                  end;
               finally
                  LOutputFile.Free;
               end;
            finally
               LConn.Free;
            end;
         end;
      end;
```

`MakeProc` returns a `TProc`, which captures the value of the `CustNo` parameter. So when we run them using the `TParallel.Join` each `TTask` has a different value for the `CustNo` variable. Nice!

Run the program and hit the button. Wait a couple of seconds and then you will get all the files created in the output folder and message dialog, which informs you that all the files have been created, all in parallel using a pooled database connection. Quite a lot of concepts and power in so few lines of code, isn't it?

There's more...

There are a lot of topics here. Here are some interesting docwiki pages about FireDAC connection definitions and multithreading:

- Different kinds of connection definitions (http://docwiki.embarcadero.com/RADStudio/en/Defining_Connection_(FireDAC)).
- Information about the TFDManager class that is responsible for connection definitions and connections management (http://docwiki.embarcadero.com/Libraries/en/FireDAC.Comp.Client.TFDManager).
- Using FireDAC in multithreading (http://docwiki.embarcadero.com/RADStudio/en/Multithreading_(FireDAC))
- Using the TParallel.For (http://docwiki.embarcadero.com/RADStudio/en/Using_TParallel.For_from_the_Parallel_Programming_Library)

6
Putting Delphi on the Server

In this chapter, we will cover the following recipes:

- Developing web client JavaScript applications with WebBroker on the server
- Converting a console service application to a Windows service
- Serializing a dataset to JSON and back
- Serializing objects to JSON and back using RTTI
- Sending a POST HTTP request encoding parameters
- Implementing a RESTful interface using WebBroker
- Controlling a remote application using UDP
- Using App tethering to create a companion app
- Creating DataSnap Apache modules
- Creating a WebBroker Apache module and publishing it under HTTPS
- Using a cross-platform HTTPS client

Introduction

In this chapter, we'll see how well Delphi can behave when it runs on the server. Most server-side technology today is scripted or managed, and in many cases it's a good choice. However, Delphi can be used to create very powerful enterprise servers with no external dependencies and great performance, and to do all these things, you need much less hardware power and memory to run it compared to, let's say, a J2EE server. Moreover, we'll see how to handle some of the most common problems when facing web servers, such as serialization, mime types, HTML encoding, and so on.

Developing web client JavaScript applications with WebBroker on the server

Many Delphi developers think that if you need to develop a web solution you have to look for something different to Delphi. So they give up years of Delphi knowledge and start to create a web solution with another technology. Although there are cases where Delphi is not the best choice (for instance, if you are developing a classic website with server-side dynamic generated pages), in most scenarios, Delphi can behave even better than many of the web-only technologies available today. What you need is a good framework to work with. In this recipe, we'll see the WebBroker technology, available since Delphi 4, and will consume it from a JavaScript application. Let's start!

Getting ready

This recipe uses two external open source projects:

- DelphiMVCFramework:
    - A powerful Delphi framework to develop RESTful web services
    - Project website: `https://github.com/danieleteti/delphimvcframework`
    - Written by Daniele Teti (me) and a lot of good contributors from all over the world

- jTable:
    - A JQuery plugin to create AJAX-based **Create Retrieve Update and Delete** (**CRUD**) tables
    - Written by Halil İbrahim Kalkan
    - Project website: `http://jtable.org/`

We'll start by downloading these libraries and putting each ZIP file in a folder, let's say `C:\DelphiBook\Libs`.

To download **DelphiMVCFramework** (**DMVCFramework**), go to the project website and clone the repository using a Git client. There are a lot of Git clients. A good general-purpose solution is TortoiseGit, a well-integrated Windows shell extension able to access remote and local Git repositories directly from Windows Explorer (TortoiseGit is downloadable from `https://tortoisegit.org/`). You can also use the command-line version and then use the following command lines:

```
git clone https://github.com/danieleteti/delphimvcframework.git delphimvcframework
git submodule update --init --recursive
```

Or, you can use Delphi to directly download the repository. Navigate to **File | Open from version control | Git**.

Then, in the window that appears, write the following information and click **OK**:

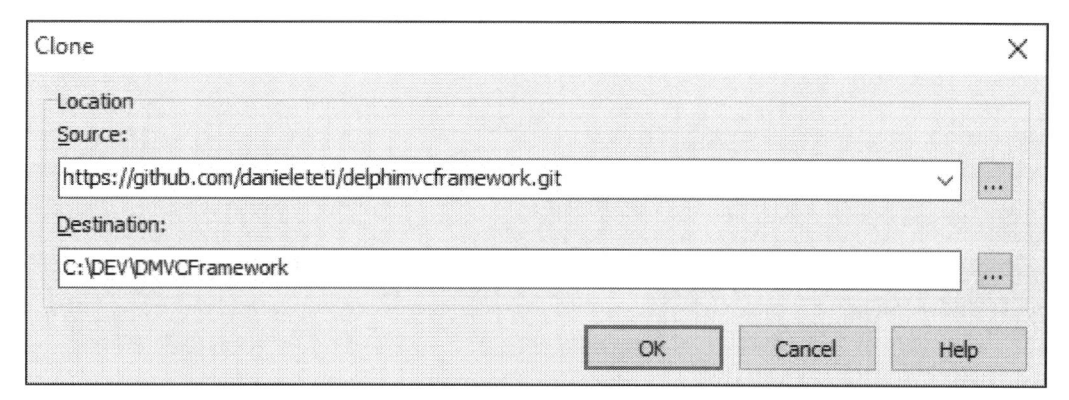

The dialog used to download the DMVCFramework project from its GitHub repository

Now the integrated Git client will clone the repository, downloading all the necessary files. At the end of the process, the wizard asks about which project we want to open. Click **Cancel** and close the dialog. The `DelphiMVCFramework` files have been downloaded in `C:\DEV\DMVCFramework`; configure the Delphi library path to point there.

Being hosted in GitHub `DelphiMVCFramework`, the latest version of the code is also available as a zip file. Look for a button labeled **Download ZIP** in the project page. However, the preferred way to get the source code is cloning the Git repo, and I strongly suggest you get confident using Git. Moreover, the ZIP file doesn't contain the submodules code; that you have to retrieve by hand from the Internet.

The same procedure needs to be done for `jTable`. Go to the GitHub project page (https://github.com/hikalkan/jtable/) and clone the repository on your machine.

As for `DelphiMVCFramework`, if you want, you can download the zip file instead.

Put the `jTable` code in `C:\DelphiBook\Libs\jtable`.

> In the recipe project, there is a downloaded copy of the sources; however, you can use this procedure if you want to download a fresher version of the sources.

Now that you know how and where to retrieve the external projects used in this recipe, let's start with the explanation.

How it works...

Open the recipe project `PhoneBookServer.dproj` from this chapter's recipe folder. This is a WebBroker project. WebBroker is a technology available since Delphi 4 to help create web server applications exposing an HTTP/HTTPS interface. More information about WebBroker can be found at the following URLs:

- `http://docwiki.embarcadero.com/RADStudio/en/Creating_Internet_server_applications_Index`
- `http://docwiki.embarcadero.com/RADStudio/en/Using_Web_Broker_Index`

In this recipe we'll see a simple CRUD for an Interbase database table. Here's the final application running in a browser:

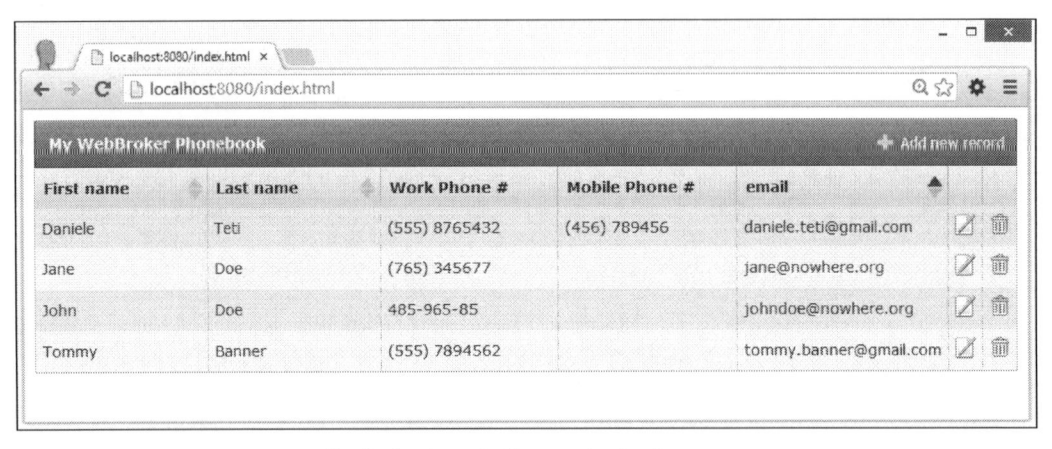

The final web application running in a browser

Take a look at the project folder. When you write WebBroker applications, the relative position of the static files used by the web application is important, and we have to deliver some static files to our clients:

```
DCU
www
MainDM.dfm
MainDM.pas
PhoneBookServer.dpr
PhoneBookServer.dproj
PhoneBookServer.exe
PhoneBookServer.res
WebModuleU.dfm
WebModuleU.pas
```

The project folder layout

The `DCU` folder contains all the generated DCUs, while the `www` folder will be our document root for the static files. In the `www` folder, you have an `index.html` file and a `lib` folder. In the `lib` folder, there is the folder containing the `jTable` library. Our application is a web client app; that means that what the user sees in their browser is not completely generated by the server and then sent to the client, but the client has an initial HTML and then it will use JavaScript code to request data to the server using AJAX. When the server data is on the client (usually transferred as JSON) the JavaScript code assemble data and HTML to generate the final DOM. In this recipe, we'll use `jTable` to avoid all the boring HTML writing to create a simple CRUD interface.

Let's start from the initial HTML file retrieved by the client. This is the file that *starts* our application, and the JavaScript inside it will download the actual data to show. If you open it using a normal text editor (better if with syntax highlighting), you will see that the following files are loaded:

- jQuery library from the Google CDN
- jQuery-UI library from `code.jquery.com`
- jTable from a local copy
- jQuery-UI CSS for a specific theme from `code.jquery.com`
- jTable CSS theme from our local copy

These files are required by our web client app.

Putting Delphi on the Server

The `jTable` library allows you to generate a complete grid with embedded editing functionalities, only providing specific URLs to invoke. We'll provide the following URLs in the WebBroker server:

- `/index.html`: Delivers the main file
- `/getpeople`: Returns a JSON array of JSON objects with the database data
- `/saveperson`: Can be invoked to create or update a person on the database. If there is an ID field, then the person will be updated; otherwise, they will be created and a new ID will be provided by the database
- `/deleteperson`: Deletes a person with a specified ID

Note that this server is not a RESTful server. All the HTTP resources are invoked using a POST method. We are using plain WebBroker here, and `DelphiMVCFramework` is used only to easily serialize data retrieved from the database. A real RESTful server will be developed in *Sending a POST HTTP request encoding parameters* recipe of this chapter.

Back to Delphi and the recipe project. Open the WebModule and the **Show its Actions** property; you should see something similar to this:

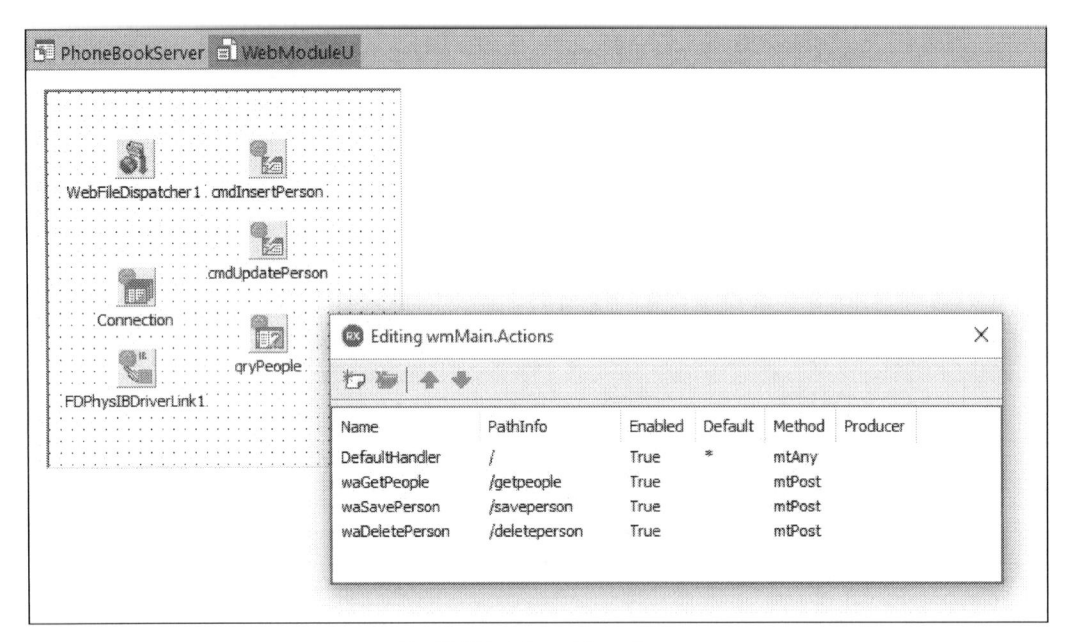

Name	PathInfo	Enabled	Default	Method	Producer
DefaultHandler	/	True	*	mtAny	
waGetPeople	/getpeople	True		mtPost	
waSavePerson	/saveperson	True		mtPost	
waDeletePerson	/deleteperson	True		mtPost	

The WebModule and its actions

The `WebFileDispatcher` is configured to point to the `www` folder as its main `root` folder. In this way, all the files in that folder (that have permitted extensions) will be visible to the client.

FireDAC components are used to access the database. There's a `TFDConnection` pointing to a local Interbase database placed in the `DATA` folder (to run this project, you have to start the Interbase Service from the Service Control Panel). For each SQL statement, there is a component dedicated, apart from DELETE, which is executed directly on the connection.

At startup, we have to activate the database connection. Here's the `TFDConnection BeforeConnect` event handler:

```
procedure TwmMain.ConnectionBeforeConnect(Sender: TObject);
begin
  Connection.Params.Values['Database'] :=
    TPath.GetDirectoryName(WebApplicationFileName) +
      '\..\..\DATA\SAMPLES.IB';
end;
```

We have to inform the internal web server where the static files are located and what the web root is. In our case, the web `root` folder is located at the same level of the executable and is called www, so in the `WebModuleCreate` event handler, we have to write the following code:

```
procedure TwmMain.WebModuleCreate(Sender: TObject);
begin
  WebFileDispatcher1.RootDirectory := TPath.GetDirectoryName
    (WebApplicationFileName) + '\www';
end;
```

Retrieving the people list

The client will issue a request to /getpeople and the server has to respond with a JSON array of JSON objects. This request is handled by the action `waGetPeopleAction`. The event handler contains the following code:

```
procedure TwmMain.wmMainwaGetPeopleAction(Sender: TObject;
    Request: TWebRequest; Response: TWebResponse;
var Handled: Boolean);
var
  JPeople: TJSONArray;
  SQL: string;
  OrderBy: string;
begin
  SQL := 'SELECT * FROM PEOPLE ';
  OrderBy := Request.QueryFields.Values['jtSorting'].Trim.ToUpper;
  if OrderBy.IsEmpty then
  begin
    SQL := SQL + 'ORDER BY FIRST_NAME ASC';
  end
  else
```

```delphi
    begin
      if TRegEx.IsMatch(OrderBy, '^[A-Z,_]+[ ]+(ASC|DESC)$') then
      begin
        SQL := SQL + 'ORDER BY ' + OrderBy;
      end
      else
        raise Exception.Create('Invalid order clause syntax');
    end;

    // execute query and prepare response
    qryPeople.Open(SQL);
    try
      JPeople := qryPeople.AsJSONArray; //ObjectsMappers
    finally
      qryPeople.Close;
    end;
    PrepareResponse(JPeople, Response);
  end;
```

This method executes a query on the `PEOPLE` table and then serializes the dataset returned using a class helper introduced by the `ObjectsMappers.pas` unit (part of the `DMVCFramework`).

`jTable` can also handle sorting on the grid columns. To do this, send another request to the server with a parameter named `jSorting`, containing the field and the direction of the order by in the form: `first_name asc` or `last_name desc`. This is a nice feature; however, we cannot simply concatenate this string to the SQL. We have to sanitize it to avoid a SQL injection attack. So, there is a regular expression to check whether the `jSorting` parameter contains only allowed characters and is composed of two words. We do not control if the field on which ordinate is a valid field because the select will issue an error in that case.

The `PrepareResponse` method is needed to correctly prepare the response to communicate with `jTable`. If you want to understand the details, check the *jTable Getting Started* here: http://jtable.org/GettingStarted.

Creating or updating a person

`jTable` allows the user to create a new record or modify a record that has already been created. Here's the GUI used in the case of a modify request:

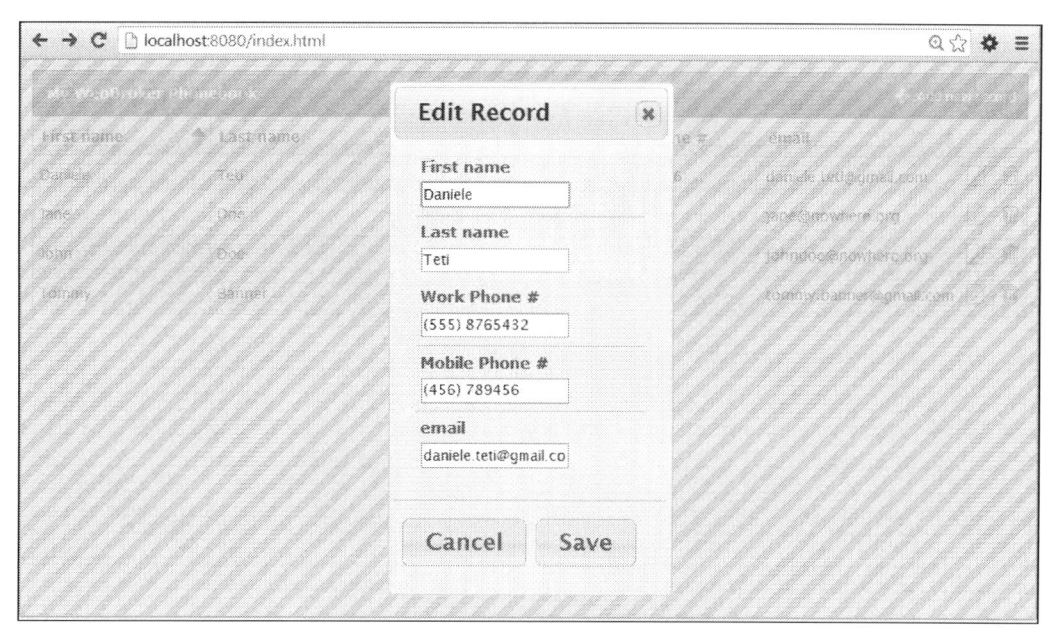

The edit dialog generated by the web client app

When the data has been filled in, the user can click **Save**, and then all the data is sent to the server in a `POST` request. This request is handled by the action `waSavePersonAction` invoked with the `/saveperson` path. Here's the code used to create or update a record:

```
procedure TwmMain.wmMainwaSavePersonAction(Sender: TObject;
  Request: TWebRequest; Response: TWebResponse;
  var Handled: Boolean);
var
  InsertMode: Boolean;
  JObj: TJSONObject;
  LastID: Integer;
  HTTPFields: TStrings;
  procedure MapStringsToParams(AStrings: TStrings;
   AFDParams: TFDParams);
  var
     i: Integer;
  begin
    for i := 0 to HTTPFields.Count - 1 do
    begin
```

```
      if AStrings.ValueFromIndex[i].IsEmpty then
        AFDParams.ParamByName(AStrings.Names[i].ToUpper).Clear()
      else
        AFDParams.ParamByName(AStrings.Names[i].ToUpper).Value :=
          AStrings.ValueFromIndex[i];
    end;
  end;

begin
  HTTPFields := Request.ContentFields;
  InsertMode := HTTPFields.IndexOfName('id') = -1;
  if InsertMode then
  begin
    MapStringsToParams(HTTPFields, cmdInsertPerson.Params);
    cmdInsertPerson.Execute();
    LastID := Connection.GetLastAutoGenValue('GEN_PEOPLE_ID');
  end
  else
  begin
    MapStringsToParams(HTTPFields, cmdUpdatePerson.Params);
    cmdUpdatePerson.Execute();
    LastID := HTTPFields.Values['id'].ToInteger;
  end;

  // execute query and prepare response
  qryPeople.Open('SELECT * FROM PEOPLE WHERE ID = ?', [LastID]);
  try
    PrepareResponse(qryPeople.AsJSONObject, Response);
  finally
    qryPeople.Close;
  end;
end;
```

The simple trick used in this code to determine if an insert or an update is requested is to check if a field named ID is present in the POSTed fields. If an ID field is present, then we have to generate an update; otherwise an insert.

Deleting a person record is the simplest method. The code of the `waDeletePerson` action is invoked with the `/deleteperson` path. Here's the code:

```
procedure TwmMain.wmMainwaDeletePersonAction(Sender: TObject;
  Request: TWebRequest; Response: TWebResponse;
  var Handled: Boolean);
begin
```

```
  Connection.ExecSQL('DELETE FROM PEOPLE WHERE ID = ?',
[Request.ContentFields.Values['id']]);
  PrepareResponse(nil, Response);
end;
```

There is only one thing to note: we didn't use a specific command to issue the SQL statement but the connection directly.

Running the application

Hitting *F9*, you should see a console window informing you that a server is started. Open the browser and point it to `http://localhost:8080`. You should see what is shown in *figure 1.1*.

If not, try checking the following:

- Is port 8080 free?
- Is the Interbase database running correctly?
- Is the URL written correctly?

There's more...

This is only a small introduction to what you can do with WebBroker and a bounce of good JavaScript libraries. There are a lot of articles about WebBroker; some of them are a bit old but most are still applicable the last version of Delphi Seattle. After reading the current documentation on the Embarcadero docwiki, have a look at the following article: `http://delphi.about.com/library/bluc/text/uc060901a.html`.

WebBroker can also create an ISAPI dll for Microsoft Internet Information Server and an Apache module dll for the Apache httpd web server. If you plan to deploy your web application on a production public server, you should consider putting your application behind a full-fledged web server such as Apache or IIS.

Another solution is to use the simple webserver created by Delphi and put a reverse proxy (`http://en.wikipedia.org/wiki/Reverse_proxy`) in front of it.

However, if you'll use the application in your intranet, it is safe enough to publish it as a console application, or (better) a Windows Service, directly on a server in your LAN.

Another bit of good news is that WebBroker WebModules are really independent from the final program type where they will be linked. So, you can develop a console application, debug it, and then convert it into a Windows Service, an Apache module, or an ISAPI dll with a few clicks.

Putting Delphi on the Server

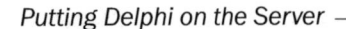

If you have trouble retrieving the `DelphiMVCFramework` project code, follow its *Getting Started* contained in the *Developer Guide*, which you can find at https://danieleteti.gitbooks.io/delphimvcframework/content/.

Converting a console application to a Windows service

Writing and debugging a Windows service can be difficult and slow. In the *Creating a Windows service* recipe in *Chapter 1, Delphi Basics* you learned how to do it from scratch, but in some cases you already have a console or VCL application that already does its job, but it would be much better if it could be recreated as a Windows service.

Getting ready

In this recipe, we'll take the WebBroker application created in the previous recipe as a console application, and convert it to a full flagged Windows service. The same approach can be used for any type of service-like application that is not currently built as a service.

As a bonus, we'll learn that, if correctly architected, a project can be compiled as a console or VCL application and, without many changes, also as a Windows service. WebBroker is particular well architected to do so, so our application will benefit from it.

How to do it...

Perform the following steps:

1. Create a new Service Application by navigating to **File | New | Other...** then **Delphi Projects | Service Application**.
2. As soon as Delphi creates the project template, save all the files with the following names:
   - Save the project as `PhoneBookService.dproj`
   - Save the Service module as `ServiceU.pas`
3. Show the object inspector for the service module and set the following properties:
   - **AllowPause = False**
   - **DisplayName = 'PhoneBookService'**
4. Now add to the project the WebModule from the Developing (the file is named `WebModuleU.pas` and should be in the `Chapter06\CODE\RECIPE01` folder). This step allows us to reuse the code written for the console application for the service application.

5. Now your Project Manager should look like the following screenshot:

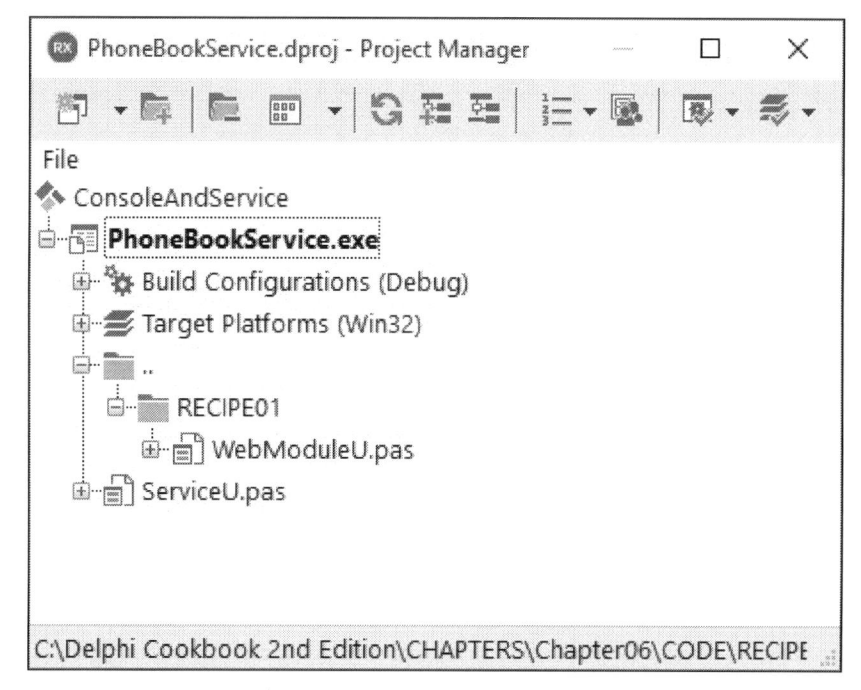

The Project Manager after adding WebModuleU.pas from the previous recipe

6. Now we have to wire some things: open `ServiceU.pas` and add the unit `IdHTTPWebBrokerBridge` in the uses clause. This allows us to create an internal HTTP service into our Windows service.

7. Now, in the private part of the `TPhoneBook` declaration, add the following line:

    private
        LServer: TIdHTTPWebBrokerBridge;

8. In the implementation section of `ServiceU.pas`, add the following uses clause:

    uses
        Web.WebReq, WebModuleU;

9. Now we have to handle the TCP server and the class registration for WebBroker. Let's create some `TPhoneService` event handlers.

10. Create the `OnCreate`, `OnStart`, and `OnStop` event handlers and fill them with the following code:

    procedure TPhoneBook.ServiceCreate(Sender: TObject);
    begin
      if WebRequestHandler <> nil **then**
        WebRequestHandler.WebModuleClass := WebModuleClass;

```
    end;

      procedure TPhoneBook.ServiceStart(Sender: TService;
        var Started: Boolean);
      begin
        LServer := TIdHTTPWebBrokerBridge.Create(nil);
        LServer.DefaultPort := 8080;
        LServer.Active := True;
      end;

      procedure TPhoneBook.ServiceStop(Sender: TService;
        var Stopped: Boolean);
      begin
        LServer.Free;
      end;
```

11. Build the project.
12. Copy the www folder from the previous recipe and put it at the same level of the compiled service.
13. OK, our service should be OK. Start a command prompt as administrator, go to the folder where the service executable is and write the following command line: `PhoneBookService.exe /install`.
14. A message dialog should inform you that the service has been installed correctly.
15. Now go to the Services management console and you should see the new service named `PhoneBookService` listed among the others. Start it and navigate with your browser to the following URL: `http://localhost:8080`.
16. Now you should see the WebBroker Phone Book page with some people listed.
17. If the people list is not loading, the service probably isn't reaching the database. Check if the database is running and if the code under `OnBeforeConnect` of the database connection is set to set the correct connection string.

How it works...

This recipe is really simple. All the dirty work is done by the WebBroker framework and by the `TIdHTTPWebBrokerBridge` class. As a general rule, when you have a TCP service that should listen while the service is running, simply start the TCP service in the `OnStart` event handler and stop it in the `OnStop` event handler. If your logic is more complex, you should be able to separate all the things that make the service available (start) and put them in the `OnStart` event handler, while all the things that make the service unavailable and free the resources (stop), in the `OnStop` event handler.

If you need to also support a paused state, you have to find out what a paused state means for your service. For this recipe, a paused state is equal to a stopped state, so I simply removed the ability to pause the service.

There's more...

Every application may have a different way of being converted into a Windows service; however, you should be aware that your service runs in a different environment with respect to your "normal" application. Two notable differences are the following:

- Services can run out of any user context, and usually do. They usually run as a **Local System Account** (as with the service in this recipe), but can be configured to run as a particular user.
- The current folder for a service is not the folder where the executable is, but the `C:\Windows\System32` folder for 64-bit services, the same for 32-bit services when run on 32-bit machines, and `C:\Windows\SysWOW64` for 32-bit services that run on 64-bit machines.

Serializing a dataset to JSON and back

At the time when almost all the Delphi program was client/server or, in general, when the Delphi program was always connected to the database server in a fully-connected scenario, dataset serialization was a niche topic. There were really only a few situations where you really needed this kind of functionality in the core of your application. Were the '90! Now, however, making your data available to other programs or getting data from other software running somewhere in the world is the norm. In some cases, the other "programs" are not written in Delphi, so the `DataSet.SaveToFile` method, or another serialization that uses a proprietary or "exotic" format, is no longer enough.

Let's say we have a JavaScript frontend for our Delphi application server. Your data should be deDelphized (I've just coined this word) and should be independent from the backend programming language or framework used. Delphi has a lot of serialization facilities, but there isn't a well-known way to serialize a DataSet in JSON standard format and deserialize a standard JSON in a DataSet (there are some units containing JSON serialization stuff but the resultant JSON is very Delphi-oriented and not well suited to be used to communicate with other non-Delphi programs). In the DataSnap framework, there are classes devoted to doing this kind of thing and they are all contained in the unit `Data.DBXJSONCommon.pas`, but at the time of writing, they are not designed to be flexible enough to be used in heterogeneous scenarios. Don't be afraid; in this recipe, we'll solve all these problems!

Putting Delphi on the Server

Getting ready

We'll use a subproject of the already mentioned `DelphiMVCFramework` (more info can be found here: https://github.com/danieleteti/delphimvcframework) called Mapper.

Mapper is a micro-framework that aim developers in mappings and conversions and will be used in this recipe and in the next.

First, get `DelphiMVCFramework` using the Git repository (a simple guide is available here: https://danieleteti.gitbooks.io/delphimvcframework/content/chapter_getting_started.html). Then create a new VCL project to do some experiments. This recipe is not a complete project, but a set of demos showing what you can do with your datasets using this open source micro framework.

The demo project is a simple list of buttons, a `TDBGrid`, and a `TMemo` to show the last JSON serialization that happened:

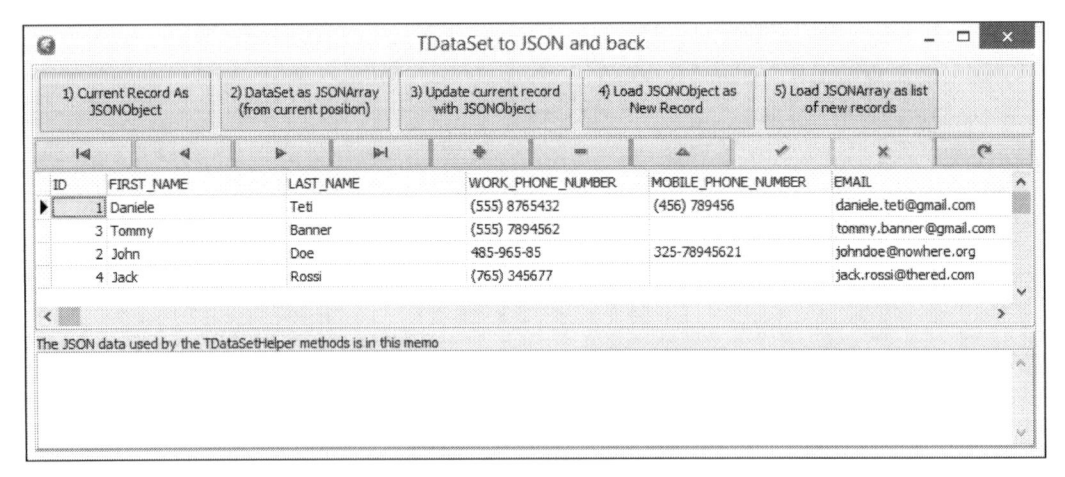

Demo for DataSet JSON serialization

How it works...

Under each button is a particular Mapper feature. The mapper serializes data in JSON format using a simple object or array of objects. To be clear, a single record will be serialized as a JSON object while a full dataset (or a set of records) is serialized as a JSON array containing JSON objects, one for each serialized record. In the uses clause of the form, there is a reference to the unit `ObjectsMappers.pas`. This unit adds some method to each `TDataSet` descendant using a class helper, and in this project, we'll use some of them.

The first button converts the current dataset record (the dataset is called `qryPeople` and is owned by a datamodule called `dm`) into a JSON object; the code used is the following:

```
Log := dm.qryPeople.AsJSONObjectString;
```

Log is a property used as a variable but in its setter, it writes its new value to the memo. So clicking button 1, you will have this situation in the form:

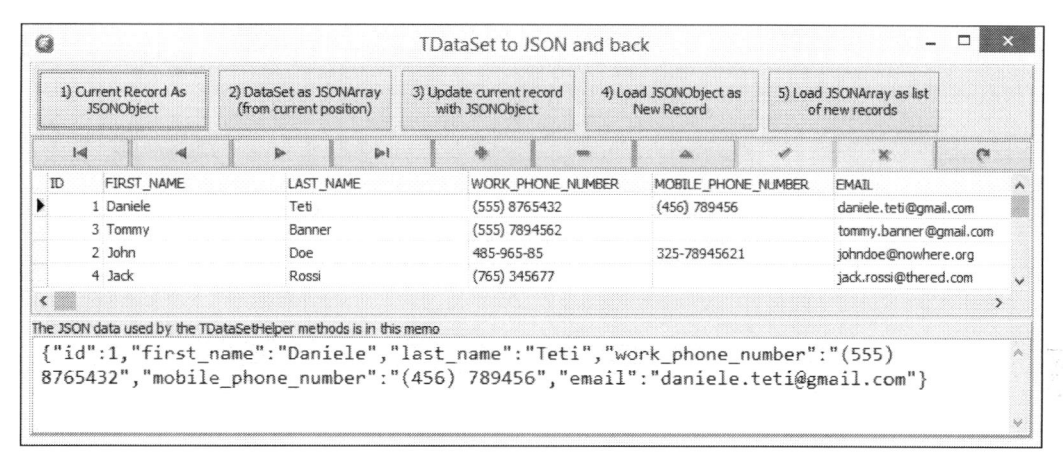

The memo shows the serialized version of the dataset current record

It is really simple! You don't even know how to access the serialization engine, just include the `ObjectsMappers` unit and all your datasets are able to serialize and deserialize themselves.

Button 2 serializes the dataset as a JSON array of JSON objects, starting from the current position:

```
Log := dm.qryPeople.AsJSONArrayString;
```

Go to the first record and click on button 2. The memo will show a JSON array like the following:

```
[{"id":1,"first_name":"Daniele","last_name":"Teti",
  "work_phone_number":"(555) 8765432",
  "mobile_phone_number":"(456) 789456",
    "email":"daniele.teti@gmail.com"},
  {"id":3,"first_name":"Tommy","last_name":"Banner",
    "work_phone_number":"(555) 7894562",
    "mobile_phone_number":null,"email":"tommy.banner@gmail.com"},
  {"id":2,"first_name":"John","last_name":"Doe",
    "work_phone_number":"485-965-85",
    "mobile_phone_number":"325-78945621",
    "email":"johndoe@nowhere.org"},
  {"id":4,"first_name":"Jack","last_name":"Rossi",
    "work_phone_number":"(765) 345677","mobile_phone_number":null,
    "email":"jack.rossi@thered.com"}]
```

As you can see, the mapper takes care of null fields and serializes them as JSON `null`. The third button does an update on the record using a JSON object:

```
dm.qryPeople.Edit;
dm.qryPeople.LoadFromJSONObjectString(
Log,
TArray<String>.Create('id'));
dm.qryPeople.Post;
```

It uses the previously serialized data (contained in the `Log` property) to update the current record. To use it, do the following:

1. Go to the first record.
2. Click button 1 (the memo fills with the serialized data as a JSON object).
3. Go to the record that you want to update.
4. Click button 3.
5. The record is updated!

You want to update all fields except the primary key, so as the second parameter of the `LoadFromJSONObjectString`, we have to pass an array of strings representing the name of the fields that we don't want to update in the dataset. In this case, we don't want to update the `id` field. So, when we call `qryPeople.Post`, the dataset sends an update to the database.

The fourth button is similar, but is used to create a new record starting from a JSON object. This is the code:

```
dm.qryPeople.Append;
dm.qryPeople.LoadFromJSONObjectString(
Log,
TArray<String>.Create('id'));
dm.qryPeople.Post;
```

To use it, do the following:

1. Go to the first record (or another record that you want to clone).
2. Click button 1 (the memo fills with the serialized data as a JSON object).
3. Click button 4.
4. A new record is created!

Obviously, you can use any JSON object to create the new record. To prove this, follow these steps:

1. Go to the first record.
2. Click button 1 (the memo fills with the serialized data as a JSON object).
3. Now, in the memo, change a JSON property, let's say `last_name`. Look for `"last_name":"some string"` and change the value (`some string`) to something else.
4. Click button 4.
5. A new record is created with the new value!

The JSON object can arrive from anywhere and can be put directly into your database using this simple `json->dataset` mapping. In the last year, I've used a lot of these techniques in real-world web and mobile applications (the next recipe will focus on a more **OO** approach compared to this one based on `TDataSet`).

The fifth button allows you to append a JSON array of JSON objects directly to the dataset:

```
dm.qryPeople.AppendFromJSONArrayString(
Log,
TArray<String>.Create('id'));
```

There's more...

Serialization and deserialization are huge topics. All the Internet services, finally, depend on some kind of serialization. The average Delphi user is very skilled with some kinds of `TDataset` descendants (`TFDMemTable`, `TClientDataSet`, or other similar datasets) and normally tends to rely on some particular functionality present in the data access components suite chosen. However, when the deserializer is not a Delphi program, some problems can arise. The Mapper framework resolves this kind of problem in a simple and elegant way (IMHO). As a real example, the JSON format doesn't provide a specific type for dates and times. If you try to blindly serialize `TDate`, `TDateTime`, and `TTime`, Delphi data types in JSON (using the underline double data type), you will get numbers that are perfectly valid for another Delphi program but completely useless for JavaScript, Java, .NET, Python, and so on. So Mapper takes care of this and other problems using standard representation where JSON doesn't provide specific data types. In this case, all datetime data is serialized and deserialized using the ISO format that can be understood by all the libraries and programming languages. Moreover, Mapper is not dependent on the regional settings of the machine, so you can generate a JSON on an English-speaking PC and deserialize it on an Italian-speaking machine without problems with decimal separators, date format, currency formatting, and so on.

Putting Delphi on the Server

Serializing objects to JSON and back using RTTI

When you are using a domain model pattern (and you should do most of the time for non-trivial applications), the entities managed by your program are contained in objects. An object has a state and methods to change its state, just like any actual object in the real world.

Getting ready

Just like the datasets in the previous recipe, the need to serialize an object in a JSON object, send the object somewhere, and then recreate that object as it was before is very common. In this recipe, we'll use the `TJson` class and extend it with new functionalities.

How to do it...

Perform the following steps:

1. Create a new VCL Forms Application.
2. Drop four TButton and a TMemo on the form. Organize the TButton in a single row as a sort of toolbar and align the TMemo to cover the remaining part of the form.
3. Name the TButton as follows:
    - btnObjToJSON
    - btnJSONtoObject
    - btnListToJSONArray
    - btnJSONArrayToList
4. Add a new unit to the project, name it `JSON.Serializer.pas` and fill it with the following code:

```
unit JSON.Serialization;

interface

uses
  REST.JSON, System.Generics.Collections, System.JSON;

type
  TJSONUtils = class(TJSON)
  public
    class function
ObjectsToJSONArray<T: class, constructor>(
```

```delphi
    AList: TObjectList<T>): TJSONArray;
    class function
JSONArrayToObjects<T: class, constructor>(
AJSONArray: TJSONArray): TObjectList<T>;
  end;

implementation

uses
  System.SysUtils;

{ TJSONHelper }

class function TJSONUtils.JSONArrayToObjects<T>(
AJSONArray: TJSONArray): TObjectList<T>;
var
  I: Integer;
begin
  Result := TObjectList<T>.Create(True);
  try
    for I := 0 to AJSONArray.Count - 1 do
      Result.Add(TJSON.JsonToObject<T>(AJSONArray.Items[I]
           as TJSONObject));
  except
    FreeAndNil(Result);
    raise;
  end;
end;

class function TJSONUtils.ObjectsToJSONArray<T>(
AList: TObjectList<T>): TJSONArray;
var
  Item: T;
begin
  Result := TJSONArray.Create;
  try
    for Item in AList do
      Result.AddElement(TJSON.ObjectToJsonObject(Item));
  except
    FreeAndNil(Result);
    raise;
  end;
end;

end.
```

5. Add another unit to the project and name it `PersonU.pas`.
6. The interface section of `PersonU.pas` must use unit `REST.Json.Types`.
7. Now declare a class as follows and let Delphi autocreate the property setters using *Ctrl +Shift + C*:

   ```
   type
     TPerson = class
     public
       property ID: Integer;
       property FirstName: String;
       property LastName: String;
       property WorkPhone: String;
       property MobilePhone: String;
       property EMail: String;
     end;
   ```

8. After *Ctrl + Shift + C*, go to the class private section and add the attribute `JsonName` to the `FID` field shown as follows:

   ```
   private
     [JsonName('id')]
     FID: Integer;
   ```

9. Save the file and go back to the main form.
10. While on the `MainForm` code, hit *Alt + F11* and add to the interface uses clause the unit `JSON.Serializer.pas`; repeat the procedure and add the unit `PersonU.pas`.
11. Now, create a read/write property named `Log` in the main form; this property does not have an internal field but reads and writes its value from the `Memo1.Lines.Text` property, acting like a proxy for it.
12. To have some objects to work with, we need some fake data. So, create a method in the private section of the form called `GetPeople` with the following code:

    ```
    private
      function GetPeople: TObjectList<TPerson>;
    ```

13. Hit *Ctrl +Shift + C* and create the method body with the following code:

    ```
    function TMainForm.GetPeople: TObjectList<TPerson>;
    var
      P: TPerson;
    begin
      Result := TObjectList<TPerson>.Create(True);
      P := TPerson.Create;
      P.ID := 1;
      P.FirstName := 'Daniele';
      P.LastName := 'Teti';
    ```

```
    P.WorkPhone := '555-4353432';
    P.MobilePhone := '(328) 7894562';
    P.EMail := 'me@danieleteti.it';
    Result.Add(P);

    P := TPerson.Create;
    P.ID := 2;
    P.FirstName := 'John';
    P.LastName := 'Doe';
    P.WorkPhone := '457-6549875';
    P.EMail := 'john@nowhere.com';
    Result.Add(P);

    P := TPerson.Create;
    P.ID := 3;
    P.FirstName := 'Jane';
    P.LastName := 'Doe';
    P.MobilePhone := '(339) 5487542';
    P.EMail := 'jane@nowhere.com';
    Result.Add(P);
end;
```

14. Now create the event handlers for the four buttons using the following code:

```
procedure TMainForm.btnJSONtoObjectClick(Sender: TObject);
var
  JObj: TJSONObject;
  Person: TPerson;
begin
  JObj := TJSONObject.ParseJSONValue(Log) as TJSONObject;
  try
    Person := TJSONUtils.JsonToObject<TPerson>(JObj);
    try
      ShowMessage(Person.FirstName + ' ' + Person.LastName);
    finally
      Person.Free;
    end;
  finally
    JObj.Free;
  end;
end;

procedure TMainForm.btnListToJSONArrayClick(Sender: TObject);
var
  People: TObjectList<TPerson>;
```

```
      JArr: TJSONArray;
    begin
      People := GetPeople;
      try
        JArr := TJSONUtils.ObjectsToJSONArray<TPerson>(People);
        try
          Log := JArr.ToJSON;
        finally
          JArr.Free;
        end;
      finally
        People.Free;
      end;
    end;

    procedure TMainForm.btnObjToJSONClick(Sender: TObject);
    var
      People: TObjectList<TPerson>;
      JObj: TJSONObject;
    begin
      People := GetPeople;
      try
        JObj := TJSONUtils.ObjectToJsonObject(People[0]);
        try
          Log := JObj.ToJSON;
        finally
          JObj.Free;
        end;
      finally
        People.Free
      end;
    end;

    procedure TMainForm.btnJSONArrayToListClick(Sender: TObject);
    var
      JArr: TJSONArray;
      People: TObjectList<TPerson>;
      Person: TPerson;
      S: String;
    begin
      JArr := TJSONObject.ParseJSONValue(Log) as TJSONArray;
      try
        People := TJSONUtils.JSONArrayToObjects<TPerson>(JArr);
        try
```

```delphi
      S := '';
      for Person in People do
        S := S + sLineBreak +
              Person.FirstName + ' ' + Person.LastName;
    finally
      People.Free;
    end;
  finally
    JArr.Free;
  end;
  ShowMessage(S);
end;
```

15. Hit *F9* and see the application running.

How it works...

The Delphi RTL class `TJSON` contains two interesting methods:

```delphi
class function ObjectToJsonObject(AObject: TObject): TJSOnObject;
```

This converts an object into its JSON representation.

```delphi
class function JsonToObject<T: class, constructor>(AJsonObject:
TJSOnObject): T;
```

This takes a JSON object and recreates the related object.

However, usually we're dealing with a list of objects and an array of JSON objects. This is because the unit `JSON.Serialization.pas` extends the `TJSON` class, because we need to serialize and deserialize lists of objects too.

Here's the public interface of `TJSONUtils`:

```delphi
type
  TJSONUtils = class(TJSON)
  public
    class function ObjectsToJSONArray<T: class, constructor>(
AList: TObjectList<T>): TJSONArray;
    class function JSONArrayToObjects<T: class, constructor>(
AJSONArray: TJSONArray): TObjectList<T>;
  end;
```

With these four methods, we have been able to do the following serializations:

- `TObject: TJSONObject`
- `TJSONObject: TObject`
- `TObjectList<T>: TJSONArray of TJSONObject`
- `TJSONArray of TJSONObject: TObjectList<T>`

What about the `JsonName` attribute on the `FID` field of `TPerson`? That attribute allows you to define a custom name for the serialized field. If you remove that attribute, the ID field is serialized as ID, which is ugly and not intuitive. The attribute allows you to serialize a nicer and standard id as JSON property name.

There's more...

The `TJSON` class allows you to define specific serialization and deserialization strategies based on data types and field names. If you want to serialize a field in a specific way, you can define a `JSONReflect` attribute on that field using the name of the class descendent from `TJSONInterceptor`. In the recipe folder, there is a bonus project called `JSONInterceptorSample` which shows how even a stream can be serialized using an interceptor and the `JSONReflect` attribute.

Sending a POST HTTP request encoding parameters

HTTP protocol supports some types of verbs. A verb is a way to ask a remote server something. Some of these verbs are `GET`, `POST`, `PUT`, `DELETE`, `HEAD`, `PATCH`, `TRACE`, and `OPTIONS`. For a detailed description of HTTP protocol, you can read the related RFCs at the following URLs:

- RFC7230, about HTTP/1.1 protocol: `https://tools.ietf.org/html/rfc7230`
- A specific section about the available verbs in the HTTP/1.1 protocol: `https://tools.ietf.org/html/rfc7231#section-4`

When you write a URL in the browser address bar and hit *Return*, you are issuing a GET request to the remote HTTP server. However, when you have to send form data to the server, usually the HTML form uses the POST method. POST is designed to allow a uniform method of sending a block of data, such as the result of submitting a form, to a data-handling process or to post a message to a bulletin board, newsgroup, mailing list, or similar group of articles. In other words, while GET is intended to retrieve a resource from the server, POST is intended to transfer data from the client to the server. When sending data to the server, the client should inform it about the type of content (in the case of body data). This information is transferred in a specific request header called content-type. If you are sending a JSON, the content type should be application/json, while if a browser is sending data that a user wrote in an HTML form, the default content type is application/x-www-form-urlencoded. The content-type is sent by the client to inform the server about the type of the content it is sending, and by the server to inform the client about the type of the content it is returning. For an overview about the different content types, check here: http://en.wikipedia.org/wiki/Internet_media_type.

In this recipe, we'll show you how to send data to a remote web server using a POST method.

Getting ready

In this recipe, we'll use the web server created in the *Developing web client JavaScript applications with WebBroker on the server* recipe but this time, we're going to create a Delphi client to post data to that server. The data sent will be stored in the database and will be available through the already present web interface.

How to do it...

This recipe is really simple. So, start the WebBroker project created in the *Developing web client JavaScript applications with WebBroker on the server* recipe (run the executable without debugging) and follow these instructions:

1. Create a new **VCL Forms Application**.

2. On the main form, drop five **TEdits**, one **TButton**, one **TRESTClient** and one **TRESTRequest**. Organize the controls as in the following screenshot:

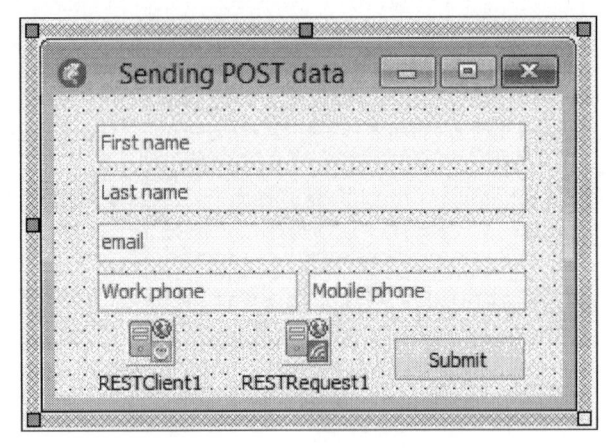

The client form used to send POST data to the web server

3. Give to the **TEdits** meaning names, to avoid confusion in the next phase.
4. Set **RESTClient1.BaseURL** to `'http://localhost:8080'`;.
5. Set the following properties on **RESTRequest1**:
    - `RESTRequest1.Client = RESTClient1`
    - `RESTRequest1.Method = rmPOST`
    - `RESTRequest1.Resource = 'saveperson'`

6. Double-click on the **TButton** and add the following code in its `OnClick` event:

```
procedure TMainForm.btnSubmitClick(Sender: TObject);
begin
   RESTRequest1.AddParameter('FIRST_NAME',
                             edtFirstName.Text);
   RESTRequest1.AddParameter('LAST_NAME',
                             edtLastName.Text);
   RESTRequest1.AddParameter('WORK_PHONE_NUMBER',
                             edtWorkPhone.Text);
   RESTRequest1.AddParameter('MOBILE_PHONE_NUMBER',
                             edtMobilePhone.Text);
   RESTRequest1.AddParameter('EMAIL', edtEmail.Text);
   RESTRequest1.Execute;
end;
```

7. Run the program, write some data in the edits and click the button. That's it! Your data has been saved on the database by the already created WebBroker application. Simple, isn't it?

The `TREST*` components were introduced in XE5 and are a fundamental part of a bigger strategic technology from Embarcadero. Moreover, while this recipe could also be realized easily with a simple `TidHTTP`, it's better to start to use `TREST*` or `TNetHTTP*` components. Why? Because `TidHTTP` relies on OpenSSL for its security layer while `TNetHTTP*` and `TREST*` (which internally uses `TNetHTTP*`) uses the native security layer offered by the operating system. So, when you need HTTPS support in your application, and believe me it will happen, you can rely on optimal support and simpler deployment compared to the INDY SSL strategy. In the recipe folder, there is also a project that uses the `TidHTTP` component; you can choose which client library to use in your projects. Moreover, in the next chapters, we'll talk about the native http/s components too.

How it works...

The URL where we have to send the data is `http://localhost:8080/saveperson`. The HTTP request is automatically created and sent to the server by the `TRESTRequest+TRESTClient` components. The `TRESTClient` defines the endpoint for all the requests, while the `TRESTRequest` defines the details for each different request. In this case, the `BaseURL` property contains the server name with the port (`http://localhost:8080`), while the request has only the `Resource` property set to the second part of the URL to `'saveperson'`.

What we're doing is adding a set of POST parameters with their values. Do you remember? `RESTRequest1.Method` is `rmPOST`, so will be created and sent as a `POST` request. The parameter names depend on what the server expects and we have to know the parameter names to correctly build a request.

As the name says, the `TREST*` components are mainly to be used with REST services, but can also be used with a normal HTTP service, as this recipe showed.

There's more...

The REST Client Library is very powerful. To get more info about it and to find out how to use it when dealing with RESTful web services, read the following entry in the docwiki: `http://docwiki.embarcadero.com/RADStudio/en/REST_Client_Library`.

If you want to see the REST Client Library in action with different kinds of services, check the RESTDemo sample here: `http://docwiki.embarcadero.com/CodeExamples/en/RESTDemo_Sample`.

Putting Delphi on the Server

Implementing a RESTful interface using WebBroker

What's REST? **Representational state transfer** (**REST**) is an architectural style consisting of a coordinated set of architectural constraints applied to components, connectors, and data elements, within a distributed hypermedia system.

The term *representational state transfer* was introduced and defined in 2000 by Roy Fielding in his doctoral dissertation at UC Irvine. If you want to know more about REST, I strongly suggest you read Fielding's dissertation here: `https://www.ics.uci.edu/~fielding/pubs/dissertation/rest_arch_style.htm`.

So, how do you build a RESTful system in Delphi? There are a lot of solutions but, according to the mentioned definitions, RESTful is not a set of libraries or algorithms, it is an architectural style, and as such, it can be respected 100%, 60%, 30%, and so on. There is a sort of scale used to measure how much a system is RESTful or not. This scale was first introduced by Leonard Richardson at the QCon conference, so it is called the **Richardson Maturity Model** (**RMM**). To get all the benefits that a RESTful approach brings, you should aim for RMM level 3. Be happy; the system we'll develop in this recipe is compliant with RMM level 3.

Getting ready

Our REST service handles a resource that is stored in a database table called `PEOPLE`. It provides CRUD methods, plus some specific features to paginate the data. Remember that RESTful doesn't mean expose method to do CRUD on a table but expose method to handle a resource. A resource can be, or cannot be, have a representation on a database table. Moreover, a resource can be also very complex with multiple nested objects, so while a table can be represented as a simple resource, generally a resource is not a mere table but an object graph stored on one, two, or more tables, or not stored at all. This is the HTTP REST interface that we'll implement:

HTTP VERB	URL	DESCRIPTION
GET	`/people`	Returns a JSON array containing one JSON object for each record present in the table `PEOPLE`. In each object the property name is the name of the field, while the property values are the value of the fields.
GET	`/people/($id)` `$id` is a URL parameter	Returns a JSON object representing the specific person who has the ID = `$id`.

HTTP VERB	URL	DESCRIPTION
POST	/people	Creates a new person in the table people. Requires a request body containing the new person to create as a JSON object. The request content-type must be `application/json`.
PUT	/people/($id)	Updates the person with `ID = $id` with the data passed in the request body. Requires a request body containing the new person to update as a JSON object. The request content-type must be `application/json`.
DELETE	/people/($id)	Deletes person with `ID = $id`
POST	/people/searches /people/searches?page=[x]	Returns a JSON array containing JSON objects. Executes a search over the `PEOPLE` table, returning only the records that match the filter passed as a JSON object in the request body. Requires a JSON object as request body. The parameter is passed as property `"TEXT"` in the request body, for example, `{"TEXT":"ele"}`.

This recipe uses DMVC, a Delphi open source framework based on WebBroker that allows you to create powerful RESTful web services. You can find the project code here: https://github.com/danieleteti/delphimvcframework.

Check out the project using the instructions on the website and put it into a folder on your file system. There are no components or controls, only units. Now you have to configure your IDE to find the DMVC units:

Navigate to **Tools** | **Options** | **Environment Options** | **Delphi Options** | **Library**.

Then click the **...** on the **Library Path edit**, and add the following paths one by one (change **C:\DEV\DMVCFramework** to the appropriate path on your machine):

```
C:\DEV\DMVCFramework\sources
C:\DEV\DMVCFramework\lib\delphistompclient
C:\DEV\DMVCFramework\lib\dmustache
```

Putting Delphi on the Server

This recipe uses many DMVC features and could be a little confusing if you don't know the basics of REST and DMVC. If so, please read the following documentation before going ahead:

- *Building Web Services the REST Way*: `http://www.xfront.com/REST-Web-Services.html`.
- *RESTful web services: The basics*: `https://www.ibm.com/developerworks/webservices/library/ws-restful/`.
- The latest information about DelphiMVCFramework is available in the *Developer Guide*: `https://danieleteti.gitbooks.io/delphimvcframework/content/`.
- The *Developer Guide* is also available as a PDF here: `https://www.gitbook.com/download/pdf/book/danieleteti/delphimvcframework`.

A valuable resource for DelphiMVCFramework is its samples, so please check the `\Samples` folder into the project `root` folder. From this point onward, I'll not repeat concepts and information already explained in the previously mentioned articles. So read them with care.

How to do it...

Perform the following steps:

1. Navigate to **Delphi Project | Web Broker | Web Server Application**.
2. Now the wizard asks you what type of web server application you want to create. This demo will be built as a console application. However, you can take advantage of the flexibility of WebBroker and add another type of application, for instance an ISAPI dll or a Windows Service. At this point, select Stand-alone console application and click **Next**.
3. The wizard proposes a TCP port where the service will listen. Click on **Test** port; if the test port succeeds, use it, otherwise change the port until the test passes. In this recipe, port 8080 is used.
4. Click **Finish**.
5. Save all. Name the project `PeopleManager.dproj` and the WebModule `WebModuleU.pas`.
6. We start from the business object classes. This web service will manage `people`, so let's create a new unit, and declare the following class:

   ```
   TPerson = class
   public
     property ID: Integer;
     property FIRST_NAME: String;
     property LAST_NAME: String;
     property WORK_PHONE_NUMBER: String;
   ```

```
    property MOBILE_PHONE_NUMBER: String;
    property EMAIL: String;
  end;
```

7. Hit *Ctrl +Shift+ C* to autocomplete the declaration; save the file as `PersonBO.pas`. Note that in projects where you have a lot of different types of classes (`businessobjects`, `controllers`, `datamodules`, and so on), it can be useful to organize the units in different folders. So, I saved `PersonBO.pas` in a folder named `BusinessObjects`. Feel free to do this as well.

8. Now it is time to create a DelphiMVCFramework controller. This is the class where there will be all the code to handle the HTTP requests and responses. Here, there should not be business logic code.

9. Create a new unit, name it `PeopleControllerU.pas` and save it into the `Controllers` folder.

10. Fill `PeopleControllerU.pas` with the following code:

```
unit PeopleControllerU;

interface

uses MVCFramework, PeopleModuleU;

type
  [MVCPath('/people')]
  TPeopleController = class(TMVCController)
  private
    FPeopleModule: TPeopleModule;
  protected
    procedure OnAfterAction(Context: TWebContext;
                           const AActionNAme: string); override;
    procedure OnBeforeAction(Context: TWebContext;
                           const AActionNAme: string;
  var Handled: Boolean); override;
  public
    [MVCPath]
    [MVCHTTPMethod([httpGET])]
    procedure GetPeople(CTX: TWebContext);

    [MVCPath('/($id)')]
    [MVCHTTPMethod([httpGET])]
    procedure GetPersonByID(CTX: TWebContext);

    [MVCPath]
    [MVCHTTPMethod([httpPOST])]
```

```
    [MVCConsumes('application/json')]
    procedure CreatePerson(CTX: TWebContext);

    [MVCPath('/($id)')]
    [MVCHTTPMethod([httpPUT])]
    [MVCConsumes('application/json')]
    procedure UpdatePerson(CTX: TWebContext);

    [MVCPath('/($id)')]
    [MVCHTTPMethod([httpDELETE])]
    procedure DeletePerson(CTX: TWebContext);

    [MVCPath('/searches')]
    [MVCHTTPMethod([httpPOST])]
    [MVCConsumes('application/json')]
    procedure SearchPeople(CTX: TWebContext);
  end;

implementation

uses
  PersonBO, SysUtils, System.JSON, ObjectsMappers, System.Math;

procedure TPeopleController.CreatePerson(CTX: TWebContext);
var
  Person: TPerson;
begin
  Person := CTX.Request.BodyAs<TPerson>;
  try
    FPeopleModule.CreatePerson(Person);
    CTX.Response.Location := '/people/' + Person.ID.ToString;
    Render(201, 'Person created');
  finally
    Person.Free;
  end;
end;

procedure TPeopleController.UpdatePerson(CTX: TWebContext);
var
  Person: TPerson;
begin
  Person := CTX.Request.BodyAs<TPerson>;
  try
    Person.ID := CTX.Request.ParamsAsInteger['id'];
```

```pascal
    FPeopleModule.UpdatePerson(Person);
    Render(200, 'Person updated');
  finally
    Person.Free;
  end;
end;

procedure TPeopleController.DeletePerson(CTX: TWebContext);
begin
  FPeopleModule.DeletePerson(CTX.Request.ParamsAsInteger['id']);
  Render(204, 'Person deleted');
end;

procedure TPeopleController.GetPersonByID(CTX: TWebContext);
var
  Person: TPerson;
begin
  Person := FPeopleModule.GetPersonByID(
CTX.Request.ParamsAsInteger['id']);
  if Assigned(Person) then
    Render(Person)
  else
    Render(404, 'Person not found');
end;

procedure TPeopleController.GetPeople(CTX: TWebContext);
begin
  Render<TPerson>(FPeopleModule.GetPeople);
end;

procedure TPeopleController.OnAfterAction(Context: TWebContext;
                                          const AActionNAme: string);
begin
  inherited;
  FPeopleModule.Free;
end;

procedure TPeopleController.OnBeforeAction(Context: TWebContext;
                                           const AActionNAme: string;
var Handled: Boolean);
begin
  inherited;
```

```
      FPeopleModule := TPeopleModule.Create(nil);
   end;

   procedure TPeopleController.SearchPeople(CTX: TWebContext);
   var
      Filters: TJSONObject;
      SearchText, PageParam: string;
      CurrPage: Integer;
   begin
      Filters := CTX.Request.BodyAsJSONObject;
      if not Assigned(Filters) then
         raise Exception.Create('Invalid search parameters');
      SearchText := Mapper.GetStringDef(Filters, 'TEXT');
      if (not TryStrToInt(CTX.Request.Params['page'], CurrPage))
         or (CurrPage < 1) then
         CurrPage := 1;
      Render<TPerson>(FPeopleModule.FindPeople(SearchText, CurrPage));
      CTX.Response.CustomHeaders.Values['dmvc-next-people-page'] :=
         Format('/people/searches?page=%d', [CurrPage + 1]);
      if CurrPage > 1 then
         CTX.Response.CustomHeaders.Values['dmvc-prev-people-page'] :=
            Format('/people/searches?page=%d', [CurrPage - 1]);
   end;

end.
```

11. Quite long, but all our RESTful interface is implemented in this unit. Now we have to write the part that actually accesses the database. In this recipe, we'll use a simple design pattern called Table Data Gateway. **Table Data Gateway** (**TDG**) was defined for the first time by *Martin Fowler* in his fundamental, and highly recommended, book *Patterns of Enterprise Application Architecture* (http://www.amazon.com/gp/product/0321127420). TDG is defined as follows: An object that acts as a Gateway to a database table. One instance handles all the rows in the table. (http://martinfowler.com/eaaCatalog/tableDataGateway.html).

12. Let's create our TDG using a `DataModule`. Add a new `DataModule`, name it `PeopleModule` and save it into the `Modules` folder as `PeopleModuleU.pas`.

13. Now your **Project Manager** should look like the following:

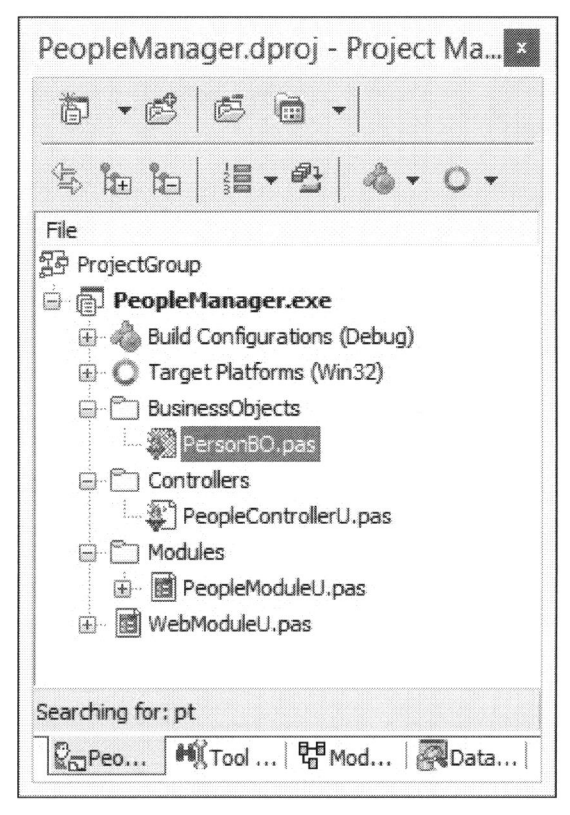

The Project Manager

14. Now, drop on the data module and link each other's, the components as follows (this is an extract of the `dfm` file):

```
object Conn: TFDConnection
  Params.Strings = (
    'Database=C:\Delphi Cookbook\BOOK\Chapter05\DATA\SAMPLES.IB'
    'User_Name=sysdba'
    'Password=masterkey'
    'DriverID=IB')
  ConnectedStoredUsage = [auDesignTime]
  Connected = True
  LoginPrompt = False
end
object qryPeople: TFDQuery
  Connection = Conn
  UpdateObject = updPeople
end
```

```
    object updPeople: TFDUpdateSQL
      Connection = Conn
    end
end
```

```
Change the FDConnection params accordingly with your machine.
```

15. Now we have to configure some data access stuff.
16. Double-click on **qryPeople**; the component editor shows up. Write the query `"SELECT * FROM PEOPLE"`, and click **Execute**. Hold the window open. This will be the query used to generate all the CRUD statements.
17. If you have correctly connected `qryPeople.UpdateObject` to `updPeople`, you should see an **UpdateSQL Editor** button on the right side of the component editor form:

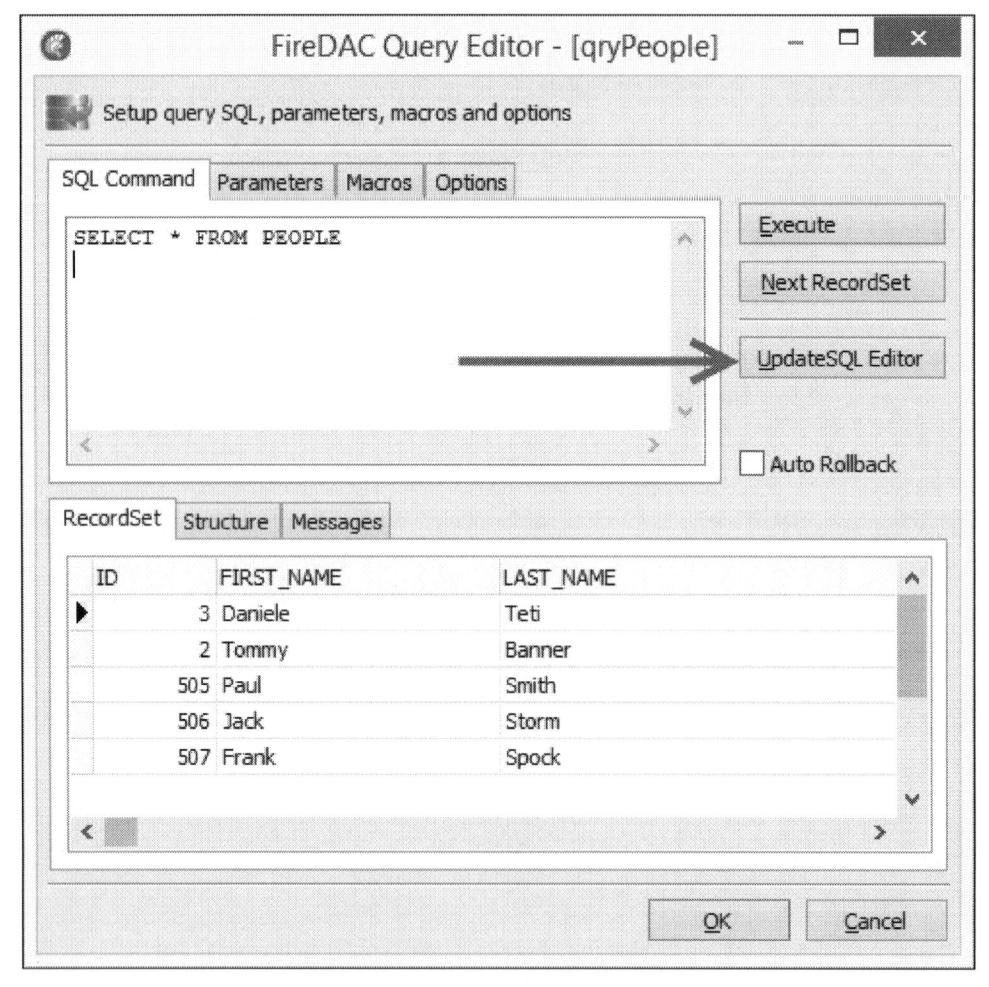

The qryPeople component editor showing the SQL and the button to configure TFDUpdateSQL linked to qryPeople

18. Click on the **UpdateSQL Editor** button and you will get another component editor. This time it is related to the `updPeople` component.

19. Select fields as shown in the image below and click **Generate SQL** and **OK**. Now your `updPeople` component has been configured with all the SQL statements needed to correctly update the `PEOPLE` table:

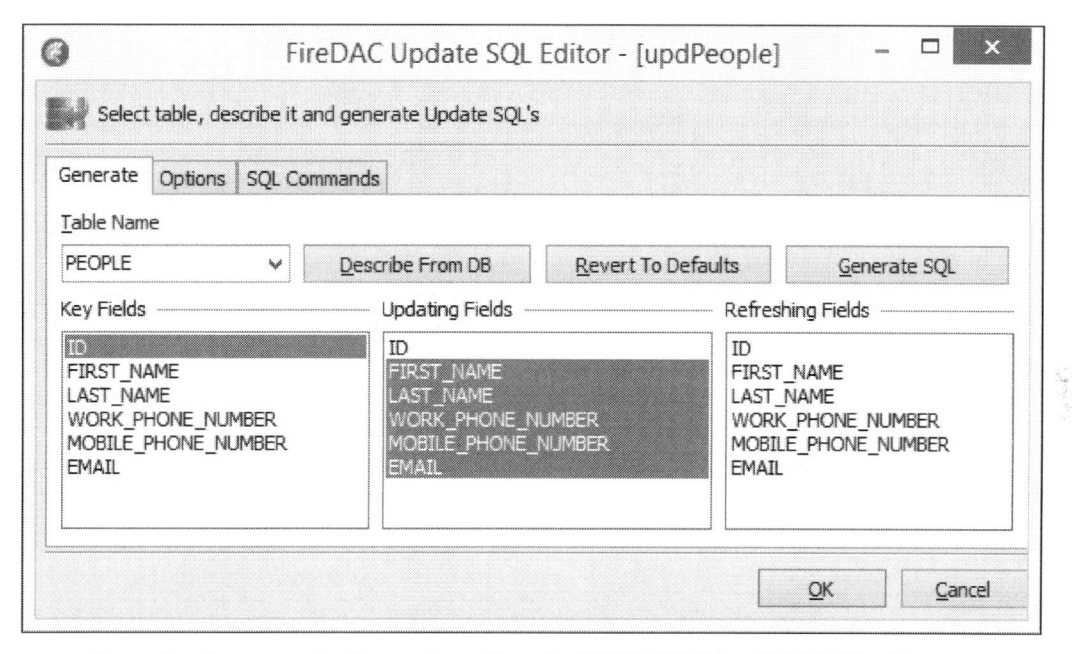

The updPeople component editor used to configure the INSERT, UPDATE and DELETE SQL statements

20. Now we have to create the methods used to CRUD records. Go to the `PeopleModuleU.pas` code view. Declare the following method in the class public section:

```
public
    procedure CreatePerson(APerson: TPerson);
    procedure DeletePerson(AID: Integer);
    procedure UpdatePerson(APerson: TPerson);
    function GetPersonByID(AID: Integer): TPerson;
    function FindPeople(ASearchText: String;
                        APage: Integer): TObjectList<TPerson>;
    function GetPeople: TObjectList<TPerson>;
end;
```

21. Hit *Ctrl* + *Shift* + *C* to autogenerate method bodies and fill them with the following code:

```
procedure TPeopleModule.CreatePerson(APerson: TPerson);
var
   InsCommand: TFDCustomCommand;
begin
   InsCommand := updPeople.Commands[arInsert];
   Mapper.ObjectToFDParameters(InsCommand.Params, APerson, 'NEW_');
   InsCommand.Execute;
   APerson.ID := Conn.GetLastAutoGenValue('gen_people_id');
end;

procedure TPeopleModule.DeletePerson(AID: Integer);
var
   DelCommand: TFDCustomCommand;
begin
   DelCommand := updPeople.Commands[arDelete];
   DelCommand.ParamByName('OLD_ID').AsInteger := AID;
   DelCommand.Execute;
end;

function TPeopleModule.FindPeople(ASearchText: String;
                                  APage: Integer): TObjectList<TPerson>;
var
   StartRec, EndRec: Integer;
begin
   Dec(APage); // page 0 => 0,9, page 1 => 10,19, page 3 => 20,29
   StartRec := (10 * APage);
   EndRec := StartRec + 10 - 1;
   qryPeople.Open('SELECT * FROM PEOPLE WHERE ' +
      'FIRST_NAME CONTAINING :SEARCH_TEXT_1 OR ' +
      'LAST_NAME CONTAINING :SEARCH_TEXT_2 OR ' +
      'EMAIL CONTAINING :SEARCH_TEXT_3 ' +
      'ORDER BY LAST_NAME, FIRST_NAME ' +
      Format('ROWS %d TO %d', [StartRec, EndRec]),
      [ASearchText, ASearchText, ASearchText]);
   Result := qryPeople.AsObjectList<TPerson>;
end;

function TPeopleModule.GetPersonByID(AID: Integer): TPerson;
begin
   qryPeople.Open('SELECT * FROM PEOPLE WHERE ID = :ID', [AID]);
```

```delphi
    Result := qryPeople.AsObject<TPerson>;
  end;

  function TPeopleModule.GetPeople: TObjectList<TPerson>;
  begin
    qryPeople.Open;
    Result := qryPeople.AsObjectList<TPerson>;
  end;

  procedure TPeopleModule.UpdatePerson(APerson: TPerson);
  var
    UpdCommand: TFDCustomCommand;
  begin
    UpdCommand := updPeople.Commands[arUpdate];
    Mapper.ObjectToFDParameters(
      UpdCommand.Params,
      APerson, 'NEW_');
    UpdCommand.ParamByName('OLD_ID').AsInteger := APerson.ID;
    UpdCommand.Execute;
  end;
```

22. These methods will be called by the controller capping data retrieved by the HTTP request. As you can see, the CRUD methods do not have references to the HTTP environment, or to JSON objects or whatever is related to the particular environment. These methods, and the whole class itself, can be used everywhere, even in a classic client/server application. Remember that the dependencies between the classes should be reduced as much as you can. More on this in the *How it works* section.

23. Add the `ObjectsMappers` unit in the implementation uses clause of `TPersonModule`.

24. Just one more thing to do in the `TPersonModule`: create the event handler `OnBeforeConnect` on the `TFDConnection` and write the following code (adapt it to point to the correct database path on your system):

```delphi
  procedure TPeopleModule.ConnBeforeConnect(Sender: TObject);
  begin
    inherited;
    Conn.Params.Values['Database'] := '..\..\..\..\DATA\SAMPLES.IB';
  end;
```

25. We're about to finish. Go back to `WebModuleU.pas` and create the `OnCreate` event handler. Here we have to configure the DelphiMVCFramework starting point. It is really simple, just two lines of code:

    ```
    procedure TwmMain.WebModuleCreate(Sender: TObject);
    begin
      FMVC := TMVCEngine.Create(Self);
      FMVC.AddController(TPeopleController);
    end;
    ```

26. The FMVC variable must be declared in the private section of the class and you have to add the `PeopleControllerU` unit in the implementation uses clause.

27. Now your project should compile. If not, check the dependencies between all the units.

28. After running the project, you get a sad console window that informs you that an HTTP server is running on port 8080. Launch a browser (better if Google Chrome or Mozilla Firefox) and request the following URL: `http://localhost:8080/people`.

29. Your browser should show all the data available in the `PEOPLE` table as a JSON array of JSON objects:

```
[{"ID":3,"FIRST_NAME":"Daniele","LAST_NAME":"Teti","WORK_PHONE_NUMBER":"
(555) 7894562 ","EMAIL":"tommy.banner@gmail.com"},
{"ID":2,"FIRST_NAME":"Tommy","LAST_NAME":"Banner","WORK_PHONE_NUMBER":"UPDAT
ED","MOBILE_PHONE_NUMBER":"UPDATED","EMAIL":"daniele.teti@gmail.com"},
{"ID":505,"FIRST_NAME":"Paul","LAST_NAME":"Smith","WORK_PHONE_NUMBER":"(555)
8765432","MOBILE_PHONE_NUMBER":"(456)
789456","EMAIL":"paul.smith@gmail.com"},
{"ID":506,"FIRST_NAME":"Jack","LAST_NAME":"Storm","WORK_PHONE_NUMBER":"(555)
1234578","MOBILE_PHONE_NUMBER":"(456)
98765432","EMAIL":"daniele.teti@gmail.com"},
{"ID":507,"FIRST_NAME":"Frank","LAST_NAME":"Spock","WORK_PHONE_NUMBER":"
(555) 1234578","MOBILE_PHONE_NUMBER":"(456)
98765432","EMAIL":"daniele.teti@gmail.com"}]
```

The JSON array of JSON objects returned by the HTTP call from the browser

30. If you want to try something different, get a valid person ID from the list of PEOPLE (look for `"ID": <some number>` in the JSON stream) and append it to the URL after a slash. This should be the effect:

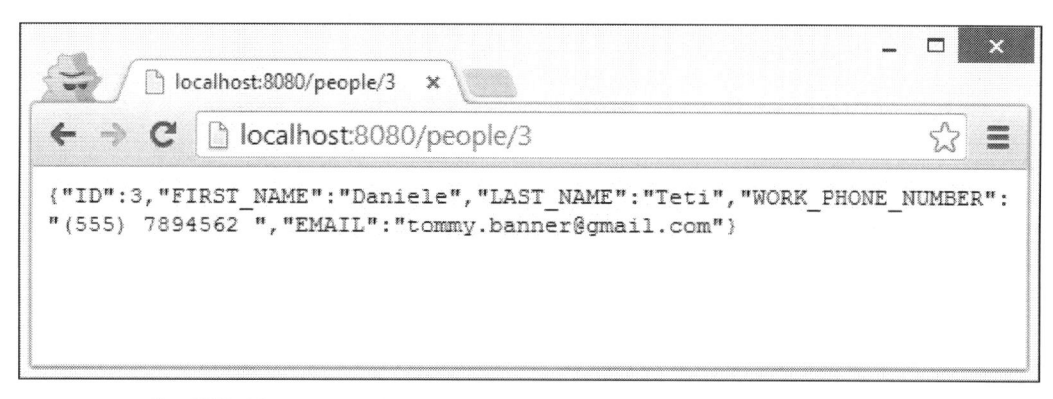

![Browser screenshot showing localhost:8080/people/3 with JSON response: {"ID":3,"FIRST_NAME":"Daniele","LAST_NAME":"Teti","WORK_PHONE_NUMBER":"(555) 7894562 ","EMAIL":"tommy.banner@gmail.com"}]

The JSON object representing a single person returned by the http call from the browser

How it works...

Wow! This recipe is very long! However, it summarizes all the concepts already seen in the previous recipes, so it's worth it.

The application is organized into three layers:

- Controller (`TPeopleController`):
    - Takes care of all the machinery needed to deserialize the JSON data into Delphi objects
    - Coordinates the job with the `Table` module
- Table Data Gateway (`TPeopleModule`):
    - Handles all the persistence needs
    - Gets objects and persists them
    - Retrieves datasets and converts them to objects
- Business Objects (`TPerson`):
    - Implements all the business logic required by the domain problem. In this sample, we don't have business logic, but if present, it should be inside the `TPerson` class.

Putting Delphi on the Server

When an HTTP request arrives at the server, the DMVCFramework router starts to find a suitable controller using the `MVCPath` attributes defined on all its controllers. When a matching controller and action is found, the request and response objects are packed in a `TWebContext` object and passed to the selected action. Here we can read information from the request and build the response accordingly.

All the action methods look like the following:

- Read information from the `http` request
- Invoke some methods on the `TPersonModule` instance
- Build the response for the client

Let's take a look at the following action used to create a new person:

```
[MVCPath]
[MVCHTTPMethod([httpPOST])]
[MVCConsumes('application/json')]
procedure CreatePerson(CTX: TWebContext);
```

. . .

```
procedure TPeopleController.CreatePerson(CTX: TWebContext);
var
   Person: TPerson;
begin
  //read information from the request
  Person := CTX.Request.BodyAs<TPerson>;
  try

     //invoke some methods on the TPeopleModule instance
     FPeopleModule.CreatePerson(Person);

     //build the response for the client
     CTX.Response.Location := '/people/' + Person.ID.ToString;
     Render(201, 'Person created');

  finally
     Person.Free;
  end;
end;
```

Chapter 6

What's that `CTX.Response.Location` line for? One of the RESTful features is the use of hypermedia controls. The point of hypermedia controls is that they tell us what we can do next, and the URI of the resource we need to manipulate to do it. Instead of having to know where to GET our newly created person, the hypermedia controls in the response tell us where to get the new person.

Another interesting action is mapped to POST `/people/searches`. Here's the code:

```
[MVCPath('/searches')]
[MVCHTTPMethod([httpPOST])]
[MVCConsumes('application/json')]
procedure SearchPeople(CTX: TWebContext);

. . .

procedure TPeopleController.SearchPeople(CTX: TWebContext);
var
  Filters: TJSONObject;
  SearchText, PageParam: string;
  CurrPage: Integer;
begin
  //read informations from the requests
  Filters := CTX.Request.BodyAsJSONObject;
  if not Assigned(Filters) then
    raise Exception.Create('Invalid search parameters');
  SearchText := Mapper.GetStringDef(Filters, 'TEXT');
  if (not TryStrToInt(CTX.Request.Params['page'], CurrPage))
                         or (CurrPage < 1) then
    CurrPage := 1;

  //call some method on the TPeopleModule
  Render<TPerson>(FPeopleModule.FindPeople(SearchText, CurrPage));

  //prepare the response (also if render has been already called)
  CTX.Response.CustomHeaders.Values['dmvc-next-people-page'] :=
    Format('/people/searches?page=%d', [CurrPage + 1]);
  if CurrPage > 1 then
    CTX.Response.CustomHeaders.Values['dmvc-prev-people-page'] :=
      Format('/people/searches?page=%d', [CurrPage - 1]);
end;
```

Putting Delphi on the Server

This action is a bit longer, but the three steps are still clearly defined. This action executes a search on the `people` table using a pagination mechanism. The URL to get the next and the previous page are returned, along with the response in the headers `dmvc-next-people-page` and `dmvc-prev-people-page`. So the client doesn't have to know which kind of call to do to get the second page, but can simply navigate through the returned info.

One last note about the `TPersonModule` that heavily uses the `DataSet` helpers introduced in the serializing a dataset to JSON and back recipe. Look at the following code used to get a person by ID:

```
function TPeopleModule.GetPersonByID(AID: Integer): TPerson;
begin
  qryPeople.Open('SELECT * FROM PEOPLE WHERE ID = :ID', [AID]);
  //uses the dataset helper to convert a record to an object
  Result := qryPeople.AsObject<TPerson>;
end;
```

It could not be simpler! Also, the method to create a new person is made really simple using some of the Mapper methods:

```
procedure TPeopleModule.CreatePerson(APerson: TPerson);
var
  InsCommand: TFDCustomCommand;
begin
  //gets the Insert statement contained in the TFDUpdateSQL
  InsCommand := updPeople.Commands[arInsert];

  //Maps the object properties to the command parameters
  Mapper.ObjectToFDParameters(InsCommand.Params, APerson, 'NEW_');

  //execute the statement
  InsCommand.Execute;

  //retrieve the last assigned ID
  APerson.ID := Conn.GetLastAutoGenValue('gen_people_id');
end;
```

There's more...

What a huge topic we covered in this recipe! To test the RESTful service that you will develop from now on, you can use the `RESTDebugger.exe` program provided within since Delphi XE5 (in the `bin` folder), or the free POSTMan Chrome extension (`http://alturl.com/6ycza`). These tools allow you to send all the HTTP VERB requests while the browser, using only the address bar, can only issue `GET` requests.

Remember that if you don't know the fundamental principle of REST well, you could break all the benefits. Don't be tempted to put verbs on the URL like this: `http://server.com/people/create` or `http://server.com/people/get`.

This is not REST, it is a sort of remote procedure call (it is not bad, but it is another thing, it's not REST).

Also, be coherent with the HTTP VERB used. All the HTTP methods must be idempotent but `POST` and `PATCH`. So, if your request is executed once or repeated two, three or a thousand times, it should not change the system further.

Read this article for a good overview on idempotence in HTTP: `http://restcookbook.com/HTTP%20Methods/idempotency/`.

Controlling remote application using UDP

What's UDP? **User Datagram Protocol**, or **UDP**, is a connectionless protocol used by everyone every day, but it seems that not too many people know it. However, it can be really useful to solve particular network problems. Like TCP, UDP works at transport layer TCP/IP model but they have very different usage. Compared to TCP, UDP is a simpler message-based connectionless protocol. Connectionless protocols do not set up a dedicated end-to-end connection, instead communication is achieved by transmitting information in one direction from source to destination without verifying the readiness or state of the receiver. However, one primary benefit of UDP over TCP is the application to **voice over internet protocol** (**VoIP**), where latency and jitter are the primary concerns. It is assumed in VoIP UDP that the end users provide any necessary real-time confirmation that the message has been received.

Here are some features of UDP:

- **Unreliable**: When a message is sent, it cannot be known if it will reach its destination; it could get lost along the way. In UDP, there is no concept of acknowledgment, retransmission, or timeout.
- **Not ordered**: If two or more messages are sent to the same recipient, the order in which they arrive is not deterministic and cannot be predicted.
- **No congestion control**: UDP itself does not avoid congestion, and it's possible for high-bandwidth applications to trigger congestion collapse, unless they implement congestion control measures at the application level.

Getting ready

In this recipe, we'll use UDP to autoconfigure an application in a LAN. Let's say you have some classic client/server applications (however, the same approach is valid for any type of application) in a LAN, a big LAN. Every application uses a database on a specific machine and uses internal web services. Usually, in this scenario, you have some kind of configuration stored somewhere on the client PC that is read at startup. But what if the database IP changes because something is changed on the network? Or, more generally, what if some part of the configuration could be subject to change for some external reasons? If the change is only about the IP, a simple internal DNS does the job. But what about a port change? And if something else changes? Ok, I think you've got the point: you have to change the configuration on all machines (if you don't have some type of software distribution, this could be a daunting and boring task). Let's think about a well-known network service, the DHCP (http://en.wikipedia.org/wiki/Dynamic_Host_Configuration_Protocol). When a machine with dynamic IP configuration starts, the operating system sends a broadcast on the network to ask for an IP. It doesn't know who will send the IP, it doesn't know if someone can reply with an IP. It doesn't know anything! In this situation, the DHCP server replies to the broadcast with the assigned IP for that machine. The machine gets its IP and can join the network. This is the same approach that we'll use in this recipe. We have a database application that doesn't know where the database it should connect to is. So it sends a broadcast on the network saying: "Hey, I'm application X, which database I should connect to?". On the network, there is another program that we call `ConfigDispatcher` that replies to the broadcast with the correct connection information for that specific application. So the client reads the `ConfigDispatcher` reply and can happily connect to the correct database. No `config` files, no "default server", no hardcoded names, but a simple autoconfiguration. Wow, this is the power of UDP.

How to do it...

This recipe is composed of two projects: the `ConfigDispatcher` and the real application. Let's start with the `ConfigDispatcher`:

1. Create a new VCL Forms Application and save it as `ConfigDispatcher`.
2. Drop three `TMemo` on the form and name them `MemoLog`, `MemoConfigApp1`, and `MemoConfigApp2`.
3. In the `MemoConfigApp1.Lines` property, add the following lines:
   ```
   Database=employee
   Server=localhost
   ```
4. In the `MemoConfigApp2.Lines` property, add the following lines:
   ```
   Database=erpdb
   Server=192.168.3.4
   ```

Chapter 6

5. In this recipe, we'll use only the first configuration, but for the sake of completeness there is also a second (fake) configuration available that will remain unused.
6. Drop a `TidUDPServer` component then drop three `TLabel` and arrange the form as shown in the following screenshot:

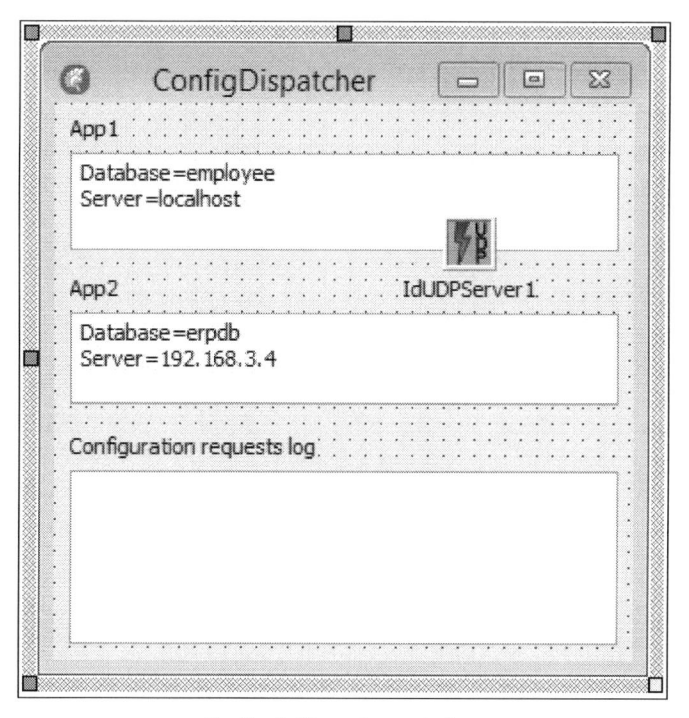

The ConfigDispatcher main form

7. Now, set the `idUDPServer1` properties as follows (this is the relevant part of the form `dfm`; it should not be difficult to read):

```
object IdUDPServer1: TIdUDPServer
  BroadcastEnabled = True
  DefaultPort = 8888
  Active = True
end
```

8. Now create the `OnUDPRead` event handler for the `idUDPServer1` component and fill it with the following code:

```
procedure TMainForm.IdUDPServer1UDPRead(
AThread: TIdUDPListenerThread;
const AData: TIdBytes;
    ABinding: TIdSocketHandle);
var
```

```
      ClientCommand, ClientConfig: string;
      CommandPieces: TArray<string>;
    begin
      ClientCommand := BytesToString(AData);
      MemoLog.Lines.Add(ClientCommand);
      CommandPieces := ClientCommand.Split(['#']);
      if (Length(CommandPieces) = 2) and
                          (CommandPieces[0] = 'GETCONFIG') then
      begin
        if CommandPieces[1] = 'APP001' then
        begin
          ClientConfig := MemoConfigApp1.Lines.Text;
        end;
        if CommandPieces[1] = 'APP002' then
        begin
          ClientConfig := MemoConfigApp2.Lines.Text;
        end;
        ABinding.Broadcast(ToBytes(ClientConfig),
                              9999, ABinding.PeerIP);
      end;
    end;
```

9. At this time, the project doesn't compile. Add unit `idGlobal` in the uses clause interface section and it should.

10. The `ConfigDispatcher` is finished. Let's start the `ClientDBApplication`.

11. Add to the project group a new VCL Forms Application (Navigate to **ProjectGroup | Add New Project | VCL Forms Application**).

12. Save the new project as `ClientDBApplication` and give a meaningful name to the form.

13. Drop the following components on the main form and set their properties as follows:

```
object FDConnection1: TFDConnection
  Params.Strings = (
    'User_Name=sysdba'
    'Password=masterkey'
    'Protocol=TCPIP'
    'DriverID=IB')
  ConnectedStoredUsage = [auDesignTime]
  LoginPrompt = False
end

object FDQuery1: TFDQuery
  Connection = FDConnection1
```

```
    SQL.Strings = ('select * from customer')
  end

  object DataSource1: TDataSource
    DataSet = FDQuery1
  end

  object FDPhysIBDriverLink1: TFDPhysIBDriverLink
  end

  object FDGUIxWaitCursor1: TFDGUIxWaitCursor
  end

  object Timer1: TTimer
    Interval = 3000
  end

  object IdUDPServer1: TIdUDPServer
    DefaultPort = 9999
    Active = True
  end
```

14. Drop a `TDBGrid` and a `TDBNavigator` and hook them to `DataSource1`.
15. Now, if you try to activate `FDQuery1`, you should see the query data in the grid.
16. Double-click on `Timer1` and fill in the `OnTimer` event with the following code:

```
procedure TMainFormClient.Timer1Timer(Sender: TObject);
begin
  Caption := 'Waiting for configuration...';
  IdUDPServer1.Broadcast(
              ToBytes('GETCONFIG#APP001'), 8888);
end;
```

17. Include `idGlobal` unit in the uses interface clause.
18. Now create the `OnUDPRead` event handler for the `idUDPServer1` component and fill it with the following code:

```
procedure TMainFormClient.IdUDPServer1UDPRead(
AThread: TIdUDPListenerThread; const AData: TIdBytes;
    ABinding: TIdSocketHandle);
var
  ServerConfig: TStringList;
  i: Integer;
begin
  Timer1.Enabled := False;
```

Putting Delphi on the Server

```
      try
        Caption := 'Configuration OK...';
        ServerConfig := TStringList.Create;
        try
          ServerConfig.Text := BytesToString(AData);
          for i := 0 to ServerConfig.Count - 1 do
          begin
            FDConnection1.Params.Values[ServerConfig.Names[i]] :=
              ServerConfig.ValueFromIndex[i];
          end;
        finally
          ServerConfig.Free;
        end;
        FDConnection1.Open;
        FDQuery1.Open;
        Caption := 'Connected';
      except
        Caption := 'Wrong configuration or cannot connect';
        Timer1.Enabled := true;
      end;
    end;
```

19. Now check that the Interbase service is started on your machine. If it's not started, start it.
20. Run the `ConfigDispatcher` without debugging and then run the `ClientDBApplication`. After 3 seconds, you should see the data in the grid. The configuration has been requested with a broadcast to the `ConfigDispatcher`, then has been parsed, understood, and used to connect to the database.
21. You can try to start the `ClientDBApplication` first, wait 6 seconds, and then start the `ConfigDispatcher`. It just works.

How it works...

This is a long recipe but the behavior is really simple. The `ConfigDispatcher` use the two memos to maintain the "strings" to send to the client that requests a specific configuration. When a client requests a configuration, the server receives a command string similar to the following:

GETCONFIG#APP001

It parses the command and replies to the client with the contents of one of the memos. For APP001, it sends the `MemoConfigApp1` content while for APP002, it sends the `MemoConfigApp2` contents. That's it, the `ConfigDispatcher` job is finished.

Chapter 6

The client is simple too. On initiation it waits 3 seconds, configured in the timer, and asks for a configuration. If some data arrives on the `UDPServer`, the `UDPRead` event handler is called. The code disables the timer, reads the data sent by the `ConfigDiaspatcher`, and tries to use it to configure its database connection. If the configuration is correct, the `ClientDBApplication` connects to its database; if not, the timer is re-enabled and after 3 seconds, another configuration request is broadcast and the cycle goes on until the client is able to connect.

As you can see, the applications talk each other without any kind of predefined knowledge or configuration. This is the power of UDP!

There's more...

Network programming and network protocols are a really large topic. As a software developer, you have to be aware - if not yet - of the possibilities that the standard networking infrastructure offers you.

The UDP protocol allows you to create *strange* applications that find and talk to each other using broadcasts. You could even create a complex application protocol based on UDP to remotely control some running applications. In the chapter devoted to mobile programming, there is another example of the power of UDP. Here are some other Delphi samples about UDP programming:

- Chat application with Delphi source: `http://delphi.about.com/library/weekly/aa101105a.htm`
- A fun utility to invoke fake and harmless BSODs on colleagues' machines: `http://www.atozed.com/indy/demos/10/index.en.aspx`

Using app tethering to create a companion app

App Tethering is one of the main features introduced in RAD Studio XE6 and since then it has been improved in security and functionalities. App tethering allows you to connect applications to exchange in a so-called *serverless* mode. In other words, it gives your applications the ability to interact with other applications running either on the same machine or on a remote machine without using a server because the applications communicate directly with each other.

App Tethering features do not depend on a specific transport or protocol, and new protocols can be implemented using the app tethering API. Currently, App Tethering can work using a network or Bluetooth Classic adapter using the same code.

Putting Delphi on the Server

To enable an application to use app tethering, only two components are required:

- `TTetheringManager`: Used to discover other applications that are using app tethering
- `TTetheringAppProfile`: Used to define the actions and data that your application shares with other applications previously paired using the TTetheringManager

The App tethering technology roughly follows the Bluetooth Classic model, where there are a set of Bluetooth devices able to interact with each other and each application exposes a set of "profiles" usable by other applications.

One of the strengths of this technology is that it is completely independent of the platform where the resultant application runs. You can use App tethering to connect a VCL application to a mobile app running on Android or iOS, or between a FireMonkey MacOSX application and an iOS app, or even more, a VCL Windows service to a FireMonkey desktop application. I think you've got the point: you can use App tethering to create an application network able to make your applications more usable.

App tethering is designed to develop so-called **companion apps**. What's a companion app? Well, a companion app is an app designed to make another application more usable. Let's say you developed a media center running on an Android TV or on a PC. You can play videos and music, but how can you control the player while you are on the sofa? You need a remote controller! Using App tethering, you can create a companion app running on your phone that is able to control the media center to play and stop a video, to go forward, or to go to the next video. The remote controller is a typical companion app of your media center.

Getting ready

There are some nice examples of app tethering on the Internet and some others have been provided by Embarcadero but in this recipe we'll talk about a completely new app. We'll develop a "presenter assistant" (I've just coined this term!). What's a presenter assistant? Well, during my training or while I'm talking at conferences or while I present the new version of Delphi to the Italian community, I use a lot of slides. So I run my MS PowerPoint presentation (or `http://www.openoffice.org/` Impress) and talk over the slides about the new Delphi features. In the last few years, I have used a presenter pointer which allows me to go to the next slide easily without going back to the PC and pressing the space key (because I walk a lot during the presentation, usually I'm too far from the PC to go back at each slide). A presenter assistant is a small device with two buttons: **Next** and **Previous**. However, I love so much to talk about programming (and Delphi) that often I run out of time. Here's the idea for this recipe: a presenter assistant app running on my Android smartphone that allows me to go to the next slide, to the previous slide and also to display how many minutes I have before the end of the speech. Here's the presenter assistant app while doing its job:

Chapter 6

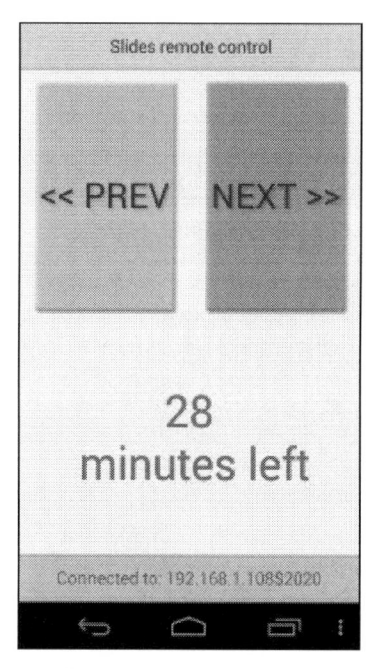

The Presenter Assistant app running on my Android phone

The Presenter VCL application is in charge of mimicking a keyboard key press when the mobile app sends the proper commands and sending the remaining minutes to the mobile app every 5 seconds (we don't need a clock; an update every 5 seconds is enough). Here's the VCL application:

The VCL application that will control the desktop application showing the slides

In the App tethering model, there isn't a server and a client. There is an application (or an app) that connects to other apps, but then the two, or more, apps are peers.

Each application can:

- **Share resources**: When other apps subscribe to a shared resource, every time the shared resource changes, all the subscribed apps are notified following the publish/subscribe model.
- **Share actions**: An app can discover and invoke actions published by other apps.
- **Send strings**: One of the apps can send a string to one of the other apps. The string can contain anything, also a complex JSON object.
- **Send streams**: One of the apps can send a stream to one of the other apps. The stream can also contain binary data such as an image or an `mp3` file.

The presenter assistant we're talking about is very simple. The mobile app needs to send two strings to the desktop application. The first when we need the next slide and the second when we need the previous slide. The VCL application running on the PC needs to publish a resource showing the remaining minutes.

How it works...

Open the project group in `Chapter6\RECIPE08`. There are two projects: `Presenter.dproj` (the VCL application) and `PresenterRemote.dproj` (the Android app).

Let's start by showing how the application works. Run the Presenter application, then run the **PresenterMobile** app on your phone and press **Connect**. If your phone is connected to the same network of your PC, you should be able to connect and see something like **Connected to: 192.168.1.101$2020** on your phone. This means that the mobile app is connected to the VCL application listening on port 2020. Now go to your desktop, write an integer number in `TSpinEdit` and press **Start Speech**. The application goes to the taskbar. Now open MS PowerPoint with a presentation (or another program which is sensible to the left and right arrow; the Delphi source code editor is also good) and repeatedly press the left or right button in the mobile app. You should see the slides (or the cursor) moving.

The following schema shows the communication between the mobile app and the VCL application after the discovering and pairing phases:

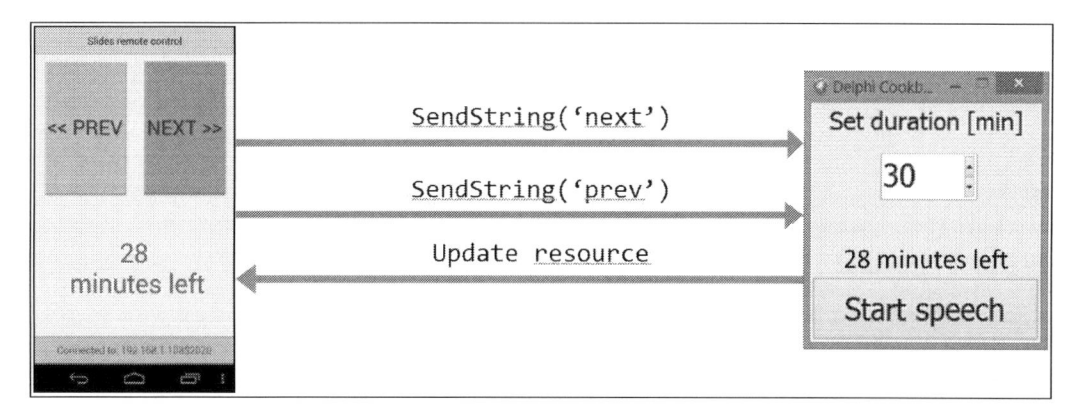

The communication between the mobile app and the VCL application

When the **PresenterMobile** app sends the NEXT command (using SendString), the Presenter application receives it and sends a VK_RIGHT Windows keyboard event. Sending a Windows keyboard event, the application is miming a user who is using the keyboard, so the key sent is intercepted by the window which has got the focus at that moment (just like how a normal keyboard works). If in the foreground, there is MS PowerPoint (or http://openoffice.org/ Impress) is showing a presentation, you get the next slide (because if you hit the right arrow during a presentation, you go to the next slide). It's the same for the PREV command, which in turn sends a VK_LEFT key to MS PowerPoint.

The relevant part of this message exchange is as follows:

```
const
  NEXT_SLIDE = Ord(VK_RIGHT);
  PREV_SLIDE = Ord(VK_LEFT);
  DEFAULT_MINUTES = 30;

procedure SendKey(const C: Word);
var
  kb: TInput;
begin
  kb.Itype := INPUT_KEYBOARD;
  kb.ki.wVk := C;
  kb.ki.wScan := MapVirtualKey(C, 0);
  kb.ki.dwFlags := 0;
  SendInput(1, kb, SizeOf(kb));
  kb.ki.dwFlags := KEYEVENTF_KEYUP;
```

Putting Delphi on the Server

```delphi
    SendInput(1, kb, SizeOf(kb));
end;

procedure TMainForm.TetheringAppProfile1ResourceReceived(
const Sender: TObject;
    const AResource: TRemoteResource);
var
  Cmd: string;
begin
  Caption := AResource.Value.AsString;
  if AResource.Hint.Equals('cmd') then
  begin
    Cmd := AResource.Value.AsString;
    if Cmd.Equals('prev') then
      SendKey(PREV_SLIDE)
    else if Cmd.Equals('next') then
      SendKey(NEXT_SLIDE);
  end;
end;
```

How about the connection between the applications? For this app, I've used the `Group` feature of App tethering. As you know, there are two ways to connect your applications:

- ▸ Define two applications as belonging to the same group and use automatic discovering and pairing. This approach is very simple, but not so flexible.
- ▸ Obtain a list of discovered applications and then request to pair with specific applications. This approach is more flexible but requires a bit of work.

Considering the scenario, I've used the `Group` property and the autoconnect feature. Here's the code under the **Connect** button in the mobile app:

```delphi
procedure TMainForm.btnConnectClick(Sender: TObject);
begin
  TetheringManager1.AutoConnect(2000);
end;
```

In order for the `AutoConnect` to work properly, both the `TetheringAppProfile` components must have the same value in the group property. In our case, the value is `com.danieleteti.presenters`.

Chapter 6

Also, the **Presenter** application shares a `Resource` with **PresenterMobile**. In order to automatically subscribe to the resource update notification, the resource name must be the same on all the paired apps:

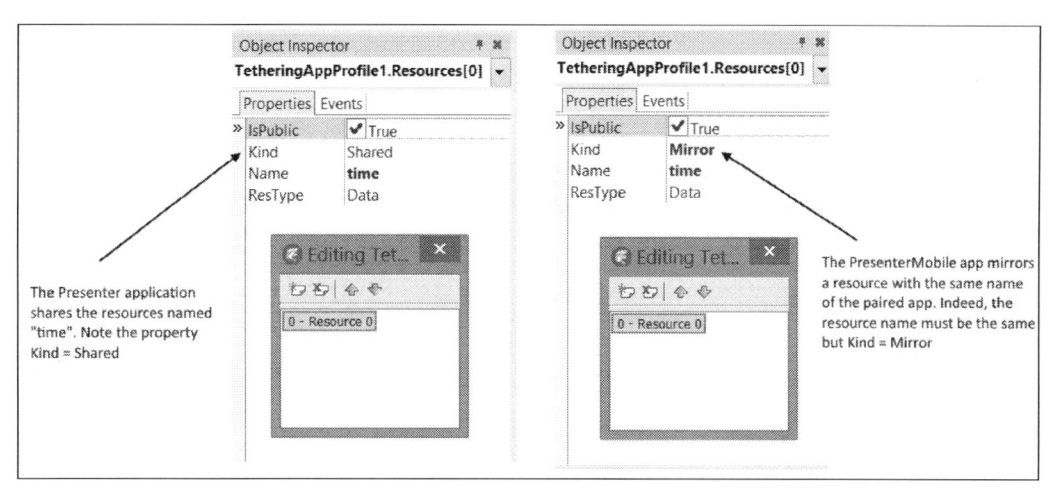

The resource configuration

Having this configuration, you can simply update the value of the resource in the desktop application using the following code:

```
TetheringAppProfile1.Resources.
   FindByName('time').Value := MinutesLeft;
```

Updating the local resource `'time'` causes an update to the remote resource with the same name and the following event handler is executed on the mobile app:

```
procedure TMainForm.TetheringAppProfile1Resources0ResourceReceived
   (const Sender: TObject; const AResource: TRemoteResource);
begin
   lblMinutes.Text := AResource.Value.AsString +
sLineBreak + ' minutes left';
end;
```

There's more...

App tethering is a nice technology. It is not a replacement for a server, but a good tool to easily create companion applications. Here's some documentation about it:

- A fast introduction to AppTethering with Delphi XE6: `https://www.youtube.com/watch?v=oeMQdvxi560`
- AppTethering with RAD Studio 10 Seattle (by Al Mannarino): `https://www.youtube.com/watch?v=da0-e38XYrk`

- Using App tethering: `http://docwiki.embarcadero.com/RADStudio/en/Using_App_Tethering`
- Adding App Tethering to Your Application: `http://docwiki.embarcadero.com/RADStudio/en/Adding_App_Tethering_to_Your_Application`
- Connecting to Remote Applications Using App Tethering: `http://docwiki.embarcadero.com/RADStudio/en/Connecting_to_Remote_Applications_Using_App_Tethering`
- Sharing and Running Actions on Remote Applications Using App Tethering: `http://docwiki.embarcadero.com/RADStudio/en/Sharing_and_Running_Actions_on_Remote_Applications_Using_App_Tethering`
- Sharing Data with Remote Applications Using App Tethering: `http://docwiki.embarcadero.com/RADStudio/en/Sharing_Data_with_Remote_Applications_Using_App_Tethering`
- Fun with Delphi XE6 App tethering and barcodes: `http://fixedbycode.blogspot.it/2014/04/fun-with-delphi-xe6-app-tethering-and.html`

Creating DataSnap Apache modules

One of the most awaited Delphi features by server-side Delphi developers is the support for the building of Apache webserver modules. Since Delphi XE6, Delphi can generate Apache modules, and this is very good news! The most recent Apache versions are supported: 2.0, 2.2, and 2.4. An Apache module is compatible only with the specific version for which has been compiled. So be sure about the Apache version you have to deploy your module before you create the project. However, it's possible to change the target Apache version by just changing a unit name.

Getting ready

In this recipe, we'll create a very simple REST service, with only one method returning a list of people. The service will be built using the Embarcadero DataSnap framework and the service itself will be packaged as an Apache webserver module. The real goal of this recipe is to show how to use the Delphi strength in creating Apache module, and a very light intro to DataSnap.

How to do it...

This recipe requires some steps, so here's the list:

1. The Apache HTTP Server (`"httpd"`) is a project of the Apache Software Foundation and has been the most popular web server on the Internet since April 1996. On Windows, one of the recommended binary distributions is maintained by the "Apache Lounge" community. Go to `http://www.apachelounge.com/download/` and download the most updated 2.4.x version as a zip file. In this recipe, we'll use the Win32 version, so download that one please.

2. Unzip the Apache distribution in a folder named Apache24 (for example, `C:\DEV\Apache24`).

3. The Apache main configuration is contained in the `C:\DEV\Apache24\conf\httpd.conf` file. Open it with a good text editor. This file contains all the main configuration and includes a bounce of other configuration files. Configuring Apache is trivial; however, in this recipe we'll configure it to let it run our module. Let's start with a very basic configuration; however, the `http.conf` syntax can be complex, so pay attention to the following steps.

4. Look for `ServerRoot`. Currently, it should look like this:

   `ServerRoot "c:/Apache24"`

5. Change the folder name to `"C:/DEV/Apache24"`. Warning, we're using `"/"` as a folder separator and not `"\"`. Also, don't terminate the folder name with a trailing slash. Now the line should look as follows:

   `ServerRoot "c:/DEV/Apache24"`

6. Look for `DocumentRoot`. This path is where static files are placed. Currently, it should look like this:

   `DocumentRoot "c:/Apache24/htdocs"`
   `<Directory "c:/Apache24/htdocs">`

7. Change the folder name to `"C:/DEV/Apache24/htdocs"` on the second line, shown as follows:

   `DocumentRoot "c:/DEV/Apache24/htdocs"`
   `<Directory "c:/DEV/Apache24/htdocs">`

8. Look for `ServerName`. The `ServerName` directive gives the name and port that the server uses to identify itself. Currently, the line is commented:

   `#ServerName www.example.com:80`

9. Just after the commented line, add the following:

   `ServerName localhost:80`

10. Let's test if our Apache is correctly configured. Open a command prompt, go to the `C:\DEV\Apache24` folder and launch the following command:

    `bin\httpd.exe`

11. Errors will be printed on the standard output. If no errors have been printed, launch a browser and navigate to `http://localhost`; you should get a `while` page with **It works!** text on it. If so, your Apache installation is running correctly. Now Apache is running in application mode. It is possible to install it as a service with a simple command that we'll see later.

12. A warning is, we are configuring Apache just to run our modules. It is not configured to be exposed on the Internet. So please read carefully the documentation about the configuration or ask an Apache expert before letting your server go into the wild!

13. Terminate Apache by pressing *Ctrl + C*, leave the command prompt for a moment, and go back to Delphi.

14. Let's create our DataSnap WebBroker project as an Apache 2.4 module.

15. Navigate to **File | New | Other** then navigate to **Delphi Projects | DataSnap Server | DataSnap WebBroker Application**.

16. The wizard asks which kind of project we're about to create; select **Apache dynamic link module** and press **Next** (shown as follows):

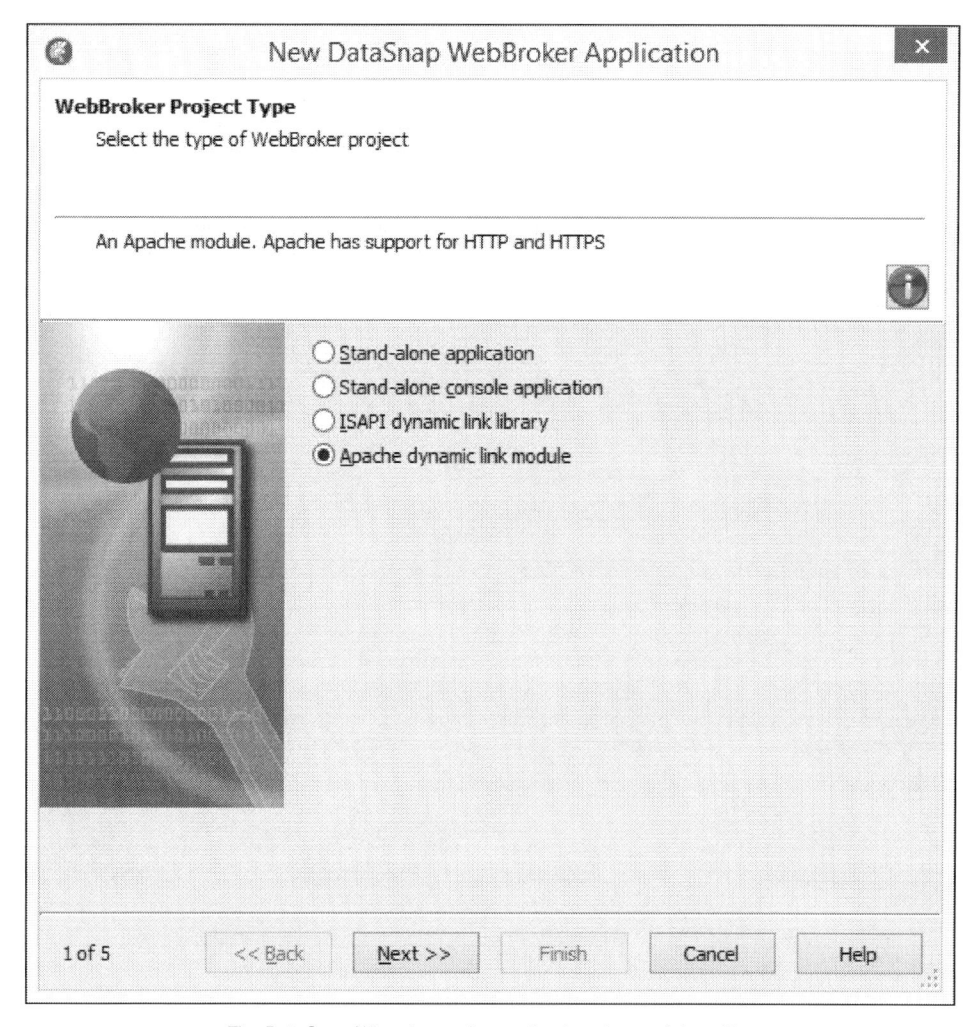

The DataSnap Wizard - we choose the Apache module option

17. Then the wizard asks which Apache version our module will be built for. Select **Apache version 2.4**, name it `datasnap_module` and press **Next**.

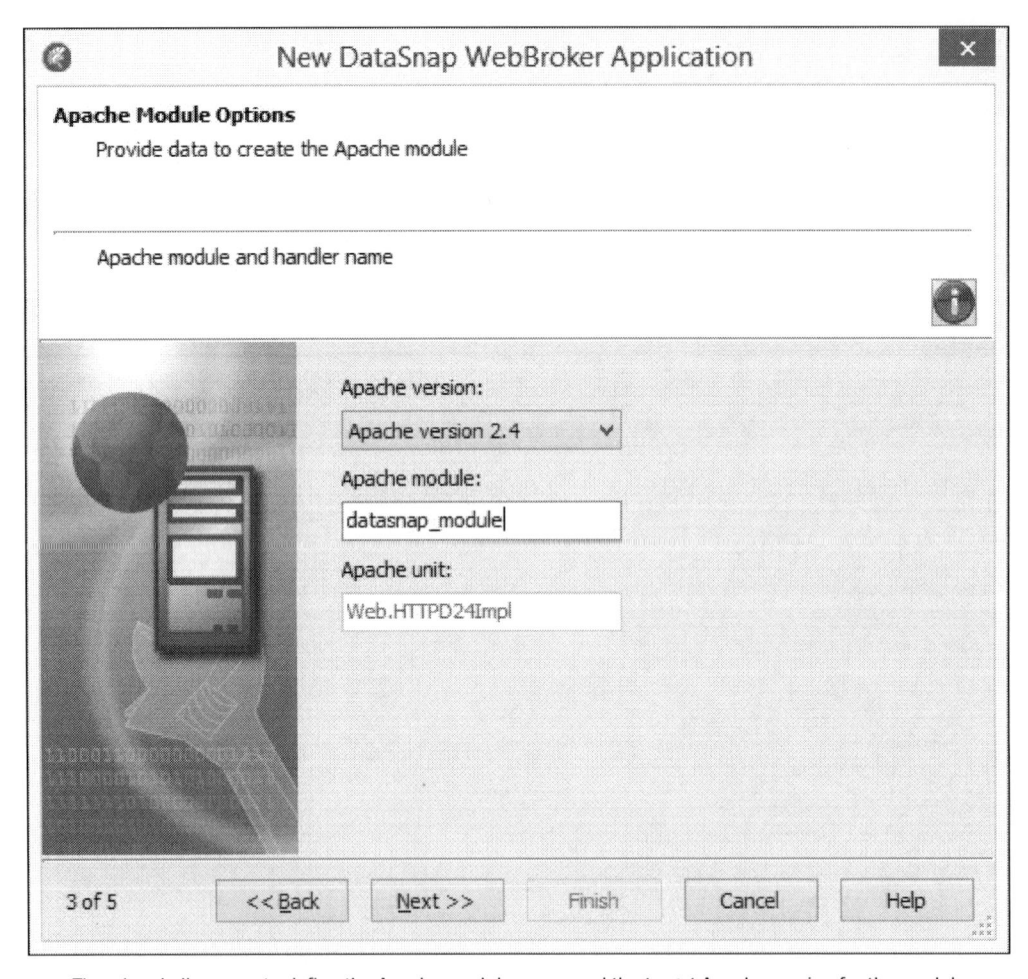

The wizard allows you to define the Apache module name and the target Apache version for the module

18. On the next screen, the wizard asks about the functionalities that we need to include in our DataSnap module. Leave the defaults and press **Next**:

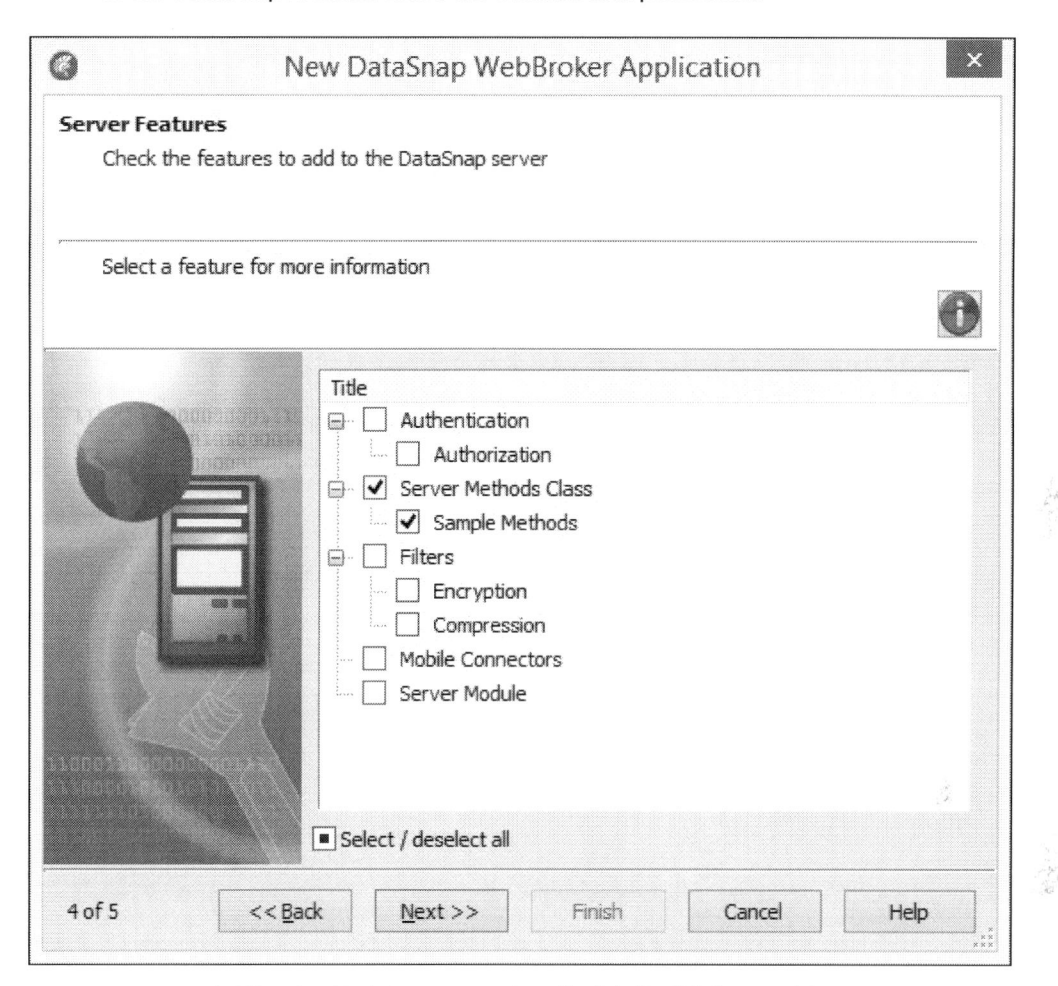

Let the wizard include some sample methods in the DataSnap module

Putting Delphi on the Server

19. At the next screen, select **TDataModule** and press **Finish**:

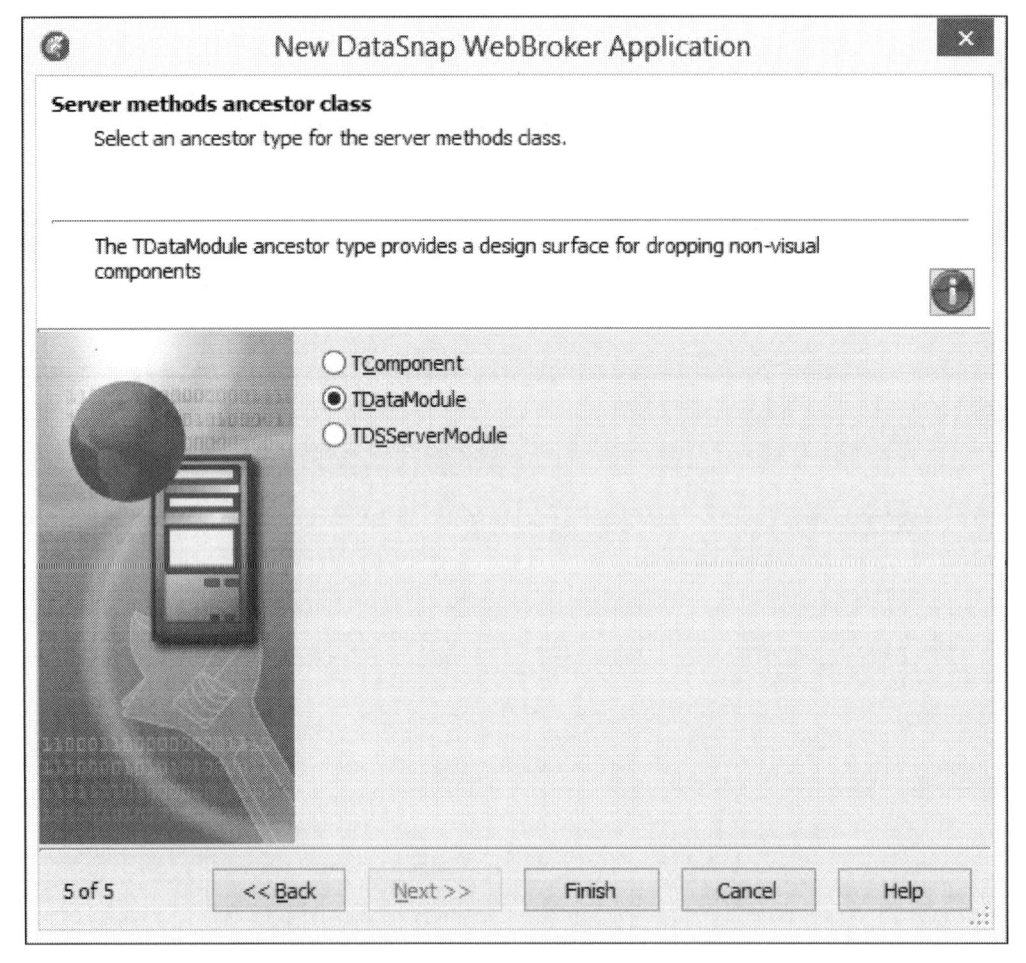

Using the TDataModule as ancestor class, we got a design surface without the overhead of the IAppServer interface that we won't use

20. Delphi has created a complete Apache 2.4 module containing a DataSnap REST server. WOW! Now let's add some features to it.
21. Save the project using the default names.

Chapter 6

22. Open `ServerMethodsUnit1.pas`, show the designer and drop on it a `TFDConnection` and a `TFDQuery`. Connect the `TFDQuery` to the `TFDConnection`, configure the `TFDConnection` to point at the sample database in the `DATA` folder contained in this recipe. The connection configuration parameters should be similar to the following:

    ```
    Database=C:\DEV\Chapter05\CODE\RECIPE08\DATA\SAMPLES.IB
    User_Name=sysdba
    Password=masterkey
    DriverID=IB
    ```

23. Go to the code editor and declare the following method in the public section of the `TDataModule`:

    public
    ```
        . . . //other methods
        function GetEmployees: TJSONArray;
    end;
    ```

24. Press *Ctrl + Shift + C* to implement the method body and fill it with the following code:

    ```
    function TServerMethods1.GetEmployees: TJSONArray;
    begin
        FDQuery1.Open('SELECT * FROM PEOPLE');
        Result := FDQuery1.AsJSONArray;
    end;
    ```

25. Go to the implementation uses clause and add the unit `ObjectsMappers` (it is a unit contained in the DelphiMVCFramework project that we'll use to do standard `DataSet` serialization).

26. Build the project. Now our Apache module is ready, but how can we test and debug it? First, we have to put the compiled dll in the right place. To allow Apache to load our module, it is useful to have it at the same level as the built-in modules. Navigate to **Project | Options | Delphi compiler** and write in the `Output` directory section the path `C:\DEV\Apache24\modules\` as shown below, then press **OK**:

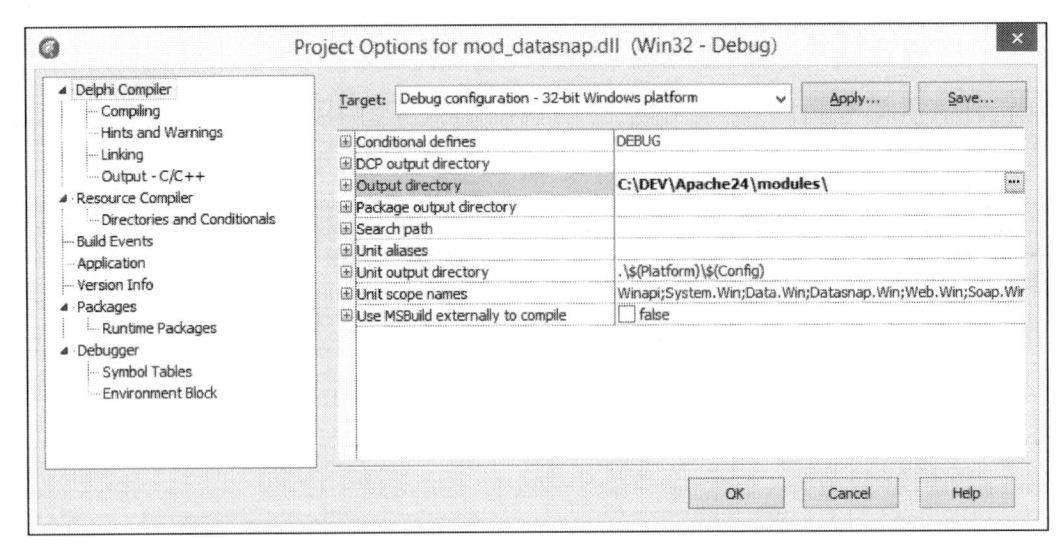

Configure the project output directory to compile directly where Apache looks for modules

27. Compile the project and go back to the `httpd.conf` file.
28. Look for `"LoadModule"` string in the file. You will find a lot of lines with this directive and many of them are commented. Just after the last `"LoadModule"` line (doesn't matter if it is commented or not), add the following lines and save the file:

    ```
    LoadModule datasnap_module modules/mod_datasnap.dll

    <Location /api>
        SetHandler mod_datasnap-handler
    </Location>
    ```

29. Now, go back to the command prompt. Go to the `C:\DEV\Apache24` folder and launch the following command:

    `bin\httpd.exe`

30. Go to a browser, and navigate to the URL `http://localhost/api/datasnap/rest/TServerMethods1/getemployees`; you should get the DataSnap JSON response from the Apache module just created.
31. How do we debug our module? Terminate Apache by pressing *Ctrl + C* from the command line and go back to Delphi.

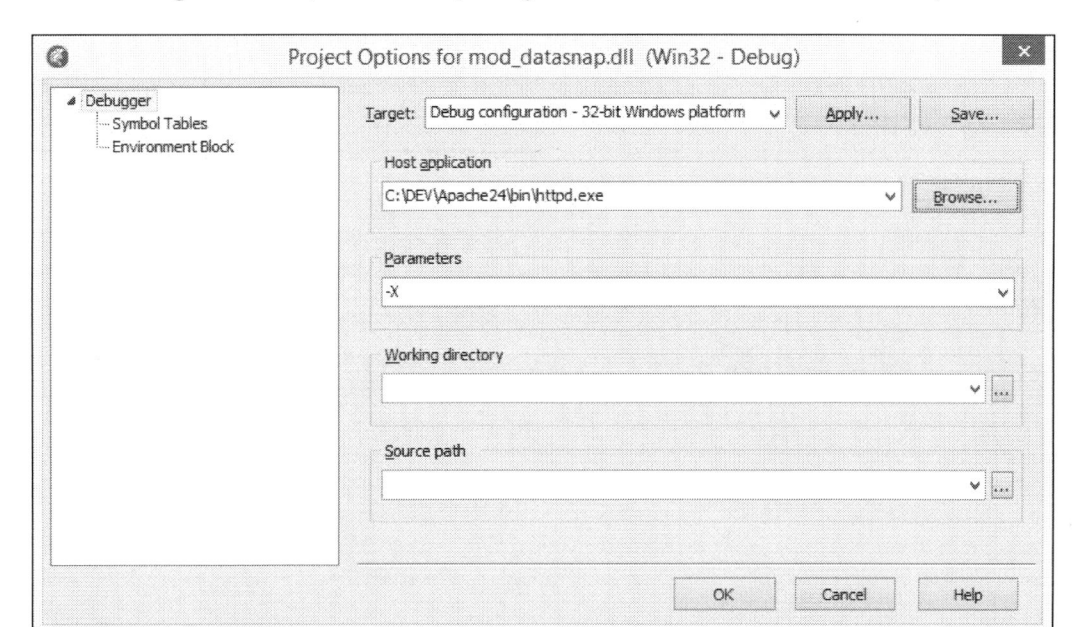

32. Navigate to **Run | Parameters**, configure the values shown as follows and press **OK**:

Let's set up the debugger to debug the module; note the -X parameter passed to the httpd.exe executable

33. Now Delphi will start Apache for us and we'll be able to debug the module as with any Delphi program. The `-X` parameter passed to `httpd.exe` launches Apache in debug mode with only one worker, so that Delphi doesn't need to debug the webserver spawned processes.
34. Run the project. Apache will silently start, launched by Delphi, and our module is loaded by the `httpd.exe` process. Now we are able to debug the module using breakpoints and all the ordinary stuff.

How it works...

Apache is configured to load our module. The source code of that module is opened in the Delphi IDE. When Delphi compiles the module dll, it writes it where Apache looks for it. Just after the compilation, Delphi launches Apache in application mode with the `-X` parameters (avoiding spawned process). Apache loads the dll as configured in the `httpd.conf` file, and Delphi attaches its debugger to the `httpd.exe` process and to its `datasnap_module.dll`. This approach is valid for any dll that is loaded at runtime by some other software, and is still valid also for every WebBroker program compiled as an Apache module or ISAPI dll.

Putting Delphi on the Server

There's more...

There are a lot of concepts in this recipe. Here are some links for those that want to go deeper. DataSnap is a complex and powerful framework from Embarcadero able to create TCP/IP and HTTP/S servers. I have held many training sessions about it, and suggest you give it a try. It is present also in Delphi Professional versions.

- *DataSnap Overview and Architecture*: http://docwiki.embarcadero.com/RADStudio/en/DataSnap_Overview_and_Architecture
- Tutorial on *Using a DataSnap Server with an Application*: http://docwiki.embarcadero.com/RADStudio/en/Tutorial:_Using_a_DataSnap_Server_with_an_Application
- Tutorial on *Using a REST DataSnap Server with an Application*: http://docwiki.embarcadero.com/RADStudio/en/Tutorial:_Using_a_REST_DataSnap_Server_with_an_Application
- And now something about the Apache webserver: Apache HTTP Server security tips: http://httpd.apache.org/docs/current/misc/security_tips.html

After you have configured and secured your Apache webserver, you can install it as a Windows Service using the following command line:

`.\bin\httpd.exe -k install -n "My DataSnap Server"`

And to uninstall:

`.\bin\httpd.exe -k uninstall -n "My DataSnap Server"`

In this way, you can package a customized Apache distribution to deploy and run your custom modules. I do it very often with my services that need to be published on the Internet, because Apache is stronger and more secure compared to the Delphi built-in webserver based on INDY (to each his work).

However, even if in this recipe we have used a dedicated Apache installation to host our module, you can also use an already deployed instance, and often you will do it. The deployment process is the same: copy your module in some path accessible from the webserver, change the `httpd.conf` file to load your module and restart the server. That's it.

Chapter 6

Creating WebBroker Apache modules

As we have already said, WebBroker is a technology available since Delphi 4 to help create web server applications exposing an HTTP/HTTPS interface. It is a very thin layer on top of HTTP/S but I love it because it doesn't try to do a lot of things, but remains at a low level, allowing you to implement the rest of the architecture as you need. Therefore, Embarcadero used WebBroker as a framework to create DataSnap and EMS. So it is very important to know it, because by knowing it, you have all the power to create web "things" such as HTTP/S services, HTML interfaces, and so on.

In this recipe, we'll create a 64bit WebBroker Apache module, install it in a custom Apache 2.4 distribution, and secure the server by configuring HTTPS access. Internally, our application uses DelphiMVCFramework, but all the steps are still valid for other frameworks or no frameworks at all (apart from WebBroker). Let's start!

Getting ready

We need to get an Apache distribution. You can use the one provided by Apache Lounge (https://www.apachelounge.com/). In this recipe, we'll use the 64 bit Apache, so go to the website and download the latest 2.4 version at 64 bit as a ZIP package. Now, follow steps 1 to 13 of the previous recipe to set up Apache.

You should be able to run Apache from the command line with the following command without any errors:

```
C:\DEV\Apache24> bin\httpd -X
```

How to do it...

Let's create the Apache module. We'll create a fake management system with a list of users. There is one resource accessible with two HTTP verbs: `GET` and `POST`:

1. Navigate to **File | New | Other**.
2. Navigate to **Delphi Projects | WebBroker | Web Server Application**.
3. In the resultant modal dialog, select **Apache dynamic link** module and click **Next**.
4. In the combo box, select **Apache version 2.4** and write `peoplemanager_module` as the module name.
5. Click **Finish**.
6. Save the project using the following filenames:
    - `mod_peoplemanager.dproj`
    - `WebModuleU.pas`

Putting Delphi on the Server

7. Add a new unit to the project, save it as `SampleControllerU.pas`, and write the following code:

```
unit SampleControllerU;

interface

uses MVCFramework;

type
  [MVCPath('/')]
  [MVCDoc('Just a sample controller')]
  TSampleController = class(TMVCController)
  public
    [MVCPath('/users')]
    [MVCHTTPMethods([httpGET])]
    [MVCDoc('Returns the users list')]
    procedure GetUsers(CTX: TWebContext);

    [MVCPath('/users')]
    [MVCHTTPMethods([httpPOST])]
    [MVCConsumes('application/json')]
    [MVCDoc('Creates a new user')]
    procedure CreateUser(CTX: TWebContext);
  end;

implementation

uses System.JSON, MVCFramework.Commons;

procedure TSampleController.CreateUser(CTX: TWebContext);
begin
  // just a fake, we don't create any user.
  // simply echo the body request as body response
  if CTX.Request.ThereIsRequestBody then
  begin
    CTX.Response.StatusCode := HTTP_STATUS.Created;
    Render(CTX.Request.BodyAsJSONObject, False)
  end
  else
    raise EMVCException.Create(HTTP_STATUS.BadRequest,
                               'Expected JSON body');
end;

procedure TSampleController.GetUsers(CTX: TWebContext);
```

```
var
  LJObj: TJSONObject;
  LJArray: TJSONArray;
begin
  LJArray := TJSONArray.Create;

  LJObj := TJSONObject.Create;
  LJObj
  .AddPair('first_name', 'Daniele')
  .AddPair('last_name', 'Teti')
    .AddPair('email', 'd.teti@bittime.it');
  LJArray.AddElement(LJObj);

  LJObj := TJSONObject.Create;
  LJObj
  .AddPair('first_name', 'Peter')
  .AddPair('last_name', 'Parker')
    .AddPair('email', 'pparker@dailybugle.com');
  LJArray.AddElement(LJObj);

  LJObj := TJSONObject.Create;
  LJObj
  .AddPair('first_name', 'Bruce')
  .AddPair('last_name', 'Banner')
    .AddPair('email', 'bbanner@angermanagement.com');
  LJArray.AddElement(LJObj);

  Render(LJArray);
end;

end.
```

8. Reopen the web module.
9. Create an event handler for the `OnCreate` event, and fill it with the following code:
   ```
   FMVCEngine := TMVCEngine.Create(self);
   FMVCEngine.AddController(TSampleController);
   ```
10. Declare `FMVCEngine` private variable as `TMVCEngine`.
11. Include `MVCFramework` in the interface uses clause.
12. Include `SampleControllerU` in the implementation uses clause.
13. Save all.

Putting Delphi on the Server

14. Right-click on the **Target Platform** node in the **Project Manager**. Select **Add Platform** and **64 bit Windows** in the dialog.

15. Be sure that the 64-bit Windows node is selected in the **Project Manager** because we have to build the module for a 64-bit Apache.

16. Navigate to **Project | Options** and select **All Configuration – All Platform** in the upper combo box.

17. Then click on the **Delphi Compiler** node and set `C:\DEV\Apache24\modules\` as `Output` directory.

18. Click **OK**, save all and build. Now your `dll` should be compiled in `C:\DEV\Apache24\modules\mod_peoplemanager.dll`.

19. Now, open file `C:\DEV\Apache24\conf\https.conf` with your preferred text editor.

20. Look for the `LoadModule` string in the file. You will find a lot of lines with this directive and many of them are commented. Just after the last `LoadModule` line (it doesn't matter if it is commented or not), add the following lines and save the file:

    ```
            LoadModule peoplemanager_module modules/mod_peoplemanager.dll
            <Location /people>
      SetHandler mod_peoplemanager-handler
         </Location>
    ```

21. Remember this location because it is a temporary configuration; we have to remove the `<location>` node before the end.

22. Now, go back to the command prompt. Go to the `C:\DEV\Apache24` folder and launch the following command:

    `bin\httpd.exe -X`

23. If some errors come up, double-check the previous steps.

24. Open a web browser (Google Chrome or Mozilla Firefox are good choices) and write down the following URL: `http://localhost/people/users`.

25. You should see a JSON array showing some user data as shown in the following screenshot:

```
[
    {
        first_name: "Daniele",
        last_name: "Teti",
        email: "d.teti@bittime.it"
    },
    {
        first_name: "Peter",
        last_name: "Parker",
        email: "pparker@dailybugle.com"
    },
    {
        first_name: "Bruce",
        last_name: "Banner",
        email: "bbanner@angermanagement.com"
    }
]
```

The resource users as JSON array; this particular formatting is because of the extension JSON View for Google Chrome

Now the Apache module works! What we still have to do is to configure HTTPS access to this service. Remember that HTTP is a textual protocol, so every byte you send or receive from an HTTP server is not encrypted and can be sniffed by anyone with a basic networking knowledge and a good sniffer. So, let's make this server secure!

To configure HTTPS on Apache, you need to generate the certificate files. OpenSSL command-line tools can do the job, and we have a copy of OpenSSL in the `Apache\bin` folder. Here's the list:

1. Shut down Apache if it is still running. You should still be in the `C:\DEV\Apache` folder; if not, go there please.
2. Enter the `bin` folder and write the following command:
   `set OPENSSL_CONF=C:\DEV\Apache24\conf\openssl.cnf`

Putting Delphi on the Server

3. This command sets the environment variable used by the `openssl.exe` executable and should contain the full path of `openssl.cnf`. Check whether the `openssl.cnf` file is actually in your Apache distribution.

4. Now we have to actually generate the certificate, which is composed of two files: the certificate file and the private key file.

5. Execute the following command line:

   ```
   openssl req -x509 -nodes -days 365 -newkey rsa:2048 -keyout
   delphicookbook.key -out delphicookbook.crt
   ```

6. You will be prompted to enter your organizational information and a common name. The common name should be the fully qualified domain name for the site you are securing (`www.mydomain.com`), or just empty in this case. You can leave the e-mail address, challenge password, and optional company name blank. When the command has finished running, it will create two files: a `delphicookbook.key` file and a `delphicookbook.crt` self-signed certificate file, valid for 365 days. Copy these files into the `C:\DEV\Apache24\conf` folder.

7. Open your Apache configuration file (`conf\httpd.conf`) in a text editor.

8. Remove the following lines, because we know that the module works but we don't need it running in HTTP:

   ```
   <Location /people>                              #REMOVE
   SetHandler mod_peoplemanager-handler            #REMOVE
   </Location>                                     #REMOVE
   ```

9. Search for line `Listen 80` and add the following lines just after it:

   ```
   Listen 443
   <VirtualHost *:443>
     ServerName localhost
     SSLEngine on
     SSLCertificateFile "conf/delphicookbook.crt"
     SSLCertificateKeyFile "conf/delphicookbook.key"
     <Location /people>
     SetHandler mod_peoplemanager-handler
     </Location>
   </VirtualHost>
   ```

10. Save the changes and exit the text editor.

11. Run Apache with the usual command (`bin/httpd -X`).

12. Now, you should be able to access the `/people/users` URI only using the HTTPS protocol; let's check it.
13. Open a browser and go to `http://localhost/people/users`.
14. You should see a big **Not Found**, good! The service is no longer accessible via the HTTP protocol.
15. Now, change the address and write `https://localhost/people/users`.
16. You should see our JSON array.
    - The browser may tell you that the certificate is not verified. We know it because it's a self-signed certificate and no Certification Authority has been contacted to obtain it. So you can accept the certificate without a problem.
17. Our WebBroker Apache module is running behind an HTTPS secured web server and is ready to rock!
18. How can we debug our module? Terminate Apache by pressing *Ctrl+C* from the command line and go back to Delphi.
19. Navigate to **Run | Parameters**, configure the values as shown in figure 9.6.
20. Now Delphi will start Apache for us and we'll be able to debug the module as for any Delphi program. The `-X` parameter passed to `httpd.exe` launches Apache in debug mode with only one worker, so that Delphi doesn't need to debug the webserver spawned processes.
21. Run the project. Apache will silently start, launched by Delphi, and our module is loaded by the `httpd.exe` process. Now we are able to debug the module using breakpoints and all the ordinary stuff.

How it works...

The project is quite simple. Using DelphiMVCFramework, we defined one resource which supports two verbs, `GET` and `POST`, with the following meanings:

URI	VERB	DESCRIPTION
`/users`	`GET`	Retrieves a JSON array of JSON objects representing fake users
`/users`	`POST`	Doesn't create anything, but echoes the JSON request body as the body response

Putting Delphi on the Server

There's more...

A lot of topics here! Now we understand how to create Apache modules and how to make them secure using HTTPS. Warning! Don't imagine to publish this server to the Internet without a proper hardening by a skilled person. This configuration is just a minimal HTTPS setup; the server could still be vulnerable in some other part.

- If you want to know more about Apache and HTTPS, check out the following article: `https://httpd.apache.org/docs/2.4/ssl/ssl_howto.html`
- Curious about OpenSSL? Check out the project's site: `https://www.openssl.org/`
- Here's a WebBroker framework introduction: `http://docwiki.embarcadero.com/RADStudio/en/Using_Web_Broker_Index`
- To get support on DelphiMVCFramework, check out the following Facebook group: `https://www.facebook.com/groups/delphimvcframework/`
- Alternatively, if you need professional support, e-mail `dmvcframework@bittime` it.

Using native HTTP(S) client libraries

The RTL provides two components that you can use to send HTTP requests to servers and handle their responses:

- `TNetHTTPClient`
- `TNetHTTPRequest`

Alternatively, as we saw in *Chapter 3, Knowing Your Friends – the Delphi RTL* you can use an instance of `THTTPClient` to manage your HTTP requests.

Why use these components instead of good old `TidHTTP` from the INDY suite? The reasons have been explained in *Chapter 3, Knowing Your Friends – the Delphi RTL* however, in this recipe we'll use the new HTTP client to show how much the deployment is simplified, also in mobile apps, using these new components instead of the INDY ones, at least for HTTP communications.

Long story short, Embarcadero developed a native HTTP client library that is not based on INDY nor OpenSSL, but then relies on the OS API to implement HTTP protocol. So, when Microsoft, Apple or Google release a new security patch, your application is already updated. Great! You simply rely on the OS security infrastructure and don't depend anymore on the OpenSSL dlls!

Getting ready

In this recipe, we'll see a simple but complete cross-platform HTTPS client able to connect to the following:

- An HTTPS service using a valid certificate provided by a certification authority
- An HTTPS service which uses a self-signed certificate

The `TNetHTTPClient` component does a great job of integrating with the underlying OS to provide a uniform development and deployment experience to the Delphi developer. This project reuses the unit `AsyncTask.pas` developed in *Using tasks to make your customer happier* of *Chapter 5, The Thousand Faces of Multithreading*. Let's see how it works.

How it works...

Open the project in `Chapter06\CODE\RECIPE11\XPlatNativeHTTPClient.dproj`. The main form is similar to the following:

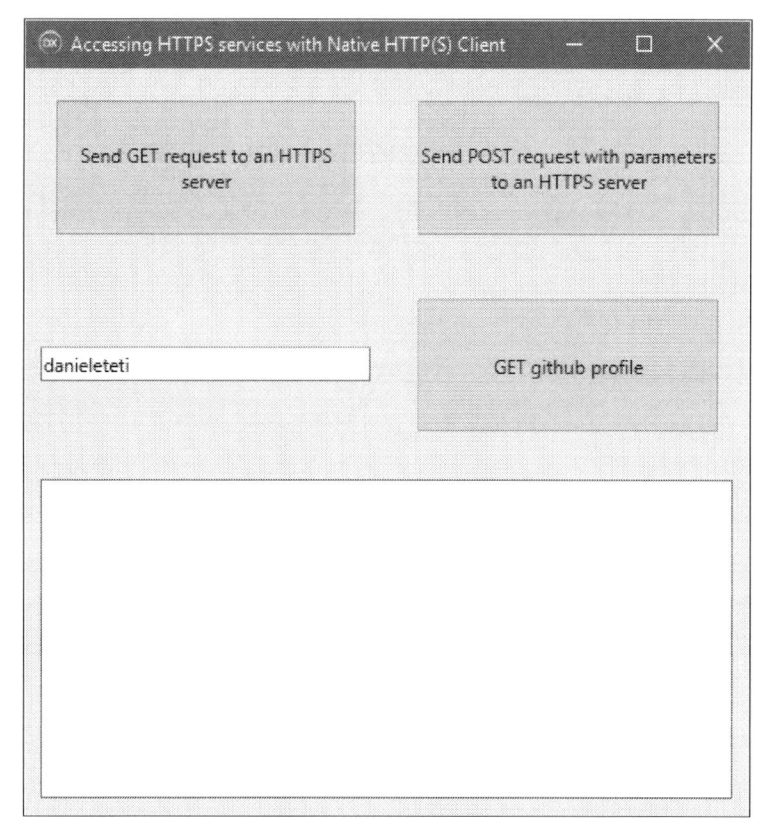

The cross-platform HTTPS client running on Windows 10

Putting Delphi on the Server

The two upper buttons send a request to the Apache HTTPS service developed in the previous recipe, while the third button sends a `GET` request to the GitHub API to get information about the username written in the edit. While the GitHub HTTPS contains a valid certificate provided by a recognized certification authority, the local service uses a self-signed certificate.

All the HTTPS requests are executed by a data module which contains an instance of `TNetHTTPClient`.

Let's check out the `THTTPDM` data module:

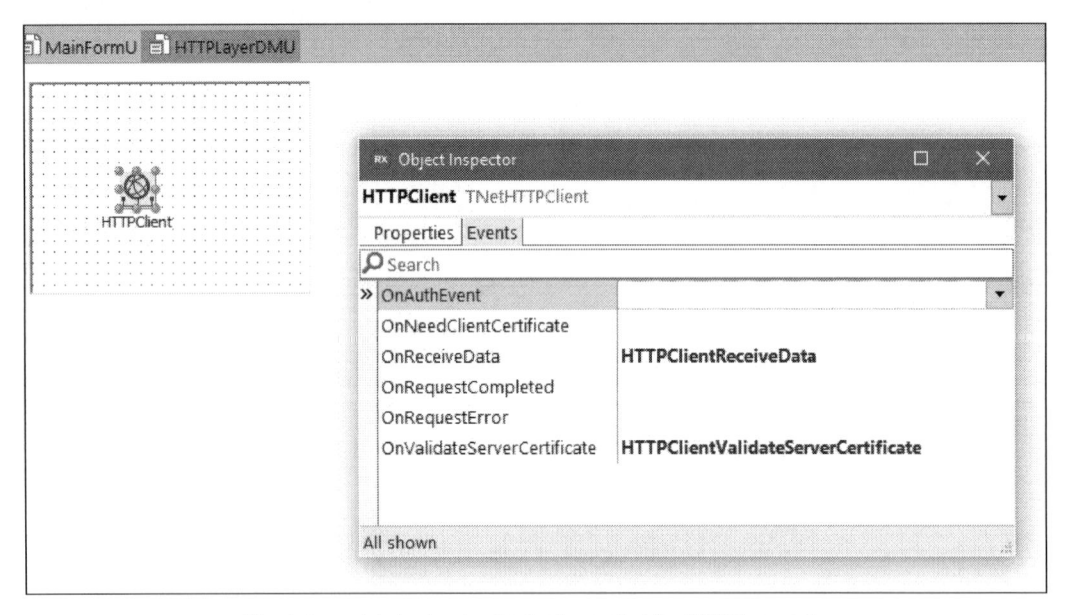

The data module in charge of actually sending the HTTPS requests

This data module contains all the methods used by the main form to do the actual HTTPS requests, plus some other helpers required to make asynchronous requests a bit simpler.

Here's the code:

```
unit HTTPLayerDMU;

interface

uses
  System.SysUtils, System.Classes, System.Net.URLClient,
  System.Net.HttpClient, System.Net.HttpClientComponent;

type
  THTTPDM = class(TDataModule)
```

```
    HttpClient: TNetHTTPClient;
    procedure HTTPClientValidateServerCertificate(
      const Sender: TObject; const ARequest: TURLRequest;
      const Certificate: TCertificate; var Accepted: Boolean);
    procedure HTTPClientReceiveData(const Sender: TObject;
      AContentLength, AReadCount: Int64; var Abort: Boolean);
  private
    FReadCount: UInt64;
    FCertificate: TCertificate;
    procedure Clear;
  public
    function Get(const URL: String): IHTTPResponse;
    function Post(const URL: String; BodyRequest: TStream;
                  Headers: TNetHeaders): IHTTPResponse;
    property ReadCount: UInt64 read FReadCount;
    property Certificate: TCertificate read FCertificate;

  type
    //a nested type used as value data object to return
    //response data from the data module to the main form
    TResponseData = record
      Response: IHTTPResponse;
      ReadedBytes: UInt64;
      Certificate: TCertificate;
      function HeadersAsStrings: TArray<String>;
    end;
  end;

implementation

{ %CLASSGROUP 'FMX.Controls.TControl' }

{$R *.dfm}

function THTTPDM.Get(const URL: String): IHTTPResponse;
begin
  Clear;
  //just forward the request to the TNetHTTPClient
  Result := HttpClient.Get(URL);
end;

procedure THTTPDM.HTTPClientReceiveData(const Sender: TObject;
  AContentLength, AReadCount: Int64; var Abort: Boolean);
begin
```

```delphi
    //As soon as the data are being read, we count it to inform the
    //main form about the total bytes read
    FReadCount := AReadCount;
  end;


procedure THTTPDM.HTTPClientValidateServerCertificate(
    const Sender: TObject; const ARequest: TURLRequest;
    const Certificate: TCertificate; var Accepted: Boolean);
begin
  //this method is executed only in case of self-signed
  //certificates, and in this code a self-signed certificate is
  //always accepted if is not expired
  Accepted := (Certificate.Start <= Now) and
              (Certificate.Expiry >= Now);
  //FCertificate contains the last self-signed certificate
  //accepted or is empty in case of valid certificates
  FCertificate := Certificate;
end;


function THTTPDM.Post(const URL: String; BodyRequest: TStream;
    Headers: TNetHeaders): IHTTPResponse;
begin
  Clear;
  //just forward the request to the TNetHTTPClient
  Result := HttpClient.Post(URL, BodyRequest, nil, Headers);
end;


procedure THTTPDM.Clear;
begin
  FReadCount := 0;
end;


function THTTPDM.TResponseData.HeadersAsStrings: TArray<String>;
var
  Pair: TNameValuePair;
begin
  Result := [];
  for Pair in Response.Headers do
  begin
    //this "insert" works like an "append" here
    Insert(Pair.Name + ':' + Pair.Value, Result, MaxLongInt);
  end;
end;

end.
```

Chapter 6

This code is quite simple and is just an high level wrapper for `TNetHTTPClient`. How does the main form use this? Let's check out the main form code:

```
unit MainFormU;

interface

uses
  System.SysUtils, System.Types, System.UITypes, System.Classes,
  System.Variants, FMX.Types, FMX.Controls, FMX.Forms,
  FMX.Graphics, FMX.Dialogs, FMX.ScrollBox, FMX.Memo,
  FMX.Controls.Presentation, FMX.StdCtrls, FMX.Layouts,
  FMX.Edit, HTTPLayerDMU;

type
  TMainForm = class(TForm)
    GridPanelLayout1: TGridPanelLayout;
    btnGet: TButton;
    btnPost: TButton;
    Layout1: TLayout;
    mmResponse: TMemo;
    EditGithubUser: TEdit;
    btnGithub: TButton;
    procedure btnGetClick(Sender: TObject);
    procedure btnPostClick(Sender: TObject);
    procedure btnGithubClick(Sender: TObject);
  private
    procedure UpdateGUI(const Value: THTTPDM.TResponseData);
  public
  end;

var
  MainForm: TMainForm;

implementation

uses
  System.JSON.Writers, System.JSON.Builders, REST.Types,
  System.Threading, FMX.Ani, System.Net.HttpClient,
  System.Net.URLClient, AsyncTask;

{$R *.fmx}

procedure TMainForm.btnGetClick(Sender: TObject);
```

```delphi
  const
    //replace this IP with your actual address
    URL = 'https://192.168.1.103/people/users';
  begin
    (Sender as TControl).Enabled := False;
    Async.Run<THTTPDM.TResponseData>(
      function: THTTPDM.TResponseData
      var
        LHTTPReq: THTTPDM;
        LResp: IHTTPResponse;
      begin
        LHTTPReq := THTTPDM.Create(nil);
        try
          LResp := LHTTPReq.Get(URL);
          if LResp.StatusCode <> 200 then
          begin
            raise Exception.CreateFmt('Error %d: %s',
                  [LResp.StatusCode, LResp.StatusText]);
          end;
          Result.ReadedBytes := LHTTPReq.ReadCount;
          Result.Certificate := LHTTPReq.Certificate;
        finally
          LHTTPReq.Free;
        end;
        Result.Response := LResp;
      end,
      procedure(const Value: THTTPDM.TResponseData)
      begin
        UpdateGUI(Value);
        (Sender as TControl).Enabled := True;
      end);

end;

procedure TMainForm.btnGithubClick(Sender: TObject);
const
  URL = 'https://api.github.com/users/%s';
var
  LGithubuser: String;
begin
  LGithubuser := EditGithubUser.Text;
  (Sender as TControl).Enabled := False;
  Async.Run<THTTPDM.TResponseData>(
```

```delphi
    function: THTTPDM.TResponseData
    var
      LHTTPReq: THTTPDM;
      LResp: IHTTPResponse;
    begin
      LHTTPReq := THTTPDM.Create(nil);
      try
        LResp := LHTTPReq.Get(Format(URL, [LGithubuser]));
        if LResp.StatusCode <> 200 then
        begin
          raise Exception.CreateFmt('Error %d: %s',
                  [LResp.StatusCode, LResp.StatusText]);
        end;
        Result.ReadedBytes := LHTTPReq.ReadCount;
        Result.Certificate := LHTTPReq.Certificate;
      finally
        LHTTPReq.Free;
      end;
      Result.Response := LResp;
    end,
    procedure(const Value: THTTPDM.TResponseData)
    begin
      UpdateGUI(Value);
      (Sender as TControl).Enabled := True;
    end);

end;

procedure TMainForm.btnPostClick(Sender: TObject);
const
  //replace this IP with your actual address
  URL = 'https://192.168.1.103/people/users';
begin
  (Sender as TControl).Enabled := False;
  Async.Run<THTTPDM.TResponseData>(
    function: THTTPDM.TResponseData
    var
      LJSONStream: TStringStream;
      LJSONWriter: TJsonWriter;
      LStreamWriter: TStreamWriter;
      LJSONObjectBuilder: TJSONObjectBuilder;
      LHeaders: TNetHeaders;
      LHTTPReq: THTTPDM;
```

```delphi
    LResp: IHTTPResponse;
begin
  LHTTPReq := THTTPDM.Create(nil);
  try
    LJSONStream := TStringStream.Create;
    try
      LStreamWriter := TStreamWriter.Create(LJSONStream);
      try
        LJSONWriter := TJsonTextWriter.Create(LStreamWriter);
        try
          LJSONObjectBuilder :=
                  TJSONObjectBuilder.Create(LJSONWriter);
          try
            LJSONObjectBuilder
              .BeginObject
                .Add('first_name', 'Daniele')
                .Add('last_name', 'Teti')
                .Add('email', 'd.teti@bittime.it')
              .EndObject;
            LJSONWriter.Flush;
            LJSONStream.Position := 0;
            LHeaders := [TNetHeader.Create('content-type',
              CONTENTTYPE_APPLICATION_JSON)];
            LResp := LHTTPReq.Post(URL, LJSONStream,
                                          LHeaders);
            if LResp.StatusCode <> 201 then
            begin
              raise Exception.CreateFmt('Error %d: %s',
                      [LResp.StatusCode,
                    LResp.StatusText]);
            end;
          finally
            LJSONObjectBuilder.Free;
          end;
        finally
          LJSONWriter.Free;
        end;
      finally
        LStreamWriter.Free;
      end;
    finally
      LJSONStream.Free;
    end;
    Result.ReadedBytes := LHTTPReq.ReadCount;
```

```
            Result.Certificate := LHTTPReq.Certificate;
         finally
            LHTTPReq.Free;
         end;
         Result.Response := LResp;
      end,
      procedure(const Value: THTTPDM.TResponseData)
      begin
         UpdateGUI(Value);
         (Sender as TControl).Enabled := True;
      end);
end;

procedure TMainForm.UpdateGUI(const Value: THTTPDM.TResponseData);
begin
   mmResponse.Lines.Clear;
   if not Value.Certificate.Subject.IsEmpty then
   begin
      mmResponse.Lines.Add('** Certificate Validity: from ' +
         DateToStr(Value.Certificate.Start) + ' to ' +
         DateToStr(Value.Certificate.Expiry));
      mmResponse.Lines.Add(sLineBreak + '** Certificate Subject: ' +
         Value.Certificate.Subject.Replace(sLineBreak, ', '));
   end
   else
   begin
      mmResponse.Lines.Add(sLineBreak +
         '** Certificate is not self-signed');
   end;
   mmResponse.Lines.Add(sLineBreak + '** Total bytes read: ' +
      Value.ReadedBytes.ToString);
   mmResponse.Lines.Add(sLineBreak + '** Headers: ' + sLineBreak +
      String.Join(sLineBreak, Value.HeadersAsStrings));
   mmResponse.Lines.Add(sLineBreak + '** Content charset: ' +
      sLineBreak + Value.Response.ContentCharSet);
   mmResponse.Lines.Add(sLineBreak + '** Response Status: ' +
      sLineBreak + Value.Response.StatusCode.ToString + ': ' +
      Value.Response.StatusText);
   mmResponse.Lines.Add(sLineBreak + '** Response body: ' +
      sLineBreak + Value.Response.ContentAsString);
end;

end.
```

Putting Delphi on the Server

Quite a lot of code, but the things to understand are few. The most important is the wrapping of `TNetHTTPClient` inside the data module. We want to isolate the event handlers needed to accept the self-signed certificates and all the helpers. Then, in the main form we can simply use the simpler interface offered by the wrapper.

All the data retrieved by the request, plus ReadBytes and Certificate, are packaged in a `TResponseData` record. All the requests simply return the `IHTTPResponse` returned by the `TNetHTTPClient`. The requests are asynchronous, so that we can use the code on Windows and on mobile platforms. The `THTTPDM` could also be more specialized with specific methods that completely hide the internals of the system, but in this case our objective is not this. Please don't use the `btnPostClick` event handler. Also, if is not really needed here; I'm using it to show how to generate JSON text using the `TJSONBuilder` object to achieve a small memory requirement, especially useful on mobile, but also in servers and in general, when your JSON may be big.

Now, try to run this project on Windows. Did it work? Try to click on the buttons and check the certificate information returned for a self-signed certificate (the one from our server) and for a proper certificate (the one from GitHub). Now, select **Android**, or **iOS** as **Target Platform** and try to run the project as a mobile app, as shown in the following screenshot (remember to change the hardcoded IP address to yours):

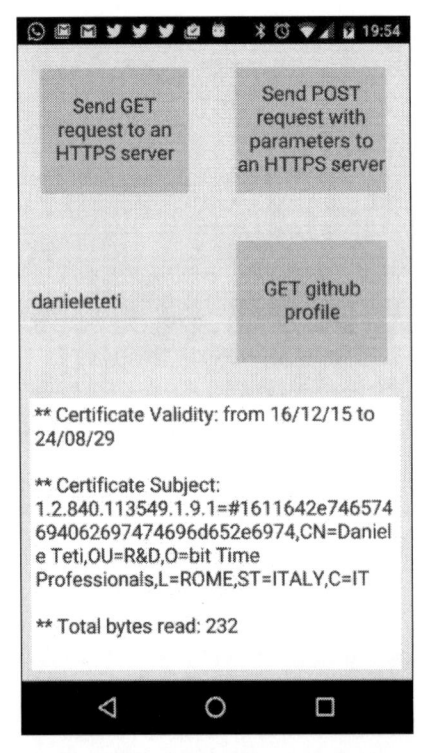

The HTTPS client running on Android

Chapter 6

As you can see, it simply works! You don't need to deploy OpenSSL dll or object code, like it was usual to do with INDY. Moreover, I quite love this integration between the OS HTTP layer and mine; it makes a lot of things simpler and is completely cross-platform.

There's more...

The `TNetHTTP*` components are a must if you want to build HTTP-enabled applications, especially on mobile, so you have to know them. Play with them, use them; If you have HTTP-enabled apps using INDY, consider switching to `TNetHTTPClient`; you will simplify deployment and development and take advantage of the deeper integration with the OS.

Here's a well-written document about the TNetHTTP* components directly from Embarcadero WikiDoc:

- Using an HTTP Client: `http://docwiki.embarcadero.com/RADStudio/en/Using_an_HTTP_Client`

7
Riding the Mobile Revolution with FireMonkey

In this chapter, we will cover the following recipes:

- Taking a photo, applying effects, and sharing it
- Using `TListView` to show and search local data
- Using SQLite databases to handle a to-do list
- Do not block the main thread!
- Using a styled `TListView` to handle long lists of data
- Customizing `TListView`
- Taking a photo and location and sending it to a server continuously
- Talking with the backend using HTTPS
- Making a phone call from your app
- Tracking the application's lifecycle

Introduction

In this chapter, we will look at how to develop mobile apps using Delphi. The recipes in this chapter require a working development configuration for your PC and in the case of iOS, your Mac, to talk with the Android or iOS device. A detailed tutorial on how to properly configure your system for this purpose can be found on the Embarcadero DocWiki. To develop and deploy an app for iOS, you require an Apple computer and an actual iOS device, while to develop and deploy for Android, you only need to have the device. There is also an emulator in the SDK where you can deploy an app but, currently, it is very slow; if you really want to develop for Android, having an actual device where deploying is faster than using an emulator is recommended.

> Visit the following links for more information and relevant documentation that will help you to configure different environments:
> - For Android configuration: The *Set Up Your Development Environment on Windows PC (Android)* documentation can be found at: `http://docwiki.embarcadero.com/RADStudio/en/Mobile_Tutorial:_Set_Up_Your_Development_Environment_on_Windows_PC_(Android)`
> - For iOS configuration: The *Set Up Your Development Environment on the Mac (iOS)* documentation can be found at: `http://docwiki.embarcadero.com/RADStudio/en/Mobile_Tutorial:_Set_Up_Your_Development_Environment_on_the_Mac_(iOS)`
> - For Windows configuration: The *Set Up Your Development Environment on Windows PC (iOS)* documentation can be found at: `http://docwiki.embarcadero.com/RADStudio/en/Mobile_Tutorial:_Set_Up_Your_Development_Environment_on_Windows_PC_(iOS)`

Taking a photo, applying effects, and sharing it

This recipe will introduce the mobile development world using a simple app that shows how to take a photo directly from the camera or from the photo library, apply some effects to it, and then share it using one of the installed apps on the device.

Chapter 7

Getting ready

This recipe makes extensive use of Delphi **actions**. Actions are an implementation of the GoF Command design pattern and have been an important tool for the Delphi developer since the initial versions of Delphi. You can use them as much as you like. In the mobile era, actions are even more important and useful. Indeed, actions can be used to execute common tasks such as taking a photo with the camera, getting a photo from the library, or sharing some content with the other apps. Here's how our app will look:

The Photo with Effects app, with buttons on the top; three out of the four buttons are bound to standard actions

Riding the Mobile Revolution with FireMonkey

How to do it...

Now we are about to create our first FireMonkey mobile app. Let's start!

1. Create a new mobile app by navigating to **File | New | Multi-Device Application - Delphi**.
2. Select the **Header/Footer** template and click on **OK**.
3. In the upper-left corner of the form designer, there is a combo box which allows you to select the OS style used by the form designer to show the form. Select **Android** from the drop-down menu.
4. The IDE has just created a base for us. Name the form `MainForm` and let's add our logic and adapt the UI.
5. Select the **HeaderLabel** label and change its **Text** property to **Photos with Effects**.
6. Select the **TToolbar** component named **Footer** and delete it.
7. Now, drop a **TPanel** component and align it to the **Top** so that it'll be just below the header.
8. Add four buttons to the just dropped **TPanel** component. Align three of them to the left-hand side and the other one to the right-hand side. Now, starting from the left-hand side, set the following values for their **StyleLookup** property:
   - **cameratoolbutton**
   - **organizetoolbutton**
   - **composetoolbutton**
   - **actiontoolbutton**
9. Now, the buttons should look like the one in the previous screenshot.
10. Drop a **TImage** component in the center of the form and align it to **Client**. This component will be our main working area.
11. Set **TImage.MarginWrapMode** to **Fit**.
12. Drop a **TListView** component at the center of the form, make it a bit wider, and name it `lvEffects`. This listview will be used to show the available effects to the user.
13. Select the **lvEffects** control and set `ItemAppearanceObjects.ItemObjects.Accessory.Visible = false`.
14. Drop a **TActionList** component, double-click on it, and then, from the little menu button on the left-hand side, click on **New Standard Action** (or you can use *Ctrl + Ins*).
15. From the resultant window, select **TTakePhotoFromCameraAction** and click on **OK**. Repeat the process and add the **TTakePhotoFromLibraryAction** and **TShowShareSheetAction** actions. Note that these actions are actually invisible components with properties and events just like a persistent field in a dataset. In a few moments, we will go back to these components to customize their default behaviors.

16. Starting from the left-hand side, connect the following actions to the buttons placed in the **TPanel** component at the top.
    1. Set the first button, **Action = TakePhotoFromCameraAction1**.
    2. Set the second button, **Action = TakePhotoFromLibraryAction1**.
    3. Do not assign an action to the third button, but name it `btnEffects`.
    4. Set the fourth button, **Action = ShowShareSheetAction1**.

17. In the app, there will be a mechanism to dynamically load the available effects by inspecting the **TFilterEffect** descendants placed on the form. So, we can simply drop some effects on the form and the app will automatically load them in a list allowing the user to use them. Drop the following effects on the form: **TEmbossEffect, TRadialBlurEffect, TContrastEffect, TColorKeyAlphaEffect, TInvertEffect, TSepiaEffect, TTilerEffect, TPixelateEffect, TToonEffect, TPencilStrokeEffect, TRippleEffect, TWaveEffect, TWrapEffect**, and **TInnerGlowEffect**.

18. Now we've to write some code. In the `private` section of the `TMainForm` class, declare the following instance members:

    private
    ```
    FItemsEffectsMap: TDictionary<Integer, TFilterEffect>;
    FUndoEffectsList: TObjectStack<TFilterEffect>;
    FUndoEffectItem: TListViewItem;
    FTopWhenShown: Extended;
    procedure LoadPhoto(AImage: TBitmap);
    procedure RecalcMenuPosition;
    procedure RemoveCurrentEffect(ARemoveFromList: boolean);
    function EffectNameByClassName(
                 const AClassName: String): String;
    ```

19. Hit *Ctrl + Shift + C* to create empty methods and fill them with the following code:

    ```
    procedure TMainForm.LoadPhoto(AImage: TBitmap);
    begin
      Label1.Text := '';
      RemoveCurrentEffect(False);
      FUndoEffectsList.Clear;
      Image1.Bitmap.Assign(AImage);
    end;

    procedure TMainForm.RecalcMenuPosition;
    begin
      FTopWhenShown := ClientHeight / 2 - lvEffects.Height / 2;
      lvEffects.Height := ClientHeight / 2;
      lvEffects.Position.X := ClientWidth / 2 -
              lvEffects.Width / 2;
    ```

```
    end;

    procedure TMainForm.RemoveCurrentEffect(ARemoveFromList:
      boolean);
    begin
      if FUndoEffectsList.Count = 0 then
        Exit;
      Image1.RemoveObject(FUndoEffectsList.Peek);
      if ARemoveFromList then
        FUndoEffectsList.Pop;
      Image1.Repaint;
    end;

    function TMainForm.EffectNameByClassName(
        const AClassName: String): String;
    begin
      Result := AClassName.Substring(1);
      Result := TRegEx.Replace(Result, '[A-Z]',
    ' $0').TrimLeft;
    end;
```

20. To compile this code, add `System.Generics.Collections` in the uses `interface` section and `System.RegularExpressions` in the uses `implementation` section. Build the project just to ensure that everything is alright.

21. Now, create the `OnCreate` event handler for the form and add the following code:

```
    procedure TMainForm.FormCreate(Sender: TObject);
    var
      eff: TFmxObject;
      lbi: TListViewItem;
    begin
      FItemsEffectsMap := TDictionary<Integer,
        TFilterEffect>.Create;
      FUndoEffectsList := TObjectStack<TFilterEffect>
        .Create(False);
      lvEffects.Position.Y := -lvEffects.Height;
      lvEffects.BeginUpdate;
      try
        FUndoEffectItem := lvEffects.Items.Add;
        FUndoEffectItem.Text := 'Undo';

        for eff in Children do
        begin
          //if it's an effect, add it to the listview
          //and to the dictionary. Use the classname
```

```
            //to create a friendly name
            if eff is TFilterEffect then
            begin
               lbi := lvEffects.Items.Add;
               lbi.Text := EffectNameByClassName(eff.ClassName);
               FItemsEffectsMap.Add(lbi.Index,
                     TFilterEffect(eff));
            end;
         end;
      finally
         lvEffects.EndUpdate;
      end;
      lvEffects.ApplyStyleLookup;
end;
```

22. Now, create the `FormResize` and `FormShow` event handlers. In the body section of these event handlers, call the `RecalcMenuPosition` procedure.

23. Select the listview and create the `OnItemClick` event handler. This event will be called when the user selects an effect from the list. Now, we have to remove, with an animation, the list from the form and apply the effect. Fill the event handler with this code:

```
procedure TMainForm.lvEffectsItemClick(const Sender:
   TObject; const AItem: TListViewItem);
begin
   TAnimator.AnimateFloatDelay(
      lvEffects, 'Position.Y', -lvEffects.Height, 0.3, 0.1,
      TAnimationType.&In, TInterpolationType.Back);

   if AItem = FUndoEffectItem then
   begin
      //undo and revert to the previous one
      RemoveCurrentEffect(true);
      if FUndoEffectsList.Count > 0 then
         Image1.AddObject(FUndoEffectsList.Peek);
   end
   else
   begin
      // apply new effect
      RemoveCurrentEffect(False);
      FUndoEffectsList.Push(FItemsEffectsMap[AItem.Index]);
      Image1.AddObject(FUndoEffectsList.Peek);
   end;
end;
```

24. Now, we've to create something that is able to show the list of available effects when the user needs to apply one of them. The effect list will drop down from the top of the form with a little bouncing effect and will go away in the same way (but in reverse).

25. Create `btnEffects` on the `click` event handler and fill it with the following code:

    ```
    procedure TMainForm.btnEffectsClick(Sender: TObject);
    begin
      if FUndoEffectsList.Count = 0 then
        FUndoEffectItem.Text := '<No effect to undo>'
      else
        FUndoEffectItem.Text := '[Undo ' +
          EffectNameByClassName(
        FUndoEffectsList.Peek.ClassName) + ']';

      TAnimator.AnimateFloat(lvEffects, 'Position.Y',
        FTopWhenShown, 0.4, TAnimationType.Out,
        TInterpolationType.Back);
    end;
    ```

26. We've got to customize the actions' behaviors. Double-click on **TActionList1**, select the **ShowShareSheet1** action, create the `OnBeforeExecute` event handler, and then fill it with the following code:

    ```
    procedure TMainForm.ShowShareSheetAction1BeforeExecute(
      Sender: TObject);
    begin
      if FUndoEffectsList.Count > 0 then
      begin
        //actually apply the effect to the bitmap
        FUndoEffectsList.Peek.ProcessEffect(nil,
          Image1.Bitmap, 0);
      end;
      ShowShareSheetAction1.Bitmap.Assign(Image1.Bitmap);
    end;
    ```

27. Create the `OnDidFinishTaking` event handler for the **TakePhotoFromCameraAction1** and **TakePhotoFromLibraryAction1** actions and fill both with the following code:

    ```
    procedure TMainForm
      .TakePhotoFromCameraAction1DidFinishTaking(
        Image: TBitmap);
    begin
      LoadPhoto(Image);
    ```

```
end;

procedure TMainForm
   .TakePhotoFromLibraryAction1DidFinishTaking(
      Image: TBitmap);
begin
   LoadPhoto(Image);
end;
```

28. Select an available target in the **Project Manager** window (in your phone or an available emulator in the case of Android) and run the app.

Tap the first button from the left-hand side and take a photo. The image should be placed in the main area. Tap on the **btnEffects** button, and you should see the listview falling from the top to allow you to choose effects. The first item should be **<No effect to undo>**. Select an effect, let's say **Contrast Effect** and see how the effect is applied to the photo. Tap **btnEffect** again, and you should see the first item saying **[Undo Contrast Effect]**. Play with the app by adding effects and using the undo features to sequentially go back to the beginning. Note that the effects will not be added (so you cannot have **Emboss** along with **Blur** applied at the same time) but applied singularly. When you are satisfied with the result, tap on the button on the right-hand side to share the photo with effects applied using an installed app:

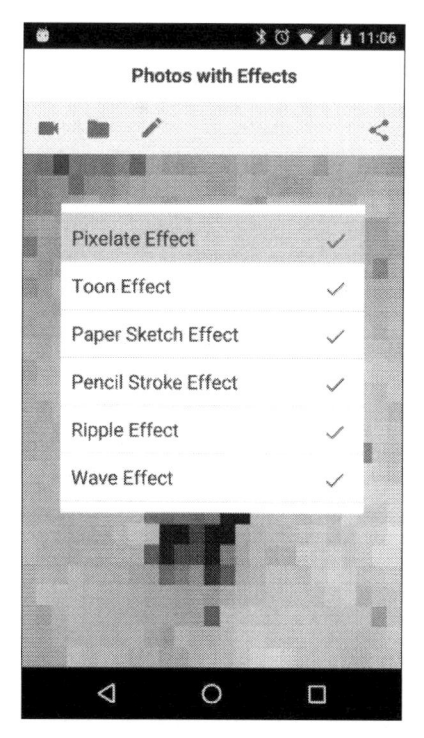

A photo taken from the camera with the Pixelate effect applied; the menu is visible and ready to apply another effect.

How it works...

When launched, the app loads the available effects, inspecting all the **TEffectFilter** descendants placed on the form, and stores the component reference in a dictionary indexed with the **ListItem** index in the list. To create a friendly effect name for the UI, the effect's class name is used. Indeed, all the effect classes have the typical Pascal case naming convention (just like all the other things in Delphi) and the `EffectNameByClassName` method uses a regular expression to make a string such as `TRadialBlurEffect` into something like the **Radial Blur** effect. To do this, the initial `T` is removed and then it is used as a regular expression, and the words are split as shown in the following code:

```
function TMainForm.EffectNameByClassName(
                const AClassName: String): String;
begin
  Result := AClassName.Substring(1);
  Result := TRegEx.Replace(Result, '[A-Z]', ' $0').TrimLeft;
end;
```

Another nice feature implemented is the **Undo** stack. Each time a new effect is applied to the Image, the current one is pushed onto the stack. So, when you tap on **Undo <current effect>**, the current effect is removed and the top of the stack is used to retrieve the last effect. With this approach, which is used in multiple scenarios, we can go back to the beginning without losing any steps.

The last note goes to the share functionality. The effects are applied, adding the related components to the image child controls list. Following the parenting relation, FireMonkey performs all of the drawing jobs; however, the image itself is not transformed, only its visual representation is "effected." Now, if you try to read the bitmap contained by the **TImage** control programmatically, the image is not "effected" and you get the original image. So how do we actually apply the effect to the image? Check the `ShowShareSheetAction1BeforeExecute` event handler:

```
procedure TMainForm.ShowShareSheetAction1BeforeExecute(
                                  Sender: TObject);
begin
  if FUndoEffectsList.Count > 0 then
  begin
    FUndoEffectsList.Peek.ProcessEffect(nil, Image1.Bitmap, 0);
  end;
  ShowShareSheetAction1.Bitmap.Assign(Image1.Bitmap);
end;
```

As you can see, the `effect` component has a `ProcessEffect` method that actually takes an image and applies the transformation to it. In this case, the effect is not only visually applied, but is actually applied. So, when you share the effected image, the image is really affected.

Chapter 7

There's more...

Many concepts are covered in this first mobile recipe. As you will see, the base approach to mobile development is no different from a normal FireMonkey application. This is an extraordinary feature of FireMonkey: one framework for all platforms. If you are good at FireMonkey, you are at least 80 percent good at all the supported platforms. However, in the mobile scope, all things get a bit slower and more difficult due to the platform limits and the inherently slower `edit/run/test` loop.

To get more info about effects, you can check the following articles:

- `http://docwiki.embarcadero.com/RADStudio/en/FireMonkey_Image_Effects`
- `http://docwiki.embarcadero.com/RADStudio/en/Applying_FireMonkey_Image_Effects`

To get more information about regular expressions as implemented in Delphi, check the following articles:

- `http://docwiki.embarcadero.com/RADStudio/en/Regular_Expressions`
- `http://docwiki.embarcadero.com/CodeExamples/en/RTL.RegExpression_Sample`

To get some information about the **Command** design pattern and the other 22 fundamental patterns, you can read the classic book, *Design Patterns: Elements of Reusable Object-Oriented Software, Erich Gamma, Richard Helm, Ralph Johnson,* and *John Vlissides, Addison Wesley Professional* (`http://www.amazon.com/Design-Patterns-Elements-Reusable-Object-Oriented/dp/0201633612`).

Using TListView to show and search local data

In many cases with mobile apps, data is read from remote servers and then stored locally to make it available even without an Internet connection. In this recipe, you'll see how to read and write to a file as well as how to show and search that data in a `TListView`.

Riding the Mobile Revolution with FireMonkey

Getting ready

This recipe is short and simple, but it is really useful because the concepts exposed are reusable and allow you to gain confidence with some very important best practices. The final aspect of the app is shown in the following screenshot. Note that the remove button is visible only when an item is selected:

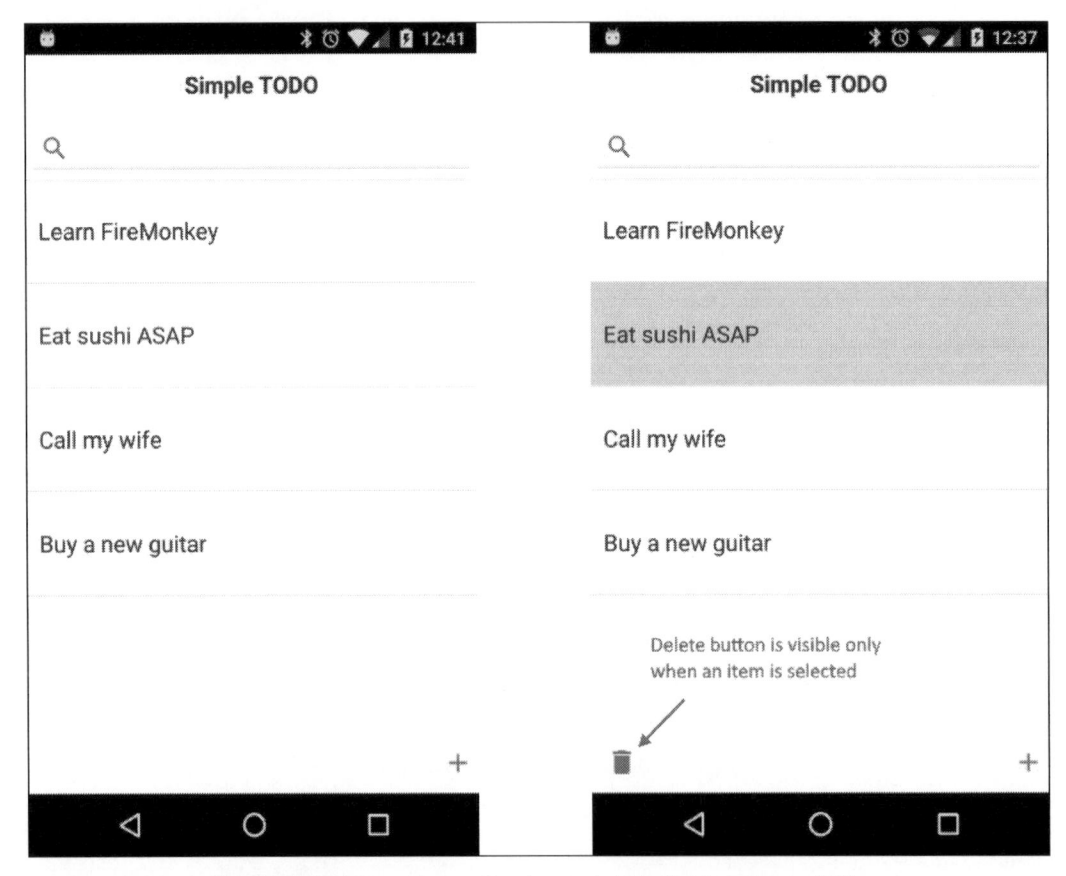

The Simple to-do app; when an item is selected, the Delete button is visible

How to do it...

1. Create a new mobile app by navigating to **File** | **New** | **Other...** | **Delphi Projects** | **Multi-Device Application**.
2. Choose the **Header/Footer** template and click on **OK**.

3. As soon as Delphi creates the project template, save all the files with the following names:
   - Save the project as `SimpleTODO.dproj`
   - Save the form as `MainFormU.pas`

4. Drop a **TListView** component on the form and set the following properties (the relevant properties are extracted from the `MainFormU.fmx` file):

   ```
   object ListView1: TListView
     Align = Client
     ItemAppearance.ItemHeight = 80
     ItemAppearanceObjects.ItemObjects.Text.WordWrap = True
     ItemAppearanceObjects.ItemObjects.Accessory.Visible = False
     SearchVisible = True
   end
   ```

5. Drop a **TActionList** component on the form and add two actions. Name them `acNew` and `acDelete`.

6. Create the `OnExecute` event handler for the two actions using the following code:

   ```
   procedure TMainForm.acDeleteExecute(Sender: TObject);
   begin
     if Assigned(ListView1.Selected) then
       ListView1.Items.Delete(ListView1.Selected.Index);
   end;

   procedure TMainForm.acNewExecute(Sender: TObject);
   begin
     //check "There's more" section
     //about InputQuery deprecation
     InputQuery('TODO', 'Write your new TODO', '',
       procedure (const AResult: TModalResult;
         const AValue: string)
       var
         LValue: string;
       begin
         LValue := AValue;
         if (AResult = mrOk) and (LValue.Trim.Length > 0) then
           AddItem(LValue);
       end);
   end;
   ```

7. Directly on the **ActionList1** component, create the `OnUpdate` event handler and fill it with the following code. This code makes the **Delete** button invisible when no item is selected on the list.

   ```
   procedure TMainForm.ActionList1Update(Action: TBasicAction;
                                        var Handled: Boolean);
   begin
     acDelete.Visible := Assigned(ListView1.Selected);
   end;
   ```

8. Go to the main form declaration and in the `private` section, declare the following variables:

   ```
   private
     FDataFileName: String;
     procedure LoadFromFile;
     procedure SaveToFile;
     procedure AddItem(const TODO: String);
   ```

9. Hit *Ctrl + Shift + C* and fill the method bodies with the following code:

   ```
   procedure TMainForm.LoadFromFile;
   var
     LFileReader: TStreamReader;
   begin
     ListView1.Items.Clear;
     if TFile.Exists(FDataFileName) then
     begin
       LFileReader := TFile.OpenText(FDataFileName);
       try
         while not LFileReader.EndOfStream do
         begin
           AddItem(LFileReader.ReadLine);
         end;
       finally
         LFileReader.Close;
       end;
     end;
   end;

   procedure TMainForm.SaveToFile;
   var
     LItem: TListViewItem;
     LFileWriter: TStreamWriter;
   begin
     LFileWriter := TFile.CreateText(FDataFileName);
     try
   ```

```
        for LItem in ListView1.Items do
        begin
          LFileWriter.WriteLine(LItem.Text);
        end;
      finally
        LFileWriter.Close;
      end;
    end;

    procedure TMainForm.AddItem(const TODO: String);
    var
      LItem: TListViewItem;
    begin
      LItem := ListView1.Items.Add;
      LItem.Text := TODO;
      ListView1.ItemIndex := LItem.Index;
    end;
```

10. As you can see, the name of the file used to store the data is in the `FDataFileName` variable.

11. Create the `OnCreate` and `OnSaveState` event handlers for the form:

    ```
    procedure TMainForm.FormCreate(Sender: TObject);
    begin
      FDataFileName := TPath.Combine(
           TPath.GetDocumentsPath, 'datafile.txt');
      LoadFromFile;
    end;
    procedure TMainForm.FormSaveState(Sender: TObject);
    begin
      SaveToFile;
    end;
    ```

12. The last thing to do is to connect the `acNew` and `acDelete` actions to two buttons. Drop two **TButton** components on the lower **TToolbar** named **Footer**, name them `btnDelete` and `btnNew`, and set the following properties:

    ```
        object btnDelete: TButton
          Action = acDelete
          Align = alLeft
          StyleLookup = 'trashtoolbutton'
        end
        object btnNew: TButton
          Action = acNew
          Align = alRight
          StyleLookup = 'additembutton'
        end
    ```

13. Run the app. For testing purposes, you can run the app using the **32-bit Windows** target.

How it works...

When the app starts, it looks in its documents path for a file named `datafile.txt`. If it exists, it is loaded and all the lines become items in the `TListView`. Remember that Delphi allows you to write cross-platform applications, so you must be aware of the way Delphi allows you to normalize the differences between operating systems; otherwise, you risk thwarting the power of Delphi and FireMonkey. The `TPath` class is useful for keeping us ignorant about system default paths, path separators, and other stuff related to the filesystem. We want to put our data into the `documents` folder. However, in Android, the `document` folder is different from the iOS one (and if your code has to run in the desktop environment as well, the paths are also different). Therefore, using the `TPath` class, we can be completely ignorant about where actually the file is stored. We can know the path, but we do not want to explicitly define it; let `TPath` do its job. These are some well-known paths that `TPath` already knows. Whenever you need the specific path, ask `TPath`:

```
class function GetHomePath: string; static;
class function GetDocumentsPath: string; static;
class function GetSharedDocumentsPath: string; static;
class function GetLibraryPath: string; static;
class function GetCachePath: string; static;
class function GetPublicPath: string; static;
class function GetPicturesPath: string; static;
class function GetSharedPicturesPath: string; static;
class function GetCameraPath: string; static;
class function GetSharedCameraPath: string; static;
class function GetMusicPath: string; static;
class function GetSharedMusicPath: string; static;
class function GetMoviesPath: string; static;
class function GetSharedMoviesPath: string; static;
class function GetAlarmsPath: string; static;
class function GetSharedAlarmsPath: string; static;
class function GetDownloadsPath: string; static;
class function GetSharedDownloadsPath: string; static;
class function GetRingtonesPath: string; static;
class function GetSharedRingtonesPath: string; static;
```

Let's go back to our app. When the items are loaded into the listview, the `acNew` and `acDelete` actions allow the user to add and remove items from the list. When the form is about to go in background, the `FormSaveState` event saves all the items—one item for a line—into the `datafile.txt` file.

In a more complex situation, it is much better to have an in-memory representation of your data model that isn't bound to any visual control. Suppose you need to access the data in another form. How do we do that? If your data is bound to the GUI, you are bound to it too! The state of your app should not be stored only on the visual controls. However, for a simple situation like this recipe, it is not a big problem.

There's more...

The power of Delphi is a great advantage in mobile development. In many cases some fundamental features of mobile apps can be tested also as a desktop app. For instance, if you need to test the usual cycle:

- Get data from a remote web service
- Organize and save data in local storage
- Retrieve data and show it in the GUI

There are chances that you can test these features as a desktop application, simplifying and speeding up the deployment and the debug phase, and then when these fundamental parts work as expected, focus on the mobile-related problems. If you have ever developed using other environments (apart from the scripted ones) you will definitely appreciate this possibility.

Another important note for an Android developer is the modal dialogs. Android OS doesn't support modal dialog boxes. Instead of calling `ShowModal` (or `InputBox`, `InputQuery`, and so on), you should call `Show` (or one of the overloaded versions of `InputBox`, `InputQuery`, and so on) and have the form return and call your event. Embarcadero recommends that we don't use modal dialog boxes on either of the mobile platforms because unexpected behavior can result. Avoiding the usage of modal dialog boxes eliminates potential problems in debugging and supporting your mobile apps.

Moreover, while still used in this recipe code for backward compatibility, since Delphi 10.1 Berlin, `InputBox`, `InputQuery`, and `MessageDlg` are deprecated in FireMonkey. If your code must compile only on Berlin or later, you should use the new `TDialogService` class which contains the following methods:

- `ShowMessage`
- `InputQuery`
- `MessageDialog`

These three methods work in a similar way but show different dialogs. For instance, `TDialogService.MessageDialog` displays a dialog box with a custom message, dialog type, set of buttons, and help context ID. `MessageDialog` can work synchronously or asynchronously depending on the preferred mode. `MessageDialog` internally calls `MessageDialogAsync` or `MessageDialogSync`. When `PreferredMode` is set to `Platform`:

- On desktop platforms (Windows and OS X), `MessageDialog` behaves synchronously. The call finishes only when the user closes the dialog box.
- On mobile platforms (Android and iOS), `MessageDialog` behaves asynchronously. The call finishes instantaneously; it does not wait for the user to close the dialog box.

To force a specific behavior for the different platforms, set `PreferredMode` to `Sync` or `ASync` (but `ASync` is not supported by Android).

Going back to our recipe, here is the `acNewExecute` method using a conditional compilation to use the `TDialogService` class if present. Remember, new projects should only use the `TDialogService` (defined in `FMX.DialogService.pas`).

```
procedure TMainForm.acNewExecute(Sender: TObject);
begin
{$IF CompilerVersion >= 24}
  // "Berlin" (or better) specific code
  TDialogService.InputQuery('TODO', ['Write your new TODO'], [''],
    procedure(const AResult: TModalResult;
      const AValues: array of string)
    var
      LValue: string;
    begin
      LValue := AValues[0];
      if (AResult = mrOk) and (LValue.Trim.Length > 0) then
        AddItem(LValue);
    end);
{$ELSE}
  //"Seattle" and previous versions up to XE7
  InputQuery('TODO', 'Write your new TODO', '',
    procedure(const AResult: TModalResult; const AValue: string)
    var
      LValue: string;
    begin
      LValue := AValue;
      if (AResult = mrOk) and (LValue.Trim.Length > 0) then
   w    AddItem(LValue);
    end);
{$ENDIF}
end;
```

Using SQLite databases to handle a to-do list

Usually, the mobile apps read or write data using the network. In many cases, however, you need local storage to save your data. A local database can be useful for a number of things:

- To buffer information while the Internet connection is not available
- To save information that will be realigned on the central server when back at the office
- To allow you a fast search on a relatively small set of data retrieved from the central databases and stored on the device
- To store some structured data

In all these cases, you have to handle a database. This recipe will show how to do it.

Getting ready

This recipe is about a to-do list. It is similar to the *Using TListView to show and search local data* recipe, but in this case, we'll use a SQL database and will show data to the user using LiveBindings. Moreover, we'll see how to create output converters for LiveBindings.

How to do it...

When you need a mobile database, you have two choices in Delphi: SQLite (an open source embedded database) and InterBase ToGo.

Since version XE6, RAD Studio has included InterBase ToGo and IBLite editions for embedded application development. You can deploy your mobile applications to iOS or Android devices with an InterBase ToGo license (at a cost) or IBLite license (free).

If your app is a bit more complex; needs encryption, stored procedures, or a number of data types, you definitely have to go for InterBase ToGo. Otherwise, you can use SQLite. Consider that IBLite is the same engine as InterBase ToGo, but limited to some extent. The biggest limit is the lack of encryption. However, an app that uses IBLite doesn't require code updates if you need to scale to InterBase ToGo, change the license and you are okay.

This recipe is very simple in terms of database requirements, so we'll use SQLite. However, the same concepts are applicable to InterBase ToGo and IBLite.

Open the `TODOList.dproj` project. The main form has all the components that are required to access the database (in a real-world app, consider using a data module for this, just like the desktop applications). The app has been created using the **Header/Footer** mobile template. The first `TabItem` contains the to-do lists, while the second `TabItem` allows you to update an existing to-do list or create a new to-do list.

When the application starts, the **TFDConnection** components connect to the database. If the database file doesn't exist, the SQLite engine is configured to create a new database file from scratch. This feature is very useful and can be configured by setting the `OpenMode` parameter to `CreateUTF8`. (The UTF8 encoding is almost always the best choice for international applications; in this case, it is the default setting for the **TFDConnection** components.) Here's the relevant part of the **TFDConnection** parameters:

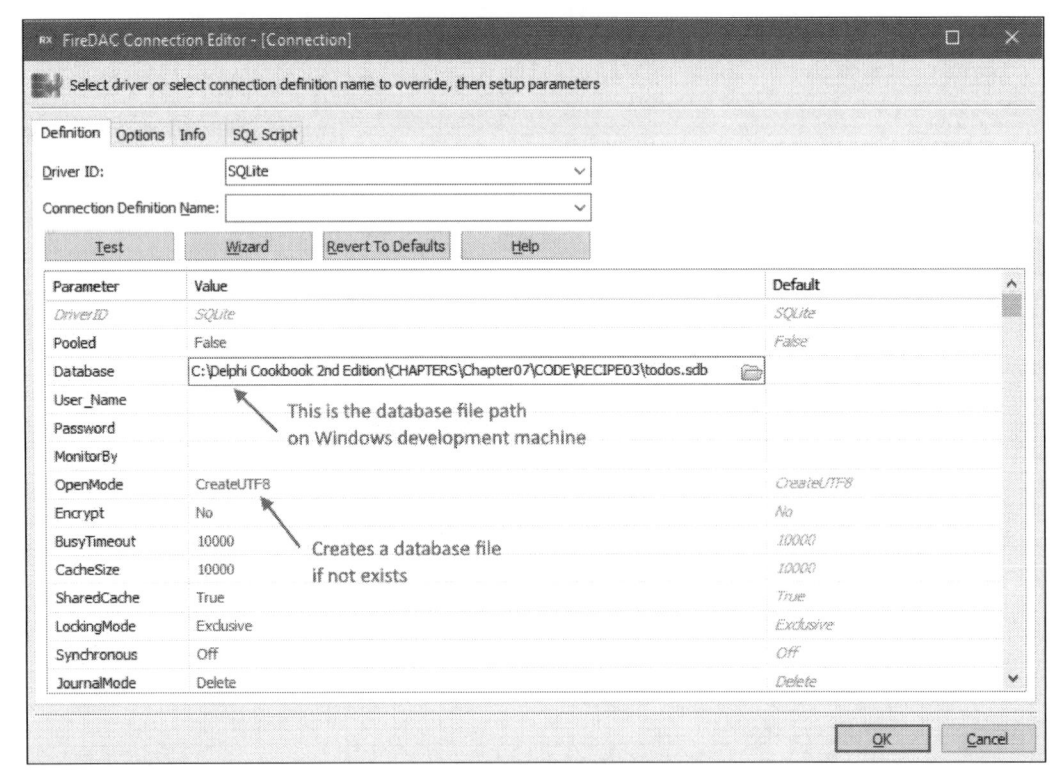

The connection parameters

Another problem to solve is related to the database path. In Windows, you can develop your mobile app using the **32 bit – Windows** target and a local path on your system; however, when the app runs on the device, you have to use another path. How do we solve this? In the connection's `BeforeConnect` event handler, consider the following code:

```
procedure TMainForm.ConnectionBeforeConnect(Sender: TObject);
begin
{$IF DEFINED(IOS) or DEFINED(ANDROID)}
  Connection.Params.Values['Database'] :=
        TPath.GetDocumentsPath + PathDelim + 'todos.sdb';
{$ENDIF}
end;
```

With this code, the database will be created in the proper iOS or Android document folder.

The next problem is related to the database structure. When and how do we create the table that we need? Let's check the `AfterConnect` event handler on the connection:

```
procedure TMainForm.ConnectionAfterConnect(Sender: TObject);
begin
  Connection.ExecSQL('CREATE TABLE IF NOT EXISTS TODOS( ' +
    ' ID INTEGER PRIMARY KEY AUTOINCREMENT NOT NULL, ' +
    ' DESCRIPTION   CHAR(50) NOT NULL, ' +
    ' DONE          INTEGER  NOT NULL  ' +
    ')');
  qryTODOs.Active := True;
end;
```

Just after the database is created, and at any subsequent run, the app tries to create the database table if it doesn't yet exist. Then, open the dataset connected to the bind source to show the data present. The listview is configured with the following code:

```
ItemAppearance.ItemAppearance = 'ListItemRightDetail'
ItemAppearance.ItemHeight = 100
SearchVisible = True
```

Riding the Mobile Revolution with FireMonkey

The second tab contains a **TMemo** component, a **TSwitch** component, and two **TLabel** components. The `TBindSourceDB` data source connected to the `qryTODO` dataset is connected to the list and to the `detail` component placed on the second `TabItem` as well. This is shown in the following screenshot (integrated with some clarifying text):

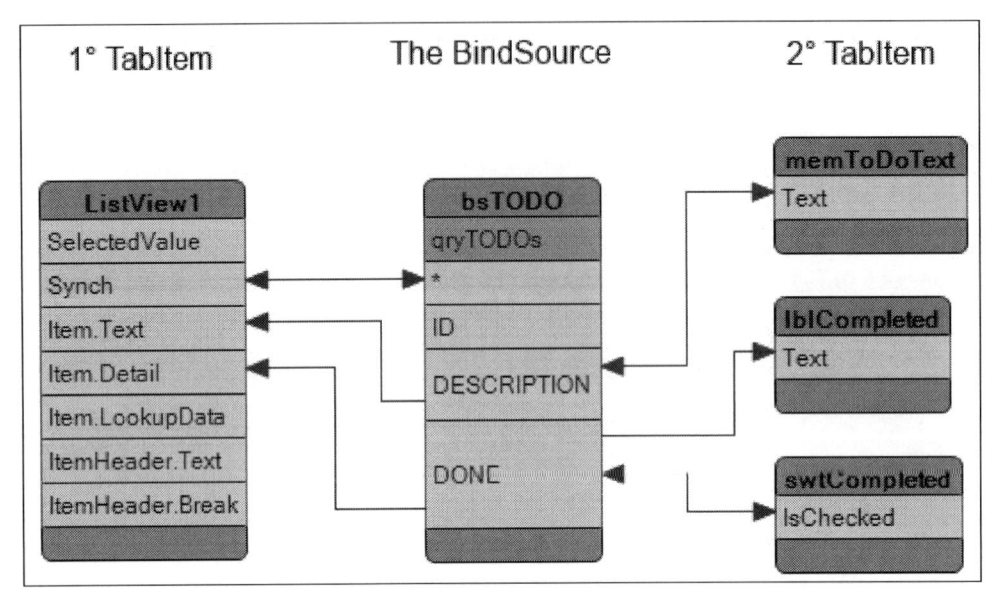

The LiveBinding designer showing the binding connections between the Bindsource, the listview, and the detail components.

All the code used to handle the dataset is normal dataset-oriented code, just like the code used to manage datasets on a desktop application.

This recipe shows a nasty problem. SQLite doesn't have the Boolean field type, so the **DONE** field in the **TODO** table is of type integer, where 1 means `true` and 0 means `false`. However, we want to connect the **DONE** field to a `TSwitch.IsChecked` property of type Boolean. In this situation, when you try to change the switch value, you will get an error like the following:

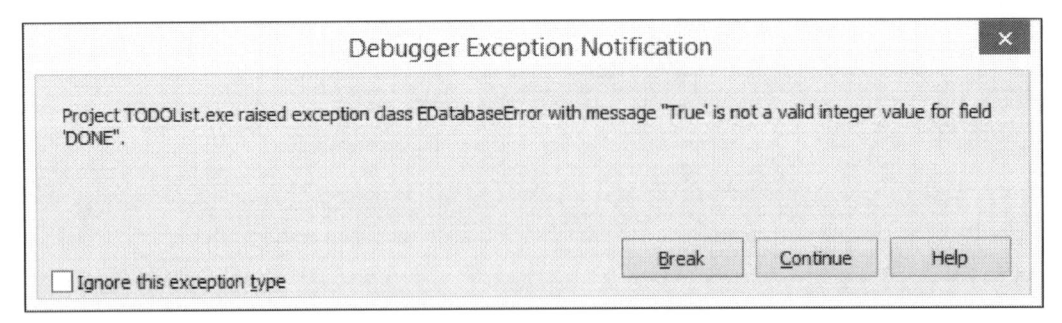

The exception raised by Delphi when you try to connect an Integer field to a Boolean component property

How do we solve this? The LiveBinding engine has a powerful mechanism to convert data from one type to another. When the result of an expression is of type X and the property where that value needs to be written is of type Y, the engine looks for a valid output converter that is able to convert type X to type Y. The available output converters are shown on the `BindingList1.OutputConverters` property. As you can see yourself, there isn't an `OutputConverter` from string to Boolean which acts as we need. To solve our problem, we've to register another `OutputConverter` object able to convert a Boolean value (`swtCompleted.IsChecked`) to a string value (because LiveBinding uses the `TField.SetText` method to set a value of a field). This output converter is registered in the `BoolToStringConverterU.pas` unit. The procedure used to register the new converter and makes it visible to the LiveBinding engine is shown in the following code:

```
const
  sBoolToString = 'BoolToString';

procedure RegisterOutputConversions;
begin
  //unregister the default converter bool->string
  TValueRefConverterFactory.UnRegisterConversion(
TypeInfo(Boolean), TypeInfo(String));

  //register the new converter bool->string
  //This converter is able to handle 1=true and 0=false
  TValueRefConverterFactory.RegisterConversion(
       TypeInfo(Boolean), TypeInfo(String),
         TConverterDescription.Create(
    procedure(const InValue: TValue; var OutValue: TValue)
    begin
      if InValue.AsBoolean then
        OutValue := '1'
      else
        OutValue := '0';
    end, sBoolToString, sBoolToString, '',
                    True, sBoolToString, nil));
end;
```

Now the app works correctly. However, be careful, now all the conversions from Boolean to string will be considered `true` when `1` and `false` when `0`. This internal mechanism of LiveBindings needs to be clearly understood, because it can cause a lot of headaches in non-trivial cases. Full code of this `OutputConverter` is available in the unit `BoolToStringConverterU.pas`.

On the second tab, there is a label that describes the meaning of the switch. When the switch is checked, the label says **The task is completed**; otherwise, it says **The task is not completed**. This feature has been implemented using LiveBinding expressions. Go to the LiveBinding designer and select the arrow that connects the **DONE** field to the `lblCompleted.Text` property. Now hit *F11* to show the **Object Inspector** window and check the `CustomFormat` property. Here, a logic has been used by the label. The expression is reported as follows:

```
"The task is " + IfThen(value = 1, "completed","not completed")
```

This code is a relational expression that transforms a value read from a dataset field to a text value shown in a label. Normally, the value is read from the source component and written on the target property component. However, using the `CustomFormat` property, you can change this default behavior to get more complex and useful information. This expression is a good example of that.

There's more...

As you can see, mobile development is a mix of well-known things and new things. The LiveBindings framework is a big new thing, and you can be frightened by it. However, don't be afraid, all your needs are there. Here are some useful links to go deeper with the concepts exposed in this recipe:

- Another approach to the Integer-As-Boolean problem can be found at: `http://www.malcolmgroves.com/blog/?p=1490`
- Information on formatting fields using LiveBindings can be found at: `http://www.malcolmgroves.com/blog/?p=1226`
- Documentation about output converters can be found at: `http://docwiki.embarcadero.com/RADStudio/en/LiveBindings_Output_Converters`
- Some tutorials on LiveBindings in RAD Studio can be found at: `http://docwiki.embarcadero.com/RADStudio/en/LiveBindings_in_RAD_Studio`

Do not block the main thread!

Long requests to external systems such as storage, databases, hardware, and networks have always been difficult to handle from a user experience point of view. For the programmers, it is simple to run the long request and, when finished (after seconds, minutes, or hours), inform the user that their data is there. However, we should care about user experience even more in the mobile world.

Getting ready

If your app runs a long-running request and the UI is frozen, the user might think that something is going wrong and start to tap here and there to try to unblock the app. After some seconds, either the operating system itself will close the app, or the user will push the **Home** button to close your app and then, usually, uninstall it. Yes, user experience is one of the most important things on mobile. Consider that, like a desktop, the user experience should be of primary importance, but what I want to emphasize is that while on desktop you may have patient users because they are sitting in front of a PC (or a Mac), on a mobile, you will certainly have impatient users who want immediate feedback from your app. Mobile apps can be used on the move, so the user may be busy doing something else while they are using your app, and the app must be fast and should give feedback as soon as possible. If a long operation is running, the app should inform the user and the GUI should never be frozen. In this recipe, we will see, not how to have 0 seconds latency, but how to inform the user that something completely regular is going on and that the app is actually working as expected, and so, the only thing that the user should do is wait!

How to do it...

The scenarios exposed in this recipe are very frequent, so this demo will have to face real timings and real problems. We'll do, as a long-running request, a REST call to an open web service that provides weather forecasts. I've used this app for a while and the forecasts even seem accurate! Cool!

The service is provided by http://openweathermap.org/ and we will issue the REST request at this endpoint: http://api.openweathermap.org/data/2.5/forecast.

All the parameters required for the request will be defined at runtime by the app.
To use this service, you need an API key. To get the API key, follow the instructions here http://openweathermap.org/appid. After having obtained the API key, we can start to create the app.

1. Create a new mobile app by navigating to **File** | **New** | **Other...** | **Delphi Projects** | **Multi-Device Application**.
2. Choose the **Header/Footer** template and click on **OK**.
3. As soon as Delphi creates the project template, save all the files with the following names:
    - Save the project as `WeatherForecasts.dproj`
    - Save the form as `MainFormU.pas`
4. Drop a **TPanel** component just below the header toolbar and align it to **alTop**.

5. Into the panel just dropped, drop two **TEdit** components and a **TButton** component and name them `EditCity`, `EditCountry`, and `btnGetForecasts` respectively. Then, set the other properties as shown in the following code:

   ```
   object btnGetForecasts: TButton
     Align = Right
     Size.PlatformDefault = False
     StyleLookup = 'refreshtoolbutton'
   end
   object EditCity: TEdit
     Align = Client
     Margins.Left = 10.000000000000000000
     Margins.Top = 10.000000000000000000
     Margins.Bottom = 10.000000000000000000
     TextPrompt = 'City'
   end
   object EditCountry: TEdit
     Align = Right
     Margins.Top = 10.000000000000000000
     Margins.Bottom = 10.000000000000000000
     TextPrompt = 'Country'
   End
   ```

6. Drop a **TAniIndicator** component into the header toolbar and align it to the **Right**. Set its **Margins** property to `10` for each side.

7. Drop a `TListView` component on the form's center and set the following properties (the relevant properties extracted from the `MainFormU.fmx` file):

   ```
   object ListView1: TListView
     AllowSelection = False
     Align = Client
     ItemAppearanceObjects.ItemObjects.Text.WordWrap = True
     ItemAppearanceObjects.ItemObjects.Text.Height = 50
     ItemAppearanceObjects.ItemObjects.Accessory.Visible =
       False
     CanSwipeDelete = False
   end
   ```

8. Drop a **TLabel** component into the footer toolbar, align it to **Client**, and name it `lblInfo`.

9. Drop the **TRESTClient** and **TRESTResponse** components and leave the default properties and names.

10. Your form at design time should look like the following:

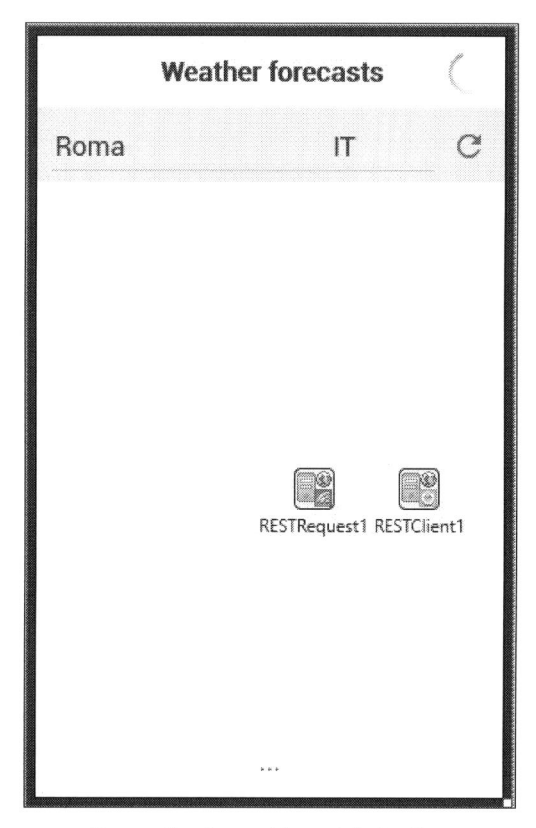

The weather forecast form at design time

11. Now, let's write some code. In the `private` section of the form, declare a string instance field called `FOSLang`. This variable will contain the current operating system language so that we can request from the service, the proper localized text.

12. Create the `FormCreate` event handler and fill it with the following code:

```
procedure TMainForm.FormCreate(Sender: TObject);
var
  LLocaleService: IFMXLocaleService;
begin
  if TPlatformServices.Current
    .SupportsPlatformService(IFMXLocaleService) then
  begin
    LLocaleService := TPlatformServices.Current
      .GetPlatformService(IFMXLocaleService)
        as IFMXLocaleService;
    FOSLang := LLocaleService.GetCurrentLangID;
```

```
      end
    else
      FOSLang := 'US';

    EditCountry.Text := FOSLang;
    RESTClient1.BaseURL :=
      'http://api.openweathermap.org/data/2.5';
    RESTRequest1.Resource :=
      'forecast?q={country}&mode=json&lang={lang}' +
      '&units=metric&APPID={APPID}';
    RESTRequest1.Params.ParameterByName('APPID')
      .Value := APPID;
    AniIndicator1.Visible := False;
  end;
```

13. In the `implementation` section of `uses`, add the following units:

    uses
    ```
    System.JSON, System.DateUtils, FMX.Platform;
    ```

14. Create an OnClick event handler for the **btnGetForecasts** button and fill it with the following code:

    ```
    procedure TMainForm.btnGetForecastsClick(Sender: TObject);
    begin
      ListView1.Items.Clear;
      RESTRequest1.Params.ParameterByName('country').Value :=
        string.Join(',', [EditCity.Text, EditCountry.Text]);
      RESTRequest1.Params.ParameterByName('lang')
        .Value := FOSLang;
      AniIndicator1.Visible := True;
      AniIndicator1.Enabled := True;
      btnGetForecasts.Enabled := False;
      RESTRequest1.ExecuteAsync(
        procedure
        var
          LForecastDateTime: TDateTime;
          LJValue: TJSONValue;
          LJObj, LMainForecast, LForecastItem, LJObjCity:
            TJSONObject;
          LJArrWeather, LJArrForecasts: TJSONArray;
          LTempMin, LTempMax: Double;
          LDay, LLastDay: string;
          LItem: TListViewItem;
    ```

```
    LWeatherDescription: string;
    LAppRespCode: string;



begin
  LJObj := RESTRequest1.Response.JSONValue
    as TJSONObject;

  // check for errors
  LAppRespCode := LJObj.GetValue('cod').Value;
  if LAppRespCode.Equals('404') then
  begin
    lblInfo.Text := 'City not found';
    Exit;
  end;
  if not LAppRespCode.Equals('200') then
  begin
    lblInfo.Text := 'Error ' + LAppRespCode;
    Exit;
  end;

  // parsing response...
  LJArrForecasts := LJObj.GetValue('list')
    as TJSONArray;
  for LJValue in LJArrForecasts do
  begin
    LForecastItem := LJValue as TJSONObject;
    LForecastDateTime := UnixToDateTime((LForecastItem
      .GetValue('dt') as TJSONNumber).AsInt64);
    LMainForecast := LForecastItem.GetValue('main')
      as TJSONObject;
    LTempMin := (LMainForecast.GetValue('temp_min')
      as TJSONNumber).AsDouble;
    LTempMax := (LMainForecast.GetValue('temp_max')
      as TJSONNumber).AsDouble;
    LJArrWeather := LForecastItem.GetValue('weather')
      as TJSONArray;
    LWeatherDescription :=
      TJSONObject(LJArrWeather.Items[0])
       .GetValue('description').Value;
    LDay := FormatDateTime('ddd d mmm yyyy',
      DateOf(LForecastDateTime));
    if LDay <> LLastDay then
```

```
      begin
        LItem := ListView1.Items.Add;
        LItem.Purpose := TListItemPurpose.Header;
        LItem.Text := LDay;
      end;
      LLastDay := LDay;
      LItem := ListView1.Items.Add;
      LItem.Text := FormatDateTime('HH',
        LForecastDateTime) + ' ' +
      LWeatherDescription +
      Format(' (min %2.2f max %2.2f)',
        [LTempMin, LTempMax]);
    end;

    // display the city name at the bottom
    LJObjCity := LJObj.GetValue('city') as TJSONObject;
    lblInfo.Text := LJObjCity.GetValue('name').Value +
      ', ' + LJObjCity.GetValue('country').Value;

    // stop the waiting animation
    AniIndicator1.Visible := False;
    AniIndicator1.Enabled := False;
    btnGetForecasts.Enabled := True;
  end);
end;
```

15. The parsing code is not simple, but now you should have all the information needed to correctly understand what's going on with this code.

16. Hit *F9* and see the application running.

17. Insert a city name and a state code (such as `Roma` and `IT` or `London` and `GB`), and you will get the weather forecasts for the upcoming days organized day by day.

How it works...

This recipe is simple from an architectural point of view. There are two parameters the user can enter. These parameters affect the request to the server that will respond with a JSON structure. Apart from the parsing code, the interesting things happen when the request is sent to the server. If we had sent a normal synchronous request to the server, the UI would be blocked until the response arrives at the client. Using the `ExecuteAsynch` method executes the actual request on a background thread so that the main thread remains free to update the UI. When the request finishes the execution, then an anonymous method is called in the main thread context. The **TAniIndicator** component is started just before the request starts and is stopped after the parsing is finished. In this way, the user is aware that something is happening. Consider that any request to an external system could potentially last for hours. Be aware of this!

The code used to fill the list uses the grouping feature of the **TListView** component to show the forecasts organized day by day.

Another thing to note is that the web service can use a localized response for descriptive text. Therefore, in the `FormCreate` event, we use the `IFMXLocaleService` service to read the current system language. Later, we use that language code to inform the remote service about the preferred localization language.

Here's the app running in the mobile preview on an Italian PC:

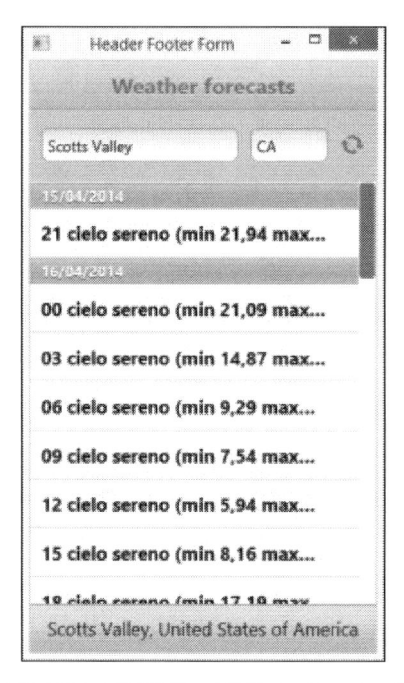

The weather forecasts app running in the mobile preview on an Italian Windows PC

There's more...

Multithreading can be difficult, but the built-in features in the REST client library allow you to send HTTP requests in a background thread in a very simple manner. You can use it as much as you want. If you are not so confident with the REST client library, here's some documentation:

- *Delphi XE5 Mobile REST Client Demo* at `https://www.youtube.com/watch?v=OkRVbgF4VMI`
- *REST Client Library* at `http://docwiki.embarcadero.com/RADStudio/en/REST_Client_Library`

Another topic that should be deeply understood to correctly design and implement FireMonkey applications (and mobile apps are only a particular type of FireMonkey applications) is the FireMonkey platform services. More info on platform services can be found at: `http://docwiki.embarcadero.com/RADStudio/en/FireMonkey_Platform_Services`.

Using a styled TListView to handle long lists of data

The **TListBox** control is very flexible. You can customize every aspect of each item in the list. However, it is not suitable if you want to handle a long list of data, because flexibility comes at the cost of system being slow when the number of data rows grows. Embarcadero specifies that you should use **TListView** to display a collection of items in a list that is optimized for LiveBindings and for fast and smooth scrolling.

Getting ready

In this recipe, we will use the *Do not block main thread!* recipe as a base to customize a listview using custom styles. In that recipe, we got a list of weather forecasts from a REST web service and then filled the listview with that data using a standard style. In this recipe, that data will be nicely inserted in to a custom listview with colors, alignment, and a summary footer. There is no design-time support with this approach, because all the controls created in each item are created at runtime; however, this approach can be very useful if you want complete control over the look and feel of your list. To be clear, the recommended approach in this case is to write a custom style for the **TListView** component; put the component in a package, install it into the IDE, and then use it from the **Object Inspector** window. To have two samples of this approach, check the following projects provided as samples (the `Sample` folder on my machine is `C:\Users\Public\Documents\Embarcadero\Studio\18.0\Samples` where 18.0 is the version of the IDE).

Within the `Sample` folder, open `Object Pascal\Multi-Device Samples\User Interface\ListView\`.

In this folder, you have a number of projects and packages that show you how to use some advanced stuff related the **TListView** components. To see the new style, you have to install the package and open the related demo project.

The package to install the `RatingListItem` list item style is `SampleListViewRatingsAppearancePackage.dproj`. The project that shows how to use the `RatingListItem` style is `SampleListViewRatingsAppearanceProject.dproj`. The package to install the `MultiDetailItem` list item style is `SampleListViewMultiDetailAppearancePackage.dproj`. The project that show how to use the `MultiDetailItem` style is `SampleListViewMultiDetailAppearanceProject.dproj`.

It is not too complex to create a custom list item style, and we'll see how to do it in the next recipe. In this recipe, we'll create the list item style element directly in the code. When you are satisfied with the result, you can create the proper package as shown in the next recipe.

Since RAD Studio 10.1 Berlin there is the ListView Items Editor which helps in case you want to define the aspect of your list view items at design time. The approach defined in this and the following chapters is more general and applicable to previous RAD Studio versions as well.

How to do it...

1. Copy the *Do not block main thread... please!* recipe in a new folder.
2. Open the project and save it as `WeatherForecastsEx.dproj`.
3. Change the code as shown in the next steps.
4. In the `private` section of the form declaration, add the following methods:

   ```
   private
     Lang: string;
     procedure AddFooter(AItems: TAppearanceListViewItems;
       const LMinInTheDay, LMaxInTheDay: Double);
     procedure AddHeader(AItems: TAppearanceListViewItems;
       const ADay: String);
     procedure AddForecastItem(AItems:
       TAppearanceListViewItems;
       const AForecastDateTime: TDateTime;
       const AWeatherDescription: String;
       const ATempMin, ATempMax: Double);
   ```

5. Press *Ctrl + Shift + C* to create the method bodies, and then add the following code:

   ```
   procedure TMainForm.AddHeader(AItems:
     TAppearanceListViewItems;
     const ADay: String);
   var
   ```

```
      LItem: TListViewItem;
    begin
      LItem := AItems.Add;
      LItem.Purpose := TListItemPurpose.Header;
      LItem.Objects.FindDrawable('HeaderLabel').Data := ADay;
    end;

    procedure TMainForm.AddForecastItem(AItems:
      TAppearanceListViewItems;
      const AForecastDateTime: TDateTime;
      const AWeatherDescription: String;
      const ATempMin, ATempMax: Double);
    var
      LItem: TListViewItem;
    begin
      LItem := AItems.Add;
      LItem.Objects.FindDrawable('WeatherDescription').Data :=
        FormatDateTime('HH', AForecastDateTime) + ' ' +
          AWeatherDescription;
      LItem.Objects.FindDrawable('MinTemp').Data :=
        FormatFloat('#0.00', ATempMin) + '°';
      LItem.Objects.FindDrawable('MaxTemp').Data :=
        FormatFloat('#0.00', ATempMax) + '°';
    end;

    procedure TMainForm.AddFooter(AItems:
      TAppearanceListViewItems;
      const LMinInTheDay, LMaxInTheDay: Double);
    var
      LItem: TListViewItem;
    begin
      LItem := AItems.Add;
      LItem.Purpose := TListItemPurpose.Footer;
      LItem.Text := Format('min %2.2f°C max %2.2f°C',
        [LMinInTheDay, LMaxInTheDay]);
    end;
```

6. Now we've to use these methods of the form. In the `btnGetForecastsClick` method, substitute the code with the following:

```
    procedure TMainForm.btnGetForecastsClick(Sender: TObject);
    begin
      ListView1.Items.Clear;
      RESTRequest1.Params.ParameterByName('country').Value :=
```

```
      String.Join(',', [EditCity.Text, EditCountry.Text]);
RESTRequest1.Params.ParameterByName('lang').Value :=
  Lang;
AniIndicator1.Visible := True;
AniIndicator1.Enabled := True;
btnGetForecasts.Enabled := False;
RESTRequest1.ExecuteAsync(
  procedure
  var
    LForecastDateTime: TDateTime;
    LJValue: TJSONValue;
    LJObj, LMainForecast, LForecastItem, LJObjCity:
      TJSONObject;
    LJArrWeather, LJArrForecasts: TJSONArray;
    LTempMin, LTempMax: Double;
    LDay, LLastDay: string;
    LWeatherDescription: string;
    LAppRespCode: string;
    LMinInTheDay: Double;
    LMaxInTheDay: Double;

  begin
    LJObj := RESTRequest1.Response.JSONValue as
      TJSONObject;

    // check for errors
    LAppRespCode := LJObj.GetValue('cod').Value;
    if LAppRespCode.Equals('404') then
    begin
      lblInfo.Text := 'City not found';
      Exit;
    end;
    if not LAppRespCode.Equals('200') then
    begin
      lblInfo.Text := 'Error ' + LAppRespCode;
      Exit;
    end;

    // parsing forecasts
    LMinInTheDay := 1000;
    LMaxInTheDay := -LMinInTheDay;
```

```
      LJArrForecasts := LJObj.GetValue('list') as
        TJSONArray;
      for LJValue in LJArrForecasts do
      begin
        LForecastItem := LJValue as TJSONObject;
        LForecastDateTime :=
          UnixToDateTime((LForecastItem
            .GetValue('dt') as TJSONNumber).AsInt64);
        LMainForecast := LForecastItem.GetValue('main')
          as TJSONObject;
        LTempMin := (LMainForecast.GetValue('temp_min')
          as TJSONNumber).AsDouble;
        LTempMax := (LMainForecast.GetValue('temp_max')
          as TJSONNumber).AsDouble;
        LJArrWeather := LForecastItem
          .GetValue('weather') as TJSONArray;
        LWeatherDescription := TJSONObject(LJArrWeather
          .Items[0]).GetValue('description').Value;
        LDay := FormatDateTime('ddd d mmm yyyy',
          DateOf(LForecastDateTime));
        if LDay <> LLastDay then
        begin
          if not LLastDay.IsEmpty then
          begin
            AddFooter(ListView1.Items, LMinInTheDay,
              LMaxInTheDay);
          end;
          AddHeader(ListView1.Items, LDay);
          LMinInTheDay := 1000;
          LMaxInTheDay := -LMinInTheDay;
        end;
        LLastDay := LDay;
        LMinInTheDay := Min(LMinInTheDay, LTempMin);
        LMaxInTheDay := Max(LMaxInTheDay, LTempMax);

        AddForecastItem(ListView1.Items, LForecastDateTime,
          LWeatherDescription, LTempMin, LTempMax);
      end; // for in

      if not LLastDay.IsEmpty then
        AddFooter(ListView1.Items, LMinInTheDay,
```

```
            LMaxInTheDay);

        LJObjCity := LJObj.GetValue('city') as TJSONObject;
        lblInfo.Text := LJObjCity.GetValue('name').Value +
          ', ' + LJObjCity.GetValue('country').Value;
        AniIndicator1.Visible := False;
        AniIndicator1.Enabled := False;
        btnGetForecasts.Enabled := True;
      end);
end;
```

7. The main difference between the *Using SQLite databases to handle a to-do list* recipe and this recipe is the complete flexibility of data visualization. To get this flexibility, we added individual controls to each list item. We defined all the needed properties, width, alignment, colors, and so on. When the device switches to landscape orientation, some alignment needs to be changed according to the larger horizontal space available. For this situation, a very handy listbox `UpdateObjects` event handler is available. Create an `UpdateObjects` event handler on the listbox and add this code:

```
procedure TMainForm.ListView1UpdateObjects(
  const Sender: TObject;
  const AItem: TListViewItem);
var
  AQuarter: Double;
  lb: TListItemText;
begin
  case AItem.Purpose of
    TListItemPurpose.None:
      begin
        AQuarter := (AItem.Parent.Width -
          TListView(AItem.Parent).ItemSpaces.Left -
          TListView(AItem.Parent).ItemSpaces.Right) / 4;

        // AItem.Objects.Clear;
        AItem.Height := 24;

        lb := TListItemText.Create(AItem);
        lb.PlaceOffset.X := 0;
        lb.TextAlign := TTextAlign.Leading;
        lb.Name := 'WeatherDescription';

        lb := TListItemText.Create(AItem);
        lb.TextAlign := TTextAlign.Trailing;
```

```
        lb.TextColor := TAlphaColorRec.Blue;
        lb.Name := 'MinTemp';
        lb.PlaceOffset.X := AQuarter * 2;
        lb.Width := AQuarter;

        lb := TListItemText.Create(AItem);
        lb.TextAlign := TTextAlign.Trailing;
        lb.TextColor := TAlphaColorRec.Red;
        lb.Name := 'MaxTemp';
        lb.PlaceOffset.X := AQuarter * 3;
        lb.Width := AQuarter;
      end;

      TListItemPurpose.Header:
      begin
        AItem.Height := 48;
        lb := TListItemText.Create(AItem);
        lb.TextAlign := TTextAlign.Center;
        lb.Align := TListItemAlign.Center;
        lb.TextColor := TAlphaColorRec.Red;
        lb.PlaceOffset.Y := AItem.Height / 4;
        lb.Name := 'HeaderLabel';
      end;

      TListItemPurpose.Footer:
      begin
        AItem.Objects.TextObject
          .TextAlign := TTextAlign.Trailing;
      end;
    end;
```

8. With this adjustment, text inside the list item is always aligned correctly.

9. Run the app. For testing purposes, you can run the app using the **32bit - Windows** target. Here's the app running on an Android phone:

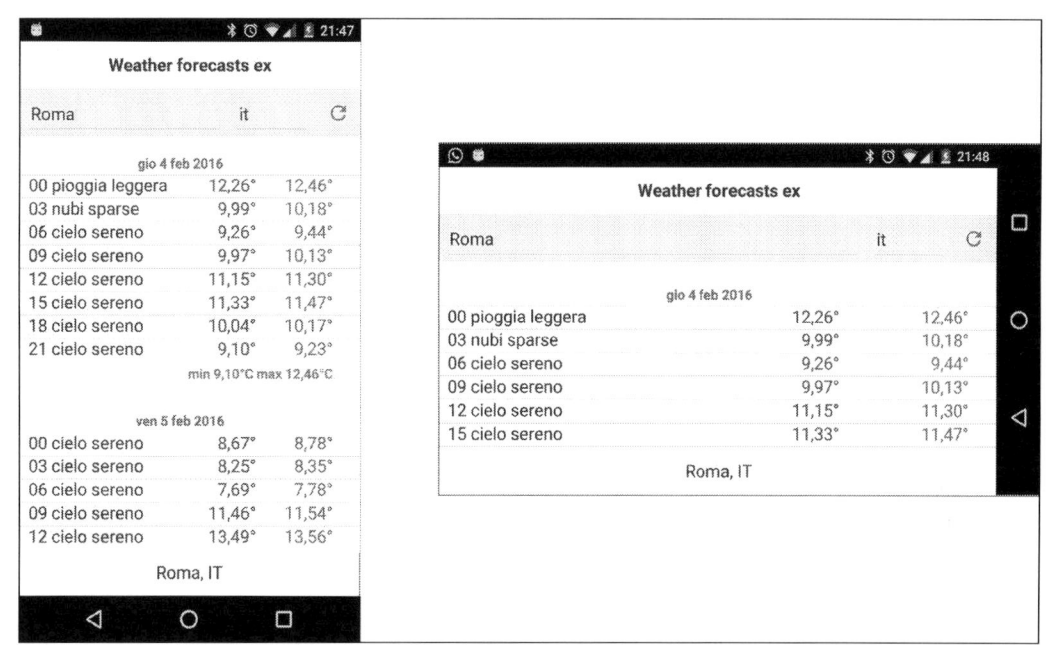

The weather forecasts app running in portrait and in landscape modes on an
Italian Android phone; note how the temperature columns are realigned between the two orientations

How it works...

After reading the JSON using the `TRESTClient` component, in the parsing code we added controls to each item to represent the three columns we require. You cannot add every kind of control to the **TListViewItem** component, add only those that inherit from **TListItemDrawable**. However, you can inherit your own class from **TListViewItem** to implement all the advanced visualizations you require.

The relevant part of the customization happens in the `ListView1UpdateObjects` method:

```
procedure TMainForm.ListView1UpdateObjects(
  const Sender: TObject;
  const AItem: TListViewItem);
var
  AQuarter: Double;
  lb: TListItemText;
  lListView: TListView;
begin
```

```delphi
lListView := Sender as TListView;
//different item purpose, different customization.
case AItem.Purpose of
  TListItemPurpose.None:
    begin
      //calculate ¼ of the available horizontal space
      AQuarter := (lListView.Width - lListView.ItemSpaces.Left -
          lListView.ItemSpaces.Right) / 4;
      AItem.Height := 24;
      //1st column, the textual description
      //Check if the item is already created. This check
      //saves resource and make the app faster
      lb :=   TListItemText(AItem.Objects
              .FindDrawable('WeatherDescription'));
      if not Assigned(lb) then
      begin
        //if needed, create and initialize the component
        lb := TListItemText.Create(AItem);
        lb.PlaceOffset.X := 0;
        lb.TextAlign := TTextAlign.Leading;
        lb.Name := 'WeatherDescription';
      end;
      //offset must be always updated depending
      //on device orientation
      lb.PlaceOffset.X := 0;

      //2nd column, the min temperature
      lb := TListItemText(AItem.Objects
              .FindDrawable('MinTemp'));
      if not Assigned(lb) then
      begin
        lb := TListItemText.Create(AItem);
        lb.TextAlign := TTextAlign.Trailing;
        lb.TextColor := TAlphaColorRec.Blue;
        lb.Name := 'MinTemp';
      end;
      //offset and width must be updated
      lb.PlaceOffset.X := AQuarter * 2;
      lb.Width := AQuarter;

      //3rd column, max temperature
      lb := TListItemText(AItem.Objects
              .FindDrawable('MaxTemp'));
```

```delphi
      if not Assigned(lb) then
      begin
        lb := TListItemText.Create(AItem);
        lb.TextAlign := TTextAlign.Trailing;
        lb.TextColor := TAlphaColorRec.Red;
        lb.Name := 'MaxTemp';
      end;
      lb.PlaceOffset.X := AQuarter * 3;
      lb.Width := AQuarter;
    end;

  TListItemPurpose.Header:
    begin
      AItem.Height := 48;
      //headers have only one itemtext
      lb := TListItemText(AItem.Objects
          .FindDrawable('HeaderLabel'));
      if not Assigned(lb) then
      begin
        lb := TListItemText.Create(AItem);
        lb.TextAlign := TTextAlign.Center;
        lb.Align := TListItemAlign.Center;
        lb.TextColor := TAlphaColorRec.Red;
        lb.Name := 'HeaderLabel';
      end;
      lb.PlaceOffset.Y := AItem.Height / 4;
    end;
  TListItemPurpose.Footer:
    begin
      //footer item doesn't have heavy
      //customization, only alignment
      AItem.Objects.TextObject.TextAlign := TTextAlign.Trailing;
    end;
  end;
end;
```

Here, as a first thing, we check that objects are already created. When you change the device orientation, objects are still there. So, if possible, it is better to reuse them than destroy and recreate from scratch. Then, all the new items are created and added to the `ListViewItem` instance. Note that each control has a name. This name is used to check their existence, and by the parsing code, to write the actual text into the `Data` property of the control. So, just to be clear, if in the item you add a **TListItemText** control named `MinTemp`, you can use `Item.Objects.FindDrawable('MinTemp').Data` to read and write (it depends on the actual object, but technically it is possible) generic data on the `MinTemp.Data` property. As you know, the `Data` property is handled by each control with a different meaning. In this specific case, all the `Data` properties represent the text written in the controls.

Then, the problem related to the orientation change is handled by the very useful `UpdateObjects` event on the listview. Here, we organize the horizontal space to split it into four columns and give the first two columns to the weather description, the third to the minimum temperature, and the fourth to the maximum temperature. You can organize all the cool things you need in this event, because it's called every time there is an update in the object visualization.

There's more...

Listviews are tremendously helpful in mobile development and you must be familiar with them to implement good looking and efficient apps. Using the custom list item style in a package, you also get LiveBinding support, while the solution exposed in this recipe doesn't provide this support. Consider developing a custom list item style and packaging it in a package if you want design-time support. This recipe gives you the starting point for developing a custom style for the listview items, when you are satisfied by the result, create the proper package as shown in the samples provided by Embarcadero.

Customizing the TListView

As we have already said in the recipe, *Using a styled TListView to handle long list of data*, the `TListView` is the best control for handling long lists of data. We already know how to change the default style using the `UpdateObjects` event, however this approach lacks the Delphi RADness approach; no visual preview, no object inspector, no Visual LiveBindings, no live data. In this recipe we'll look at how to create a `TListView` style which can be installed in the Delphi IDE and used at design time in the object inspector and in the Visual LiveBindings designer.

Getting ready

`TListView` uses the **Appearance Class** to define how it looks at runtime. An **Appearance Class** is nothing more than a class derived from `TAppearanceObjects` (or one of its inherited classes). You can create and install a new customized appearance class and use it in your design, by installing a new package. This package defines the classes that implement a custom appearance for listview items. You can customize the fields as necessary, to implement specialized graphics or texts.

How it works...

Open the project group **Chapter07\CODE\RECIPE06\CustomAppearanceGroup.groupproj**.

The group is composed of the following two projects:

- **DelphiCookbookListViewAppearance.dproj**: This is a package containing the appearance class that we defined for our purpose. This package need to be installed and its path must be in the Delphi library path for all the needed platforms.
- **WeatherForecastCustomAppearance.dproj**: The actual application. It uses the appearance class defined in the previous package and uses LiveBindings to show the weather forecasts.

Let's talk about the appearance class. Open the file, `DelphiCookbookListViewAppearanceU.pas` contained in the package. The main class in this unit is `TDelphiCookbookItemAppearance`. As you can see, this file is declared in the implementation section so that no one can directly use it. So who can never use it? Check the unit initialization and finalization section.

initialization
```
TAppearancesRegistry.RegisterAppearance(
TDelphiCookbookItemAppearance,
TDelphiCookbookAppearanceNames.ListItem,
[TRegisterAppearanceOption.Item],
sThisUnit);
```

finalization
```
TAppearancesRegistry.UnregisterAppearances(
TArray<TItemAppearanceObjectsClass>
.Create(TDelphiCookbookItemAppearance));
```
end.

Using the initialization and finalization sections the new appearance class is registered as soon as the package, and the units contained, are loaded in the IDE. But what does `TDelphiCookbookItemAppearance` look like?

Here's its declaration.

```
type
  TDelphiCookbookItemAppearance = class(TPresetItemObjects)
  public
    const DEFAULT_HEIGHT = 40;
  private
    FMinTemp: TTextObjectAppearance;
    FMaxTemp: TTextObjectAppearance;
    procedure SetMinTemp(const Value: TTextObjectAppearance);
    procedure SetMaxTemp(const Value: TTextObjectAppearance);
  protected
    function DefaultHeight: Integer; override;
    procedure UpdateSizes(const FinalSize: TSizeF);
override;
    function GetGroupClass: TPresetItemObjects.TGroupClass;
override;
  public
    constructor Create(const Owner: TControl); override;
    destructor Destroy; override;
  published
    property Accessory;
    property Text;
    property MinTemp: TTextObjectAppearance
read FMinTemp write SetMinTemp;
    property MaxTemp: TTextObjectAppearance
read FMaxTemp write SetMaxTemp;
  end;
```

As any appearance class, it inherits from `TPresetItemObjects` which defines the standard behavior for a generic `TListViewItem`. Then we added two more text objects: `MinTemp` and `MaxTemp`. These objects are not real controls but a set of properties used internally to define actual graphical objects. Into an appearance class, it is possible to add a number of custom elements. See the following list for all the available elements:

- `TTextObjectAppearance`: A text label.
- `TImageObjectAppearance`: An image.
- `TAccessoryObjectAppearance`: A flexible graphical indicator which provides different predefined icons. It is used to graphically inform the user that more information is available if the item is tapped/clicked.
- `TTextButtonObjectAppearance`: This is a button with a predefined label. It is used in the standard item when delete on swipe is used.
- `TGlyphButtonObjectAppearance`: This is another kind of button but has an icon instead of text.

The appearance class can define the default height for every item, in our case the default height is 40. Two methods require particular attention: the constructor, where all the objects must be initialized, and the `UpdateSize`, which is called when an item is added into the list and every time you rotate the device, or resize the listview.

Here's the constructor:

```delphi
constructor TDelphiCookbookItemAppearance.Create(
const Owner: TControl);
var
   LInitTextObject: TProc<TTextObjectAppearance>;
begin
  inherited;

  //The 2 text objects are initialized in the same way, so let's
  //create an anonymous method to initialize them
  LInitTextObject := procedure(pTextObject: TTextObjectAppearance)
    begin
      //initialization is quite standard for all objects. There
      //are however some fundamental steps...

      //notify the container when the control change
      pTextObject.OnChange := ItemPropertyChange;

      //setting the default properties
      pTextObject.DefaultValues.Align := TListItemAlign.Leading;
      pTextObject.DefaultValues
.VertAlign := TListItemAlign.Center;
      pTextObject.DefaultValues
.TextVertAlign := TTextAlign.Center;
      pTextObject.DefaultValues
.TextAlign := TTextAlign.Trailing;
      pTextObject.DefaultValues.PlaceOffset.Y := 0;
      pTextObject.DefaultValues.PlaceOffset.X := 0;
      pTextObject.DefaultValues.Width := 80;
      pTextObject.DefaultValues.Visible := True;

      //reset the control to the default just defined
      pTextObject.RestoreDefaults;

      //the object is owned by the appearance object instance
      pTextObject.Owner := Self;
    end;

  //create and initialize the text label
```

```delphi
//for the min temperature
FMinTemp := TTextObjectAppearance.Create;
FMinTemp.Name := TDelphiCookbookAppearanceNames.MinTemp;
//by default the text is blue
FMinTemp.DefaultValues.TextColor := TAlphaColorRec.Blue;
LInitTextObject(FMinTemp);

//create and initialize the text label
//for the max temperature
FMaxTemp := TTextObjectAppearance.Create;
FMaxTemp.Name := TDelphiCookbookAppearanceNames.MaxTemp;
//by default this text will be red
FMaxTemp.DefaultValues.TextColor := TAlphaColorRec.Red;
LInitTextObject(FMaxTemp);

//Now we've to define LiveBindings members for this appearance
//class. Remember, the Visual LiveBinding designer
//will show the members defined here and will use these
//expressions to set the value of the member at runtime.

//define LiveBindings members related to mintemp
FMinTemp.DataMembers := TObjectAppearance.TDataMembers.Create
  (TObjectAppearance.TDataMember.Create(MIN_TEMP_MEMBER,
  // Displayed by LiveBindings
  Format('Data["%s"]',
    [TDelphiCookbookAppearanceNames.MinTemp])));
  // Expression to access value from TListViewItem


//define LiveBindings members related to maxtemp
FMaxTemp.DataMembers := TObjectAppearance.TDataMembers.Create
  (TObjectAppearance.TDataMember.Create(MAX_TEMP_MEMBER,
  // Displayed by LiveBindings
  Format('Data["%s"]',
    [TDelphiCookbookAppearanceNames.MaxTemp])));
  // Expression to access value from TListViewItem

// Define the appearance objects
AddObject(Text, True);
AddObject(MinTemp, True);
AddObject(MaxTemp, True);
end;
```

As you can see in the constructor, there is no information about size. We set alignments, colors, and so on, but no size. Where are sizes defined? In the `UpdateSizes` method which is called whenever the `TListView` needs to know how big each component is. Moreover, we can set visibility and other details in this method. In this case, we want to hide the `MinTemp` text if the width of the control is not enough. This change is done automatically because the `UpdateSizes` is called repeatedly.

```delphi
procedure TDelphiCookbookItemAppearance.UpdateSizes(
const FinalSize: TSizeF);
var
  LColWidth: Extended;
  LFullWidth: Boolean;
begin
  BeginUpdate;
  try
    inherited;
    //we define a virtual layout of 12 columns based on
    //current listitem width
    LColWidth := FinalSize.Width / 12;

    //is the listitem wide enough to contain the full
    //set of information?
    LFullWidth := LColWidth * 4 >= MinTemp.Width;


    if LFullWidth then
    begin
      //mintemp is visible, the default text is large 6 virtual
      //columns and the other texts are 2 columns wide
      MinTemp.Visible := True;
      Text.InternalWidth := LColWidth * 6;
      MinTemp.PlaceOffset.X := LColWidth * 6;
      MinTemp.InternalWidth := LColWidth * 2;
      MaxTemp.PlaceOffset.X := LColWidth * 9;
      MaxTemp.InternalWidth := LColWidth * 2;
    end
    else
    begin
      //mintemp is not visible, the default text is large 8
      //virtual columns and the maxtemp texts is 4 columns wide
      MinTemp.Visible := False;
      Text.InternalWidth := LColWidth * 8;
      MaxTemp.PlaceOffset.X := LColWidth * 8;
      MaxTemp.InternalWidth := LColWidth * 4;
```

```
      end;
   finally
      EndUpdate;
   end;
end;
```

It is time to see this app running! Install the package (right-click on the project inside the **Project Manager** and click on **Install**). Just after the IDE confirms the correct installation, add into the **Delphi Library Path**, the path of the file; `DelphiCookbookListViewAppearanceU.pas`. From now on, for every `TListView` that you drop in a form, in the property `ItemAppearance.ItemAppearance` there will be a new value selectable named `DelphiCookbookWeatherAppearance`. That is the appearance class registered by the package.

Now, select the project `WeatherForecastCustomAppearance.dproj`, select a suitable target (on mobile you can see also what has happened by rotating the device, while on Windows you can mimic it resizing the windows) and run the project. Here's how the app looks on an Android phone:

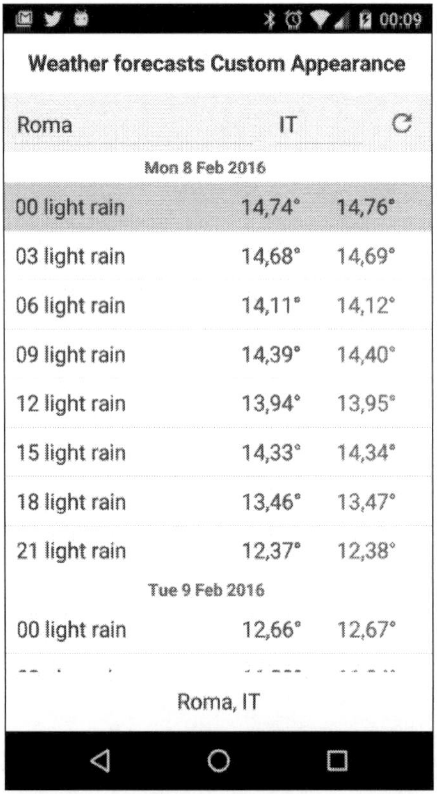

Fig. 7.1 The app running on an Android phone. Note the columns right-aligned.

If you try to rotate the phone or resize the window, in case you are doing your test on a Windows machine, you can see how the columns are correctly repositioned.

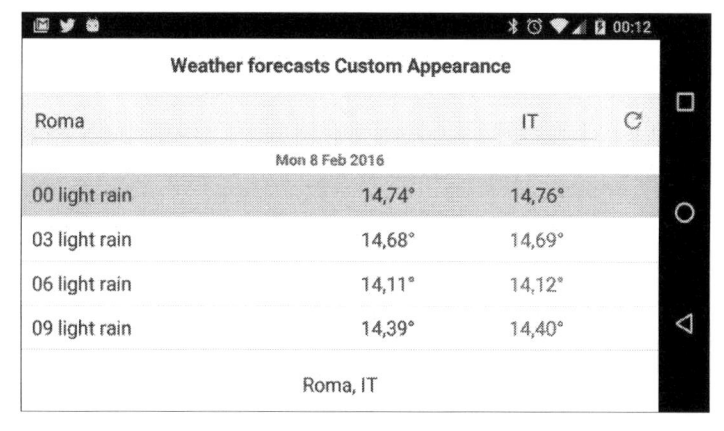

Fig. 7.2 The app in landscape mode

If not enough room is available, the `mintemp` columns are hidden. Try to resize the application when it runs on a Windows machine. You will get a layout similar to the following:

Fig. 7.3 The application running on a Windows machine. If there is not enough space when resizing the window, the mintemp column is automatically hidden

Riding the Mobile Revolution with FireMonkey

Remember, from now on, the new appearance class is available for all the `TListView` at design time as well. You can create all the styles that you need, install them into the IDE as a package, and then use them in your application, on mobile and desktop. The property `ItemAppearance.ItemAppearance` will show all the available styles, as shown in the next image:

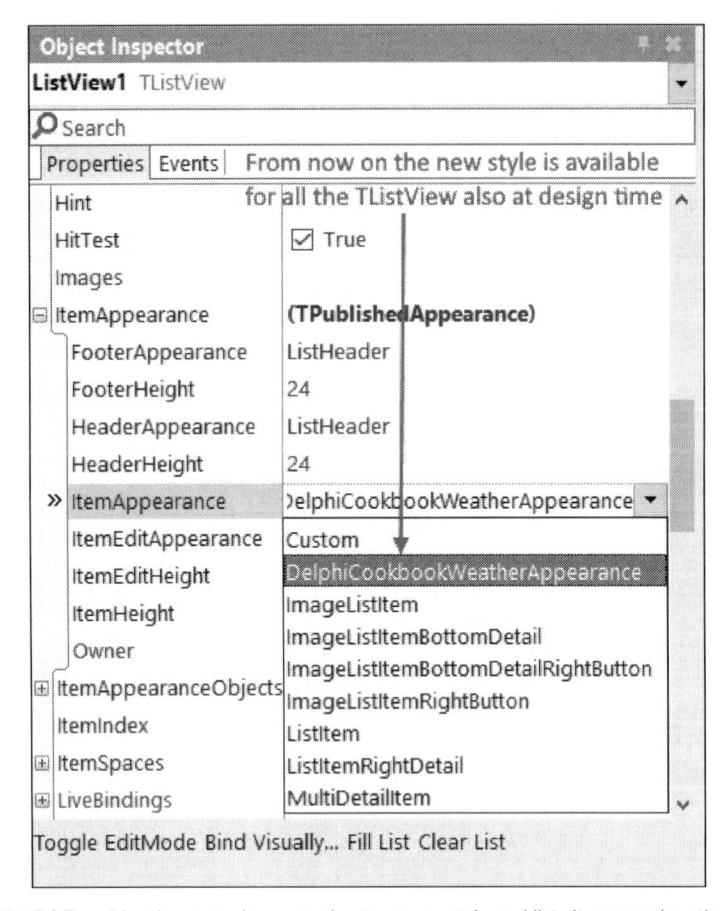

Fig. 7.4 The object inspector is aware about our new style and lists it among the others

Moreover, each element defined in the appearance class as a published property is available in the **Object Inspector** as a single editable property under the `ItemAppearanceObjects.ItemObjects` property as well:

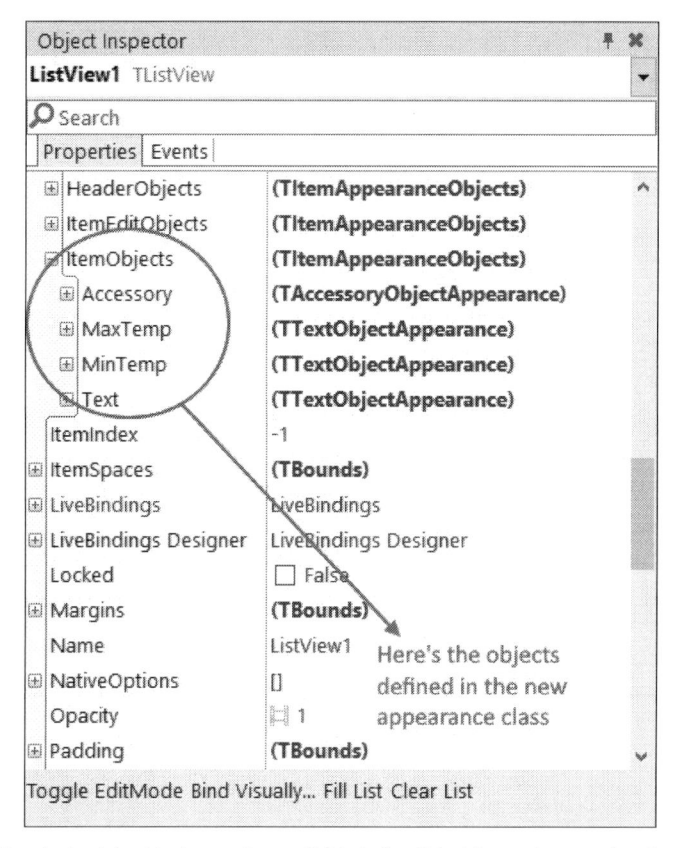

Fig. 7.5 The single style objects are also available in the Object Inspector as a singular property.

There's more...

Appearance class development can be very difficult. The style designed in this recipe is a read-only style and provides only the `ItemAppearance` variation. However, you can also create:

- `HeaderAppearance`
- `FooterAppearance`
- `ItemEditAppearance`

The good news is that the development process is the same, so after this recipe you are ready to create completely customized list views.

Since Delphi 10.1 Berlin Embarcadero added a new ListView Item Designer which greatly simplify the customization of list item. Before start a new Appearance Class developmern, check if the flexibility offered by the list view item designer is enough for your needs.

Riding the Mobile Revolution with FireMonkey

Taking a photo and location and sending it to a server continuously

In this recipe, we will talk about many things. We will see how to continuously get an image from the camera, how to get location information, and how to send binary data to a web server. Then, moving on to the server side, we will see how to read binary data from the client and how to generate content on the fly. All these things will be used to implement a simple monitoring system.

Getting ready

This recipe is divided into client and server sides. The client side is a mobile app acting as a *special* camera able to get image and location and then send it to a remote server. There is also a live preview on the main form, so you can see what you are sending to the server. The server simply gets the information and stores it in the filesystem. This recipe is quite complex, so I avoided an actual SQL (or NoSQL) database to store all the information and used the filesystem.

How to do it...

Launch two instances of Delphi and open one project in each of them (this will help in the debug phase). The server project is `MonitorServer.dproj`, while the client app is `MonitorMobile.dproj`.

Let's start with the client side.

The client side

On the main form, there are the **TCameraComponent** and **TLocationSensor** components; the **TButton** control on the top of the form is used to activate them. As soon as the camera has enough data to create a frame, the **TCameraComponent** calls its `SampleBufferReady` event handler, and now the process begins. Here's the code in the `SampleBufferReady` event handler:

```
procedure TMainForm.CameraComponent1SampleBufferReady(
  Sender: TObject; const ATime: TMediaTime);
var
  lFrame: TFrameInfo;
  lBitmapToSend: TBitmap;
begin
  CameraComponent1.SampleBufferToBitmap(FSnapshot, True);
  Image1.Bitmap.Assign(FSnapshot);

  if SecondsBetween(Now, FLastSent) >= 4 then
```

```
      begin
        lBitmapToSend := GetResizedBitmap(FSnapshot);
        try
          lFrame := TFrameInfo.Create;
          lFrame.TimeStamp := now;
          lFrame.Lat := CurrLocation.Latitude;
          lFrame.Lon := CurrLocation.Longitude;
          lBitmapToSend.SaveToStream(lFrame.Stream);
          lFrame.Stream.Position := 0;
          FSenderThread.ImagesQueue.PushItem(lFrame);
        finally
          lBitmapToSend.Free;
        end;
        FLastSent := now;
      end;
    end;
```

Information retrieved by the camera is converted into an actual bitmap using the handy `SampleBufferToBitmap` method provided by **TCameraComponent** itself. Now we've an image. Where does the location information come from? The `TLocationSensor` component has the `OnLocationChanged` event that is called whenever the actual location, considering the different ways to get the location (such as GPS, Wi-Fi, and GPS combined with Wi-Fi), actually changes. In the `LocationSensor1LocationChanged` procedure, we save the new location in a form field as shown in the following code:

```
    procedure TMainForm.LocationSensor1LocationChanged(
       Sender: TObject; const OldLocation,
       NewLocation: TLocationCoord2D);
    begin
      CurrLocation := NewLocation;
    end;
```

Now, go back to the `CameraComponent1SampleBufferReady` event handler. The information is used to fill an instance of `TFrameInfo` and then this instance is pushed to the `TThreadedQueue<TFrameInfo>` thread property. The main thread pushes the `TFrameInfo` instances into the queue, while the background thread reads the `TFrameInfo` instances, creates a proper HTTP request, and then sends it to the server. The `TFrameInfo` type contains all the information required by the server:

```
    type
      TFrameInfo = class
      private
        { . . . some private declarations . . . }
      public
        constructor Create;
```

```
    property Stream: TStream read FStream;
    property Lat: Double read FLat write SetLat;
    property Lon: Double read FLon write SetLon;
    property TimeStamp: TDateTime read FTimeStamp
                               write SetTimeStamp;
  end;
```

The complex stuff actually runs on the background thread. Let's see its `Execute` method:

```
procedure TImageSenderThread.Execute;
var
  lHTTPClient: THTTPClient;
  lFrameInfo: TFrameInfo;
  lEncodedParams: string;
begin
  inherited;
  FFilesToDelete := TList<String>.Create;
  lHTTPClient := THTTPClient.Create;
  lHTTPClient.ConnectionTimeout := 2000;
  lHTTPClient.ResponseTimeout := 1000;
  while not Terminated do
  begin
    try
      if FImagesQueue.PopItem(lFrameInfo) <> wrTimeout then
      begin
        //prepare the request parameters
        lEncodedParams := Format('ts=%s&lat=%s&lon=%s', [
          FormatDateTime('YYYY-MM-DD HH-NN-SS',
            lFrameInfo.TimeStamp),
          FormatFloat('##0.00000000', lFrameInfo.Lat,
            FFormatSettings),
          FormatFloat('##0.00000000', lFrameInfo.Lon,
            FFormatSettings)]);

        TNetEncoding.URL.EncodeQuery(lEncodedParams);

        //actually send the http request
        lHTTPClient.ContentType := 'image/png';
        lHTTPClient.Post(MONITORSERVERURL + '/photo?' +
          lEncodedParams, lFrameInfo.Stream);
      end;
    except
      //the best way to handle this exception, and keep this
```

```
              //code simple, is to send the next frame.
              //The same approach of the video
              //streaming protocols: "in case of error, send the next
              //frame" so, do nothing
      end;
   end;
end;
```

In the usual thread loop, we try to read the next `TFrameInfo` instance from the queue. If such an instance is present, we create an HTTP request using a simple HTTP `POST` method with the image file in the `request` body and the other information in the `querystring` parameter. In order to avoid unnecessary I/O operations, the file is not saved on the file system but the stream itself is sent. In this code, you might note some suppressed exceptions (`try...except` with an empty `except` block). Usually, this is not good. However, in this case, if we lose a frame for some reason, the best way to fix the problem is to send the next one. So in some places, the exceptions are suppressed because the next frame will solve the problem. Moreover, the threaded queue has a size of only two elements. If the main thread tries to append a third `FrameInfo` object in the queue, it is stopped for 10 milliseconds; if it still cannot append the data, that data is lost. This is one of the approaches available when you are dealing with queues: if the queue is full, new data is discarded until the queue consumes its current content. To save space and battery energy, the image is resized before sending. The actual resizing is done by the `GetResizedBitmap` method just before the image taken by the camera is assigned to the stream property of the `TFrameInfo` instance:

```
   function TMainForm.GetResizedBitmap(const Value: TBitmap;
      const MaxSize: UInt16 = 640): TBitmap;
   var
      lProp: Extended;
      lLongerSide: Double;
   begin
      Result := TBitmap.Create;
      Result.Assign(Value);
      lLongerSide := Max(Value.Width, Value.Height);
      if lLongerSide > MaxSize then
      begin
         lProp := MaxSize / lLongerSide;
         Result.Resize(Trunc(Value.Width * lProp),
            Trunc(Value.Height * lProp));
      end;
   end;
```

The server-side

The server-side is a WebBroker project with only two actions configured, as shown in the following table:

Action name	PathInfo	HTTP method
DefaultHandler	/	mtGet
waPhoto	/photo	mtPost

The `waPhoto` action receives the client request, reads the data, and saves it on the filesystem. This action saves two files:

- The actual image file as a `.png` image file
- Another file containing all the location information in JSON format

Here's the code for the `waPhoto` action:

```
procedure TwmMain.wmMainwaPhotoAction(Sender: TObject;
  Request: TWebRequest; Response: TWebResponse;
  var Handled: Boolean);
var
  lFileStream: TFileStream;
  lByteStream: TBytesStream;
  lFileName: string;
  lLat: Double;
  lLon: Double;
  lInfoObject: TJSONObject;

  procedure SaveInfoFile;
  begin
    lInfoObject := TJSONObject.Create;
    if TryStrToFloat(Request.QueryFields.Values['lat'], lLat,
      FFormatSettings) then
      lInfoObject.AddPair('lat', TJSONNumber.Create(lLat));
    if TryStrToFloat(Request.QueryFields.Values['lon'], lLon,
      FFormatSettings) then
      lInfoObject.AddPair('lon', TJSONNumber.Create(lLon));
    TFile.WriteAllText('images' + PathDelim + lFileName + '.info',
      lInfoObject.ToString);
  end;

  function QueryFieldsValidation: Boolean;
  begin
    Result := true;
```

```
      Result := Result and (not
        Request.QueryFields.Values['ts'].IsEmpty);
      Result := Result and (not
        Request.QueryFields.Values['lat'].IsEmpty);
      Result := Result and (not
        Request.QueryFields.Values['lon'].IsEmpty);
    end;

begin
  if not QueryFieldsValidation then
  begin
    Response.StatusCode := 400;
    Response.Content := 'Invalid query fields';
    Exit;
  end;
  if not SameText(Request.ContentType, 'image/png') then
  begin
    Response.StatusCode := 400;
    Response.Content := 'Invalid content type';
    Exit;
  end;

  TDirectory.CreateDirectory('images');
  lFileName := Request.QueryFields.Values['ts'] + '.png';
  lFileStream := TFileStream.Create('images' + PathDelim +
    lFileName, fmCreate);
  try
    lByteStream := TBytesStream.Create(Request.RawContent);
    try
      lFileStream.CopyFrom(lByteStream, 0);
    finally
      lByteStream.Free;
    end;
  finally
    lFileStream.Free;
  end;
  SaveInfoFile;
  Response.StatusCode := 200;
  DeleteFiles;
end;
```

Now, data is saved in a couple of files with names similar to the following:

- `2016-04-27 23-14-53.png`: This is a plain `.png` image file
- `2016-04-27 23-14-53.png.info`: This is a JSON text file containing location information related to the previous file

Now, the `DefaultHandler` action is used to generate some HTML to let the remote user see the image and location information. Here's the code for this action:

```
procedure TwmMain.WebModule1DefaultHandlerAction(Sender: TObject;
  Request: TWebRequest; Response: TWebResponse;
  var Handled: Boolean);
var
  lHTMLOut: TStringBuilder;
  lFileName, lJSONInfoString: string;
  lStart, lFileTimeStamp: TDateTime;
  lTimes: Integer;
  lJSONInfo: TJSONObject;
  lLat, lLon: Double;
const
  MONITORED_MINUTES = 5;
begin
  lHTMLOut := TStringBuilder.Create;
  try
    lHTMLOut.AppendLine('<!doctype html><html><head>');
    lHTMLOut.AppendLine('<style>');
    lHTMLOut.AppendLine('  body {font-family: Verdana; padding: '+
      '40px 10px 0px 50px; }');
    lHTMLOut.AppendLine('  pre {font-size: 200%;}');
    lHTMLOut.AppendLine('</style>');
    lHTMLOut.AppendLine(
      '<meta http-equiv = "refresh" Content = "4">');
    lHTMLOut.AppendLine('</head><body>');
    lHTMLOut.AppendLine(
      '<h1>Delphi Cookbook Mobile Monitor</h1>');
    lStart := Now;
    lTimes := 0;
    while true do
    begin
      lTimes := lTimes + 1;
      lFileTimeStamp := lStart - OneSecond * lTimes;
      lFileName := 'images' + PathDelim +
        FormatDateTime(DATEFORMAT, lFileTimeStamp) + '.png';
      if TFile.Exists(lFileName) then
      begin
```

```
            lHTMLOut.AppendFormat('<h3>Last update %s</h3>',
              [DateTimeToStr(lFileTimeStamp)]);
            lHTMLOut.AppendFormat('<img src="%s"><br>', [lFileName]);
            if TFile.Exists(lFileName + '.info') then
            begin
              try
                lJSONInfoString := TFile.ReadAllText(
                  lFileName + '.info');
                lJSONInfo :=
                  TJSONObject.ParseJSONValue(lJSONInfoString)
                    as TJSONObject;
                if Assigned(lJSONInfo) then
                begin
                  lLat := (lJSONInfo.GetValue('lat') as
                    TJSONNumber).AsDouble;
                  lLon := (lJSONInfo.GetValue('lon') as
                    TJSONNumber).AsDouble;
                  lHTMLOut.AppendFormat(
                    '<pre>Lat: %3.8f Lon: %3.8f</pre>', [lLat, lLon]);
                end
                else
                  lHTMLOut.Append(
                    '<pre>Invalid metadata information');
              except
                on E: Exception do
                begin
                  lHTMLOut.AppendFormat(
                    '<pre>Invalid metadata information: %s',
                    [E.Message]);
                end;
              end;
            end
            else
            begin
              lHTMLOut.Append('<pre>No others info available</pre>');
            end;
            break;
          end
          else if lTimes >= 60 * MONITORED_MINUTES then
          begin
            lHTMLOut.AppendFormat(
              '<h2>No image available in the last %d minutes</h2>',
              [MONITORED_MINUTES]);
            break;
```

```
        end;
      end;
      lHTMLOut.AppendLine('</body></html>');
      Response.Content := lHTMLOut.ToString;
    finally
      lHTMLOut.Free;
    end;
  end;
```

This method creates some HTML on the fly and looks for the most recent snapshot saved on the server. When it finds an image, it inserts the image filename into the HTML to let the browser request it. Then, it opens the `.info` JSON file, reads the location information, and inserts it in to the HTML as well. Note, that this monitoring app doesn't have a proper synchronization mechanism between file writing and file reading, so in many parts of the code, you see an empty `try...except` block. For this recipe, it is enough. However, in more critical systems, a proper mechanism (such as critical sections, monitors, or mutex) is required to synchronize file access and avoid empty frames, especially with multiple clients.

To update the image displayed on the HTML page, there is a special meta tag in the HTML document header, as follows:

```
<meta http-equiv = "refresh" Content = "4">
```

With this line, the page is updated every 4 seconds (more information about the `http-equiv` meta tags can be found at: `http://www.w3schools.com/Tags/att_meta_http_equiv.asp`).

To try the application, launch the server and navigate to the URL `http://localhost:8080` on your browser. You should see a page like the following:

The monitoring system page when it hasn't found images for the last 5 minutes.

Now, in the mobile project, open the `ImageSenderThreadU.pas` unit and locate `const MONITORSERVERURL`. Change the `const` value to point to your machine IP. Note that the phone (or the tablet) and your PC must be on the same Wi-Fi network. In my case, the constant is configured as follows:

```
const
   MONITORSERVERURL = 'http://192.168.1.100:8080';
```

Replace the IP with yours, and leave the protocol (`http`) and the port (`8080`) as is. In a real-world app, put a small configuration section in the mobile app to let the user enter the actual URL where the server listens.

Run the mobile app, activate the camera using the button in the upper-right corner, and after a couple of seconds you should see an image and the location information coming up in the web page. The final web page should look like the following:

The monitoring system running while showing a sort of recursive image of itself

There's more...

This recipe acts like training for a lot of concepts. If you want to go deeper into them, you can read the following articles and information:

- *Using Location Sensors* at: http://docwiki.embarcadero.com/RADStudio/en/Mobile_Tutorial:_Using_Location_Sensors_(iOS_and_Android)
- *Uses Permissions* at: http://docwiki.embarcadero.com/RADStudio/en/Uses_Permissions
- *FMX.Media.TCameraComponent* at: http://docwiki.embarcadero.com/Libraries/en/FMX.Media.TCameraComponent

Talking with the backend

This recipe will introduce you to real-world business mobile apps and their related application servers. It is not a simple world. It is full of well-known and specific traps related to your infrastructure, your business logic, your application transactions, and so on. Just to be clear, you have to take care of your design and the way you implement it to a greater extent compared to a classic client/server application. On going deeper into the mobile programming (and in general, in all asynchronous scenarios), you will see that things become harder than usual. In the mobile world, things can get messy really fast and your customers will complain even faster. Be warned!

This recipe is a mobile client for the **People Manager** application server developed in the *Implementing a RESTful interface using WebBroker* recipe in *Chapter 6, Putting Delphi on the Server*.

Getting ready

As already mentioned, this recipe is composed of the application server and the mobile client. The UI is not blocking so that all the REST requests are executed in a background thread using the built-in features of `TRESTClient`.

How to do it...

The app is based on the **Header/Footer with Navigation** mobile template. In the first `TTabItem` object, there is a list of people. In the second `TTabItem` object, there are the selected person's details. Data is read from the `REST` services exposed by the `PeopleManager.dproj` server.

The client implements a simple CRUD operation and uses a subset of the server services. The service used and the relative URL are mentioned in the following table (you can implement search functionality as an exercise):

HTTP verb	URL	Description
GET	/people	This returns a JSON array containing one JSON object for each record present in the PEOPLE table. In each object, the property name is the name of the field, while the property values are the values of the fields.
POST	/people	This creates a new person in the PEOPLE table. This requires a request body containing the new person's data to create a JSON object. The content-type request must be application/json.
PUT	/people/{id}	This updates the person with id with the data passed in the request body. This requires a request body containing the person to update as a JSON object. The content-type request must be application/json.
DELETE	/people/{id}	This deletes the person with id.

The GET people/:id method is available from the server too, but the client doesn't use it because the GET /people method already returns an array with all the complete entities. In a real-world app, you perhaps have lots of entities, or a lot of entity attributes or nested objects, so it makes sense to use the GET verb to get the full single entity representation.

Locally, the data is stored in a TDataSet component, a TFDMemTable component (yes, I love it) to be precise, and are loaded using the class helper declared in ObjectsMappers.pas (contained in the DelphiMVCFramework project and already used in *Chapter 6, Putting Delphi on the Server*).

All the logic is implemented in a data module created before the main form is created (navigate to **Project | Options | Forms** to check the form creation order). Methods provided by the data module to the main form are as follows:

```
public
  procedure SavePerson(AOnSuccess: TProc;
            AOnError: TProc<Integer, String> = nil);
  procedure DeletePerson(AOnSuccess: TProc;
            AOnError: TProc<Integer, String> = nil);
  procedure LoadAll(AOnSuccess: TProc;
            AOnError: TProc<Integer, String> = nil);
  function CanSave: Boolean;
```

Riding the Mobile Revolution with FireMonkey

`CanSave` is used to enable or disable UI actions depending on the `dsPeople` dataset state. The `LoadAll` method is called from the `FormShow` event handler, and it requests data for the server and populates the in-memory dataset. Seeing that all remote requests are asynchronous, we need some callback to update the UI after the request is finished in order to show data in the case of success, or to show error messages in the case of errors. Here's the code for the data module `LoadAll` method:

```
procedure TdmMain.LoadAll(AOnSuccess: TProc; AOnError:
                          TProc<Integer, String>);
begin
  if dsPeople.State in [dsInsert, dsEdit] then
    dsPeople.Cancel;    //cancel all unposted data
  dsPeople.Close;

  RESTRequest.ClearBody;
  RESTRequest.Resource := 'people';
  RESTRequest.Method   := TRESTRequestMethod.rmGET;

  //execute remote request asynchronously
  //WARNING! The anonymous method passed as parameter to the
  //ExecuteAsynch is execute within the main thread, so there is
  //no need to synchronize UI access
  RESTRequest.ExecuteAsync(
    procedure
    begin
      if RESTRequest.Response.StatusCode = 200 then
      begin
        //load response jsonarray in the dataset
        dsPeople.Active := True;
        dsPeople.AppendFromJSONArrayString(
            RESTRequest.Response.JSONValue.ToString);
        dsPeople.First;
        if Assigned(AOnSuccess) then
        //call the 'success' user callback
        AOnSuccess();
      end
      else
      begin
        if Assigned(AOnError) then
          //call the 'error' user callback
          AOnError(RESTRequest.Response.StatusCode,
                   RESTRequest.Response.StatusText);
      end;
    end);
end;
```

This method is declared in the data module. How can we call this method in the `acRefreshData` action within the main form? Here's the code:

```
procedure TMainForm.acRefreshDataExecute(Sender: TObject);
begin
  DoStartWait('Please wait while retrieving the people list');
  dmMain.LoadAll(
    procedure
    begin
      DoEndWait;
    end,
    procedure(StatusCode: Integer; StatusText: String)
    begin
      DoEndWait;
      ShowError(Format('Error [%d]: %s',
                [StatusCode, StatusText]));
    end);
end;
```

Remember, a call to the `LoadAll` method is not blocking for the main thread. So, any code after a call to `LoadAll` is executed as soon as possible (as the OS decides) and not after the data is retrieved. This is the reason why we need the callbacks. The first anonymous method is our success callback, and it is executed when data is already in the dataset and the user can see them in the listview. The second anonymous method is our error callback, and it is executed if some errors occur in the call. The other remote calls work in the same manner.

If you, for some reason, would like to use a different HTTP component to do the REST HTTP calls, and this library doesn't support asynchronous client requests, you can always rely on the good old anonymous thread (or PPL since Delphi XE7). The following code is included in the `LoadAll` method, but it is commented to show an alternative way to do remote calls without using the `ExecuteAsynch` method:

```
TThread.CreateAnonymousThread(
  procedure
  begin
    try
      //synch call, but executed in an anonymous thread
      RESTRequest.Execute;
      TThread.Synchronize(nil,
        procedure
        begin
          if RESTRequest.Response.StatusCode = 200 then
          begin
            dsPeople.Active := True;
            dsPeople.AppendFromJSONArrayString(
```

```
              RESTRequest.Response.JSONValue.ToString);
          if Assigned(AOnSuccess) then
            AOnSuccess();
        end
        else
          AOnError(RESTRequest.Response.StatusCode,
                  RESTRequest.Response.StatusText);
      end);
    except
      on E: Exception do
      begin
        if Assigned(AOnError) then
        begin
          ErrMsg := E.Message;
          TThread.Synchronize(nil,
            procedure
            begin
          //Passing 'Zero' to the callback means that some
              //non-protocol related exception has been raised
              AOnError(0, ErrMsg);
            end);
        end
      end;
    end;
  end).Start;
```

An important feature of well-designed mobile apps is the feedback to the user. Your user *must* know what your application is doing after his input; otherwise, he/she would probably stop it. Therefore, we need to show a **Please wait** screen. To do so, this app uses a TPopup component. This component has a property called IsOpen that is used to show it or hide it. Just before each request, we set an instance form variable to true and after the request, when the response is visible somewhere in the UI, we set that variable to false. Here's the code to handle the **Please wait** screen:

```
procedure TMainForm.DoEndWait;
begin
  BackgroundOperationRunning := False;
end;

procedure TMainForm.DoStartWait(AWaitMessage: String);
begin
  //this label is placed inside the "Please wait" screen
  lblMessage.Text := AWaitMessage;
  BackgroundOperationRunning := True;
end;
```

How do we actually show the `TPopup` component? The setter of the `BackgroundOperationRunning` is a good place to do so. Here's the code:

```
procedure TMainForm.SetBackgroundOperationRunning(
  const Value: Boolean);
begin
  FBackgroundOperationRunning := Value;
  acRefreshData.Enabled := not FBackgroundOperationRunning;
  AniIndicator1.Visible := FBackgroundOperationRunning;
  TabItem1.Enabled := not FBackgroundOperationRunning;
  ppMessage.IsOpen := FBackgroundOperationRunning;
end;
```

Data is linked to the UI using the LiveBindings engine. Here's the LiveBindings designer showing the links:

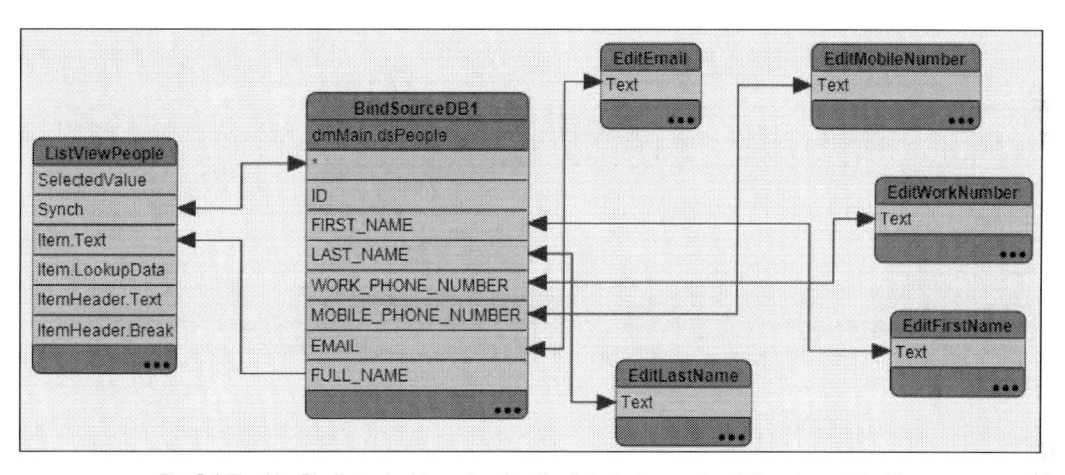

Fig. 8.1 The LiveBindings designer showing the links between the dsPeople and the UI

Riding the Mobile Revolution with FireMonkey

After launching the app, you will get this wait screen:

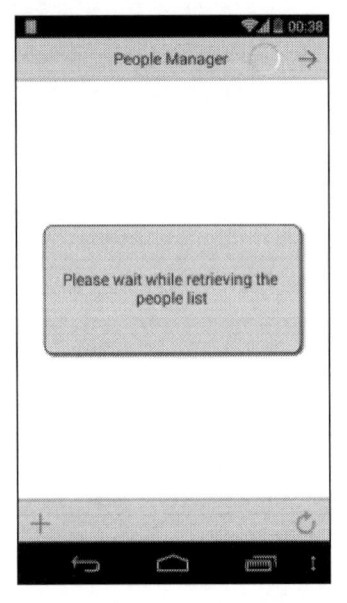

The wait screen

Then, when the data is retrieved, parsed, and loaded, this is the screen you will get:

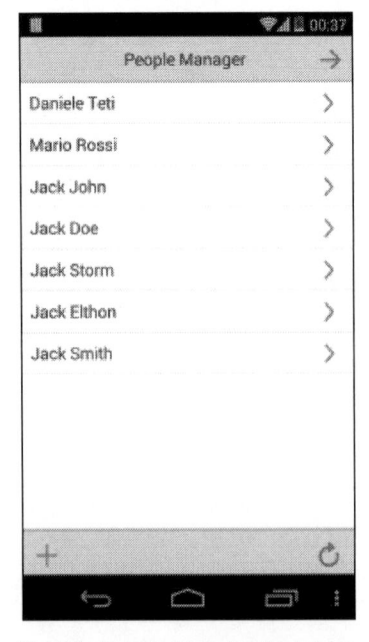

The list of people loaded in the listview

If you tap an item, you will get the editing screen:

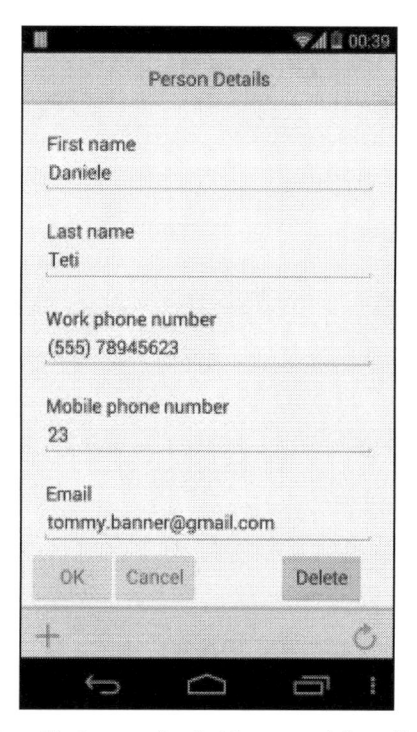

The editing screen showing the person information

There's more...

A lot of topics in this recipe! Mobile apps can be really complex as this simple example demonstrates. However, using the LiveBindings engine, the local storage offered by SQLite and IBLite, and the nice Delphi components to load data in memory, you can create mobile apps easily enough. Here are some other demos about the technologies involved in developing this type of app:

- *FireDAC IBLite with Delphi XE6* at: `https://www.youtube.com/watch?v=jbRJCqNgNDc`
- *Delphi XE5 Mobile REST Client Demo* at: `https://www.youtube.com/watch?v=OkRVbgF4VMI`
- *Delphi XE5 Mobile REST Client Demo Source* at: `http://delphi.org/2013/09/delphi-xe5-mobile-rest-client-demo-source/`
- *The New REST Client Library, A Tool of Many Trades* at: `https://www.youtube.com/watch?v=nPXYLK4JZvM`

Making a phone call from your app!

Many mobile devices, especially in the consumer market, are phones or devices that can make phone calls. In some cases, your mobile app may have the ability to make a call or just monitor the incoming or outgoing calls.

Getting ready

In this recipe, we'll see how to make a call and how to monitor the current calls as well. Also, in this case, the useful FireMonkey platform services framework comes in handy.

How to do it...

1. Create a new mobile app by navigating to **File | New | Multi-Device Application Delphi**.
2. Select the **Header/Footer** template and click on **OK**.
3. Drop the following components on the main form:
    - **TEdit** (edtPhoneNumber)
    - **TButton** (btnCall)
    - **TListBox** (lbCalls)
    - **TListBox** (lbInfo)

4. Arrange the components as shown in the following screenshot:

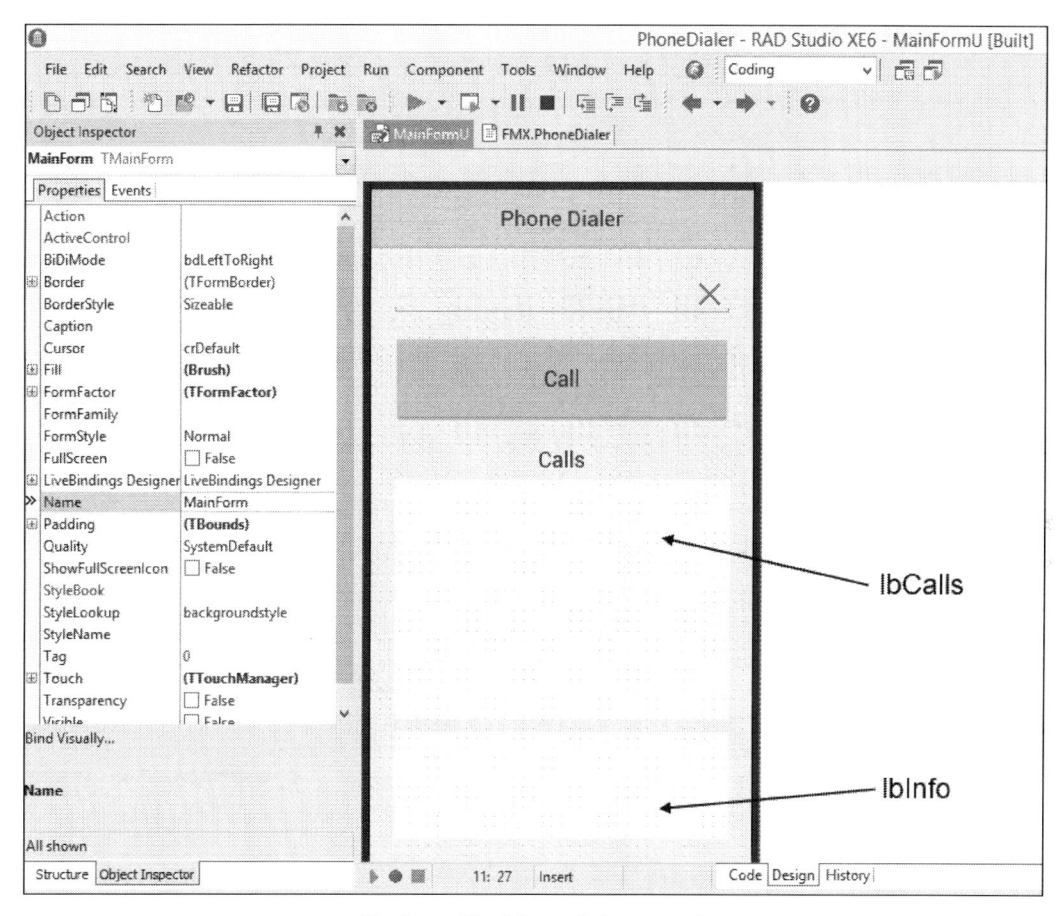

The form with all the controls arranged

5. Put in some labels to explain what the listboxes will contain, as shown in the preceding screenshot.

6. Now, create the `FormCreate` event handler and fill it with this code:

```
procedure TMainForm.FormCreate(Sender: TObject);
begin
   lbInfo.Clear;
   if TPlatformServices.Current.
       SupportsPlatformService(IFMXPhoneDialerService,
                        IInterface(FPhoneDialerService))
   then
   begin
      FPhoneDialerService.OnCallStateChanged :=
                                       CallStateChanged;
```

```
        lbInfo.ItemHeight := lbInfo.ClientHeight / 4;
        lbInfo.Items.Add('Carrier Name: ' +
          FPhoneDialerService.GetCarrier.GetCarrierName);
        lbInfo.Items.Add('ISO Country Code: ' +
          FPhoneDialerService.GetCarrier.GetIsoCountryCode);
        lbInfo.Items.Add('Network Code: ' +
          FPhoneDialerService.GetCarrier.GetMobileCountryCode);
        lbInfo.Items.Add('Mobile Network: ' +
          FPhoneDialerService.GetCarrier.GetMobileNetwork);
        btnCall.Enabled := True;
      end
    else
      lbInfo.Items.Add('No Phone Dialer Service');
  end;
```

7. In the form's `private` section, declare the following methods:

```
  private
    FPhoneDialerService: IFMXPhoneDialerService;
    procedure CallStateChanged(const ACallID: string;
                    const AState: TCallState);
    function CallStateAsString(AState: TCallState): String;
```

8. Press *Ctrl* + *Shift* + *C* and fill the methods just created with the following code:

```
function TMainForm.CallStateAsString(
AState: TCallState): String;
begin
  case AState of
    TCallState.None:
      Result := 'None';
    TCallState.Connected:
      Result := 'Connected';
    TCallState.Incoming:
      Result := 'Incoming';
    TCallState.Dialing:
      Result := 'Dialing';
    TCallState.Disconnected:
      Result := 'Disconnected';
    else
      Result := '<unknown>';
  end;
end;

procedure TMainForm.CallStateChanged(const ACallID: string;
  const AState: TCallState);
```

```
begin
  lbCalls.Items.Add(Format('%-16s %s',
                [ACallID, CallStateAsString(AState)]));
end;
```

9. Now, create the `OnClick` event for the `btnCall` method and fill it with this code:

```
procedure TMainForm.btnCallClick(Sender: TObject);
begin
  if not edtPhoneNumber.Text.IsEmpty then
    FPhoneDialerService.Call(edtPhoneNumber.Text)
  else
  begin
    ShowMessage('No number to call, please type a phone number.');
    edtPhoneNumber.SetFocus;
  end;
end;
```

10. Run the app on your phone. Note the `lbInfo` method showing all the information about your mobile network. Write a phone number in the editing area and click the **Call** button. Note what happens to the `lbCalls` method during the outgoing calls and during the incoming calls. This activity is shown in the following screenshot:

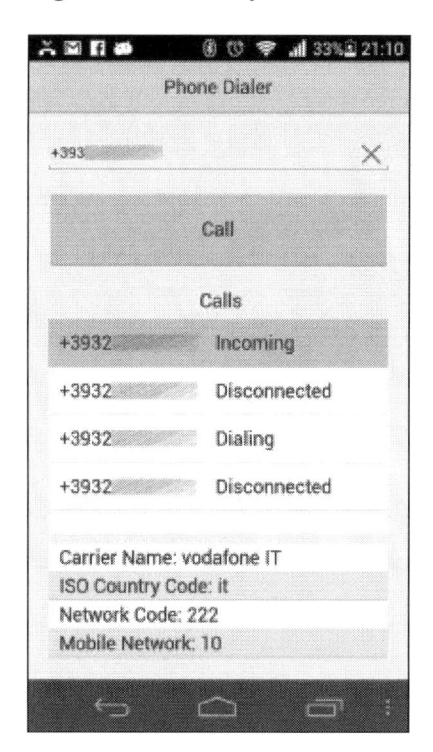

The Phone Dialer app running on a phone, after some in/out calls; note the events in the first list

How it works...

This recipe is very simple. All the work is done at the beginning when the `FormCreate` event handler asks the system whether it supports the `IFMXPhoneDialerService` interface. This interface has the following methods:

```
{ Interface of Phone Dialer }
IFMXPhoneDialerService = interface (IInterface)
  ['{61EE0E7A-7643-4966-873E-384CF798E694}']
  // Make a call by specified number
  function Call(const APhoneNumber: string): Boolean;
  // Get current carrier
  function GetCarrier: TCarrier;
  // Get all currrent calls. If the current calls aren't
  // present, the array will be empty
  // The developer shall delete array cells after use
  function GetCurrentCalls: TCalls;
  // Getter, Setter and property for work with event of tracing
  // of state change of a call
  function GetOnCallStateChanged: TOnCallStateChanged;
  procedure SetOnCallStateChanged(
            const AEvent: TOnCallStateChanged);
  property OnCallStateChanged: TOnCallStateChanged
          read GetOnCallStateChanged
          write SetOnCallStateChanged;
end;
```

There's more...

Using the monitoring functionality, you can implement a system to track the phone call duration and type (incoming or outgoing). Using this service, you can implement a list of contacts centralized on a server and allow your user to call those contacts without having the contact in the phone's address book. Another utilization is to monitor allowed incoming calls, and if a special blocked number calls, you can send a notification to a remote server. There are endless possibilities—explore them yourself.

Tracking the application's lifecycle

In the "safe" MS Windows desktop application development land, our application has a lifecycle, but it is not crucial to take care of it. Usually, you have a set of events to handle such as `FormCreate`, `FormClose` (at the form level), or `Application OnRestore`, or `Application OnTerminate`. In some cases, you have to handle the state where the main application window is minimized, and this is still simple. In the mobile world, as usual, things are a bit more complex. The concept of lifecycle is evidence. Just to make things messier, an Android activity's lifecycle is different from an iOS view lifecycle. Remember, when an app is in the background, it can be completely destroyed.

Getting ready

But, hey! Why I should care about the lifecycle? That's a very good point! There are a lot of things that you should, or must, do while your application is switching from one state to another.

Here are some examples:

- Handle the current input control's state. You can save or discard data, but you cannot send the **Do you want to save?** message to the user. If a user touches the **Home** button, you cannot stop them. For this specific situation, it could be useful to have the `OnSaveState` form event too, which is an abstraction of what we are talking about.
- Stop or restart CPU intensive work related to a calculation.
- Look for some previously saved data on the filesystem.
- Search Bluetooth devices or AppTethering-enabled applications.
- Update a remote resource more frequently than when the app was running in the background. In the background, you may check a particular HTTP resource once an hour, while if the app is in foreground, you can decide to check that resource once a minute.
- Append a system notification to remind the user of something just before terminating an app.
- Stop the audio output (if applicable for your app).
- Stop the GPS monitoring (if applicable to your app).
- Go into power saving mode, whatever it means for your app, and many more.

As you can see, the application lifecycle is very important. Let's see how we can hook up to it.

How to do it...

This recipe is not a standard recipe. We will not build a complete app, but a reference app. You can launch this app every time you want to know which event (app event or form event) is fired and when.

As the first thing, in the `FormCreate` event, we've to hook to the system FireMonkey messaging system and subscribe to the `TApplicationEventMessage` message type:

```
procedure TMainForm.FormCreate(Sender: TObject);
begin
  TPlatformServices.Current.SupportsPlatformService(
    IFMXLoggingService, IInterface(FLoggingService));

  FSubscrID := TMessageManager.DefaultManager.
   SubscribeToMessage(TApplicationEventMessage,
     procedure(const Sender: TObject;
               const Msg: TMessage)
     var
      AppEvent: TApplicationEventMessage;
     begin
       AppEvent := TApplicationEventMessage(Msg);
       case AppEvent.Value.Event of
         TApplicationEvent.FinishedLaunching:
           LogEvent('App Finished Launching');
         TApplicationEvent.BecameActive:
           LogEvent('App Became Active');
         TApplicationEvent.WillBecomeInactive:
           LogEvent('App Will Become Inactive');
         TApplicationEvent.EnteredBackground:
           LogEvent('App Entered Background');
         TApplicationEvent.WillBecomeForeground:
           LogEvent('App Will Become Foreground');
         TApplicationEvent.WillTerminate:
           LogEvent('App Will Terminate');
         TApplicationEvent.LowMemory:
           LogEvent('App Low Memory');
         TApplicationEvent.TimeChange:
           LogEvent('App Time Change');
         TApplicationEvent.OpenURL:
           LogEvent('App Open URL');
       end;
     end);
  LogEvent('Event FormCreate');
end;
```

Chapter 7

With this code, every time the system raises a message regarding our app, we'll be informed. The `System.Messaging.pas` unit, added in the `implementation` uses clause, contains the classes needed to access the system's messaging system.

How does this messaging system work? Once you have an instance of `TMessageManager`, you can subscribe message-handling methods to specific types of messages. Message-handling methods may be methods of an object or anonymous methods. In our case, we have used an anonymous method. This messaging mechanism can also be used in your app or component as an independent messaging system. However, FireMonkey also uses it to send system messages using the default messaging manager instance. In this recipe, we're using it to subscribe to the system messages.

An instance of `TApplicationEvent`, the type on which we're doing the big case statement, represents the application-related messages and may have any of the following values:

Event	Description
`BecameActive`	This indicates that an application has gained the focus.
`EnteredBackground`	This indicates that the application is running in the background because the user is no longer using it.
`FinishedLaunching`	This indicates that the application has been launched.
`LowMemory`	This event is a warning to the application that the device is running out of memory.
	In this case, the application should reduce memory usage, freeing structures and data that are not fundamental or that can be reloaded as per requirements at a later point.
`OpenURL`	This indicates that the application has received a request to open a URL (only for iOS).
`TimeChange`	This indicates that there has been a significant change in time (only for iOS).
	This event might happen, for example, when the day changes or when the device changes to or from daylight savings time.
`WillBecomeForeground`	This indicates that the user is now using the application, which was previously running in the background.
`WillBecomeInactive`	This indicates that the application is going to lose the focus and become inactive.
`WillTerminate`	This indicates that the user or the operating system is quitting the application.

Riding the Mobile Revolution with FireMonkey

Remember to be a good FireMonkey citizen, when you subscribe to a system notification, you have to unsubscribe to it too. We do it in the `FormDestroy` event just after logging - the last thing:

```
procedure TMainForm.FormDestroy(Sender: TObject);
begin
   LogEvent('Event FormDestroy');
   TMessageManager.DefaultManager.Unsubscribe(
TApplicationEventMessage, FSubscrID, True);
end;
```

The `LogEvent` method appends the message text to the listbox and writes the same message to the system log as well using the reference to `IFMXLoggingService` retrieved in the `FormCreate` event handler. Moreover, whereas the form events could be many, there is a checkbox to exclude them from the logging. Here's the code for the `LogEvent` method:

```
procedure TMainForm.LogEvent(Msg: string);
begin
   if (not CheckBox1.IsChecked) and
     Msg.StartsWith('event', True) then Exit;
   Memo1.Lines.Add(Format('%s: %s', [TimeToStr(Now), Msg]));
   Memo1.GoToTextEnd; //memo goes to the last line
   if Assigned(FLoggingService) then
     FLoggingService.Log('LifeCycle: %s', [Msg]); //syslog
end;
```

This is the infrastructure code, but what events are we waiting for? In the main form, there are some test buttons that raise specific system and form events. Here's the app while it is logging form events and system messages:

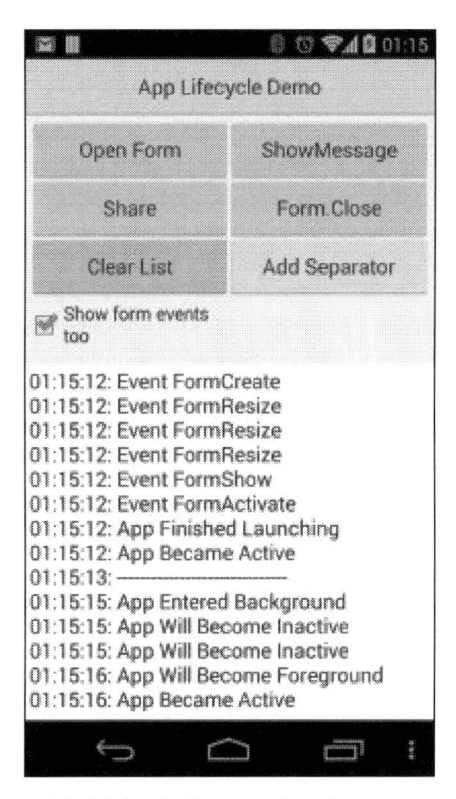

Chapter 7

The app while it is logging form events and system messages

In the main form, every interesting event that could be raised, whether the app state changes or not, is filled with code similar to the following one:

```
procedure TMainForm.FormActivate(Sender: TObject);
begin
   LogEvent('Event FormActivate');
end;
```

Now everything is traced, including app state changes and form events. Now you can connect your device, if it's not already connected, and launch the proper tool to see the device logger (launch `Monitor.bat` for Android devices or see the device console for iOS devices). Start the app and play with the buttons.

Try to tap the **Open Form** button and then close the newly opened form by tapping on the **Close** button. As you can see in the list, only form events are called (`FormDeactivate` and `FormActivate`), and this is reasonable. Now tap on the **ShowMessage** button and see what happens. Form events are not raised but an app message arrives. Look! The app goes into the inactive state for a `ShowMessage` call! This is a case where this sort of testing tool is very handy. If you don't know exactly when an app switches its state from one to another, you cannot rely on this state change to do anything useful and reliable. But now you have the right tool!

There's more...

Experimenting with the lifecycle, you can find interesting utilization that makes your user happy with your app.

Another interesting thing that I suggest you study is the messaging system, based on a variation of the well-known and more general **Observer** design pattern of GoF fame. Simply speaking, this messaging system is just something that triggers an event to which anyone can listen. Different libraries offer different implementations and for different purposes, but the basic idea is to provide a framework for issuing events and subscribing to them.

More information about the `System.Messaging.pas` unit can be found in the following articles:

- *Sending and Receiving Messages Using the RTL* at: `http://docwiki.embarcadero.com/RADStudio/en/Sending_and_Receiving_Messages_Using_the_RTL`
- *List of FireMonkey Message Types* at: `http://docwiki.embarcadero.com/RADStudio/en/List_of_FireMonkey_Message_Types`
- *System.Messaging (Delphi)* at: `http://docwiki.embarcadero.com/CodeExamples/en/System.Messaging_(Delphi)`
- Where the messaging system began; the Observer design pattern at: `http://en.wikipedia.org/wiki/Observer_pattern`

8
Using Specific Platform Features

In this chapter, we will cover:

- Using Android SDK Java classes
- Using iOS Objective C SDK classes
- Displaying PDF files in your app
- Sending Android intents
- Letting your phone talk – using the Android TextToSpeech engine
- Using Java classes in Android apps with Java2OP
- Doing it in the background, the right way – Android services

Introduction

There are situations where if you need a particular Android or iOS feature, FireMonkey does not help you. FireMonkey does a very good job in supporting all the common mobile features, but not all the APIs have been already imported, polished, and wrapped in nice Object Pascal reusable classes or components. What can you do in these cases? The good news is that you can import classes from the underlying SDK (and NDK in case of Android) and wrap them just like Embarcadero did in the FireMonkey platform.

In this chapter, we will see some classes import examples. Keep in mind that the code using imported classes is not cross-platform. That is, if you import an Android SDK class and your code uses it, you lost the possibility to compile that specific code for iOS. However, you can, as usual, use some IFDEFs to statically select the Android specific code from the iOS specific code. Moreover, in the last recipe, we'll see how to use one of the most powerful Android features: the services.

Using Android SDK Java classes

In this section, we'll talk about the mechanisms that the compiler offers to import classes from the Android SDK and NDK. This is not a standard recipe but is more of a show-case showing the possibilities offered by the Delphi compiler and the process needed to fully use them when dealing with OS built-in libraries.

Getting ready

What we will do is import a well-known Android class used everywhere in the Android ecosystem: the `Toast`. As the Android documentation says:

> "A toast provides simple feedback about an operation in a small popup. It only fills the amount of space required for the message and the current activity remains visible and interactive."

`Toasts` are used to inform users about something in an unobtrusive way. They do not have an **OK** or **Close** button because they automatically disappears after a defined timeout.

Well, how to use a `Toast` in a Delphi app?

The first thing to do is to have a clear vision of the class methods and all the other types involved in their definition. Going to the official documentation on the `http://developer.android.com/reference/android/widget/Toast.html` website, you can get this information. Here are the most relevant as the Android Java SDK documentation explains them.

The following table shows `Toast` class constants:

Type	Constant
int	LENGTH_LONG
int	LENGTH_SHORT

The following table shows `Toast` public instance methods

Type	Method
void	cancel()
int	getDuration()
int	getGravity()
float	getHorizontalMargin()
float	getVerticalMargin()
View	getView()
int	getXOffset()

Type	Method
int	getYOffset()
void	setDuration(int duration)
void	setGravity(int gravity, int xOffset, int yOffset)
void	setMargin(float horizontalMargin, float verticalMargin)
void	setText(int resId)
void	setText(CharSequence s)
void	setView(View view)
void	show()

The following table shows `Toast` public static methods (like the class methods in Delphi):

Type	Method
Toast	makeText(Context context, int resId, int duration)
Toast	makeText(Context context, CharSequence text, int duration)

This is the typical usage of the `Toast` class inside an Android activity:

```
Toast.makeText(getContext(),
"Hello Toast World",
Toast.LENGTH_LONG).show();
```

Now with this information, we can start to define our import Delphi class.

How to do it...

The Android Delphi compiler allows you to declare a specific class as a Generic Java Import of an SDK Java class. The class that does this magic is declared within the `Androidapi.JNIBridge.pas` unit and is declared as follows:

```
TJavaGenericImport<C: IJavaClass; T: IJavaInstance>
```

The `TJavaGenericImport` is a generic class which we can use to make the declaration of imported Java object factories easier. Using this class, we split the class methods and instance methods into two interfaces. This class blends the two interfaces into one factory that can produce instances of Java objects, or provide a reference to an instance representing the Java class. Moreover, Android Java SDK uses Java Strings objects, while Delphi uses strings. If you need to pass a string to a method imported from the SDK that expects a `JString` (the type used by the Delphi compiler to match the Java String object) you have to use the `StringToJString` function defined in `Androidapi.Helpers.pas` to convert it.

Using Specific Platform Features

So, the next step to use the `Toast` class is to define two interfaces. The first one declares all the class methods (static in Java) with the same signature as the Java ones. The second one, declares all the instance methods with the same Java signature as well. How to map Java types to the Delphi types? In the Delphi RTL, there are a lot of samples of imported Java classes and this is a small summary of what you can understand from the already imported classes and from the `api-version.xml` file present in the Android SDK, which contains the declaration of all the SDK classes (using RAD Studio 10.1 Berlin, the path is `<Public Documents>\Embarcadero\Studio\18.0\CatalogRepository\AndroidSDK-24.3.3\platform-tools\api\api-version.xml`).

Java Type	Delphi Type
`boolean`	`Boolean`
`byte`	`ShortInt`
`char`	`WideChar`
`double`	`Double`
`float`	`Single`
`int`	`Integer`
`long`	`Int64`
`short`	`SmallInt`
`void`	If used as a return type, use procedure instead of function
`java/lang/CharSequence`	`JCharSequence`
`android/view/View`	`JView`
`java/lang/String`	`JString`

All methods must be declared with the `cdecl` calling convention to be compatible with the Java calling convention. Moreover, the interface declaring the interface methods must be decorated with the `JavaSignature` RTTI attribute, which defines the full Java package where the mapped class is declared in the SDK. It may seem complex, but the resultant code is not. Here, is the final import declaration for the `Toast` class:

```
type
  [JavaSignature('android/widget/Toast')]
  JToast = interface(JObject)
    ['{AC116FB8-FE4D-47E8-BEC9-96E919A01CC7}']
    procedure cancel; cdecl;
    function getDuration: Integer; cdecl;
    function getGravity: Integer; cdecl;
    function getHorizontalMargin: Single; cdecl;
    function getVerticalMargin: Single; cdecl;
    function getView: JView; cdecl;
    function getXOffset: Integer; cdecl;
```

```
    function getYOffset: Integer; cdecl;
    procedure setDuration(duration: Integer); cdecl;
    procedure setGravity(gravity: Integer; xOffset:
Integer; yOffset: Integer); cdecl;
    procedure setMargin(horizontalMargin: Single;
verticalMargin: Single); cdecl;
    procedure setText(resId: Integer); cdecl; overload;
    procedure setText(s: JCharSequence); cdecl; overload;
    procedure setView(view: JView); cdecl;
    procedure show; cdecl;
  end;

  JToastClass = interface(JObjectClass)
  ['{127EA3ED-B569-4DBF-9BCA-FE1491FC615E}']
    function init(context: JContext): JToast; cdecl;
    function makeText(context: JContext; resId: Integer;
duration: Integer): JToast; cdecl; overload;
    function makeText(context: JContext;
text: JCharSequence;
duration: Integer): JToast; cdecl; overload;
  end;
```

Now, with these two interfaces, we can declare our `TJToast` class inheriting from the `TJavaGenericImport` using this code:

```
TJToast = class(TJavaGenericImport<JToastClass, JToast>)
const
  LENGTH_LONG = 1;
  LENGTH_SHORT = 0;
end;
```

As you can see, the body of the class is almost empty because all the methods will be used by an internal created object returning an interface reference. `LENGTH_LONG` and `LENGTH_SHORT` are simple constants in Java, so I added them as `const` in the `TJToast` declaration. `TJToast` can be used as follows, using the same methods documented for the Android Java SDK:

```
procedure TMainForm.Button3Click(Sender: TObject);
var
  Toast: JToast;
begin
  Toast := TJToast.JavaClass.makeText(TAndroidHelper.Context,
    StrToJCharSequence('Hello World'), TJToast.LENGTH_SHORT);
  Toast.show();
end;
```

Using Specific Platform Features

However, if you run this code, you will get the following exception:

```
Java.lang.RuntimeException: Can't create handler inside thread that
has not called Looper.prepare()
```

This is because the `Toast` must be synchronized with the UI thread. So using the `CallInUIThread` function declared in `FMX.Helpers.Android.pas`, we can synchronize the call with the main thread. Here is the complete code:

```delphi
procedure TMainForm.Button1Click(Sender: TObject);
begin
  CallInUiThread(
    procedure
    var
      Toast: JToast;
    begin
      Toast := TJToast.JavaClass.makeText(TAndroidHelper.Context,
        StrToJCharSequence('Hello World'), TJToast.LENGTH_SHORT);
      Toast.show();
    end);
end;
```

Now the code works, but the utilization pattern is not very Delphi-like. Indeed, we're using Java classes and methods, but using the Delphi syntax. However, we can write some helper code to make the `Toast` utilization more similar to the Delphi RTL and the Delphi programmer mindset:

```delphi
interface

{$SCOPEDENUMS ON}

type
  TToastDuration = (Short = 0, Long = 1);
  TToastPosition = (Default = 0, TOP = 48,
BOTTOM = 80, CENTER = 17,
VerticalCenter = 16, HorizontalCenter = 1);
  procedure ShowToast(const AText: string;
      const ADuration: TToastDuration = TToastDuration.Short;
    const APosition: TToastPosition = TToastPosition.Default);

implementation

uses
  FMX.Helpers.Android, AndroidAPI.Helpers;

procedure ShowToast(const AText: string;
```

```delphi
  const ADuration: TToastDuration;
  const APosition: TToastPosition);
begin
  CallInUiThread(
    procedure
    var
      Toast: JToast;
    begin
      Toast := TJToast.JavaClass.makeText(TAndroidHelper.Context,
        StrToJCharSequence(AText), Integer(ADuration));
      if APosition <> TToastPosition.Default then
        Toast.setGravity(Integer(APosition), 0, 0);
      Toast.show();
    end);
end;
```

In this version, we've also used the `setGravity` method to define the `Toast` position on the screen. To do this, we have used an enumerated type mapped to the same integer values defined in the `android.view.Gravity` class. Also, check the call to the `TAndroidHelper.Context` to get the activity context needed by the method.

Now, we can use the `Toast` class using a very Delphi-styled function. Here are some sample calls:

```delphi
ShowToast('Hello Toast World');
ShowToast('Hello Toast World', TToastDuration.Long,
TToastPosition.Center);
ShowToast('Hello Toast World', TToastDuration.Short);
```

As a suggestion, try to make your imports as intuitive as possible for your Delphi users (even if you are the only user) because all the rest of your code is written using the Delphi libraries. Stay as homogeneous as possible; it is a good principle whatever language you use. Encapsulate the imported classes in proper Delphi code structures (including classes, records, functions, and whatever is appropriate) and the style of your code will benefit from it, being much more coherent with itself.

In the recipe code, there is the full app showing the different kinds of `Toast` utilization.

There's more...

Complex classes require more work to be imported but there are tools that can help in this hard work. Some tools available for the Delphi versions before XE8 are as follows:

- **Java2Pas**: http://www.softwareunion.lu/en/downloads/

Using Specific Platform Features

For users of newer version, Embarcadero released `Java2OP` that does a very good job. One of the next recipes will talk about it.

These tools do a good job and help in the boring methods declaration phase. However, you cannot simply import a class and use it in your Delphi code. In many cases, you have to do additional work to arrange a good class structure in your units to get around units' circular references.

However, if you are interested and want to know more, I suggest checking the good presentation held by Brian Long at the CodeRage 8 conference where he talks about accessing Android and iOS API (http://blog.blong.com/2013/10/my-coderage-session-files.html).

Since Delphi XE7 is it possible to use your own or third-party Java libraries in RAD Studio applications in a simpler way. Check out this link for more information http://docwiki.embarcadero.com/RADStudio/en/Using_a_Custom_Set_of_Java_Libraries_In_Your_RAD_Studio_Android_Apps.

As FireMonkey and the mobile "soul" of Delphi matures, third-party mobile components start to be available on the market. Even if you are not interested in native widgets, you can study the code from the project "D.P.F Delphi Android Native Components" which can help you understand how this kind of interfacing job works (http://sourceforge.net/projects/dpfdelphiandroid/).

Moreover, you can also use native NDK `.so` files. To get an idea on how to do it, check the `Androidapi.Log.pas` unit where the function used by the `IFMXLoggingService` service on Android is declared. As you will see, there is a declaration very similar to the declaration usually used for the Windows dll:

```
function __android_log_write(Priority: android_LogPriority;
  const Tag, Text: MarshaledAString): Integer; cdecl;
  external AndroidLogLib name '__android_log_write';
```

As time goes by, Embarcadero will add more and more wrappers for the Android SDK classes and functionalities, but until then, if you need to use specific SDK classes or third-party Java classes (that will require a bit of work to be packaged in the generated APK) you can rely on the compiler support and the RTL class `TJavaGenericImport` to declare and use it.

Using iOS Objective C SDK classes

Just as we saw about Android in the previous recipe, Delphi is able to access the iOS SDK as well. In this section, we'll talk about the mechanisms that the compiler offers to import classes from the iOS SDK. This is not a standard recipe but is more of a show-case showing the possibilities offered by the Delphi compiler and the process needed to fully use them when dealing with OS built-in libraries. The mechanism is similar to the Android ones, but there are some notable differences.

Getting ready

In Objective-C, all classes have `NSObject` as a common ancestor. iOS SDK is composed of some frameworks. An iOS framework is a number of classes specialized for a single purpose. For example, UIKit is the framework containing all the basic classes related to the UI, the iAd framework contains all the stuff related to the advertising and MapKit wraps up all the mapping related classes.

Note that Objective-C uses the `NSString` objects while Delphi uses strings. If you need to pass a string to an iOS API that expects an `NSString` you can use the `StrToNSStr` function defined in `Macapi.Helpers.pas` to convert it.

Let's say we need to use the `UIDevice` class from the iOS SDK (the process is applicable for every class in the SDK). As the Apple documentation says:

> "The UIDevice class provides a singleton instance representing the current device. From this instance you can obtain information about the device such as assigned name, device model, and operating-system name and version."

How it works...

The iOS Delphi compiler allows you to declare a specific class as a Generic `ObjectiveC` Import of an SDK class. The class that does this magic is declared within the `Macapi.ObjectiveC.pas` unit and is declared as follows:

```
TOCGenericImport<C: IObjectiveCClass; T: IObjectiveCInstance>
```

The `TOCGenericImport` is a generic class that we can use to make the declaration of imported `ObjectiveC` object factories easier. Using this class, we split the class methods and instance methods into two interfaces. This class blends the two interfaces into one factory that can produce instances of `ObjectiveC` objects, or provide a reference to an instance representing the `ObjectiveC` class.

But, how do we define the methods in the two interfaces?

Reading the iOS documentation for the `UIDevice` class, you read method and property signatures. Let's translate some of the most significant ones.

The first property we want to translate is `model`. The `model` property returns the model of the device (can be "iPhone," "iPod touch," or other values identifying the device model). The property is read only.

This is the complete signature:

```
@property(nonatomic, readonly, retain) NSString *model
```

Using Specific Platform Features

In Object, Pascal is translated as follows:

```
function model: NSString; cdecl;
```

As you can see, a read only property is mapped to a function with the name of the property as the function name, and with the ObjectiveC property type as the ObjectPascal return value. But, what about **R/W (read/write)** properties?

The next property we want to translate is proximityMonitoringEnabled, a R/W property of the type Boolean indicating whether proximity monitoring is enabled or not.

This is the complete signature:

```
@property(nonatomic,getter=isProximityMonitoringEnabled)
BOOL proximityMonitoringEnabled
```

In Object, Pascal is translated as follows:

```
procedure setProximityMonitoringEnabled(
proximityMonitoringEnabled: Boolean); cdecl;
function isProximityMonitoringEnabled: Boolean; cdecl;
```

A R/W property is mapped to a procedure (the setter) and a function (the getter). The procedure name starts with "set" followed by the ObjectiveC property name (proximityMonitoringEnabled becomes setProximityMonitoringEnabled) and accepts a parameter of the same type of the property. The function name is defined by the property signature; in this case it is isProximityMonitoringEnabled, returning a value of the same type of the property type. If the property signature does not impose the getter name, the translation is similar to the following.

In ObjectiveC it is as follows:

```
@property(nonatomic, retain) NSString *accessibilityLabel
```

In Delphi, it is as follows:

```
function accessibilityLabel: NSString; cdecl;
procedure setAccessibilityLabel(accessibilityLabel: NSString); cdecl;
```

The UIDevice import will look like the following (only some methods were imported):

```
UIDeviceClass = interface(NSObjectClass)
    ['{A2DCE998-BF3A-4AB0-9B8D-4182B341C9DF}']
    function currentDevice: Pointer; cdecl;
end;

UIDevice = interface(NSObject)
    ['{70BB371D-314A-4BA9-912E-2EF72EB0F558}']
```

```
    function batteryLevel: Single; cdecl;
    function batteryState: UIDeviceBatteryState; cdecl;
    function isBatteryMonitoringEnabled: Boolean; cdecl;
    function isMultitaskingSupported: Boolean; cdecl;
    function isProximityMonitoringEnabled: Boolean; cdecl;
    function localizedModel: NSString; cdecl;
    function model: NSString; cdecl;
    function name: NSString; cdecl;
    function orientation: UIDeviceOrientation; cdecl;
    procedure playInputClick; cdecl;
    function proximityState: Boolean; cdecl;
    function systemName: NSString; cdecl;
    function systemVersion: NSString; cdecl;
    function uniqueIdentifier: NSString; cdecl;
  end;
  TUIDevice = class(TOCGenericImport<UIDeviceClass, UIDevice>)
  end;
```

Now the `UIDevice` class is usable as the following (however, the suggested use is as a singleton using the `currentDevice` property. Here it is used as a normal instance just for example):

```
var
  device: UIDevice;
begin
  device := TUIDevice.Create;
  ShowMessage(NSStrToStr(device.model));
end;
```

Note that the class methods defined in the `UIDevice` class can also be used by Delphi. You don't need to create an instance (just like normal class methods) but the returning pointer must be wrapped in the proper class type:

```
var
  device: UIDevice;
  model: string;
begin
  //wraps the pointer to the proper type using the Wrap method
  device := TUIDevice.Wrap(TUIDevice.OCClass.currentDevice);
  model := NSStrToStr(device.model);
  ShowMessage(model);
end;
```

Using Specific Platform Features

There's more...

The topic about the `ObjectiveC` class imports is very huge and a deep explanation of it is out of the scope of this book. However, if you are interested and want to know more, I suggest you check out the presentation held by Brian Long at the CodeRage 8 conference where he talks about accessing iOS and Android API (`http://blog.blong.com/2013/10/my-coderage-session-files.html`).

As FireMonkey and the mobile "soul" of Delphi matures, third-party mobile components start to be available on the market. Even if you are not interested in native widgets, you can study the code from the project "D.P.F Delphi iOS Native Components" (`http://sourceforge.net/projects/dpfdelphiios/`).

Displaying PDF files in your app

In the mobile world, often you need to show your user PDF files. Maybe these PDF files are used as reports (usually generated by some reporting tool on the remote server), as a statement about something that the user should do, which is in the form of a small book, or simply as a products catalog. So, how do we display a PDF deployed within the app, or downloaded from some remote server and stored locally? How do we do it on Android and iOS? This is the topic of this recipe.

Getting ready

Let's say we have to create an app that contains some PDF files. In this case, we don't download the files, but simply deliver them within the app. Later, we'll see how to download them from the network.

To deploy additional files within our app, we've to use the Deployment Manager accessible by navigating to **Project | Deployment**. If you need to know how to use it, check the Embarcadero documentation (`http://docwiki.embarcadero.com/RADStudio/en/Deployment_Manager`).

The additional file will be deployed in the private documents folder. Under Android, the private documents folder is identified as `./asset/internal` while on iOS, it is identified as `.\Startup\Documents`. Using the Deployment Manager, put a PDF file in these folders for each platform so it will be included in the generated app package.

How it works...

All that's required to show the PDF is encapsulated in a single unit called `xPlat.OpenPDF.pas`. The main form contains a button that once clicked calls the function `OpenPDF`, passing the name of the file to be shown:

```
procedure TMainForm.btnOpenPDFClick(Sender: TObject);
begin
  OpenPDF('samplefile.pdf');
end;
```

Let's analyze the `OpenPDF` function in the `xPlat.OpenPDF.pas` unit. Here's the full code:

```
unit xPlat.OpenPDF;

interface

procedure OpenPDF(const APDFFileName: string);

implementation

uses
  System.SysUtils, IdURI, FMX.Forms, System.Classes,
  System.IOUtils, FMX.WebBrowser, FMX.Types, FMX.StdCtrls
{$IF defined(ANDROID)}
    , Androidapi.JNI.GraphicsContentViewText
    , FMX.Helpers.Android
    , Androidapi.Helpers
    , AndroidSDK.Toast
    , Androidapi.JNI.Net
    , Androidapi.JNI.JavaTypes
{$ENDIF}
{$IF defined(IOS)}
    , iOSapi.Foundation
    , Macapi.Helpers
    , FMX.Helpers.iOS
    , FMX.Dialogs
{$ENDIF}
    ;

{$IF defined(ANDROID)}

procedure OpenPDF(const APDFFileName: string);
```

Using Specific Platform Features

```
    var
      Intent: JIntent;
      FilePath, SharedFilePath: string;
    begin
      FilePath := TPath.Combine(TPath.GetDocumentsPath, APDFFileName);
      SharedFilePath := TPath.Combine(
    TPath.GetSharedDocumentsPath, APDFFileName);
      if TFile.Exists(SharedFilePath) then
        TFile.Delete(SharedFilePath);
      TFile.Copy(FilePath, SharedFilePath);

      Intent := TJIntent.Create;
      Intent.setAction(TJIntent.JavaClass.ACTION_VIEW);
      Intent.setDataAndType(
    StrToJURI('file://' + SharedFilePath),
    StringToJString('application/pdf'));
      try
        SharedActivity.startActivity(Intent);
      except
        on E: Exception do
          ShowToast('Cannot open PDF' + sLineBreak +
            Format('[%s] %s', [E.ClassName, E.Message]),
            TToastDuration.Long);
      end;
    end;
    {$ENDIF}

    {$IF defined(IOS)}
    type
      TCloseParentFormHelper = class
      public
        procedure OnClickClose(Sender: TObject);
      end;

    procedure TCloseParentFormHelper.OnClickClose(Sender: TObject);
    begin
      TForm(TComponent(Sender).Owner).Close();
    end;

    procedure OpenPDF(const APDFFileName: string);
    var
      NSU: NSUrl;
      OK: Boolean;
      frm: TForm;
```

```
    WebBrowser: TWebBrowser;
    btn: TButton;
    evnt: TCloseParentFormHelper;
begin
    frm := TForm.CreateNew(nil);
    btn := TButton.Create(frm);
    btn.Align := TAlignLayout.Top;
    btn.Text := 'Close';
    btn.Parent := frm;
    evnt := TCloseParentFormHelper.Create;
    btn.OnClick := evnt.OnClickClose;
    WebBrowser := TWebBrowser.Create(frm);
    WebBrowser.Parent := frm;
    WebBrowser.Align := TAlignLayout.Client;
    WebBrowser.Navigate('file://' + APDFFileName);
    frm.ShowModal();
end;
{$ENDIF}

end.
```

Showing the PDF file on Android

To display the PDF on Android, we have used an Android-specific mechanism called intents (check the specific recipe to know more about Android intents). The file is actually shown by an external app already installed on the device; if such an app is not present, the PDF cannot be shown and a message is shown to the user. You can install Adobe PDF Reader or another app that is able to display PDF, which is "intent-compatible" with the one from Adobe. In accordance with Android I/O security, to let another app read the PDF file bounded in our `assets/internal` folder, we have to copy the file from the private documents folder, which is private to the app and not accessible from other apps, to the shared documents folder (readable from all the other apps installed on the device).

Just after the copy, we create an Intent and configure it to launch an app able to show that PDF. The configuration is simple enough:

```
//create the Intent directly from the Android SDK
Intent := TJIntent.Create;
//We need to show the PDF, so ACTION_VIEW is ok
Intent.setAction(TJIntent.JavaClass.ACTION_VIEW);
//Where is the file? Which mime type?
Intent.setDataAndType(
StrToJURI('file://' + SharedFilePath),
StringToJString('application/pdf'));
```

Using Specific Platform Features

```
try
   //ask to the OS to find a proper app to handle the intent
   SharedActivity.startActivity(Intent);
except
   //TODO: there aren't apps able to show the PDF. Inform the user!
end;
```

Showing the PDF file on iOS

On iOS, there aren't any Intents, but we can use another mechanism to show our PDF. The iOS WebView component is able to show PDFs, so we create a form on the fly containing a WebView and a button to close the form. The OpenPDF iOS implementation does not use iOS specific mechanisms, apart from the WebView capabilities.

After having created the form at run-time (remember that if you don't have an `fmx` file associated with the `TForm` instance, you cannot use `TForm.Create()` to create the form but `TForm.CreateNew()`. The code is reported here, with some comments:

```
//create the form without an fmx
frm := TForm.CreateNew(nil);
//create the button used to close the form.
//On iOS there is not a "back" button as in Android
btn := TButton.Create(frm);
btn.Align := TAlignLayout.Top;
btn.Text := 'Close';
btn.Parent := frm;
evnt := TCloseParentFormHelper.Create;
//set the Button OnClick event handler
btn.OnClick := evnt.OnClickClose;
//create the TWebBroser component wich wraps the iOS WebView
WebBrowser := TWebBrowser.Create(frm);
WebBrowser.Parent := frm;
WebBrowser.Align := TAlignLayout.Client;
//point the webbroser to the local file under the private folder
WebBrowser.Navigate('file://' + APDFFileName);
frm.ShowModal();
```

There's more...

This code does its job. However, Android and iOS users do not have the same user experience. On Android, you can use whatever app you have installed on the device to show the PDF, so you could also change the file with annotations, highlights, and drawings directly on the file. Note that the file is readable also from other apps than yours. This can be a problem in some situations. On iOS, conversely, you cannot modify the PDF with annotations and do not have a full control on the file, and the file remains "private" for your app. These facts must be but be carefully analyzed and you have to be aware of the pros and cons about every choice you make. If you want to provide a uniform set of functionalities, additional work and third-party components and libraries are needed.

One particular mention is worth for the TMS iCL component suite (http://www.tmssoftware.com/site/tmsicl.asp). It is specific for FireMonkey on iOS (so it doesn't compile on Android) but contains a component called TTMSFMXNativePDFLib that is able to create new PDF documents, open existing PDF documents, and do many other things.

> **Using Google Docs Viewer**
>
> If your PDF is located at a public URL, you can also use the PDF visualizer included in Google Docs. Point a WebView to the following URL and your PDF will show up:
>
> ```
> "https://docs.google.com/gview?embedded=true&url=" +
> PDFURL;
> ```

Download the PDF file from the server

Let's say we have an application server that generates reports from some database data and saves them as PDF files.

We can download these files using a simply `TidHTTP` component and store them locally using code similar to the following:

```
var
   FileStream: TStream;
   FilePath: String;
begin
FilePath := TPath.Combine(
TPath.GetSharedDocumentsPath, 'myreport.pdf');
FileStream := TFileStream.Create(FilePath, fmCreate);
IdHttp1.Get(
'http://www.myserver.com/reports/myreport.pdf', FileStream);
end;
```

Sending Android Intents

One of the most useful things about Android development is the intents dispatching mechanism. As Google says: "An intent is an abstract description of an operation to be performed", and just to be clearer, continues saying, "An Intent provides a facility for performing late runtime binding between the code in different applications. Its most significant use is in the launching of activities, where it can be thought of as the glue between activities. It is basically a passive data structure holding an abstract description of an action to be performed." (http://developer.android.com/reference/android/content/Intent.html).

Intents are widely used in Android, and if you want to fully integrate your Delphi app with the Android OS, probably you have to deal with Intents. Delphi uses intents internally to deal with some fundamental Android services (`TShareSheetAction`, `TTakePhotoFromCameraAction`, and so on). In this recipe, we'll see how to directly use intents in our app, with many examples.

Getting ready

The primary, and mandatory, pieces of information in an intent are:

- `action`: This is the general action to be performed, such as `ACTION_VIEW`, `ACTION_EDIT`, `ACTION_MAIN`, and so on
- `data`: This is the data to operate on, such as a person record in the contacts database, expressed as a URI

There are two kinds of intent, explicit and implicit intents:

- **Explicit intent**: The app defines the target component directly in the intent
- **Implicit intent**: The app asks the Android system to evaluate registered components based on the intent data and other optional information (implicit intents)

Using Java and the Android SDK, you can send an implicit intent with the following code:

```
Intent myIntent = new Intent(
Intent.ACTION_VIEW, Uri.parse("http://www.danieleteti.it"));
startActivity(myIntent);
```

This code asks the Android system to view a web page. If the OS finds an activity able to handle this kind of information (based on action and data), then that activity will be started and the intent data passed to it.

Intents are available also to the Delphi users. The previous Java code can be translated in Delphi as follows:

```
var
  Intent: JIntent;
begin
  Intent := TJIntent.Create;
  Intent.setAction(TJIntent.JavaClass.ACTION_VIEW);
  Intent.setData(StringToJString('http://www.danieleteti.it'));
  TAndroidHelper.Activity.startActivity(Intent);
end;
```

As you can see, the code is very similar to the Java version. Note that this code cannot be compiled on any platform but Android, so if you want to add this code in a cross platform app (for Android, iOS, or also Windows and MacOSX) you have to surround it with some IFDEFs.

There are many components able to respond to some kind of intents; the Android documentations is very good on this topic. In this recipe, we'll open a web page, start Google Maps by pointing to a specific address, open an e-mail client, open the Twitter app, and ask for speech-to-text recognition.

How it works...

In the main form, there are six buttons, a listbox, and some labels. Here's how the form is rendered at runtime (after using it to recognize the phrase "this is a book").

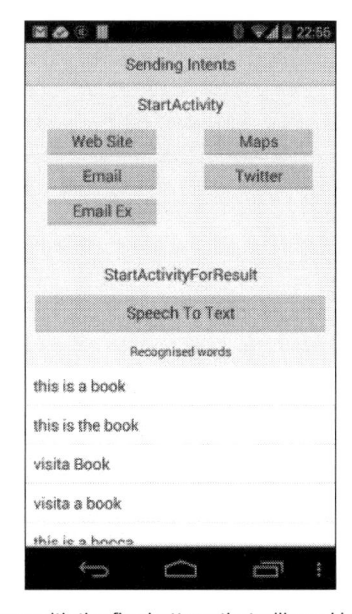

The app with the five buttons that will send intents

Using Specific Platform Features

Let's open the project `SendingAndroidIntents.dproj` and study it. The first four buttons, as you can see while reading the events handler, call a form method called `LaunchViewIntent` after passing a URI:

```
procedure TMainForm.btnMapsClick(Sender: TObject);
begin
   //launch Google Maps (or similar app)
   LaunchViewIntent(
'geo://0,0?q=Piazza del Colosseo 1,00184 Roma');
end;

procedure TMainForm.btnEmailClick(Sender: TObject);
begin
   //launch an email client with an empty email
   LaunchViewIntent('mailto:daniele.teti@gmail.com', false);
end;

procedure TMainForm.btnTwitterClick(Sender: TObject);
begin
   //launch twitter client (if installed)
   LaunchViewIntent('http://twitter.com/danieleteti');
end;
```

The procedure `LaunchViewIntent` is defined as follows:

```
procedure TMainForm.LaunchViewIntent(AURI: string;
AEncodeURL: boolean);
var
   Intent: JIntent;
   URI: JString;
begin
   if AEncodeURL then
      AURI := TIdURI.URLEncode(AURI);
   Intent := TJIntent.Create;
   Intent.setAction(TJIntent.JavaClass.ACTION_VIEW);
   URI := StringToJString(AURI);
   Intent.setData(TJnet_Uri.JavaClass.parse(URI));
   TAndroidHelper.Context.startActivity(Intent);
end;
```

This method executes all the steps needed to create an intent for the purpose of displaying something; indeed, the action `ACTION_VIEW` means, "I want to view something" and asks the OS to show the information described in the `data` property (and other intent properties if present).

Chapter 8

Firstly, we check whether the URI needs to be encoded; if so, we use the `TidURI.URLEncode` method from the `INDY` library to do the encoding. Then, an intent is created and configured with `ACTION_VIEW` as the action and the passed URI as the data. Having the intent configured, the last thing to do is to ask the OS what that intent is for. In this case, we want to start an activity to do the work defined in the intent. The Android context used by the FireMonkey framework is accessible using the `TAndroidHelper.Context` static method. So the last line uses `TAndroidHelper.Context.startActivity(Intent)` to actually send the intent. This kind of intent is the most simple.

More complex intent – sending a full flagged e-mail

The fifth button, named **Email Ex**, sends an e-mail just like the **Email** button, but is more powerful because the prepared e-mail will also have the subject, the body, and the CC and BCC fields correctly filled. Let's see how this is possible.

In this case, the simple `ACTION_VIEW` with some data is not enough. Here's the code used to send a more complex e-mail:

```
procedure TMainForm.btnEmailExClick(Sender: TObject);
var
  Intent: JIntent;
  URI: JString;
  AddressesTo: TJavaObjectArray<JString>;
  AddressesCC, AddressesBCC: TJavaObjectArray<JString>;
begin
  Intent := TJIntent.Create;
  Intent.setAction(TJIntent.JavaClass.ACTION_SENDTO);
  Intent.setData(
TJnet_Uri.JavaClass.parse(StringToJString('mailto:')));
  AddressesTo := TJavaObjectArray<JString>.Create(2);
  AddressesTo.Items[0] := StringToJString('daniele.teti@gmail.com');
  AddressesTo.Items[1] := StringToJString('john.doe@nowhere.com');

  AddressesCC := TJavaObjectArray<JString>.Create(1);
  AddressesCC.Items[0] := StringToJString('jane.doe@nowhere.com');

  AddressesBCC := TJavaObjectArray<JString>.Create(1);
  AddressesBCC.Items[0] :=
StringToJString('backup@mywebsite.com');

  Intent.putExtra(TJIntent.JavaClass.EXTRA_EMAIL, AddressesTo);
  Intent.putExtra(TJIntent.JavaClass.EXTRA_CC, AddressesCC);
  Intent.putExtra(TJIntent.JavaClass.EXTRA_BCC, AddressesBCC);
  Intent.putExtra(TJIntent.JavaClass.EXTRA_SUBJECT,
StringToJString('Greetings from Italy'));
```

Using Specific Platform Features

```
    Intent.putExtra(TJIntent.JavaClass.EXTRA_TEXT,
      StringToJString('I''m learning how to use Android Intents!'+
sLineBreak + 'They are very powerful!' +
sLineBreak + sLineBreak + 'See you...'));
    SharedActivity.startActivity(Intent);
end;
```

As you can see, we set more properties in the intent than in the previous example. Also, a `TJavaObjectArray<JString>` is used to pass a Delphi wrapper of a Java array to the intent. Also note how generics can be used while talking to the Android SDK.

Tapping this button, you will get a fully prepared e-mail as in the following screenshot. Note how the subject, the CC, and the BCC tabs have been filled using information sent by the intent.

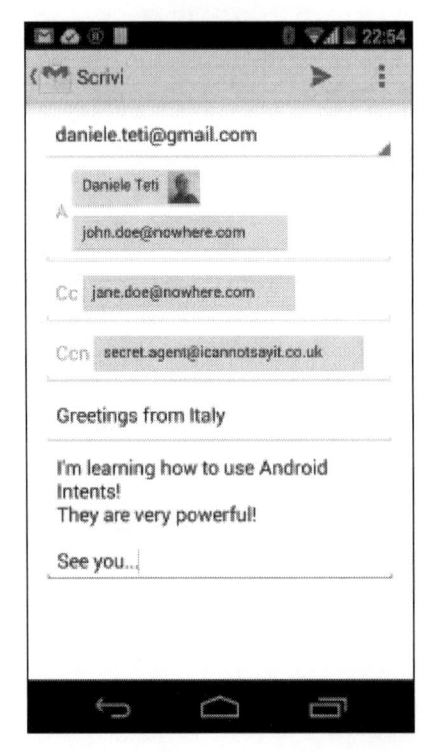

Gmail ready to send the e-mail prepared by our app

Starting an activity for result – the speech to text engine

Sometimes, you want to get a result back from an activity when it ends its job. For example, you may start an activity that lets the user pick a photo in a photo gallery and when it ends, it returns the selected image or a person in a list of contacts and when it ends, it returns the person that was selected.

To do this, we call the `TAndroidHelper.Activity.startActivityForResult` method. The result will come back through a FireMonkey message readable using the global `TMessageManager` instance.

`startActivityForResult` gets two parameters, the first one is the intent itself, while the second is an integer value identifying the request code. This request code will be passed to the message handler when the activity ends. Yes, since the `startActivityForResult` is not blocking, when the launched activity ends you have to know from which request it has been launched.

When an activity exits, some data should be returned back to its parent. It must always supply a result code, which can be the standard results `RESULT_CANCELED`, `RESULT_OK`, or any custom values starting with `RESULT_FIRST_USER` (all these values are defined in the Android documentation here http://developer.android.com/reference/android/app/Activity.html). In addition, it can optionally return an Intent containing any additional data it wants. All of this information appears back on the parent message handler along with the integer identifier it originally supplied.

The last button launches the `SpeechToText` engine activity, asks the user to say something, then ends and sends the possible recognized phrases to the parent activity:

```
procedure TMainForm.btnSTTClick(Sender: TObject);
var
   Intent: JIntent;
   ReqCode: Integer;
const
   STT_REQUEST = 1001;
   ACTION_RECOGNIZE_SPEECH = 'android.speech.action.RECOGNIZE_SPEECH';
   EXTRA_LANGUAGE_MODEL = 'android.speech.extra.LANGUAGE_MODEL';
   EXTRA_RESULTS = 'android.speech.extra.RESULTS';
begin

   //assign a code to this request
   ReqCode := STT_REQUEST;
   //create and configure the intent (check android SDK docs)
   Intent := TJIntent.Create;
   Intent.setAction(StringToJString(ACTION_RECOGNIZE_SPEECH));
   Intent.putExtra(StringToJString(EXTRA_LANGUAGE_MODEL),
StringToJString('en-US'));
   //when the launched activity ends, this handler will be called.
   //Here we've to read the data sent back from the launched activity
   TMessageManager.DefaultManager.SubscribeToMessage(
     TMessageResultNotification,
     procedure(const Sender: TObject; const Message: TMessage)
     var
```

```delphi
      M: TMessageResultNotification;
      i: Integer;
      Words: JArrayList;
      TheWord: string;
    begin
      M := TMessageResultNotification(message);
      //is this request the right one?
if M.RequestCode = ReqCode then
      begin
        //The request returned OK?
        if (M.ResultCode = TJActivity.JavaClass.RESULT_OK) then
        begin
          Words := M.Value.getStringArrayListExtra(
StringToJString(EXTRA_RESULTS));
          ListBox1.Clear;
        //if there are recognized words, fill the listbox
          if Words.size > 0 then
          begin
            ListBox1.BeginUpdate;
            try
              for i := 0 to Words.size - 1 do
              begin
                TheWord := JStringToString(JString(Words.get(i)));
                ListBox1.Items.Add(TheWord);
              end;
            finally
              ListBox1.EndUpdate;
            end;
          end
          else
            ShowToast('Some problems occurred');
        end
        else
          ShowToast('Nothing to recognise');
      end;
    end);

  //start the activity for result passing the specific ReqCode
  TAndroidHelper.Activity.startActivityForResult(Intent, ReqCode);
end;
```

The code is not trivial, but the main parts are clearly identifiable. Firstly, we configure the intent to launch the speech recognizer. Then, before launching the intent, we subscribe to system messages of the type `TMessageResultNotification`. This kind of message is sent by FireMonkey when an Android activity has been launched with `startActivityForResult`. Inside the message handler, we've to check whether the message is from our launched activity (so we check the `ReqCode`) and whether the activity returned with no errors (so we check the `RESULT_OK`). If everything is okay, we can read the information contained in the returned intent (this time the intent is used to send back information from the launched activity to the parent app).

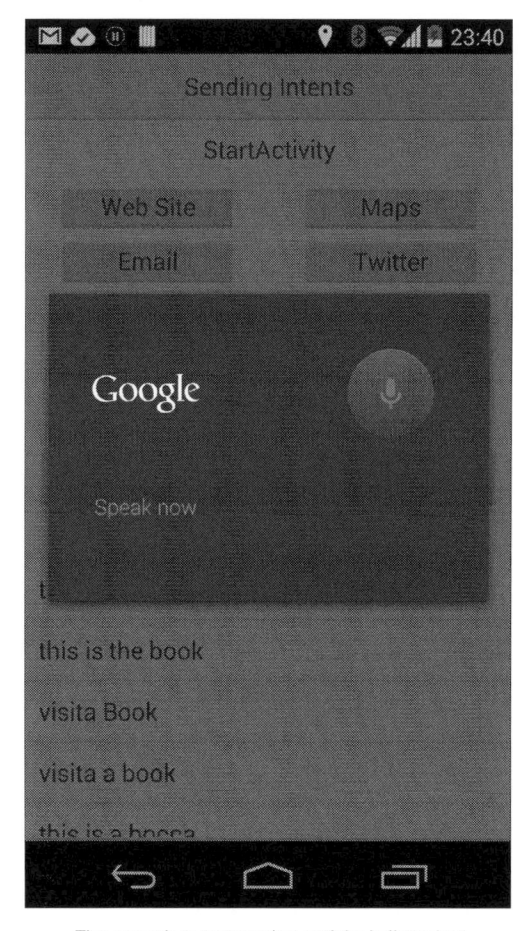

The speech to text engine activity is listening

Play with the app and discover how the different kinds of intent work.

There's more...

Intents are fundamental parts of the Android ecosystem. FireMonkey uses them in the components and in the RTL, and a developer who wants to deeply integrate their app with the Android OS must know how they work and the possibilities that they open up. Think, every app installed on your device can be elegantly integrated in your app without too much effort. A good point can be, study all the common intents available and usable in your Android device. You will learn useful things and will get in touch with many practical uses of intents.

All the available common intents are explained in this article: http://developer.android.com/guide/components/intents-common.html.

Letting your phone talk – using the Android TextToSpeech engine

In this recipe, we'll do some very fun stuff. On your Android phone, run an app with a listening UDP server on it. When another application, in our case a VCL application, sends a UDP broadcast with some text, the android app will pronounce the text using the android TTS engine.

Getting ready

The first thing to do is to import the TTS classes from the android SDK in our Delphi project. That is not a simple task; however, luckily, someone already did the job. Indeed, Jeff Overcash, the maintainer of the **InterBase Express Components** (**IBX**), wrote the Android Text To Speech JNI Translation. His translation with a simple demo app is available on CodeCentral (http://cc.embarcadero.com/item/29594).

In this recipe, we'll use the imported classes to let our android device read the text sent via UDP broadcast. Note that the message will be read by each device that receives it. Thus, if you have 2, 3, or 4 phones, you will listen to the message read by all the phones almost simultaneously.

How it works...

Open the project group containing the mobile app and the VCL application.

In the mobile app, we have an empty form with a label on it aligned to the client. At the form startup (1 second after the form creation), we configure the TTS engine with the following code:

```
procedure TMainForm.Timer1Timer(Sender: TObject);
begin
  Timer1.Enabled := False;
```

```
    FTTS := TJTextToSpeech.JavaClass.init(
  TAndroidHelper.Context, FTTSListener);
  end;
```

The `FTTSListener` instance is a `TJavaLocal` descendent implementing the required `JTextToSpeech_OnInitListener` interface. The TTS system is getting initialized and when done, the listener `onInit` method is called (check the unit `TTSListenerU.pas`). However, if the TTS engine is correctly initialized, we've to configure it by setting the language to be used when it talks. So, in the listener constructor, I've added an anonymous method that will be called by the listener to configure the engine after the initialization. The code is written inside the `FormCreate` event handler as shown here:

```
constructor TMainForm.Create(AOwner: TComponent);
begin
  inherited;
  FTTSListener := TttsOnInitListener.Create(
    procedure (AInitOK: boolean)
    var
      Res: Integer;
    begin
      if AInitOK then
      begin
        Res := FTTS.setLanguage(TJLocale.JavaClass.ENGLISH);
        if (Res = TJTextToSpeech.JavaClass.LANG_MISSING_DATA) or
           (Res = TJTextToSpeech.JavaClass.LANG_NOT_SUPPORTED) then
          Label1.Text := 'Selected language is not supported'
        else
        begin
          Label1.Text := 'READY To SPEAK!';
          IdUDPServer1.Active := True;
        end;
      end
      else
        Label1.Text := 'Initialization Failed!';
    end);
end;
```

If the configuration goes well, the `TidUDPServer`, configured to listen on all interfaces on port 9999, is activated. In the `idUDPServer1.OnUDPRead` event handler, there is a hook between the data sent over the network and the TTS engine:

```
procedure TMainForm.IdUDPServer1UDPRead(
AThread: TIdUDPListenerThread;
const AData: TIdBytes; ABinding: TIdSocketHandle);
```

```
var
  bytes: TBytes;
begin
  bytes := TBytes(AData);
  Speak(TEncoding.ASCII.GetString(bytes));
end;

procedure TMainForm.Speak(const AText: string);
begin
  FTTS.Speak(
    StringToJString(AText),
    TJTextToSpeech.JavaClass.QUEUE_FLUSH, nil);
end;
```

The method Speak is the entry point to the TTS engine. The mobile app is completed. Now, let's talk about the VCL application that has to send the UDP packets.

Open the `VCLTTSClient` project, and you will see a form like the following:

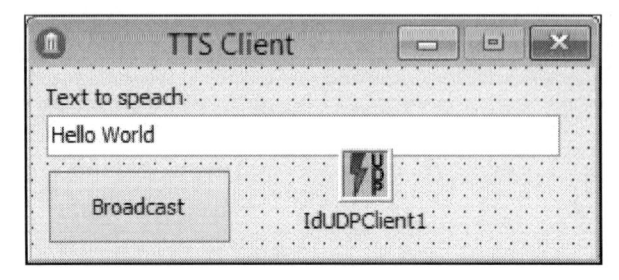

The simple VCL form that will send the UDP messages to the mobile app

This application is even simpler than the mobile one. Shortly, when the user clicks on the button, the event handler sends the text entered in the edit to all the available broadcast addresses (considering its subnet as a Class C network). In other words, if the PC where the application is running, has a single IP address, let's say 192.168.1.50, the UDP packet is sent to the broadcast address 192.168.1.255, and so on for each Ethernet interface configured on the Windows machine (to get all the IP addresses, I've used a handy class named `TIdStackLocalAddressList` that comes with INDY. Moreover, this is just a demo, but if you want to be sure about the broadcast addresses, you should do additional work but this is a network specific topic out of the scope of this book). To replace the last address part (for example, .50 must become .255) I've used a simple regular expression to replace the last octet. Note that this code actually works only for IPv4 addresses:

```
procedure TMainForm.btnSendClick(Sender: TObject);
var
  CurrIP, BrdcstIP: string;
  i: Integer;
begin
```

```delphi
    for i := 0 to FAddressesList.Count - 1 do
    begin
      if FAddressesList.Addresses[i].IPVersion = Id_IPv4 then
      begin
        CurrIP := FAddressesList.Addresses[i].IPAddress;
        BrdcstIP := FToIPv4Broadcast.Replace(CurrIP, '.255');
        IdUDPClient1.Broadcast(Edit1.Text, 9999, BrdcstIP);
      end;
    end;
end;

procedure TMainForm.FormCreate(Sender: TObject);
begin
  FAddressesList := TIdStackLocalAddressList.Create;
  GStack.GetLocalAddressList(FAddressesList);
  FToIPv4Broadcast := TRegEx.Create('\.\d{1,3}$');
end;
```

That's it! Run the mobile app on you android phone and verify that it is currently connected to the same WiFi where the PC is connected. Then, run the VCL application on your PC, write something on the edit, and hit the button. You android device should start to talk.

There's more...

The ability to setup TCP or UDP servers on our mobile devices opens a great range of possibilities. However, you should open ports on your phone conscientiously.

Thanks to Jeff Overcash, the TTS wrapper had greatly simplified the work required to let the android phone talk. If you want to go deeper on using the TTS engine, you should read the following Android documentation:

- Java documentation about the main class used in this recipe: http://developer.android.com/reference/android/speech/tts/TextToSpeech.html
- The Java package where the classes has been imported from: http://developer.android.com/reference/android/speech/tts/package-summary.html
- An introduction to the TTS engine on Android: http://android-developers.blogspot.it/2009/09/introduction-to-text-to-speech-in.html

Using Java classes in Android apps with Java2OP

In this recipe, we will talk about the `Java2OP` command line utility. `Java2OP.exe` ("Java To Object Pascal") is a command-line tool that you can use to generate Delphi native bridge files from Java libraries (JAR or class files). Once having generated the Object Pascal files describing the Java needed classes, you can use them to provide your Delphi applications access to those Java libraries on Android.

`Java2OP.exe` is included in the most recent Delphi versions and is available at the following path: `<RAD Studio>\bin\converters\java2op\java2op.exe`.

Getting ready

This recipe is an upgraded version of the *Using Android SDK Java classes* recipe. Indeed, while in the first recipe, we created the Object Pascal files by hand reading the Android documentation, here we'll use the `Java2OP.exe` utility to automatically generate them. This is the process that you will use 90% of the time (if you have a modern version of Delphi); however, the first recipe is still relevant to correctly understand the process and eventually, changes something in the generated files if needed.

How to do it...

We start with a copy of the recipe *Using Android SDK Java classes*. Our objective is to recreate the same app using a generated interface file instead of the file created manually. Copy the project with all the files and put it in another folder, open it in the RAD Studio IDE and remove the file `AndroidSDK.Toast.pas` from the project. Also, remove all reference to the file in the other units. Change the project name from `ToastDemo` to `ToastDemoWithJava2OP`.

Now, open the command prompt and go to `<RAD Studio>\bin\converters\java2op\` (for example `C:\Program Files (x86)\Embarcadero\Studio\18.0\bin\converters\java2op\`).

`Java2OP` can generate Object Pascal interface files from compiled Java classes and from JAR files. However, consider that the output files do not include members that are part of the built-in RAD Studio Java libraries for Android unless you explicitly specify those members using the `-classes` parameter. Moreover, if any of the classes that you specified depend on members from the built-in RAD Studio Java libraries for Android, the resulting native bridge file does not redeclare those members, but it includes the RAD Studio units that already declare those members.

Being in the `java2op` folder, run the following command line:

`Java2OP.exe -classes android.widget.Toast -unit AndroidSDK.Java2OP.Toast`

Chapter 8

Now you should see a new file called `AndroidSDK.Java2OP.Toast.pas` containing the generated Object Pascal interfaces. We asked the `Java2OP` to generate the interface file for the class `android.widget.Toast` and to generate it in a unit called `AndroidSDK.Java2OP.Toasp.pas`.

Copy this file into the project folder and add it to the project (you can also change the PATH environment variable to be able to call `Java2OP.exe` directly inside the project folder). Go to the main form and add this new file in the uses clause. Try to recompile. You should see some compiler errors. In the original recipe we've created some utility function to simplify the utilization of the imported class. Now, we've got to do the same, but we should not change the generated file, instead we'll create another unit that uses the generated one and declares the utility functions. Let's create the new unit and name it `AndroidSDK.Toast.Utils.pas`. As you can see, we are using simple conventions for unit names. If the unit has been generated by the `Java2OP`, the name respects the following format:

```
AndroidSDK.Java2OP.<OriginalClassName>.pas
```

While the relative unit that contains the hand-written code is relative to the class utilization, respect the following format:

```
AndroidSDK.<OriginalClassName>.Utils.pas
```

However, any convention is good as far as it makes it simple to understand whether the file has been generated by `Java2OP` or handwritten.

In the new file, we have to declare some types and functions to make the raw Java interfaces more usable and more Delphi-like. The cose is functionally the same as the first handwritten version. Here are the file contents:

```
unit AndroidSDK.Toast.Utils;

interface

{$SCOPEDENUMS ON}

type
   TToastDuration = (Short = 0, Long = 1);
   TToastPosition = (default = 0, Top = 48,
     Bottom = 80, Center = 17,
     VerticalCenter = 16, HorizontalCenter = 1);
procedure ShowToast(const AText: string;
   const ADuration: TToastDuration = TToastDuration.Short;
   const APosition: TToastPosition = TToastPosition.Default);

implementation

uses
```

Using Specific Platform Features

```
      FMX.Helpers.Android,
      AndroidAPI.Helpers,
      AndroidSDK.Java2OP.Toast;

procedure ShowToast(const AText: string;
    const ADuration: TToastDuration = TToastDuration.Short;
    const APosition: TToastPosition = TToastPosition.Default);
begin
    CallInUiThread(
        procedure
        var
            Toast: JToast;
        begin
            Toast := TJToast.JavaClass.makeText(TAndroidHelper.Context,
                StrToJCharSequence(AText), Integer(ADuration));
            if APosition <> TToastPosition.Default then
                Toast.setGravity(Integer(APosition), 0, 0);
            Toast.show();
        end);
end;
end.
```

Now, if you try to recompile, you should get some compiler errors because `TJToast.LENGTH_SHORT` is no more defined. This is because the `Java2OP` generated file has this identifier defined as `TJToast.JavaClass.LENGTH_SHORT`. Change it as now the project should compile and run as with the previous one but using an auto generated class interface from the Java android classes.

There's more...

`Java2OP` is quite powerful. It can generate interfaces from classes, JAR files, or plain Java source files. At the command prompt, type `Java2OP` without parameters to get a list of the available switches.

Also, you can check the official documentation to properly understand the possibilities: http://docwiki.embarcadero.com/RADStudio/en/Java2OP.exe,_the_Native_Bridge_File_Generator_for_Android.

Just as side note, in some Delphi installations Java2OP doesn't generate the correct interfaces. If you have experienced this behavior, try to download the following version directly from code central: http://cc.embarcadero.com/item/30007.

Doing it in the background, the right way – Android services

In this recipe, we'll be introduced to the fantastic world of Android services! As you probably know, Android is multitasking from the very first version. Multitasking is not a simple thing for an operating system running on limited hardware. Let's think about the memory that could be allocated for days, or weeks, to some specific processes with the user that runs new apps over and over again. At some point, the memory will finish and the OS has to decide whether to prevent a new app from starting or to eliminate some old processes that the user hasn't used for a while. Obviously, the second option is the best; to allow new apps to run, the OS needs to free some memory still allocated to other apps. At this point, there is another question: which apps can be removed from the memory?

Let's leave this question unanswered for a moment and talk about the Android OS components. Android is a complex OS composed of a lot of different components, but the principals are activities and services. As Google says (source: http://developer.android.com/guide/components/activities.html):

> "An Activity is an application component that provides a screen with which users can interact in order to do something, such as dial the phone, take a photo, send an email, or view a map. Each activity is given a window in which to draw its user interface. The window typically fills the screen, but may be smaller than the screen and float on top of other windows. representation of a screen."

Let's say that, in Delphi terminology, an activity could be defined as a "form" from the user's point of view (but technically speaking, for the Android OS, a Delphi app is composed of only one activity, which will contain all the created forms). What we've created so far using Delphi, are owner-drawn forms that are hosted in a special "native" activity provided by Embarcadero able to render Firemonkey graphics. Using the designer, we define the graphical aspect of the Firemonkey-based activity. What are services? Again, Google says (source: http://developer.android.com/guide/components/services.html):

> "A Service is an application component that can perform long-running operations in the background and does not provide a user interface. Another application component can start a service and it will continue to run in the background even if the user switches to another application. Additionally, a component can bind to a service to interact with it and even perform interprocess communication (IPC). For example, a service might handle network transactions, play music, perform file I/O, or interact with a content provider, all from the background."

As they have experienced it, Android developers very well know, there is a clear criteria and priority to decide which apps' components can be killed to recover the memory. The simplified criteria are as follows:

- Activities have more chances to be destroyed than services
- Background activities have more chances to be destroyed than foreground activities

After this long introduction, let's talk about the recipe we'll analyze in this section. It is a simple app provided to a virtual newspaper reporter that has to collect people's answers about some facts. The virtual newspaper reporter walks in the main city streets and asks people some questions, then he has to send this data to the central editorial staff for statistical analysis in real time. Obviously, this is a demo, and in a real-world app, it could be better to have a local database, acting as the queue storage for the information to be sent; but now, we want to keep things simple enough just to show you how to interact with the Android service. If you need a more robust solution, you can always integrate a database using the concept we already saw in the recipe about database on mobile.

Getting ready

Our app will have an activity to get the information and a service to push that information to the remote server. Using a service, we also know that if the reporter will stop for lunch and his phone's memory is running low, Android will not kill the process where the service is running too fast.

As we mentioned, an Android service is an application without a user interface that performs background tasks.

There are essentially two types of service:

- **A started service**: This kind of service is started by an Android application. The service can run in the background indefinitely, even if the application is closed. This type of service usually performs a single task and automatically stops after finishing.
- **A bound service**: This kind of service only runs while it is bound to an Android application. There is an interaction between the application and the service, and it remains active until the application unbinds. More than one application can bind to the same service.

Keep in mind that your service can work both ways. It can be started (to run indefinitely) and also allow binding.

Chapter 8

Remember that a service is simply a component that can run in the background even when the user is not interacting with your application. Thus, you should create a service only if you really need it. In other words, if you need to perform work outside your main thread while the user is interacting with your application, then you should probably use a background thread using `TThread` or the PPL and not a service. For example, if you want to play some music, but only while your app is in the foreground, you might create a thread and do it. In this case, a service is not necessary.

We chose to use the started service for our needs. Android supports different kinds of service and Delphi allows us to create the following types:

- Local service
- Local intent service
- Remote service
- Remote intent service

A local service is private to an application while a remote service is public, and other applications can access it. The "intent" variations refer to the way the intent is handled by the service, and whether it is in its main thread or not (more info about Intent Services can be found here `http://developer.android.com/reference/android/app/IntentService.html`). However, remember that the `onStartCommand` service event is always called on the main application thread in any service.

In Delphi, we have to create the service and the app as two separated projects in the same project group. You can follow the detailed tutorial in the Embarcadero docwiki to create an app and a local service (`http://docwiki.embarcadero.com/RADStudio/en/Creating_Android_Services`).

How it works...

Let's open the `Chapter08\CODE\RECIPE08\SurveyGroup.groupproj` group project and analyze each part.

The group project is composed of three projects:

- The app itself
- The local service that the app uses to send data to the server
- The REST web service that collects the information sent by the service

Using Specific Platform Features

The app UI is quite simple and is shown in the following screenshot while in use:

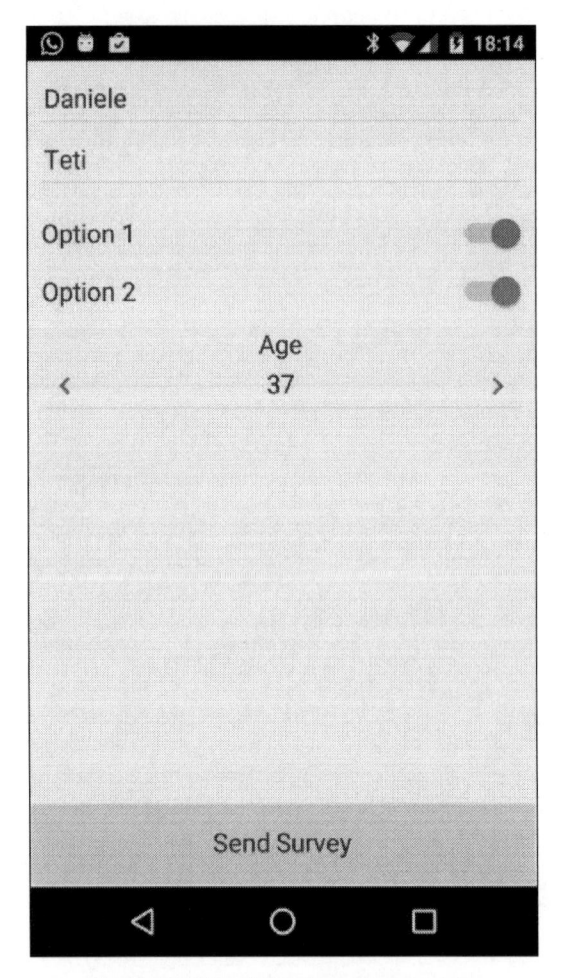

Fig. 8.5 The UI or SurveyApp with some data

When the user writes the data and clicks on **Send Survey**, the inserted data is packaged in a JSON object and then sent to the local service. Here's the code under the button and the method that actually sends data to the service:

```
procedure TMainForm.actSendSurveyExecute(Sender: TObject);
var
   LJSurvey: TJSONObject;
begin
   LJSurvey := TJSONObject.Create;
   LJSurvey.AddPair('first_name', EditFirstName.Text);
   LJSurvey.AddPair('last_name', EditLastName.Text);
   LJSurvey.AddPair('option1',
```

```
      TJSONBool.Create(SwitchOption1.IsChecked));
    LJSurvey.AddPair('option2',
      TJSONBool.Create(SwitchOption2.IsChecked));
    LJSurvey.AddPair('age', TJSONNumber.Create(SpinBoxAge.Value));
    SendSurveyInterview(LJSurvey);
end;

procedure TMainForm.SendSurveyInterview(ASurveyData: TJSONObject);
var
  LIntent: JIntent;
begin
  LIntent := TJIntent.Create;
  LIntent.putExtra(StringToJString('data'),
    StringToJString(ASurveyData.ToJSON));
  StartService('MySurveyService', LIntent);
end;

procedure TMainForm.StartService(const AServiceName: string;
  const AIntent: JIntent);
var
  LService: string;
begin
  LService := AServiceName;
  if not LService.StartsWith('com.embarcadero.services.') then
    LService := 'com.embarcadero.services.' + LService;
  AIntent.setClassName(TAndroidHelper.Context.getPackageName(),
    TAndroidHelper.StringToJString(LService));
  TAndroidHelper.Context.StartService(AIntent);
end;
```

So far, we packaged data and sent that data to the service. But we would like to know when the data was actually sent to the WebService, but only if the app is in the foreground. To do this, the service will broadcast an intent when the WebService replies. To do that, we have to register and configure a `BroadcastReceiver`. We must carefully handle this registration code because we've to keep the registration for just the needed time, not more. For instance, we cannot register the broadcast receiver and then forget about it, we have to unregister it in the `FormClose` event, so that no notification looks for a receiver no more alive:

```
procedure TMainForm.FormCreate(Sender: TObject);
var
  Filter: JIntentFilter;
begin
  //TMyReceiver is a custom     class which will
  //handle the notification
```

Using Specific Platform Features

```
    FMyListener := TMyReceiver.Create;

    //configure a new broadcastreceiver using our own listener
    FBroadcastReceiver :=
      TJFMXBroadcastReceiver.JavaClass.init(FMyListener);

    //to which intents are we interested? Let's configure
    //an intent filter to inform the Android OS
    //about our interests
    Filter := TJIntentFilter.JavaClass.init;
    //success response action
    Filter.addAction(
      StringToJString(TSurveyConstants.SURVEY_RESPONSE));
    //fail response action
    Filter.addAction(
      StringToJString(TSurveyConstants.SURVEY_RESPONSE_ERROR));

    //actually register the receiver
    TAndroidHelper.Context
      .registerReceiver(FBroadcastReceiver, Filter);
end;

procedure TMainForm.FormClose(Sender: TObject;
  var Action: TCloseAction);
begin
  //unregister the receiver
  TAndroidHelper.Context.getApplicationContext
     .unregisterReceiver(FBroadcastReceiver);
end;
```

The action constants used in these event handlers are defined in a separate shared unit named ConstantsU.pas, as follows:

```
type
  TSurveyConstants = class sealed
  public
    const
      SURVEY_RESPONSE = 'SURVEY_RESPONSE';
    const
      SURVEY_RESPONSE_ERROR = 'SURVEY_RESPONSE_ERROR';
  end;
```

Chapter 8

What about the `TMyReceiver` class, which is the actual handler for our response data coming from the service? Here it is, as declared in the `BroadcastReceiverU` unit:

```
unit BroadcastReceiverU;
interface
uses
  Androidapi.JNIBridge,
  Androidapi.JNI.Embarcadero,
  Androidapi.JNI.GraphicsContentViewText;

type
  TMyReceiver = class(TJavaLocal, JFMXBroadcastReceiverListener)
  public
    procedure onReceive(context: JContext; intent: JIntent);
      cdecl;
  end;

implementation

uses
  Androidapi.Helpers, Androidapi.JNI.JavaTypes,
  Androidapi.JNI.Widget, UtilsU, ConstantsU, LogU;

procedure TMyReceiver.onReceive(context: JContext;
  intent: JIntent);
var
  LText: string;
begin
  //if the service reply with an error, show it to the user
  //with specific info
  if JStringToString(intent.getAction) =
    TSurveyConstants.SURVEY_RESPONSE_ERROR
  then
  begin
    LText := JStringToString(
      intent.getStringExtra(StringToJString('error')));
    LText := 'Error: ' + sLineBreak + LText;
  end
  else
  begin
    //this is success response
    LText := JStringToString(
      intent.getStringExtra(StringToJString('result')));
    LText := 'Just Arrived: ' + sLineBreak + LText;
```

Using Specific Platform Features

```
    end;

    //show a toast and log it as debug
    ShowToast(LText);
    LogInfo('Broadcast Received = %s -> %s',
      [JStringToString(intent.getAction), LText], 'survey');
  end;

end.
```

In this code, there are some utility units written to help the development. We will speak about them in the next sections.

Now that we know how the app works, we can talk about the service.

We chose an Android local service for our needs. This is the most typical choice when the Android application interacts directly with the Android service, both running on the same process.

The wizard creates a `Data Module` with the `TAndroidService` class from the `System.Android.Service` unit, with the necessary events:

```
unit MainServiceU;

interface

uses
  System.SysUtils,
  System.Classes,
  System.Android.Service,
  AndroidApi.JNI.GraphicsContentViewText,
  AndroidApi.JNI.Os;

type
  TAndroidServiceDM = class(TAndroidService)
    function AndroidServiceStartCommand(const Sender: TObject;
      const Intent: JIntent; Flags, StartId: Integer): Integer;
  private
    procedure BroadcastResponse(Value: String);
    procedure BroadcastException(const E: Exception);
  public
  end;

const
```

```pascal
    BASE_URL = 'http://192.168.1.106:8080'; //put your IP

var
  AndroidServiceDM: TAndroidServiceDM;

implementation

{%CLASSGROUP 'FMX.Controls.TControl'}

{$R *.dfm}

uses
  AndroidApi.JNI.App, AndroidApi.Helpers, System.JSON,
  System.Net.HTTPClient, AndroidApi.JNI.JavaTypes,
  LogU, ConstantsU;

function TAndroidServiceDM.AndroidServiceStartCommand(
  const Sender: TObject;
  const Intent: JIntent; Flags, StartId: Integer): Integer;
var
  LJSONString: string;
Begin
  //Using START_STICKY in case of restarting the intent is not
  //redelivered, so we have to check its existence
  if Assigned(Intent) and
     Intent.hasExtra(StringToJString('data')) then
  begin
    LJSONString := JStringToString
      (Intent.getStringExtra(StringToJString('data')));
    TThread.CreateAnonymousThread(
      procedure
      var
        LHTTP: THTTPClient;
        LData: TStringStream;
        LResp: IHTTPResponse;
      begin
        LHTTP := THTTPClient.Create;
        LData := TStringStream.Create(LJSONString,
          TEncoding.UTF8);
        LData.Position := 0;
        LogInfo('Sending data to %s/surveys',
          [BASE_URL], 'surveyservice');
```

Using Specific Platform Features

```
      try
        LResp := LHTTP.Post(BASE_URL + '/surveys', LData);
        BroadcastResponse(LResp.ContentAsString);
      except
        on E: Exception do
        begin
          BroadcastException(E);
        end;
      end;
      JavaService.stopSelfResult(StartId);
      LogWarning('Stopped StartId=%d', [StartId],
        'surveyservice');
    end).Start;
  end
  else
  begin
    LogWarning('Service started, but no intent delivered', [],
      'surveyservice');
  end;

  // We want this service to continue running until it is
  // explicitly stopped and restarted if killed,
  // so return START_STICKY.
  Result := TJService.JavaClass.START_STICKY;
end;

procedure TAndroidServiceDM.BroadcastException(
  const E: Exception);
var
  LJIntent: JIntent;
begin
  LJIntent := TJIntent.Create;
  LJIntent.setAction(
    StringToJString(TSurveyConstants.SURVEY_RESPONSE_ERROR));
  LJIntent.putExtra(StringToJString('error'),
    StringToJString(E.ClassName + ': ' + E.Message));
  TAndroidHelper.Context.sendBroadcast(LJIntent);
end;

procedure TAndroidServiceDM.BroadcastResponse(Value: String);
var
  LJIntent: JIntent;
```

```
begin
  LJIntent := TJIntent.Create;
  LJIntent.setAction(
    StringToJString(TSurveyConstants.SURVEY_RESPONSE));
  LJIntent.putExtra(
    StringToJString('result'), StringToJString(Value));
  TAndroidHelper.Context.sendBroadcast(LJIntent);
end;

end.
```

All this simple service is contained inside the `OnStartCommand` event handler.

This event is called by the system every time a client explicitly starts the service by calling `startService()`, providing the arguments it supplied and a unique integer token representing the start request. Here is an explanation about their parameters.

The `Intent` parameter is the Intent supplied to `startService()` by the activity, as given. This may be null if the service is being restarted after its process has gone away. The `Flags` parameter contains additional data about this start request. The `startId` parameter is a unique integer provided by the Android OS to represent this specific request to start. It can be used with `stopSelfResult()`. The `StartCommand` event handler runs in the main thread, so we cannot perform any long operations here just like in the form code. Indeed, we first create a new background thread to do the actual work. Inside this thread, we make the actual HTTP request to the remote service and package the response for the listener.

When the response has been packaged in a proper JSON object, the thread calls `JavaService.stopSelfResult(StartId)`. What is that? Any Android service has its own lifecycle. A started service must manage its own lifecycle. The system does not stop or destroy the service, unless it must recover system memory, and the service continues to run after the `OnStartCommand()` event completes. So, the service must stop itself by calling `stopSelf()` or another component can stop it by calling `stopService()`. A started service can handle its stop independent of the activity that starts it. There are at least two ways in which a service can stop itself:

Method to stop the service	Meaning
`JavaService.stopSelf()`	Stop the service if it was previously started.
`JavaService.stopSelfResult(startId)`	Stop the service if the most recent time it was started was `startId`.

Using Specific Platform Features

Once requested to stop with `stopSelf()`, the system destroys the service as soon as possible. However, if your service handles multiple requests to `onStartCommand()` concurrently, like our service, then you shouldn't stop the service when you're done processing a start request, because you might have received a new start request since then (stopping at the end of the first request would terminate the second one). To avoid this problem, you can use `stopSelfResult(startId)` to ensure that your request to stop the service is always based on the most recent start request. That is, when you call `stopSelfResult(startId)`, you pass the `startId` of the start request (the `startId` delivered to `OnStartCommand` event handler) to which your stop request corresponds. Then, if the service received a new start request before you were able to call `JavaService.stopSelfResult(startId)`, then the `startId` will not match and the service will not stop.

As last note, let's talk about the value returned by the `OnStartCommand` event. This value is really important to understand the service life cycle. If `OnStartCommand` returns `START_STICKY`, the system will try to recreate your service after it is killed. If `OnStartCommand` returns `START_NOT_STICKY`, the system will not try to recreate your service after it is killed. As last options, among the most popular, there is `START_REDELIVER_INTENT`, which is particularly handy. If `OnStartCommand` returns `START_REDELIVER_INTENT` if this service's process is killed while it is started, then it will be scheduled for a restart and the last delivered intent redelivered to it again via a standard intent as it would be the first time.

But what about the data sent itself? Where is the serialized JSON object send? The third project in the group is called `SurveyWebService.dproj` and is a `DelphiMVCFramework` RESTful service, which has one controller called `TSurveyCollector` and one action called `CreateSurveyResponse`. This project has been created starting from a nice wizard included in the `DelphiMVCFramework`. The WebModule is quite standard, while the controller is the following:

```
unit SurveysCollectorCtrlU;

interface

uses
  MVCFramework;

type
  [MVCPath('/surveys')]
  TSurveyCollector = class(TMVCController)
  public
    [MVCPath]
    [MVCHTTPMethod([httpPOST])]
```

```
    procedure CreateSurveyResponse(ctx: TWebContext);
  end;

implementation

uses
  System.SysUtils, System.IOUtils, System.JSON,
  MVCFramework.Commons, MVCFramework.Logger;

procedure TSurveyCollector.CreateSurveyResponse(ctx: TWebContext);
begin
  Log('Request data: ' + ctx.Request.Body);
  Log('Wait a bit...');
  Sleep(5000); //just to mimic a long operation
  if ctx.Request.ThereIsRequestBody then
  begin
    //if there is a body request just send OK
    Render(HTTP_STATUS.OK,
      TJSONObject.Create(TJSONPair.Create('result', 'ok')))
  end
  else
  begin
      Render(HTTP_STATUS.BadRequest,
      TJSONObject.Create(TJSONPair.Create('result', 'ko')));
  end;
  Log('Response sent');
end;
end.
```

As you can see, the server acts like a potentially complete backend system, but it is really only a fake server, which doesn't even do anything with the sent data and is just a way to show how it is possible to communicate with a remote server from an Android service.

So, do you want to run this distributed project? Let's start:

1. Run the `SurveyWebService.dproj` without debugging.
2. Retrieve your IP address (`ipconfig` in the command prompt).
3. In the file `MainServiceU.pas`, change the constant BASE_URL according to your IP:
   ```
   const
     BASE_URL = 'http://YOUR_IP_ADDRESS_HERE:8080';
   ```

Using Specific Platform Features

4. Now, build the project `MySurveyService.dproj`.
5. Select the project `MySurveyApp.dproj`, expand the node **Target Platform**, select **Android**, and then right-click on **Android** platform and select **Add Android Service**.
6. From the resultant open dialog, select the folder where the service is. You should see two folders named `Android` and `JavaClasses`. Click on **Select** and then follow the wizard to the end. This "strange" step is required to let the app to know its service.
7. Now you can run the project `MySurveyApp.dproj`.
8. Write some data in the UI widget and tap **Send Survey**.
9. After some seconds a `Toast` should inform you that the data has been correctly sent and the WebService log should say the same thing (check the folder where the WebService executable is).

There's more...

Lot of things in this recipe! Delphi 10 Seattle is the first version of Delphi, which allows to create Android service. There is still some room for improvement, but this integration is already very powerful.

Before you start to write real-world apps using the Android service, I strongly encourage you to study the following documentation:

- Creating Android Services: http://docwiki.embarcadero.com/RADStudio/en/Creating_Android_Services
- Differences and features of each kind of Android service (in Delphi): http://docwiki.embarcadero.com/RADStudio/en/Android_Service
- Android Service introduction by Google: http://developer.android.com/reference/android/app/Service.html

As promised, I will talk about the other units involved in the project. At the time of writing the Android system logger is provided by the unit `FMX.Types`. However, the unit is not compatible with services because it looks for an activity context. Waiting for an update, I wrote the `LogU.pas`, which completely exposes the power of the Android logger and works also in Delphi 10 Seattle services. The unit `UtilsU.pas` is simpler because it's only a small wrapper around the `TJToast` class. It defines a handy `ShowToast` procedure, which is simpler to call compared to the raw `TJToast` creation. Obviously, this unit can be used outside this project too.

Index

Symbols

2D graph
 measure, displaying 203-207

A

Android
 PDF files, displaying 415
Android apps
 Java classes, using with Java2OP 430-432
Android Intents
 full flagged e-mail, sending 421, 422
 sending 418-420
 speech to text engine 422-426
Android SDK Java classes
 using 402-408
Android services 433-446
Android TextToSpeech engine
 using 426-429
animations
 used, for impressing clients 149-153
anonymous methods 72-76
app
 lifecycle, tracking 395-400
 PDF files, displaying 412, 413
App tethering
 URL 289
 using, to create companion app 283-289

B

backend
 talking with 382-389
Bitmap Style Designer
 URL 4

BSODs
 URL 283

C

callback
 types, URL 176
chat application
 with Delphi source, URL 283
classes
 helpers, creating 88-97
clients
 impressing, animations used 149-153
code
 decoupling, cross platform publish/subscribe
  mechanism used 129-135
companion app
 about 284
 creating, App Tethering used 283-289
complex vector shapes
 showing, paths used 165-170
connection
 URL 229
console application
 converting, to Windows service 242-245
content types
 URL 257
cross platform publish/subscribe mechanism
 used, for decoupling code 129-135

D

dataset
 serializing, to JSON and back 245-249
DataSnap Apache modules
 creating 290-300

Data URI schema
　URL 126
**DelphiMVCFramework
　　　(DMVCFramework)**
　about 232
　URL 246
Delphisorcery
　URL 176
duck typing
　RTTI used 84-88

E

effects
　applying 322-331
Embarcadero
　docwiki, URL 241
　URL 45, 84
embedded forms
　stack, creating 25-27
encoded Internet world
　coping with, System.NetEncodings
　　　used 119-126
enumerable types
　URL 80
　writing 76-79
events
　URL 203
eXtensible Markup Language (XML) 34

F

file extension
　associating, with application
　　　on Windows 52-58
FireDAC
　URL 229
FireMonkey (FMX)
　about 137, 138
　basics, URL 185
　controls modifying, styles used 138-144
　GUI, reinventing 177-185
　using, in VCL application 170-176
FireMonkey Style Designer (FSD) 141

futures
　used, for monitoring things 216-222

G

GUI
　reinventing 177-185

H

helpers
　creating, for classes 88-97
higher-order functions
　URL 72
　using 72-76
HTTP Client
　URL 319
HTTP TRACE
　verifying 118, 119
HTTP verbs 117, 118
Hypertext Transfer Protocol (HTTP)
　considerations 107

I

InterBase Express Components (IBX) 426
I/O
　in 21st Century 44-47
iOS Objective C SDK classes
　using 408-411

J

Java classes
　using, in Android apps with
　　　Java2OP 430-432
JSON and back
　dataset, serializing to 245-249
　objects serializing to, RTTI used 250-256
JSON (JavaScript Object Notation)
　manipulating 28-33
JSON parser
　URL 33
jTable
　about 232
　URL 233, 238

L

LiveBindings
  master/details (M/D) using 153-163
  URL 164
location
  sending, to server continuously 372-375
  server-side 376-378

M

master/details (M/D)
  using, with LiveBindings 153-163
measure
  displaying, on 2D graph 203-207
Method Draw
  URL 170
Microsoft © Message Compiler 52
monitor
  URL 195
MonkeyMixer
  URL 176
Multiple Document Interface (MDI) paradigm 58
multiple threads
  synchronizing, TEvent used 199-203
multithreading 187

N

native HTTP(S) client libraries
  used, for consuming RESTful services 106-116
  using 308-319

O

Object Inspector 60
objects
  serializing to JSON and back, RTTI used 250-256
observer. *See* **publish/subscribe pattern**
Observer design pattern
  about 400
  URL 28
OmniThreadLibrary
  URL 207
oscilloscope 203

owner draw combos
  using 16-18
owner draw control
  making aware, of VCL styles 19-24
owner draw listboxes
  using 16-18

P

parallel for loop
  used, for parallelizing 222-229
Parallel Programming Library (PPL) 188, 208
Pascal Sets Intersect 15
paths
  used, for showing complex vector shapes 165-169
PDF files
  displaying, in app 412
  displaying, on Android 415
  displaying, on iOS 416, 417
  downloading, from server 417
phone call
  making, from app 390-394
photo
  sending, to server continuously 372-375
  taking 322-331
Plain Old Delphi Object (PODO) 79
POST HTTP request
  sending, request encoding parameters used 256-259
PPL
  URL 215
publish/subscribe pattern 129

R

regular expression (RegEx)
  samples, URL 106
  syntax, URL 106
  URL 100
  used, for checking strings 100-106
remote application
  controlling, UDP used 277-283
REST Client Library
  URL 259
RESTDemo sample
  URL 259

RESTful interface
   implementing, WebBroker used 260-277
RESTful service
   consuming, native HTTP(s) client
      libraries 106-116
   URL 218
reverse proxy
   URL 241
Richardson Maturity Model (RMM) 260
RTTI
   about 80-84
   used, for duck typing 84-88

S

Scalable Vector Graphics (SVG) 165
shared resources
   synchronizing, TMonitor used 188-195
space
   saving, System.Zip used 126-129
SQLite databases
   used, for handling to-do list 339-344
stack overflow
   URL 97
strings
   checking, regular expressions (RegEX)
      used 100-106
styled TListView
   using, to handle long lists of data 352-362
styles
   used, for modifying FireMonkey
      controls 138-144
SuperObject
   URL 33
System.NetEncodings
   used, for coping with encoded
      Internet world 119-126
System.Zip
   used, for saving space 126-129

T

Table Data Gateway (TDG) 266
tasks
   used, for making customer happy 208-215
TDBGrid
   customizing 9-15

TEvent
   used, for synchronizing multiple
      threads 199-203
TFDManager class
   URL 229
TFireMonkeyContainer
   URL 176
things
   monitoring, futures used 216-222
thread!
   unblocking 344-352
thread-safe queue
   using 196-198
THTTPClient method 117, 118
TLayout
   URL 185
TListBox
   styled TListBox, creating 144-149
TListView
   customizing with 362-371
   used, for searching and saving
      local data 331-338
TMessageManager
   URL 28
TMonitor
   used, for synchronizing shared
      resources 188-195
TortoiseGit
   URL 232
TTaskDialog 58-69
TTask.IFuture
   URL 222

U

User Datagram Protocol (UDP)
   used, for controlling remote
      application 277-283

V

Visual Component Library (VCL)
   about 2
   FireMonkey, using 170-176
   runtime style, modifying 5-7
   used, for changing application
      look and feel 2-4
voice over internet protocol (VoIP) 277

W

WebBroker
  URL 234
  used, for implementing RESTful
      interface 260-277
WebBroker Apache modules
  creating 301-308
web client JavaScript applications
  application, running 241, 242
  developing, with WebBroker
      on server 232-237
  people list, retrieving 237, 238
  person, creating 239-241
Web Script library
  URL 33
Windows API
  about 58
  file extension, associating with
      application 52-58
  URL 59

Windows service
  console application, converting to 242-244
  creating 47-51
  TService.LogMessage method, using 52

X

XML documents
  manipulating 34-43
  transforming 34-43
XML markup languages
  URL 42
XSLT
  URL 43

Z

Zip 126

Printed in Great Britain
by Amazon